LEVEL 3 ALTERNATIVE ACADEMIC QUALIFICATION
CAMBRIDGE ADVANCED NATIONAL

Computing: Application Development

Student Book

Chris Charles, David Corbett & Jen Gainsford

CAMBRIDGE
UNIVERSITY PRESS & ASSESSMENT

Shaftesbury Road, Cambridge CB2 8EA, United Kingdom

One Liberty Plaza, 20th Floor, New York, NY 10006, USA

477 Williamstown Road, Port Melbourne, VIC 3207, Australia

314–321, 3rd Floor, Plot 3, Splendor Forum, Jasola District Centre, New Delhi – 110025, India

103 Penang Road, #05–06/07, Visioncrest Commercial, Singapore 238467

Cambridge University Press & Assessment is a department of the University of Cambridge.

We share the University's mission to contribute to society through the pursuit of education, learning and research at the highest international levels of excellence.

www.cambridge.org
Information on this title: www.cambridge.org/9781009817134

First published 2025
20 19 18 17 16 15 14 13 12 11 10 9 8 7 6 5 4 3 2 1

Printed in Great Britain by Ashford Colour Ltd.

A catalogue record for this publication is available from the British Library

ISBN 978-1-00-981713-4 Paperback
ISBN 978-1-00-981712-7 Digital Edition
ISBN 978-1-00-981715-8 Digital Edition (1 Year Site Licence)

Additional resources for this publication at www.cambridge.org/9781009817134

Contents

Acknowledgements

The authors and publishers acknowledge the following sources of copyright material and are grateful for the permissions granted. While every effort has been made, it has not always been possible to identify the sources of all the material used, or to trace all copyright holders. If any omissions are brought to our notice, we will be happy to include the appropriate acknowledgements on reprinting.

Thanks to the following for permission to reproduce images:

Cover oxygen/Getty Images

Inside **F160** Quantic69/GI; **TA1** Igor Zhukov/GI; Booka1/GI; Daniel Balakov/GI; **TA2** Diki Prayogo/GI; Flavia Morlachetti/GI; **TA3** AndreyPopov/GI; Artvea/GI; **TA5** Yurich84/GI; Merovingian/GI; Capuski/GI; Oscar Wong/GI; Courtneyk/GI; SpiffyJ/GI (x2); **TA6** Xavierarnau/GI; Cavan Images/GI; Portra/GI; **F161** SpicyTruffel/GI; **TA1** Gorodenkoff/GI; Mrgao/GI; Pictafolio/GI; IndiaPix/IndiaPicture/GI; Sitthiphong/GI; Yevgen Romanenko/GI (x2); Figure 2.11 Photography by Jonathan Banks for Microsoft; **TA4** Fotoscape/GI; MirageC/GI; Douglas Sacha/GI; Oscar Wong/GI; **TA5**: Ole_CNX/GI; **TA6** Sean Gladwell/GI; **F162** Korawat thatinchan/GI; **TA1** SFL Travel/ Alamy Stock Photo; Bob Riha Jr/GI; New York Daily News Archive/GI; NurPhoto/GI; Alex Ruhl/Alamy Stock Photo; **TA2** Oscar Wong/GI; CarmenMurillo/GI; Tomas Knopp/GI; Trinetuzun/GI; NicoElNino/GI; Amenic181/GI; Rawpixel/GI; **TA3** Bagi1998/GI; Figure 3.27 Reproduced with permission of Jacob Farney; **TA4** Courtneyk/GI; Figure 3.33 By permission of IntentUK.com; Sesame/GI (x2)

Key: GI = Getty Images

Adobe product screenshots reprinted with permission from Adobe.

Introduction

About your course

Working in the computing industry is very rewarding. The Level 3 Alternative Academic Qualification Cambridge Advanced National in Computing: Application Development will help you to develop key knowledge, understanding and skills that are important for jobs and careers within the sector. During the course you will be encouraged to:

- think creatively, innovatively, analytically, logically and critically
- develop valuable communication skills
- develop transferable learning and skills, such as evaluation, planning, presentation and research skills
- develop independence and confidence in applying the knowledge and skills that are vital for progression to higher education and work situations.

How you will be assessed

You can take the Level 3 Alternative Academic Qualification Cambridge Advanced National in Computing: Application Development at one of two levels:

Certificate

For this qualification, you must complete two units:

- One mandatory externally assessed unit (E)
- One mandatory non-examined assessment unit (NEA).

Unit number	Unit title	How is it assessed?	Mandatory or optional
F160	Fundamentals of application development	E	M
F162	Designing and communicating UX/UI solutions	NEA	M

Extended Certificate

For this qualification, you must complete five units:

- Two mandatory externally assessed units
- One mandatory NEA unit
- Two optional NEA units.

Unit number	Unit title	How is it assessed?	Mandatory or optional
F160	Fundamentals of application development	E	M
F161	Developing application software	E	M
F162	Designing and communicating UX/UI solutions	NEA	M
F163	Game development	NEA	O
F164	Website development	NEA	O
F165	Immersive technology solution development	NEA	O
F166	Software development	NEA	O

Computing:
Application
Development
Digital Student Book
Optional Unit F166

The **Level 3 Alternative Academic Qualification Cambridge Advanced National Computing: Application Development Student Book** will support you with your Mandatory units. Support for the Optional units can be found at **cambridge.org/cambridge-advanced-nationals.**

About the authors

Chris Charles

Chris Charles is an experienced teacher, author, educational consultant and head of digital learning. His published material includes books, schemes of work, online revision material and CPD courses. He supports a number of organisations with technical and pedagogical knowledge. Chris also works on a Subject Knowledge Enhancement programme and with trainee teachers to secure their subject knowledge. Chris is interested in promoting high-quality digital learning in all subject areas.

David Corbett

David Corbett is an experienced teacher. He graduated from the University of Wales, Aberystwyth. Beyond his classroom responsibilities, David has expanded his influence within the educational community by becoming an educational resource provider for secondary schools across the UK. He has developed and provided a diverse range of resources tailored to various courses in both England and Wales. Additionally, he has offered bespoke training sessions focused on the teaching and assessment of the Cambridge Nationals Creative iMedia course, supporting teachers in their delivery of the curriculum.

Jen Gainsford

Jen Gainsford is an experienced Head of Department who taught a range of different computing courses across the 11–18 age range during her 15 years of teaching. Since leaving teaching in 2023, Jen has worked to build digital capability and skills within a higher education institution, but still works as a trainer, examiner and moderator in her spare time. Jen has also previously authored a range of teacher resources and student textbooks.

How to use this book

Throughout this book, you will notice lots of different features that will help your learning. These are explained below.

Learning intentions – each topic begins with a set of learning intentions to show you what the topic covers.

Key words – key words are highlighted in the text and explained fully in the glossary to ensure you understand key terminology.

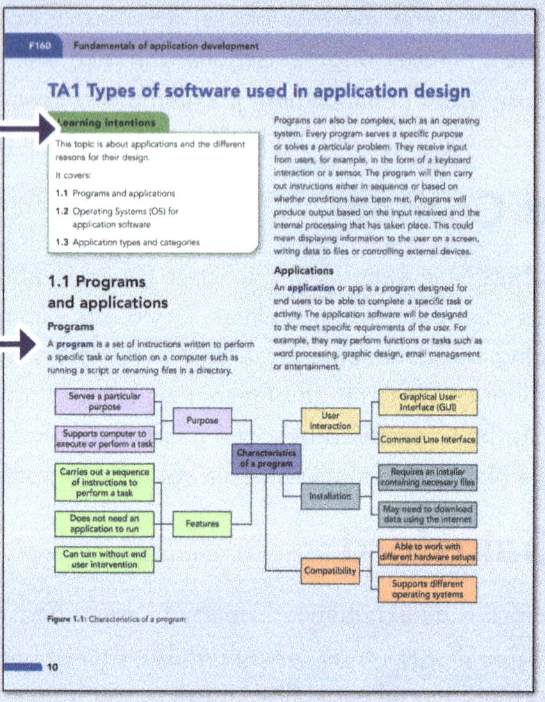

F160 Fundamentals of application development

TA1 Types of software used in application design

Learning intentions

This topic is about applications and the different reasons for their design.

It covers:

1.1 Programs and applications

1.2 Operating Systems (OS) for application software

1.3 Application types and categories

1.1 Programs and applications

Programs

A **program** is a set of instructions written to perform a specific task or function on a computer such as running a script or renaming files in a directory.

Programs can also be complex, such as an operating system. Every program serves a specific purpose or solves a particular problem. They receive input from users, for example, in the form of a keyboard interaction or a sensor. The program will then carry out instructions either in sequence or based on whether conditions have been met. Programs will produce output based on the input received and the internal processing that has taken place. This could mean displaying information to the user on a screen, writing data to files or controlling external devices.

Applications

An **application** or app is a program designed for end users to be able to complete a specific task or activity. The application software will be designed to the meet specific requirements of the user. For example, they may perform functions or tasks such as word processing, graphic design, email management or entertainment.

Characteristics of a program
Purpose
Serves a particular purpose
Supports computer to execute or perform a task
Features
Carries out a sequence of instructions to perform a task
Does not need an application to run
Can turn without end user intervention
User interaction
Graphical User Interface (GUI)
Command Line Interface
Installation
Requires an installer containing necessary files
May need to download data using the internet
Compatibility
Able to work with different hardware setups
Supports different operating systems

Figure 1.1: Characteristics of a program

10

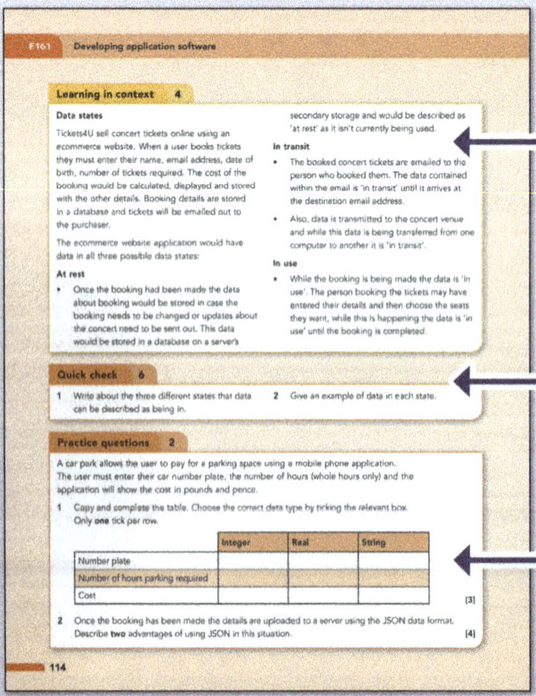

F161 Developing application software

Learning in context 4

Data states

Tickets4U sell concert tickets online using an ecommerce website. When a user books tickets they must enter their name, email address, date of birth, number of tickets required. The cost of the booking would be calculated, displayed and stored with the other details. Booking details are stored in a database and tickets will be emailed out to the purchaser.

The ecommerce website application would have data in all three possible data states:

At rest

- Once the booking had been made the data about booking would be stored in case the booking needs to be changed or updates about the concert need to be sent out. This data would be stored in a database on a server's secondary storage and would be described as 'at rest' as it isn't currently being used.

In transit

- The booked concert tickets are emailed to the person who booked them. The data contained within the email is 'in transit' until it arrives at the destination email address.
- Also, data is transmitted to the concert venue and while this data is being transferred from one computer to another it is 'in transit'.

In use

- While the booking is being made the data is 'in use'. The person booking the tickets may have entered their details and then choose the seats they want, while this is happening the data is 'in use' until the booking is completed.

Quick check 6

1 Write about the three different states that data can be described as being in.

2 Give an example of data in each state.

Practice questions 2

A car park allows the user to pay for a parking space using a mobile phone application. The user must enter their car number plate, the number of hours (whole hours only) and the application will show the cost in pounds and pence.

1 Copy and complete the table. Choose the correct data type by ticking the relevant box. Only **one** tick per row.

	Integer	Real	String
Number plate			
Number of hours parking required			
Cost			

[3]

2 Once the booking has been made the details are uploaded to a server using the JSON data format. Describe **two** advantages of using JSON in this situation. [4]

114

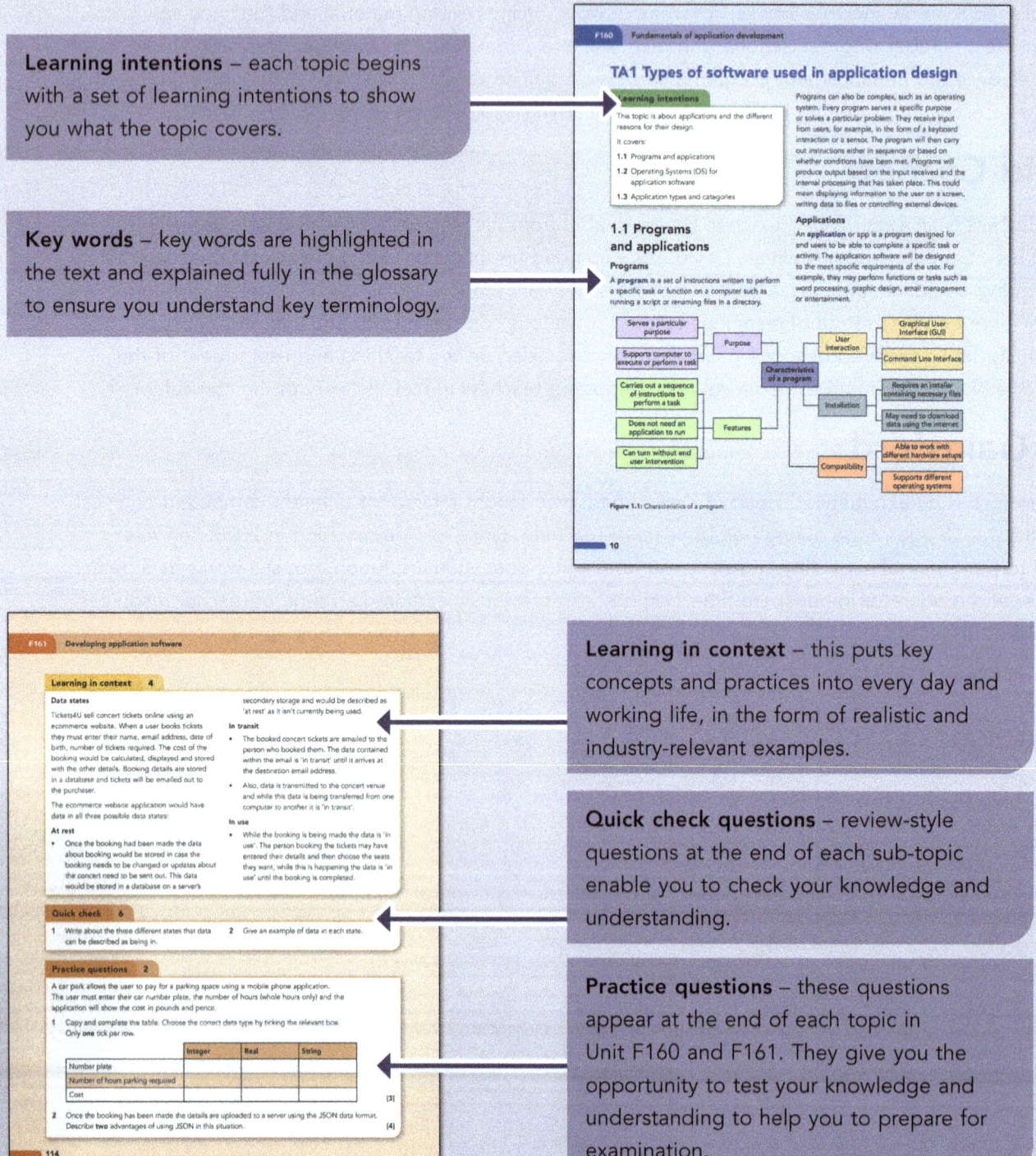

Learning in context – this puts key concepts and practices into every day and working life, in the form of realistic and industry-relevant examples.

Quick check questions – review-style questions at the end of each sub-topic enable you to check your knowledge and understanding.

Practice questions – these questions appear at the end of each topic in Unit F160 and F161. They give you the opportunity to test your knowledge and understanding to help you to prepare for examination.

F160 Fundamentals of application development

Topic Areas

TA1: Types of software used in application design
TA2: Software development models
TA3: Planning application development projects
TA4: Application design scoping
TA5: Human computer interface and interaction
TA6: Job roles and skills

In today's digital age, applications play a crucial role in various aspects of our lives, from communication and productivity to entertainment and education. Understanding the fundamentals of application development is essential for anyone aspiring to become a proficient software developer or designer.

In this unit you will learn about applications and their functions, reflecting on how client requirements can shape the software choices that are made. You will learn about the different processes that take place when designing an application, from initial planning to exploring design ideas and features. You will also learn about the variety of job roles in this area, understanding how each contributes to application development and their main roles and responsibilities.

TA1 Types of software used in application design

Learning intentions

This topic is about applications and the different reasons for their design.

It covers:

1.1 Programs and applications

1.2 Operating Systems (OS) for application software

1.3 Application types and categories

1.1 Programs and applications

Programs

A **program** is a set of instructions written to perform a specific task or function on a computer such as running a script or renaming files in a directory.

Programs can also be complex, such as an operating system. Every program serves a specific purpose or solves a particular problem. They receive input from users, for example, in the form of a keyboard interaction or a sensor. The program will then carry out instructions either in sequence or based on whether conditions have been met. Programs will produce output based on the input received and the internal processing that has taken place. This could mean displaying information to the user on a screen, writing data to files or controlling external devices.

Applications

An **application** or app is a program designed for end users to be able to complete a specific task or activity. The application software will be designed to the meet specific requirements of the user. For example, they may perform functions or tasks such as word processing, graphic design, email management or entertainment.

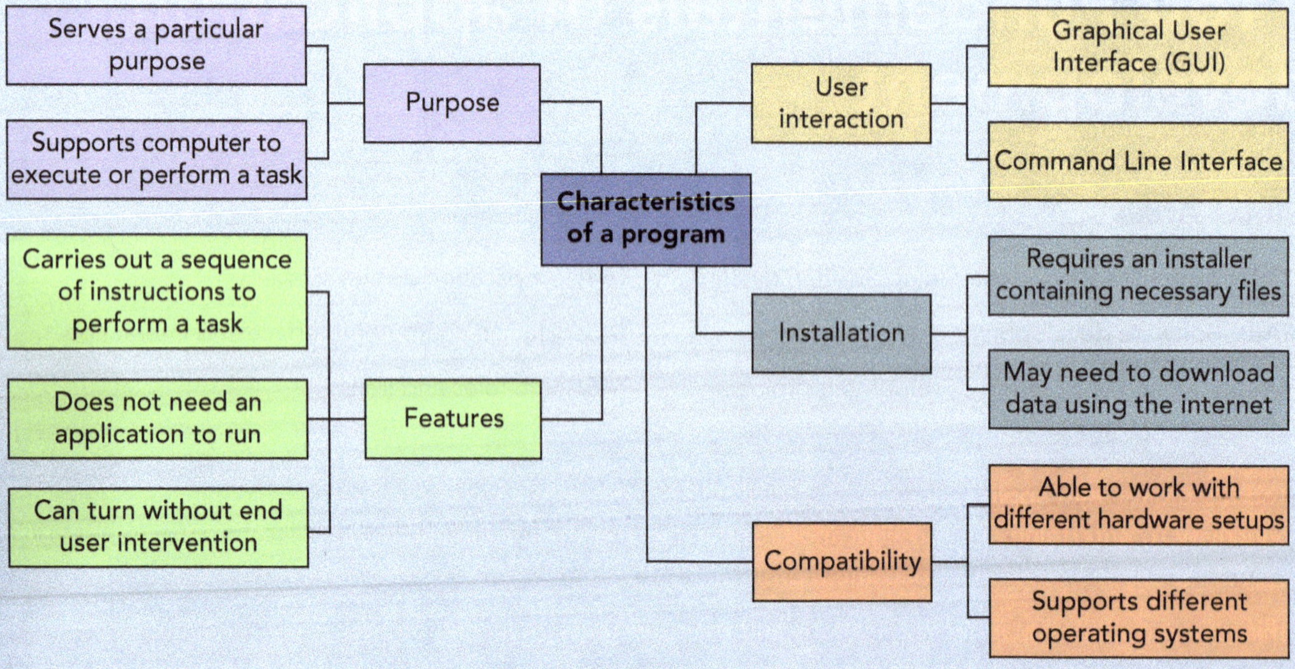
Serves a particular purpose
Supports computer to execute or perform a task
Purpose
Carries out a sequence of instructions to perform a task
Does not need an application to run
Can turn without end user intervention
Features
Characteristics of a program
User interaction
Graphical User Interface (GUI)
Command Line Interface
Installation
Requires an installer containing necessary files
May need to download data using the internet
Compatibility
Able to work with different hardware setups
Supports different operating systems

Figure 1.1: Characteristics of a program

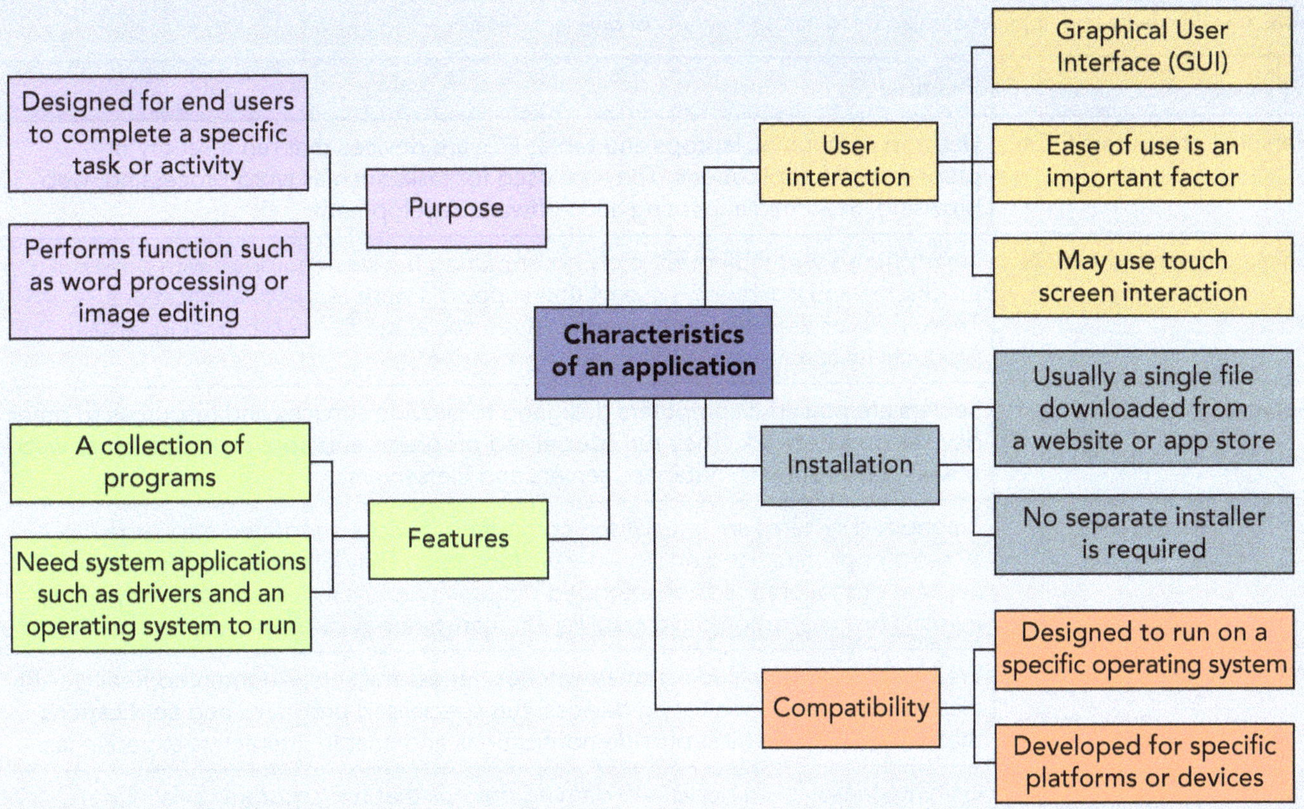
Characteristics of an application
Purpose
Designed for end users to complete a specific task or activity
Performs function such as word processing or image editing
Features
A collection of programs
Need system applications such as drivers and an operating system to run
User interaction
Graphical User Interface (GUI)
Ease of use is an important factor
May use touch screen interaction
Installation
Usually a single file downloaded from a website or app store
No separate installer is required
Compatibility
Designed to run on a specific operating system
Developed for specific platforms or devices

Figure 1.2: Characteristics of an application

Applications are developed to run on a specific operating system, utilising the operating system and other system software to function such as the file storage system. They will also be developed for specific platform or device types. An Android mobile application for an Android phone, for example, will be different to a Windows application designed to run on a desktop PC. Multiple versions of the same application may be developed to meet these differing needs.

Applications generally have a user-friendly Graphical User Interface (GUI) to make them easier to use. They require installation and can be downloaded from an app store or website.

Applications are essentially a type of program. However, not all programs are applications. Programs include a broader category of software including both applications and other types of software such as system utilities, drivers and scripts.

There are some good examples of devices using programs and application software highlighted in Table 1.1.

Table 1.1: Programs and applications can be found on a variety of different devices

Device	Example
Personal computers (PCs)	Desktop computers, laptops and tablet PCs are devices that run a variety of programs and applications. They are used for tasks such as word processing, web browsing, multimedia, gaming and software development.
Smartphones and tablets	Smartphones and tablets are mobile computing devices equipped with powerful processors and operating systems that support a wide range of applications. These devices are used for communication, social media, web browsing, email, productivity tasks, gaming, navigation and more.
Servers	Servers are powerful computers designed to provide services and resources to other devices on a network. They run specialised programs and applications, such as web servers, email servers, database servers and file servers.
Embedded systems	Embedded systems are specialised computing devices integrated into larger systems or products to perform specific functions. They often run programs and applications tailored to their intended purpose, such as industrial control systems, medical devices, automotive systems and consumer electronics.
Wearable devices	Wearable devices, including smartwatches, fitness trackers, Augmented Reality (AR) glasses and health monitoring devices, run specialised programs and applications that track fitness metrics, provide notifications and enable interactive experiences.
Gaming consoles	Gaming consoles are dedicated gaming devices that run programs and applications tailored for gaming experiences. These devices support a variety of gaming software, including console-exclusive titles, online multiplayer games and multimedia entertainment apps.
Smart home devices	Smart home devices, such as smart speakers, smart thermostats, smart locks, and smart appliances, incorporate programs and applications to automate tasks, control home functions remotely and interact with other smart devices in a connected home ecosystem.

Quick check 1

1 Discuss with a partner the similarities and differences between programs and applications.

2 Think about an application you are familiar with. Make notes on how the application meets the needs of its end user.

1.2 Operating Systems (OS) for application software

Network

Network operating systems are specifically tailored to support the functionalities of a network. The typical functions of a network operating system include:

- resource sharing across the network
- user authentication and access control
- providing communication services between networked devices
- network administration tools.

An example of a network operating system is Windows Server, Microsoft's server operating system which is widely used in enterprise environments.

Network operating systems are found in environments where there are multiple computers and devices that are connected to form a network. These devices might include:

- a server, the central computer that provides various services and resources to other computers
- workstations, individual computers that are used by users to perform tasks such as web browsing and document editing
- printers, scanners and storage devices.

Table 1.2: Advantages and disadvantages of network operating systems

Advantages	Disadvantages
• System updates can be easily rolled out across the network • Central server provides stability • Enhanced security such as user authentication.	• Initial costs for a central server, hardware and software • Ongoing costs for regular maintenance and support • Hardware and software can have compatibility issues with network operating systems.

Open OS

An **open operating system** is a software system whose source code is freely available for anyone to use, modify, and distribute under an agreed set of rules called a licence. Open operating systems encourage collaboration between users to create a system to meet their needs. Examples include Linux based systems such as Ubuntu.

Table 1.3: Advantages and disadvantages of open operating systems

Advantages	Disadvantages
• Users and developers can modify and customise the system to meet their needs • Community support, such as forums, makes it easy to access help and guidance • Many open systems are free or at a low cost compared to alternatives.	• Operating systems can be complex and need a level of technical expertise to configure, customise and maintain them • Compatibility with hardware devices or different versions of the operating system can be an issue.

Open operating systems are widely adopted across various industries and applications.

- Smartphones and tablets using the Android operating system, developed by Google offers a customisable user interface and support for a wide range of hardware configurations. Through the Google Play Store there is an extensive app ecosystem available for developers.
- Computers and laptops running Linux-based operating systems such as Ubuntu offer a customisable and secure computing environment. They are widely used in desktops, laptops, and servers with a vast selection of software packages available.
- Single-board computers such as a Raspberry Pi run on open-source operating systems providing users with a platform for learning programming and experimenting with electronics.

HDMI

Figure 1.3: Photograph of a Raspberry Pi model B board

Proprietary

A **proprietary operating system** is a software system developed and owned by a specific company or organisation. The source code is not publicly available, and the use, modification and distribution of it is not allowed. This type of system is developed to generate revenue through fees paid for a licence to use it or associated hardware. Examples of proprietary operating systems include Microsoft Windows, macOS and iOS.

There are a wide range of devices that rely on proprietary operating systems. Some common examples of devices using proprietary systems include:

- Smartphones and tablets using Apple's iOS, which is exclusive to Apple mobile devices such as iPhones and iPads. It has a sophisticated graphical user interface and seamless integration with other Apple-based products.
- Computers and laptops, for example MacBooks and iMacs, use Apple's macOS proprietary operating system. It offers a user-friendly interface, robust built-in applications, and seamless integration with other Apple devices. By contrast, a Microsoft PC or laptop would run a Windows-based operating system.
- Gaming consoles such as Sony's PlayStation and Microsoft's Xbox consoles use proprietary operating systems tailored for gaming and entertainment experiences. These include features to enable online gaming, media streaming and access to online stores.

Table 1.4: Advantages and disadvantages of proprietary operating systems

Advantages	Disadvantages
• Often prioritises ease of use and user-friendly interfaces, making them accessible to a wide range of users, including those with limited technical expertise • Include comprehensive support options to provide help for users • Optimised for specific hardware configurations, resulting in better performance and compatibility with supported devices.	• Opportunities for customisation are limited to the restrictions imposed by the company • Licencing fees or subscription costs can increase total cost of ownership and impact affordability of the system • May be more susceptible to security vulnerabilities due to the closed nature of development and limited transparency.

Operating systems and client requirements

Choosing an operating system on which to develop an application is important as it affects the reach, user experience and technical requirements of the application. Considerations might include:

- Compatibility: the most crucial factor is ensuring that the chosen operating system supports the application's required features and functions. Some applications are designed specifically for certain operating systems or may have dependencies that require a particular version.
- Performance: if an application requires real-time processing or high computational power, the operating system must be capable of efficiently managing system resources, such as the CPU and memory.

- Security: applications that deal with sensitive data or operate in regulated industries may need to have an operating system that has robust security features and a track record of addressing vulnerabilities quickly.
- User experience: different operating systems have distinct user interfaces, mechanisms of interaction and customisation options. The chosen operating system should align with the target users' preferences and provide an intuitive and seamless user experience.
- Licencing and costs: some operating systems are open-source and free to use, while others require purchasing licences or subscriptions. Clients may want cost-effective solutions that meet the application's requirements without creating unnecessary expenses.
- Support and maintenance: the availability of support and maintenance services for the chosen operating system is crucial for ensuring the application's reliability and stability. Operating systems with a large user base often have extensive documentation, community forums and professional support options available.

Learning in context 1

Selecting an operating system

Pixel Logic Inc. is a software development company specialising in image editing and enhancement applications. With a focus on providing intuitive and powerful tools for both amateur and professional photographers, Pixel Logic Inc. aims to create innovative solutions that empower users to unleash their creativity.

Pixel Logic Inc. has decided to develop a new photo editing application to meet the growing demand for versatile and user-friendly image editing tools. One of the key decisions facing the company is choosing the appropriate operating system(s) to develop the application for. The management team is debating between iOS, Android, and Windows as potential platforms for these applications are the mostly commonly used operating systems on mobile devices.

Table 1.5: Factors considered by Pixel Logic when making their choice

Factor	iOS	Android	Windows
Market share and user base	Known for its affluent user base and strong presence in the creative industry. Apple devices, such as iPhones and iPads, are popular among photographers and designers.	Dominates the global smartphone market with a wide user base, offering potential for reaching a large audience.	Less prevalent in the mobile space compared to iOS and Android but has a presence in the desktop and laptop markets, particularly among professionals and businesses.
Development environment	Development for iOS requires specialist coding knowledge. Apple's strict guidelines ensure consistency and quality across iOS apps.	The platform offers greater flexibility but may present challenges due to the range of different devices using this platform and compatibility issues.	Development for Windows can be done using Visual Studio and languages like C# or C++. Allows for building applications that run across multiple Windows devices.

(Continued)

Learning in context **Continued**

Factor	iOS	Android	Windows
Monetisation strategy	The App Store is known for higher user spending, offering potential for generating revenue through app sales and in-app purchases.	Google Play Store has a larger number of free apps and relies more on ad-based monetisation models. In-app purchases and subscriptions are also common.	The Microsoft Store provides opportunities for app distribution, but the user base may be smaller compared to iOS and Android.

Quick check 2

1 Make notes on the key differences between open and proprietary operating systems.

2 Imagine you want to create a new application for a desktop computer. What operating systems could you choose from? Consider the pros and cons of each.

1.3 Application types and categories

1.3.1 Application types

MP3
EPS
AVI
PNG
WAV
TXT
GIF
CSS
JPG
XLS
PDF
DOC
PPT
MOV
ZIP
PDF

Figure 1.4: These types of file are created and edited using applications

Communication

Communication applications are used to enable communication between users through various means such as text, voice, video calls and messaging. Characteristics include user-friendly interfaces, support for multimedia sharing, encryption for secure communication, integration with social media platforms and presence of features like group chats and video conferencing.

Educational

Educational applications are used to aid learning and increase knowledge, often through interactive lessons, quizzes, tutorials and educational resources. Characteristics include structured learning content, progress tracking, use of games and access to a wide range of subjects and topics.

Entertainment

Entertainment applications provide leisure activities and content for enjoyment and relaxation. Characteristics include content such as movies, TV shows, music, podcasts and eBooks with personalised recommendations, social sharing features, ability to download content for later. They may also use subscription-based models.

Games

Game applications give interactive experiences for entertainment and enjoyment, often involving challenges, strategy and competition. Characteristics include a huge range of game genres including action, adventure, puzzle, simulation and role-playing games. They also include engaging gameplay mechanics, high-quality graphics and sound effects, multiplayer options, in-app purchases and regular updates.

Lifestyle

Lifestyle applications assist users in managing various aspects of their daily lives, including health, fitness, finance, travel and personal organisation. Characteristics include features tailored to specific lifestyle needs such as workout tracking, budget management, travel planning tools, habit-building functions, reminders and customisation options.

Productivity

Productivity applications help users enhance efficiency and accomplish tasks effectively, both professionally and personally. Characteristics include tools for task management, note-taking, document editing, calendar integration, collaboration features, cloud storage synchronisation, cross-platform compatibility and support for integrations with other productivity tools.

Protection and utility

Protection and utility applications ensure the security, privacy and smooth functioning of devices by offering various utility functions and security features. Characteristics include antivirus and malware protection, device optimisation tools, data backup and recovery options, privacy controls, password managers, VPN services and system monitoring functionalities.

Web browsers

Web browsers enable users to access and navigate the World Wide Web, view web pages and interact with online content. Characteristics include a fast and responsive browsing experience, support for multiple tabs, bookmarking, private browsing modes, synchronisation across devices, compatibility with web standards and technologies and extensions or add ons for additional functionality.

1.3.2 Application software categories

Open

Open application software are applications that are built using open-source principles and are freely available for anyone to use, modify and distribute. They often encourage collaboration among developers and communities, leading to rapid innovation and improvement. The purpose of open application software is to provide accessible, flexible, and collaborative solutions that empower users and promote innovation in the software development ecosystem. Examples include VLC Player, Audacity and Mozilla Firefox.

Table 1.6: Advantages and disadvantages of open application software

Advantages	Disadvantages
• Flexibility: allow for a high degree of customisation and flexibility. Users can tailor applications to their specific needs, creating functionalities that may not be available in standard, closed applications. • Innovation: encourage innovation as they allow developers and users to experiment with new ideas, features and integrations. • Community collaboration: enable collaboration within developer communities. Developers can share their work, collaborate on projects and learn from each other.	• Quality control: as anyone can contribute, there may be a wide variation in the quality of applications, with some being poorly designed, insecure, or unreliable. • Security risks: if developers do not follow best practices or adequately test their code, there can be security risks that can potentially compromise the security of an entire system or network. • Lack of support: users may have to rely on community forums or self-help resources for assistance, which may not always be comprehensive enough.

Devices that use open application software include:

- personal computers such as desktops and laptops
- servers
- mobile devices such as smartphones and tablets
- embedded systems such as routers
- industrial equipment such as automation systems and robotics
- educational devices such as interactive whiteboards, educational robots.

Closed

Closed software is proprietary software developed and distributed by companies or organisations for commercial purposes. Users typically do not have access to the source code and modifications are often not allowed. The main purpose is to generate revenue through the sale of licences or subscriptions. Examples include Microsoft Office, Adobe Photoshop and AutoCAD.

Closed-source applications are commonly found in:

- personal computers such as desktops and laptops
- embedded systems such as consumer electronics and medical devices.

Shareware

Shareware software is distributed on a trial basis, allowing users to evaluate its features before purchasing a licence. Typically, shareware versions have limited features or a trial period after which users are prompted to purchase the full version. The main purpose of shareware is to encourage users to try out the software and then purchase the full version if they find it useful. It's a marketing strategy often used by independent developers or small software companies. Examples include WinRAR and WinZip.

Shareware applications are typically found in:

- Personal computers such as desktops and laptops
- Mobile devices such as smartphones and tablets.

Freeware

Freeware software is available for use at no cost. Users can download, install and use freeware without any payment required. Freeware is often distributed with an open license, allowing users to change and sell the software. Freeware is typically developed by individuals, organisations or communities for various purposes, including educational or recreational reasons. While it is offered for free, it serves a purpose for developers who may still benefit from donations, advertising revenue or by using it as a promotional tool for other products or services. Examples include VLC Media Player, Audacity and Firefox.

Freeware applications are commonly found in:

- personal computers such as desktops and laptops
- mobile devices such as smartphones and tablets
- consumer electronics such as smart TVs and digital cameras.

Embedded

Embedded software is specifically designed to perform dedicated functions within a larger system or device. It's often tightly integrated with hardware and may have limited user interaction or visibility. Embedded software is used in a wide range of devices and systems, including consumer electronics, automotive systems, medical devices, industrial equipment and more. Its purpose is to control and manage the functionality of the device or system it's embedded in. Examples include software found inside routers, operating systems in smartphones and control software in automotive systems.

Embedded applications are used in a wide range of devices and systems, including:

- consumer electronics such as smartphones, smart TVs and home appliances
- automotive systems such as infotainment systems and engine control units
- industrial machinery and equipment
- medical devices

- aerospace and defence systems
- IoT devices such as smart sensors and wearable devices.

Client requirements that affect the selection of an appropriate application software category

To select the most appropriate application software category, understanding and aligning with client requirements is essential. Software type should meet their needs while considering factors such as functionality, budget, security, scalability, support and user experience.

26.6

Figure 1.5: An example of a smart home device used to control the thermostat

Table 1.7: Advantages and disadvantages of different types of application software

Application software	Advantages	Disadvantages
Closed	• Security: may be more secure as the source code is not publicly available, making it harder for people to find vulnerabilities • Control: developers have full control over the software, allowing them to maintain quality and consistency.	• Lack of customisation: users have limited ability to customise or modify the software to suit their specific needs • Dependence: users are dependent on the developer for updates, bug fixes and support • Cost: closed-source software can be more expensive which can be a barrier for some users.
Shareware	• Evaluation: users can often try the software before purchasing, allowing them to evaluate its suitability. • Flexibility: developers can offer different pricing models, such as one-time purchases or subscriptions, to meet different user needs.	• Piracy: shareware is prone to piracy, as users can easily distribute unauthorised copies. • Limited functionality: shareware versions often come with limitations or restricted features compared to the full version, which may frustrate users.
Freeware	• Cost: freeware is free to use, making it accessible to a wide range of users. • Community support: freeware often benefits from community contributions, such as bug fixes and feature enhancements.	• Sustainability: it can be challenging for developers to sustain development and support without a direct revenue stream. • Quality: without financial incentives, developers may prioritise other projects or neglect maintenance and updates.
Embedded	• Efficiency: embedded applications are designed to run on specific hardware, resulting in optimised performance. • Reliability: embedded applications are often highly reliable, as they undergo rigorous testing and optimisation for their intended use cases.	• Limited flexibility: embedded applications designed for a specific hardware may not be adaptable for other environments. • Development complexity: developing embedded systems requires specialised knowledge of the hardware and programming skills that can increase the project cost.

Functionality – If the client requires extensive customisation and specific features tailored to their unique needs, they may prefer closed software where they can work closely with developers to implement those features. For clients who need a wide range of features but have limited budget constraints, shareware or freeware options may be suitable as they often provide a broad set of functionalities at a lower cost.

Budget constraints – Clients with limited budgets may prefer freeware or open-source software as they are usually available at no cost, reducing the cost. Alternatively, clients may choose shareware software if they are willing to pay for additional features or support, but still require cost-effective solutions.

Security and compliance requirements – Clients operating in industries with strict security and compliance regulations may prioritise closed-source software due to its enhanced security features and support. Embedded applications may also be considered for industries where security and reliability are paramount, as they are often purpose-built for specific hardware.

Scalability – Clients with scalability requirements may select closed or shareware software that offers extensive customisation options and scalability features to allow for future growth.

Support and maintenance – Clients with limited IT resources may prioritise software categories that offer comprehensive support and maintenance packages. Closed and shareware software often provide dedicated support channels and regular updates. Freeware and open-source software may still be viable options if the client is comfortable relying on community support or has in-house technical expertise.

User experience and training – Clients concerned about user experience and ease of adoption may prioritise closed or shareware software with intuitive interfaces and extensive user documentation. Freeware and open-source software may require more extensive training and support to maximize user proficiency, depending on their complexity.

1.3.3 Application software types

Off-the-shelf

Off-the-shelf software is prepackaged software that is developed and sold to a wide audience. It is ready-made and typically comes with standard features and functionalities. The purpose of off-the-shelf software is to provide solutions to common problems or meet needs in a general way across various industries. It's readily available for purchase or licencing and can be deployed relatively quickly. Examples include Microsoft Office, Adobe Photoshop and QuickBooks.

Table 1.8: Advantages and disadvantages of off-the-shelf application software

Advantages	Disadvantages
• Cost-effective: off-the-shelf software is typically cheaper than bespoke solutions as development costs are spread across a wide user base. • Fast deployment: because off-the-shelf software is pre-built, it can be deployed quickly, saving time and effort. • Established support: off-the-shelf software often comes with dedicated support from the vendor, including updates, patches and user documentation.	• Limited customisation: off-the-shelf software may not fully meet the unique requirements of every organisation. • Feature overload: some off-the-shelf software may come with features that are not relevant to a particular organisation, potentially causing confusion. • Dependency on vendor: organisations rely on the vendor for updates, support and maintenance, which may lead to issues if the vendor discontinues the product or provides inadequate support.

Custom off-the-shelf

Custom off-the-shelf software is a modified version of off-the-shelf software that has been tailored to meet the specific requirements of a particular organisation or industry. The purpose of custom off-the-shelf software is to combine the advantages of off-the-shelf solutions with the ability to address specific business needs. Organisations may customise the software to integrate with existing systems or comply with requirements of their business.

Table 1.9: Advantages and disadvantages of custom off-the-shelf application software

Advantages	Disadvantages
• Tailored solutions: custom off-the-shelf software offers a balance between standard features and customisation. • Reduced development time: typically requires less time and effort compared to building a bespoke solution from scratch, leading to faster deployment. • Lower cost: customising existing software is often more cost-effective than developing bespoke solutions since the foundation already exists, reducing development expenses.	• Limited flexibility: despite customisation options, organisations may still encounter limitations in functionality or integration capabilities. • Dependency on vendor: organisations may face challenges if the vendor does not support extensive customisation or if future updates conflict with customisations made. • Potential for over-customisation: organisations may over-customise off-the-shelf software, leading to complexity, maintenance issues and challenges in future upgrades.

Bespoke

Bespoke software is developed from scratch to meet the specific requirements of a single client or organisation. It is built to meet the client's specifications and needs. The purpose of bespoke software is to provide a highly customised solution that precisely meets the client's unique business processes and objectives. It offers complete control over features, design and functionality. Bespoke software is often used when off-the-shelf solutions cannot meet the organisation's requirements, or they want to stand out from their competition.

Table 1.10: Advantages and disadvantages of bespoke application software

Advantages	Disadvantages
• Complete customisation: bespoke software offers total flexibility and customisation, allowing organisations to tailor the solution to their unique requirements. • Competitive advantage: bespoke software can provide a competitive edge by addressing specific business needs and improving efficiency. • Ownership and control: organisations have full ownership and control over bespoke software, including intellectual property rights, allowing them to make changes and enhancements as needed.	• Higher cost: bespoke software development is typically more expensive than off-the-shelf solutions. • Longer development time: building bespoke software from scratch requires more time and resources compared to deploying off-the-shelf or customised solutions. • Higher risk: custom software development carries risks, including losing site of the aims, technical challenges and project delays, which may impact timelines and budgets.

Client requirements that affect the selection of an appropriate application software type

To find the best fit of application software type to meet the client requirements, the following factors may need to be considered:

Client specific requirements – If the client's requirements are very specific or complicated, they may need a bespoke solution. This would allow for complete customisation. However, if the requirements are more common, there may be an off-the-shelf product that will meet their needs.

Budget and time constraints – Clients with a limited budget or short time frame available may not be able to afford a custom off-the-shelf or bespoke solution. An off-the-shelf solution is cheaper and more quickly deployed, however, it would still need to be a good fit for the client's needs to be a suitable option.

Need for flexibility – Requirements can change over time, for example as the organisation grows. If this is the case then a solution that allows for flexibility, such as a custom off-the-shelf solution may offer this.

Industry-specific requirements – Clients may have industry specific needs or regulatory requirements to meet. In such cases, the client may need software that is tailored to address these requirements that could be best met by bespoke software.

Integration with existing systems – Clients with existing systems may want software solutions that seamlessly integrate with their current setup. This compatibility is best achieved through a custom off-the-shelf or bespoke solution.

User experience – Client requirements related to user experience, interface design and usability can influence the choice of application software type. Off the-shelf solutions often come with existing user interfaces and functionalities which may or may not be suitable. Bespoke solutions, however, can be tailored to provide an intuitive user experience aligned with the client's preferences and users.

Support and maintenance – Ongoing support, maintenance and updates are all important when selecting a software type. Off-the-shelf solutions typically come with vendor support and regular updates, while bespoke solutions may require dedicated maintenance resources or ongoing support contracts to provide a good experience for the end user.

Quick check 3

1 Summarise the differences between off-the-shelf, custom off-the-shelf and bespoke software application types.

2 Consider the factors affecting choice of application software type. If you were going to put them in order from the most to least important, which would be first and why?

Practice questions 1

ABC Health and Fitness is a leading wellness organisation committed to promoting healthy lifestyles through nutrition and exercise. They are seeking to develop a new mobile application called HealthPro that aims to simplify meal planning, promote balanced nutrition and empower users to make healthier food choices.

1 Explain the relationship between a program and an application. [2]

2 HealthPro will be designed for a proprietary operating system. Describe **one** advantage of this choice. [1]

3 Identify **one** type of application for HealthPro. [1]

4 Identify **two** possible characteristics of the application type chosen in **question 3**. [2]

TA2 Software development models

Learning intentions

This topic is about the different software models that may be used to create an application and their common phases.

It covers:

2.1 Software development models

2.2 The common phases of software development models

2.1 Software development models

Software development models are structured approaches to design used by software development teams to structure, plan and control the process of creating software. The models provide a framework that outlines the sequence of activities, tasks and deliverables involved in the software development lifecycle.

Software development models are used for the following reasons:

- They provide structure, outlining the activities from start to finish.
- They improve communication by making sure everyone understands their tasks and how they contribute to the final product.
- They help manage risk by identifying issues at an earlier stage.
- They support best practice and meeting quality standards.

Some common models used are highlighted in Table 1.11.

Table 1.11: Types of software development model

Traditional model	Prototyping model	Iterative model
Waterfall	• Rapid throwaway • Incremental • Evolutionary.	• Rapid Application Development (RAD) • Spiral • Agile.

Traditional model

Waterfall

The **waterfall model** is a linear and sequential approach to software development. It consists of distinct phases, such as requirements gathering, design, implementation, testing, deployment and maintenance. Each phase must be completed before moving on to the next, resembling a waterfall flowing downwards.

This model is well-suited for projects with clear and stable requirements or projects with strict regulatory or compliance requirements where documentation is crucial.

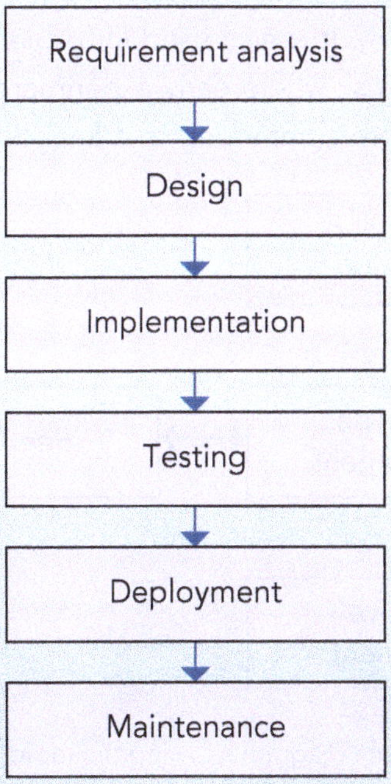
Requirement analysis
Design
Implementation
Testing
Deployment
Maintenance

Figure 1.6: Stages of a waterfall approach to software deployment

Table 1.12: Advantages and disadvantages of a waterfall software development model

Advantages	Disadvantages
• Clear and well-structured process • Easy to understand and manage • Each phase has defined deliverables, making progress measurable.	• Lack of flexibility to accommodate changes in requirements • Limited opportunities for customer feedback and validation during development.

Prototyping model

Rapid throwaway

The rapid throwaway model focuses on quickly building prototypes or mock-ups of the software to gather feedback and check requirements. **Prototype models** are often incomplete or of low quality, intended for demonstration and discussion purposes. Once feedback is received, the prototype is discarded and development begins using a different model or approach.

This approach is used for projects where the primary goal is to explore different design options or concepts quickly. It is also used for projects with high uncertainty or risk where early experimentation is necessary before committing to a final design.

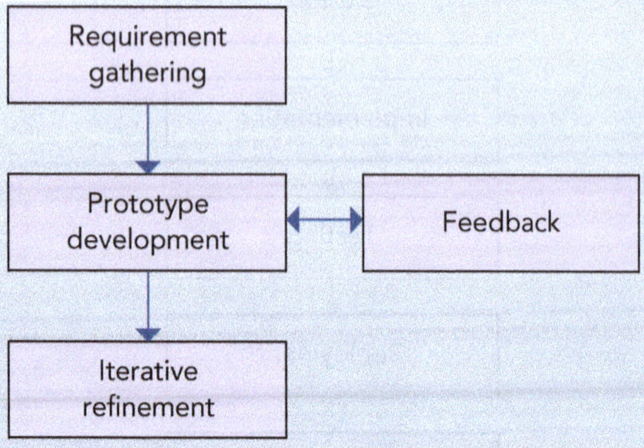

Requirement gathering
Prototype development
Feedback
Iterative refinement

Figure 1.7: Simple diagram showing the rapid throwaway model

Table 1.13: Advantages and disadvantages of a rapid throwaway software development model

Advantages	Disadvantages
• Increased speed of version development • Evolve ideas quicker • Lower labour costs/ staffing • Faster decision making • Can show client versions easier/ quicker • Reduced documentation.	• Can develop too many versions that are not needed • Increased costs by developing many versions • Confusion on feedback when many versions are created quickly • Lack of analysis at each stage of prototype development • Final product requires complete redevelopment from scratch after prototyping phase • May lead to wasted resources if prototyping reveals solution is not suitable.

Incremental

The incremental software development model involves breaking down the project into smaller, manageable modules or increments. Each increment represents a complete subset of functionality that can be developed, tested and delivered independently. Development occurs with each iteration or cycle adding new features or enhancements to the software. Stakeholders can review and provide feedback on each increment, allowing for continuous improvement and refinement.

This approach is suited to projects where requirements can be divided into distinct, prioritised increments. They might also be long-term projects with evolving requirements in which delivering early and frequently is important.

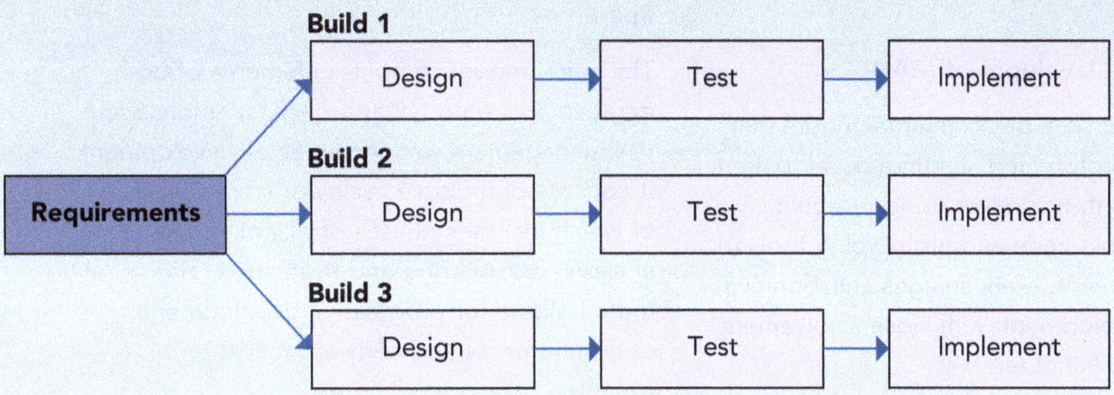
Build 1
Design
Test
Implement
Requirements
Build 2
Design
Test
Implement
Build 3
Design
Test
Implement

Figure 1.8: Diagram showing how each increment builds on work completed in previous iterations in the incremental model

Table 1.14: Advantages and disadvantages of an incremental software development model

Advantages	Disadvantages
• Flexibility to accommodate changes and adapt to evolving requirements • Opportunities for feedback at each iteration.	• Requires careful planning to define increments • Risk of scope growing too much if requirements are not managed effectively.

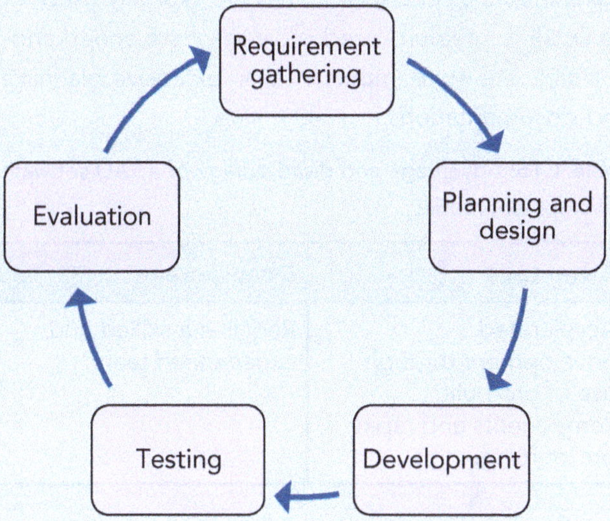
Requirement gathering
Planning and design
Development
Testing
Evaluation

Figure 1.9: In evolutionary software development, feedback from stakeholders on one cycle is incorporated into the next cycle

Evolutionary

The evolutionary model focuses on **iterative** development and refinement of the software through multiple cycles or iterations. Each iteration involves gathering requirements, designing, implementing, testing and evaluating the software. It allows for progressive development of requirements and design, with feedback from stakeholders incorporated into subsequent iterations.

This model is suitable for projects with evolving or unclear requirements where exploration and experimentation may be beneficial. They may also be used for technically complex projects or those where the solution is not clearly understood at the start.

Table 1.15: Advantages and disadvantages of an evolutionary software development model

Advantages	Disadvantages
• Iterative and incremental development allows for continuous improvement and refinement • Provides flexibility to respond to changing requirements and market conditions.	• Requires active user involvement and frequent feedback • May lead to higher initial development costs.

Iterative model

Rapid Application Development (RAD)

The RAD model is a type of incremental model that emphasises rapid prototyping, iterative development and user involvement. It involves using pre-built components, reusable code and prototyping tools to accelerate development. It encourages collaborative and interactive development, with close involvement of end users and stakeholders.

This model is used for projects with tight deadlines or those the need to gather quick feedback from stakeholders or end users. They are typically used for small to medium-sized projects where speed and flexibility are more important than extensive planning and documentation.

Table 1.16: Advantage and disadvantage of a RAD software development model

Advantage	Disadvantage
Accelerated development through use of pre-built components and rapid prototyping.	Requires a skilled and experienced team.

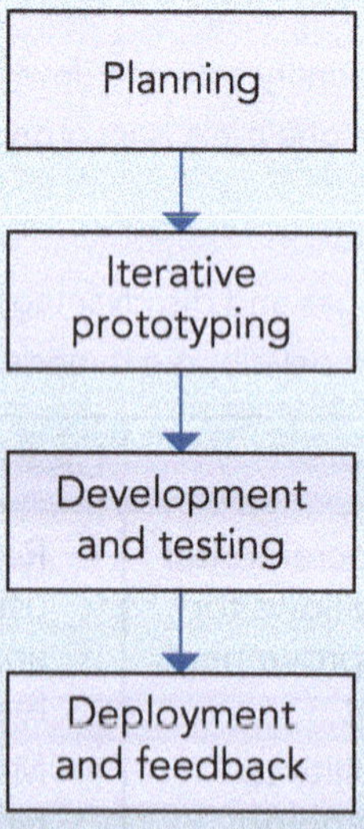
Planning
Iterative prototyping
Development and testing
Deployment and feedback

Figure 1.10: In the RAD model, development cycles are short and focused on delivering working prototypes quickly

Spiral

The spiral model combines elements of both iterative and waterfall approaches, emphasising risk management and incremental development. It consists of multiple cycles or spirals, each of which includes phases of planning, risk analysis, engineering and evaluation. The spiral model allows for progressive development of requirements and early identification of potential risks.

This model is used for projects with significant technical risks or uncertainties that need to be managed throughout the process. These may be large-scale projects where managing risk is important for success.

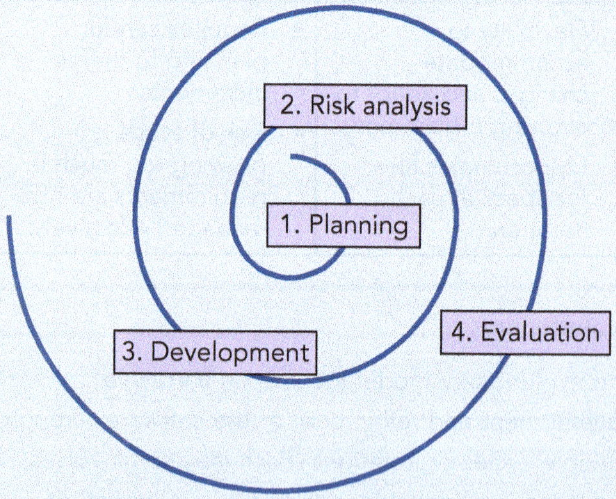
2. Risk analysis
1. Planning
4. Evaluation
3. Development

Figure 1.11: Phases within a spiral model

Table 1.17: Advantages and disadvantages of a spiral software development model

Advantages	Disadvantages
• Enables early risk identification and mitigation • Flexibility to accommodate changes and adjustments throughout the development process.	• Can be complex and resource-intensive to manage, particularly for small projects • Requires skilled and experienced team to effectively manage risk analysis.

Agile

Agile methodologies, such as Scrum and Kanban, prioritise flexibility, collaboration and iterative development. Scrum is primarily used for software development projects. Kanban, on the other hand, is more visual, using a board to represent work items moving through various stages of a process.

Agile approaches involve breaking the project into smaller iterations or sprints, typically lasting one to four weeks. Development teams work closely with stakeholders, adapt to changing requirements and deliver working software incrementally.

This model is used for projects with rapidly changing or evolving requirements where stakeholder collaboration and customer feedback are essential. It is typically used for small to medium-sized projects.

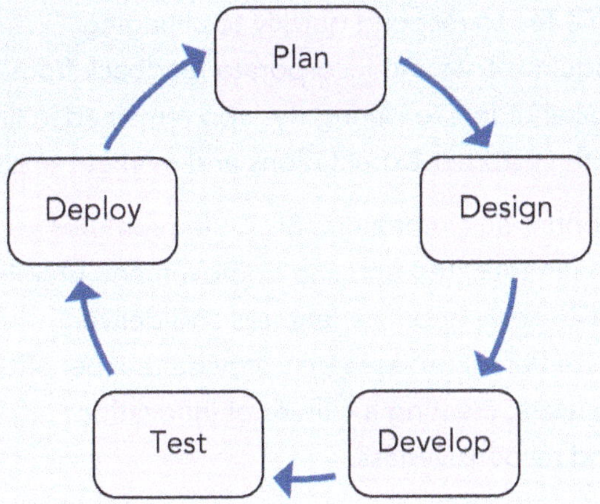
Plan
Design
Develop
Test
Deploy

Figure 1.12: In agile software development, activities are divided into small, manageable iterations

Table 1.18: Advantages and disadvantages of an agile software development model

Advantages	Disadvantages
• Emphasis on customer collaboration ensures software meets user needs and expectations • Continuous improvement and adaptation to evolving requirements.	• Requires highly collaborative team with strong communication skills • May not be suitable for projects with rigid or fixed requirements.

Using software development models offers several advantages. For example:

- Structured approach: development models provide a structured framework for organising and managing the software development process. This structured approach helps teams to plan, execute and monitor the project effectively.
- Clarity and communication: models facilitate communication and collaboration among project stakeholders by establishing a common understanding of the development process, milestones and deliverables. Clear communication helps in aligning expectations and resolving conflicts efficiently.
- Quality checking: development models emphasise quality throughout the software development lifecycle. By including testing activities at various stages, models help in identifying defects early, ensuring that the final product meets the required quality standards.

While software development models can have many advantages, there can also be many disadvantages. Some of these include:

- Rigidity: some development models, such as the waterfall model, can be rigid and inflexible, particularly when it comes to accommodating changes in requirements or responding to unexpected challenges. This rigidity may result in delays or cost overruns if not managed properly.
- Level of administration: certain models, especially those with extensive documentation and formal processes, can introduce administrative burden on the development team. This additional overhead may slow down the development process and increase project costs.

- Limited flexibility: some models, such as waterfall, follow a sequential and linear approach, which may not be well-suited for projects with evolving or unclear requirements. Such models may lack the flexibility to adapt to changing customer needs or market conditions.

These limitations will need to be carefully considered and addressed to ensure successful project outcomes.

Learning in context 2

Selecting a software model type

XYZ Tec, a leading technology company, wants to develop a new mobile application to enhance customer engagement and expand its market reach. Facing tight timelines and evolving requirements, XYZ Tec needed to carefully choose a project management model that would ensure efficient development, adaptability to changes, and timely delivery of the app.

At the start of the project, XYZ Tec chose to follow the waterfall project management model.

1. Clarity of requirements: The initial stage of the project had well-defined requirements, making it suitable for the waterfall model's linear and sequential movement through stages such as requirements gathering, design, development, testing and deployment.
2. Predictability: By following a defined plan and sequence of activities, XYZ Tec felt there would be greater predictability in project timelines and deliverables, crucial for meeting stakeholder expectations and business objectives.
3. Documentation: The waterfall model emphasises comprehensive documentation at each stage, providing clear guidelines and reference points for development teams and stakeholders, so reducing the chance of misunderstandings.

However, as the project progressed, XYZ Tec faced evolving customer needs and market changes. They felt a shift to a more adaptive and iterative project management type was required. Consequently, XYZ Tech transitioned to the agile project management model.

They made the change for the following reasons:

1. Flexibility: Agile's iterative nature allowed XYZ Tec to respond quickly to changing requirements and incorporate feedback from stakeholders, ensuring the app remained in line with customer expectations and market trends.
2. Continuous improvement: Agile promotes continuous iteration and improvement, enabling XYZ Tec to prioritise features and deliver incremental releases that provide real benefits to users, creating a culture of innovation and responsiveness.
3. Enhanced collaboration: Agile fosters close collaboration among teams, enabling communication, knowledge sharing and collective problem-solving, leading to higher-quality product and stronger team morale.

By initially adopting the waterfall model and later changing to the agile model, XYZ Tec balanced the need for structured planning with the flexibility to adapt to changing requirements and the market.

Quick check 4

1 Imagine that you are developing a new mobile app for your school or college. How would you decide which software development model to use for the project? Make a list of factors and briefly explain why they are important.

2 Create a mind map to draw out the key features of each of the following types of software development model: traditional model, prototyping model, iterative model.

2.2 The common phases of software development models

Planning

The planning phase of the software development model lays the foundation for a successful project by defining project goals, scope, resources, schedules and risk management strategies. The specifics of the planning phase will vary depending on the model chosen but will usually examine the project requirements and the **feasibility** of the project.

Requirements

In software development, the requirements provide information on what the software should do and how it should work. They are a detailed list of everything the software needs to do to be successful.

This involves gathering and analysing requirements from stakeholders, including clients, end users and other relevant parties.

The first stage is to identify stakeholders, those who have an interest in the software being developed. In addition to the client, this might include subject matter experts and regulatory bodies. To understand the requirements, you could use a range of methods such as:

- Interviews: in-person or online meetings with a series of open-ended questions to establish stakeholder perspectives and requirements
- Workshops and focus groups: in-person or online meetings with a group of people to hold collaborative discussions, encouraging active participation and engagement from a range of stakeholders
- Surveys and questionnaires: used to gather quantitative data and feedback on specific aspects of the software requirements
- Prototyping and mock-ups: develop prototypes, mock-ups or proof-of-concept demos to visualise and validate requirements with stakeholders.

As part of this phase, iteration may occur as stakeholders provide feedback or as the team gains a deeper understanding of the project scope.

Feasibility

In analysing the feasibility of a software development project, it is important to consider several factors.

- Technical feasibility: this examines whether the project is possible using the available technology, tools and resources. This includes a consideration of system functionalities and the expertise of the people available to take part in the project.
- Economic and/or commercial feasibility: this will look at whether the project would work financially when the costs of development are considered when weighed up against potential benefits. Potential benefits might include increased revenue, cost savings, improved efficiency or competitive advantages.
- Schedule feasibility: this evaluates whether the proposed project can be completed within the desired timeframe and deadlines. It involves examining the time required for each element

of the project and the availability of staff and resources. Project scheduling tools such as Gantt charts may be used.

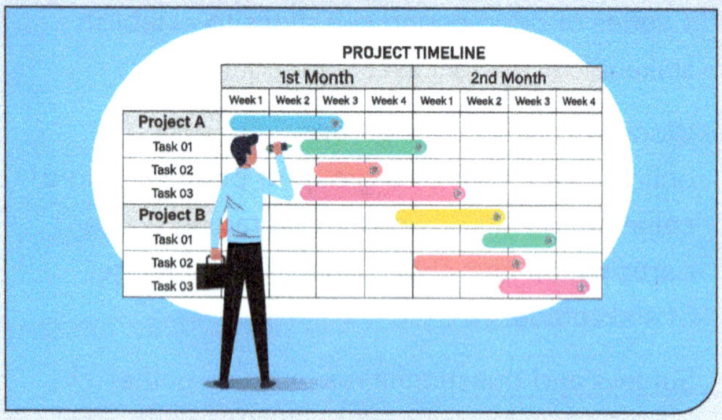
PROJECT TIMELINE
1st Month
2nd Month
Week 1
Week 2
Week 3
Week 4
Week 1
Week 2
Week 3
Week 4
Project A
Task 01
Task 02
Task 03
Project B
Task 01
Task 02
Task 03

Figure 1.13: A Gantt chart is a visual tool to show tasks, their duration and their dependencies

Design

The design phase in software development is the stage where the requirements gathered during the planning phase are translated into a detailed blueprint or design for the software system. It involves creating a comprehensive plan that outlines how the software will be structured, organised and implemented to meet the specified requirements.

Key activities involved in the design phase include Interface Design, Architectural Design and Detailed Design.

Interface design

Interface design focuses on designing the User Interface (UI) and User Experience (UX) aspects of the software. It involves creating layouts, navigation flows and interaction patterns that are intuitive, visually appealing and user-friendly.

Interface design considers factors such as usability, accessibility and responsiveness to ensure that the software is easy to use and accessible to a diverse range of users.

Common tasks in interface design include:

- Wireframing: creating simplified sketches or mock-ups of the UI to visualise the layout and structure of screens or pages.
- Prototyping: building interactive prototypes or mock-ups to simulate the behaviour and functionality of the UI.
- User testing: conducting testing with real users to gather feedback and refine the UI design based on their preferences and needs. The aim of this is to uncover issues with user interaction with the software, understand user behaviour and get feedback to improve the overall user experience.
- Graphic design: designing visual elements such as icons, images, colours and typography to enhance the aesthetic appeal and branding of the software.

Figure 1.14: Wireframes can be used to plan the layout of screens on mobile applications

During this phase, iteration may occur as initial designs are reviewed, refined and adjusted based on feedback or changing requirements.

Architectural design

Architectural design focuses on defining the overall structure and organisation of the software system. It identifies the main parts of the system and how they work together. It is focused on making sure the system can grow, be fixed easily, work fast and stay safe.

Common tasks in architectural design include:

- System decomposition: breaking down the system into smaller, manageable components or modules that can be developed and maintained independently

- Design patterns: developing common solutions to recurring problems that are encountered when building programs
- Dependency management: managing dependencies between components and modules to ensure they are not too reliant on one another
- Trade-off analysis: checking that design choices match what the project needs and can handle.

Detailed design

Detailed design is like drawing a detailed map for building software. It's about figuring out how each part of the software will work inside and what it needs to do its job. This includes designing how the different pieces will talk to each other and making sure they're set up correctly.

Some common tasks in detailed design are:

- Component design: defining the structure and connections of each part of the software
- Algorithm design: creating step-by-step instructions for the software to solve specific problems
- Data design: deciding how information will be organised and stored
- Error handling: planning how the software will handle mistakes or problems to make sure it keeps running smoothly.

Constructing/creation

The construction phase of a software development project focuses on turning design concepts into a working software solution. This includes coding, testing, debugging, documentation and version control, so users can go back to previous versions if needed. This is a crucial stage where the software product begins to take shape.

Tasks involved in the construction phase include coding, testing and debugging.

- Coding: developers write the code according to the specifications outlined in the design documents. This involves translating design concepts into programming languages and creating algorithms to build the software solution.
- Testing: as code is written in the construction/creation phase, developers perform tests to ensure that the software behaves as expected. Testing helps identify and fix defects early in the development process, improving code quality and reliability.
- Debugging: developers troubleshoot and debug issues identified during testing. This involves identifying the causes of problems, fixing errors in the code and ensuring that the software behaves as expected under various conditions.

Testing

In addition to testing during the construction phase, the software will also go through a thorough evaluation to ensure it meets quality standards, functions correctly and meets user requirements.

During this phase, functional testing will take place. This involves checking that each function or feature of the software performs as it is supposed to according to specified requirements. It might also include regression testing. This is the process of retesting the software after code changes or modifications have been made to make sure that existing functionalities are not negatively affected.

Examples of tasks that may be included in the testing phase include:

- Unit testing: testing individual parts of the software to ensure they work correctly
- Integration testing: checking that different parts of the software work together as expected
- Compatibility testing: ensuring the software works correctly across different devices, browsers, and operating systems
- Usability testing: evaluating the user interface and user experience to make sure it is intuitive and user-friendly.

Implementation

Once the system has been thoroughly tested, it is ready for implementation.

The implementation phase is when the software is deployed and integrated into an organisation's existing systems and processes. This phase may include the installation, configuration and testing to ensure it works as expected. It may also include training users on how the software works and providing initial support to ensure the software features are being used successfully.

There are three different approaches to implementation: phased, parallel and big bang implementation, each with its own advantages and disadvantages.

Phased

Phased implementation involves rolling out the new software or changes gradually, in phases or stages. There might be certain features or functionalities that will be delivered in chunks over time. This reduces risk as testing can be carried out at each stage and eases the transition for users by allowing them to adapt gradually to the new system. However, this will prolong the overall implementation timeline as each phase requires time and resources and could cause frustration for the end user.

Parallel

Parallel implementation involves running both the old and new systems alongside one another for a period of time. This provides a safety net by allowing users to go back to the old system if issues arise with the new system. It also means that users can gradually transition to the new system at their own pace, which reduces disruption. However, organisations have the cost of two systems to maintain and support, which can be expensive. It can also be confusing for end users to have two systems at the same time.

Big bang (crash)

Big bang implementation involves delivering the new system or changes all at once, replacing the old system entirely in a single operation. This approach offers the fastest implementation timeline as the new system is deployed in one step. It also simplifies management and coordination as the focus is on a single switchover event. However, it is high risk as, if issues arise with the new system, there is no fallback option. It also forces users to adapt quickly to the new system without a transition period.

During this phase, iteration may occur as issues are identified and addressed, or as user feedback leads to updates or enhancements for the software.

Common tasks during the implementation phase include:

- Implementation plan: outline the steps, timeline and resources needed for the implementation phase
- Training: organise and deliver training to ensure users are comfortable and able to use the new system
- User support: offer helpdesk services and troubleshooting to aid users during the transition period.

Documentation creation

To support implementation of the software, user documentation needs to be created to guide end users through the software interface, features and functionalities. Clear, well written documentation is key to improving the user experience and supporting the successful adoption of the software.

Tasks might include:

- **Audience:** understanding the needs, skill level and preferences of the target audience
- **Planning:** deciding the scope of the content of the documentation by consulting with the target audience
- **Writing content:** writing clear and concise content, avoiding technical terms and jargon.
- **Visual aids:** creating visual aids such as screenshots, diagrams and videos to make the documentation more engaging and accessible.

Maintenance

Once the software has been implemented, maintenance is important to ensure the ongoing functionality, stability and usability of the software. This is essential for ensuring the long-term success of the project.

Here are the main tasks involved in the maintenance phase:

- **Bug fixing:** identifying, prioritising and fixing any bugs, errors or issues that occur in the software. This may involve troubleshooting reported problems, analysing causes and resolving the issues.
- **Enhancements:** adding new features, functionalities or improvements based on user feedback, changing requirements or advances in technology.
- **Performance optimisation:** identifying and addressing performance issues that affect its speed, responsiveness or scalability, for example.
- **Security updates:** monitoring and addressing security vulnerabilities, threats and risks to ensure the software remains secure and protected against potential cyberattacks or data breaches.
- **Compatibility maintenance:** ensure that the software remains compatible with changing platforms, operating systems, browsers and third-party integrations.

During this phase, iteration may occur as new features are added, existing features are improved or as bugs are reported and resolved.

Quick check 5

1 Create an infographic that summarises each of the phases of software development and highlights **at least two** tasks that might feature in each phase.

2 Explain to someone the differences between the three approaches to implementation.

Practice questions 2

Nimble Motors is a leading car dealership and service centre dedicated to providing high-quality vehicles and exceptional customer service. They want to update their existing mobile application to allow them to showcase their latest vehicle stock and enable customers to conveniently book their cars for repair and maintenance services. Their goal is to enhance the customer experience, streamline their operations and strengthen their online presence.

1 Discuss whether Nimble Motors should use the waterfall model for the development of the application. **[9]**

In your answers, you **must** write about:

- any advantages to Nimble Motors
- any disadvantages to Nimble Motors
- whether you would recommend that Nimble Motors use the waterfall model and your reasons.

2 Nimble Motors have decided on a big bang implementation approach.

Describe what is meant by big bang implementation. **[2]**

TA3 Planning application development projects

Learning intentions

This topic is about why planning a project is important, planning considerations and the impact of planning on application development. It also explores the component parts of a variety of planning tools that might be used, their advantages and disadvantages and how they can be used effectively.

It covers:

3.1 Planning projects

3.2 Project planning tools

3.1 Planning projects

Purpose of planning projects

Project planning is crucial to the success of an application development project for several reasons. First, it provides a clear vision and **objectives** for the project. This means that all stakeholders have an understanding about what needs to be done. A project plan will also set out the timeline for the project and **milestones** that need to be met along the way. This helps track progress and make sure that the project is completed on time.

A project plan will also identify and allocate **resources** such as time for different tasks and activities, **budget** and **personnel** needed. This means that resources can be used as efficiently as possible, and wastage reduced. This also helps to accurately control costs and manage expenses across the project lifecycle.

Planning also helps in identifying potential risks and developing strategies to reduce or remove them. By foreseeing and tackling risks early on, the project stands a better chance of success. Planning also helps with quality assurance by defining quality standards and procedures. This ensures that the final product meets the desired quality criteria and satisfies user requirements.

Finally, a project plan facilitates better communication and collaboration among team members and stakeholders. It ensures that everyone involved in the project understands their roles and responsibilities and those of others within the project.

Impact of not planning a project

Overall, it is preferable to plan carefully for a project for it to be successful. If a project is not adequately planned, it can result in the partial or total failure of a project to deliver a suitable final product.

For example, if project objectives are vague or poorly defined this can lead to confusion among team members and stakeholders. This might result in delays to the project or an unsuitable final product. If a project timeline is not established, it's easy for projects to fall behind schedule, leading to missed deadlines and potential business impacts such as increased costs or loss of revenue.

Resource management is key to project success. Where this is not considered, there may be an inefficient allocation of resources, leading to delays and poor-quality outcomes. This can also lead to unexpected expenses, resulting in budget overruns and financial strain on the organisation. Additionally, where risks are not considered at the outset of a project, it becomes more vulnerable to unexpected challenges, which can derail progress and impact success.

Finally, without adequate project planning, communication among team members and stakeholders can suffer. This can lead to misunderstandings and conflict about the project and its direction.

Table 1.19: Advantages and disadvantages of planning application development projects

Advantages	Disadvantages
• Clarity of objectives: planning helps to define clear project objectives and scope, ensuring that all stakeholders understand what needs to be achieved. • Resource optimisation: proper planning enables efficient allocation and use of resources such as time, budget and manpower, reducing wastage and maximising productivity. • Risk mitigation: planning involves identifying and addressing potential risks early in the project lifecycle, reducing the likelihood of costly setbacks and delays. • Timeline management: planning allows for the setting of realistic timelines and milestones, enabling better tracking of progress and ensuring timely delivery of the project. • Quality assurance: planning includes defining quality standards and processes, ensuring that the final product meets the desired level of quality and user requirements. • Cost control: by estimating costs accurately and controlling expenses throughout the project, planning helps prevent budget overruns and financial issues.	• Time consuming: planning can be time-consuming, especially for complex projects, which may delay the start of a project. • Overplanning: excessive planning, where too much time is spent planning and not enough on actual execution, can result in project delays. • Inflexibility: overly rigid plans may not be flexible enough to reflect changes or unforeseen circumstances, leading to difficulties in adapting to evolving project requirements. • Costly changes: if planning is not done thoroughly, it may lead to costly changes later in the project lifecycle, increasing expenses and delaying delivery. • Dependency on assumptions: plans are often based on assumptions about future events or conditions, which may turn out to be incorrect, leading to deviations from the planned course of action.

Planning considerations

To successfully plan a project, the following areas must be considered:

- budget
- constraints
- legislation
- resources
- success criteria
- time.

Budget

The budget is the amount of money that is available for the project. The project plan should ensure that the overall development budget is not exceeded. The budget directly affects the scope and scale of the application development. It influences the size of the development team, the technology that can be used and the level of customisation or features that can be implemented. A limited budget may require prioritising certain features over others or seeking cost-effective solutions.

Constraints

Constraints are limitations or boundaries that may affect the project and could be technological, environmental, regulatory or organisational constraints. Within the project plan it is important to understand and address constraints to ensure project success. Constraints influence decision-making throughout the development process. Technological constraints may dictate the choice of platforms or tools, while regulatory constraints such as data protection laws may affect how user data is handled. Ignoring constraints can lead to compliance issues, project delays or unexpected costs.

Legislation

Legislation refers to laws or a set of laws that have been passed by a government. Within the planning phase of the project, it is vital relevant legal and ethical issues are considered.

The following areas of legislation may be relevant to application software development:

- Copyright
- Data protection
- Electronic communications.

Copyright law protects original works of authorship, including software code, images, videos and sound. It ensures that developers have exclusive rights to their code and prevents unauthorised copying, distribution or modification of their work. Developers need to be mindful of copyright law when creating software to avoid infringing on others' intellectual property rights. Failure to comply with copyright law can lead to legal disputes, fines and damage to reputation.

Data protection legislation aims to protect individuals' privacy rights and regulate the processing of personal data. In software development, compliance with data protection laws is crucial when handling personal user information such as name, email address and location data, for example. Software developers must use appropriate data protection measures such as encryption and CAPTCHA to ensure the confidentiality, integrity and availability of user data.

Different countries have different data protection laws and regulations. For example, the European Union's General Data Protection Regulation (GDPR) has strict requirements for data protection, while other countries may have less strict rules. Organisations must follow the data protection laws of all countries involved in the data transfer. This can be made more complicated when data is transferred across borders and requires a thorough understanding of international regulations.

Electronic communications are also subject to legislation, including email, messaging and electronic marketing. Software developers must comply with electronic communications legislation when developing applications that involve electronic messaging or marketing activities. This includes obtaining consent from users before sending commercial communications, providing means of opting out and ensuring compliance with rules regarding spam emails and electronic marketing.

Making sure the application complies with legislation is critical for legal and ethical reasons. Failure to stick to relevant laws and regulations can lead to financial penalties, and damage to the organisation's reputation.

Resources

Resources include the human, technological and physical assets required to complete the project successfully. These should be carefully considered as part of the project plan so there are enough skilled personnel, hardware and software, and support systems for efficient application development. Inadequate resources may lead to project delays, increased costs and impact on quality.

Success criteria

Success criteria define the measurable factors that determine project success. When planning a project these need to be identified (see TA2.2), so that progress to the desired outcome can be measured allowing those involved to track the progress and make any adjustments if needed. Success criteria guide decision-making and project priorities during application development. They help ensure that the developed application meets user needs, achieves business objectives and delivers expected benefits.

Time

Time is a critical constraint in project management. When planning, meeting deadlines and delivering the project on schedule is essential to meet stakeholder expectations and minimising additional costs. Time constraints may mean prioritising essential features to ensure deadlines are met. Failure to manage time effectively can lead to project delays, missed opportunities and dissatisfaction among stakeholders.

Quick check 6

1. Summarise the reasons why planning a project is important.
2. Create a mind map to draw out key points about factors to consider when planning a project.

3.2 Project planning tools

Each of these project management tools offers unique advantages and disadvantages, and the choice of tool(s) depends on the specific needs, complexity and goals of the project, as well as the preferences and expertise of the project team.

Often, a combination of tools may be used to address different aspects of project planning to ensure a successful outcome.

Arrow diagram

An **arrow diagram** is a graphical representation used in project planning to show the order of activities and their dependencies within a project. It consists of nodes (or circles) that represent events and arrows that represent activities. The arrows show the relationships between activities and the direction of travel. Dummy arrows can also be used to represent relationships between activities where there is no direct link. Dummy arrows are drawn as dashed lines.

Arrow diagrams are often used together with **Critical Path Method (CPM)** or **Program Evaluation and Review Technique (PERT)** to analyse project schedules, identify critical paths and work out the earliest and latest start and finish times for activities. They provide a visual representation of the project's workflow, helping project managers and teams understand the project's structure and dependencies, and helping to schedule and plan resource allocation.

Table 1.20: Advantages and disadvantages of arrow diagrams

Advantages	Disadvantages
• Provides a visual representation of the project's tasks and their dependencies • Helps in identifying the critical path and understanding the sequence of tasks • Useful for complex projects with numerous tasks.	• Can become complex and difficult to understand for large projects • May not clearly show task durations or resource allocation • Less commonly used compared to other tools.

Critical Path Analysis (CPA)/Critical Path Method (CPM)

Critical Path Analysis (CPA) or Critical Path Method (CPM) is a project management technique used to plan and manage complex projects. It helps project managers identify the longest sequence of dependent activities and work out the shortest possible time for completing a project.

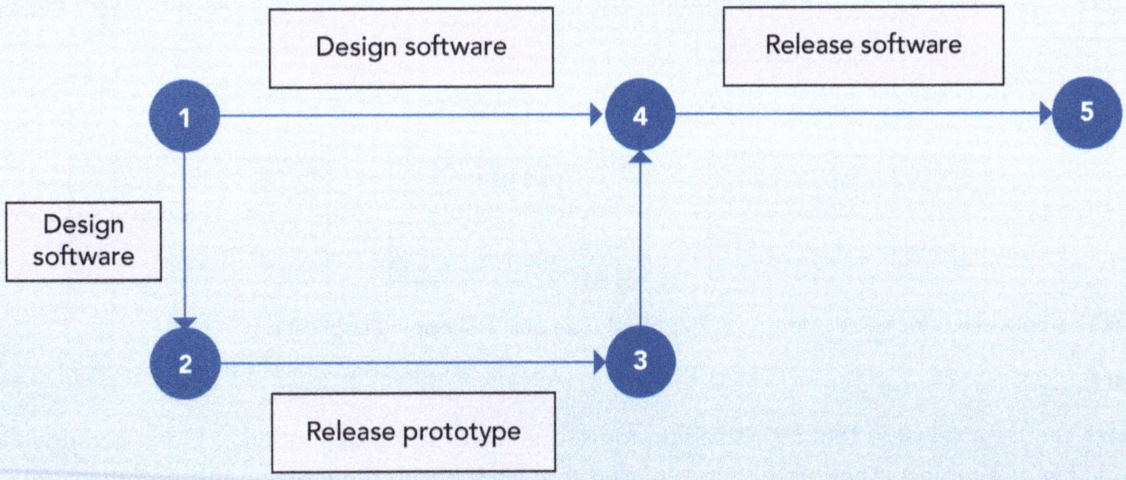
Design software
Release software
1
4
5
Design
software
2
3
Release prototype

Figure 1.15: Example of an arrow diagram with event nodes and arrows to show path through a project

The key features are:

- Tasks and activities: the work required to complete the project, clearly defined, with specific start and end points.
- Dependencies: tasks often depend on each other, meaning that the start or completion of one task may affect the start or completion of another.
- Duration: the time required to complete each task. This can be estimated based on historical data, expert judgment or other estimation techniques.

A visual representation of these elements is plotted on a network diagram. It can be constructed using nodes (representing tasks) and arrows (representing dependencies). Network diagrams help in identifying the critical path and understanding the sequence of tasks. The critical path is the longest sequence of tasks through the project network, meaning that if any task on the critical path is delayed, the entire project will be delayed.

Table 1.21: Advantages and disadvantages of CPA

Advantages	Disadvantages
• Identifies the critical path, helping to prioritise tasks and focus resources on critical activities • Provides a clear understanding of project dependencies and the shortest possible duration for project completion • Helps in scheduling, resource allocation and risk management.	• Requires accurate task duration estimates, which can be challenging to establish • Does not account for uncertainties or variations in task duration • Can be complex to implement and may require specialised software.

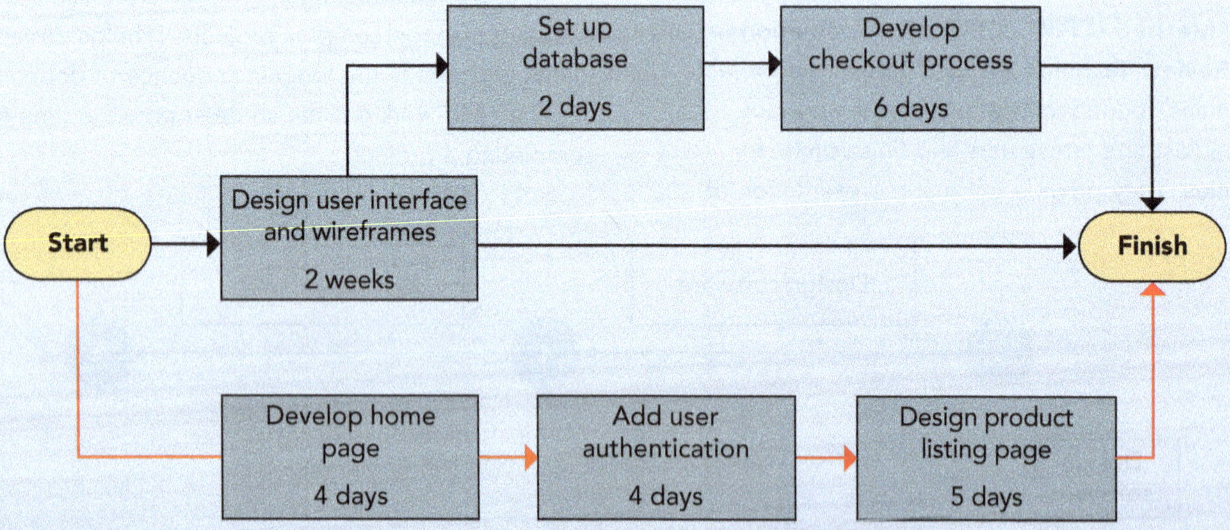
Set up database
2 days
Develop checkout process
6 days
Start
Design user interface and wireframes
2 weeks
Finish
Develop home page
4 days
Add user authentication
4 days
Design product listing page
5 days

Figure 1.16: Example of a Critical Path Method (CPM) plan for an online shopping application

Flowchart

A **flowchart** can be a valuable tool for visualising the sequence of tasks, dependencies, decision points and overall workflow of a project. They are commonly used to communicate the logic and flow of the software's processes. They support the planning process by providing a clear visual roadmap of the stages in the project from the initial idea to completion.

Table 1.22: Commonly used symbols used on a flowchart when mapping out a process within a project

Symbol	Symbol name	Description
 Start / End	Start/End	These symbols represent the beginning and end of the project flowchart.
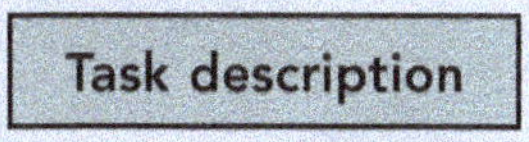 Task description	Process/Task	These symbols represent specific tasks or activities within the project.
 Decision	Decision	These symbols represent points in the project where a decision needs to be made, leading to different paths or outcomes.
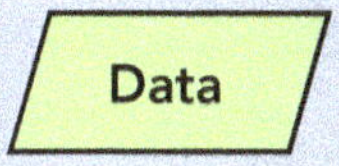 Data	Data Input/Output	These symbols indicate where data is entered into or extracted from the project.
	Arrows	These connect the various symbols in the flowchart, indicating the sequence of tasks and the flow of the project.

Table 1.23: Advantages and disadvantages of flowcharts

Advantages	Disadvantages
• Offer a visual representation of project workflows, decision points and process sequences • Easy to understand and communicate, making them useful for team collaboration and stakeholder engagement.	• May become too complex for large projects • Limited in their ability to represent detailed task durations, resource allocations or dependencies • Not specifically designed for project management.

Gantt charts

Gantt charts are often found within project management software. They play an important role in project planning as they visually represent the schedule of tasks, their durations, dependencies and progress over time. This helps plan the timeframe for the project, how tasks should be ordered and how resources should be allocated across the project.

The key components and conventions include:

- Task list: a column on the left side of the Gantt chart that outlines all the tasks or activities involved in the project. Each task is typically listed as a row in the chart.
- Time scale: the horizontal axis of the Gantt chart represents time, usually broken down into days, week, or months, depending on the project's timeline. The time scale provides a reference for scheduling tasks and tracking progress over time.
- Bars/blocks: bars or blocks represent individual tasks or activities. Each task is depicted as a horizontal bar covering the duration of the task along the time axis. The length of the bar linked to the task's duration. Shading may also be used to show task completion.

- Dependencies: dependencies, shown by arrows or lines connecting tasks, indicate the sequence in which tasks must be completed.
- Milestones: significant events or achievements within the project timeline, represented on the Gantt chart as diamond-shaped symbols placed at specific points along the time axis.

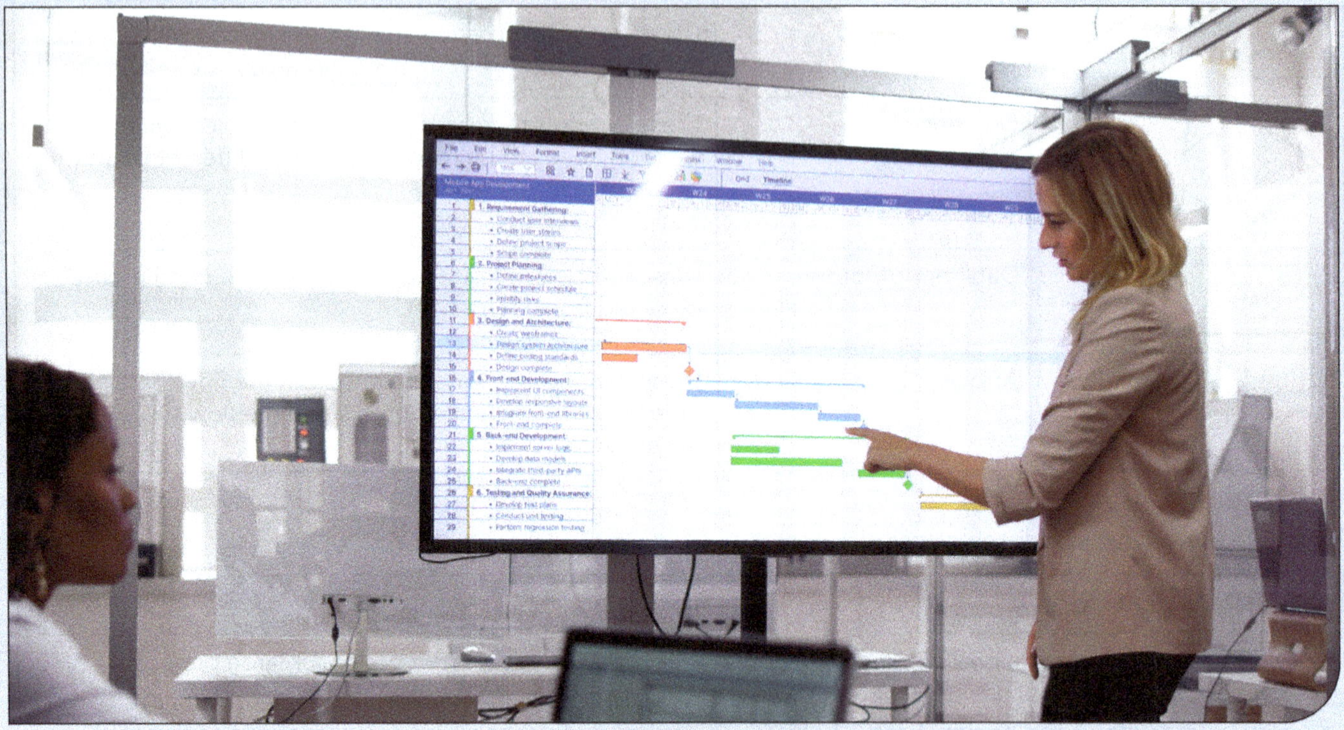

Figure 1.17: Gantt charts give a visual representation of the project schedule, task dependencies, milestones and progress

Table 1.24: Advantages and disadvantages of Gantt charts

Advantages	Disadvantages
• Provide a visual timeline of project tasks, durations and dependencies • Clearly show task dependencies, overlaps and milestones • Help in resource planning, scheduling and tracking progress.	• May oversimplify complex project workflows • Can be challenging to manage for large projects with lots of tasks or changes.

PERT charts

Program Evaluation and Review Technique (PERT) charts are another tool used in project management to visualise and schedule tasks. During the planning phase, PERT charts provide an idea of the time required to complete a project, which can help with resource allocation and risk management. They are designed to produce estimates of the shortest, longest and most likely time frame for a project. PERT charts are particularly useful for projects with uncertain durations or where several activities can run at the same time.

Features of a PERT chart include:

- **Nodes**: these represent tasks or activities within the project. Each node typically contains the task name, as well as other relevant information such as duration estimates, dependencies and responsible individuals or teams.
- Directed arrows: these connect the nodes in the PERT chart, representing the dependencies between tasks. Arrows indicate the sequence in which tasks must be completed.
- Event points: event points (also called circles or bubbles) represent milestones or key events within the project timeline, such as project start.
- Duration estimates: each task or activity in the PERT chart is associated with how long each task is likely to take, for example: Optimistic (O), Most Likely (M) and Pessimistic (P) durations. These estimates are used to calculate the Expected Time (ET) of each task. Note that, in Figure 1.18, durations are not included as each project will be different.

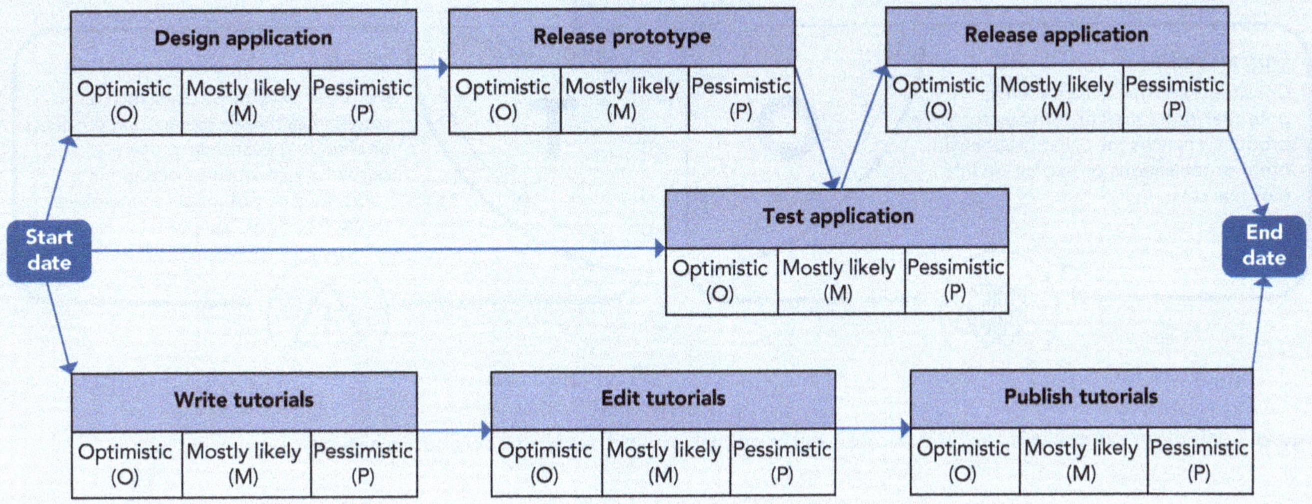
Start date
Design application
Optimistic (O)
Mostly likely (M)
Pessimistic (P)
Release prototype
Optimistic (O)
Mostly likely (M)
Pessimistic (P)
Release application
Optimistic (O)
Mostly likely (M)
Pessimistic (P)
Test application
Optimistic (O)
Mostly likely (M)
Pessimistic (P)
End date
Write tutorials
Optimistic (O)
Mostly likely (M)
Pessimistic (P)
Edit tutorials
Optimistic (O)
Mostly likely (M)
Pessimistic (P)
Publish tutorials
Optimistic (O)
Mostly likely (M)
Pessimistic (P)

Figure 1.18: PERT is focused on managing uncertainty in project duration

Table 1.25: Advantages and disadvantages of PERT

Advantages	Disadvantages
• Uses estimates for task durations, allowing for uncertainty and variability • Helps in risk analysis by considering optimistic, pessimistic and most likely scenarios • Provides a visual representation of project timelines and dependencies.	• Requires expertise to accurately estimate optimistic, pessimistic and most likely durations for tasks • Can be time-consuming to create and manage, especially for large projects • May not provide as clear a view of the critical path as other tools.

Strengths/Weaknesses/Opportunities/Threats (SWOT) analysis

A **SWOT analysis** (Strengths, Weaknesses, Opportunities, Threats) is a strategic planning tool commonly used in business to assess the internal and external factors that may affect a project or organisation. It can provide valuable insights into various aspects of the project, helping to inform decision-making and planning.

A SWOT analysis is typically shown in a 2×2 grid with a quadrant for each element. Each section is then completed as in Figure 1.19.

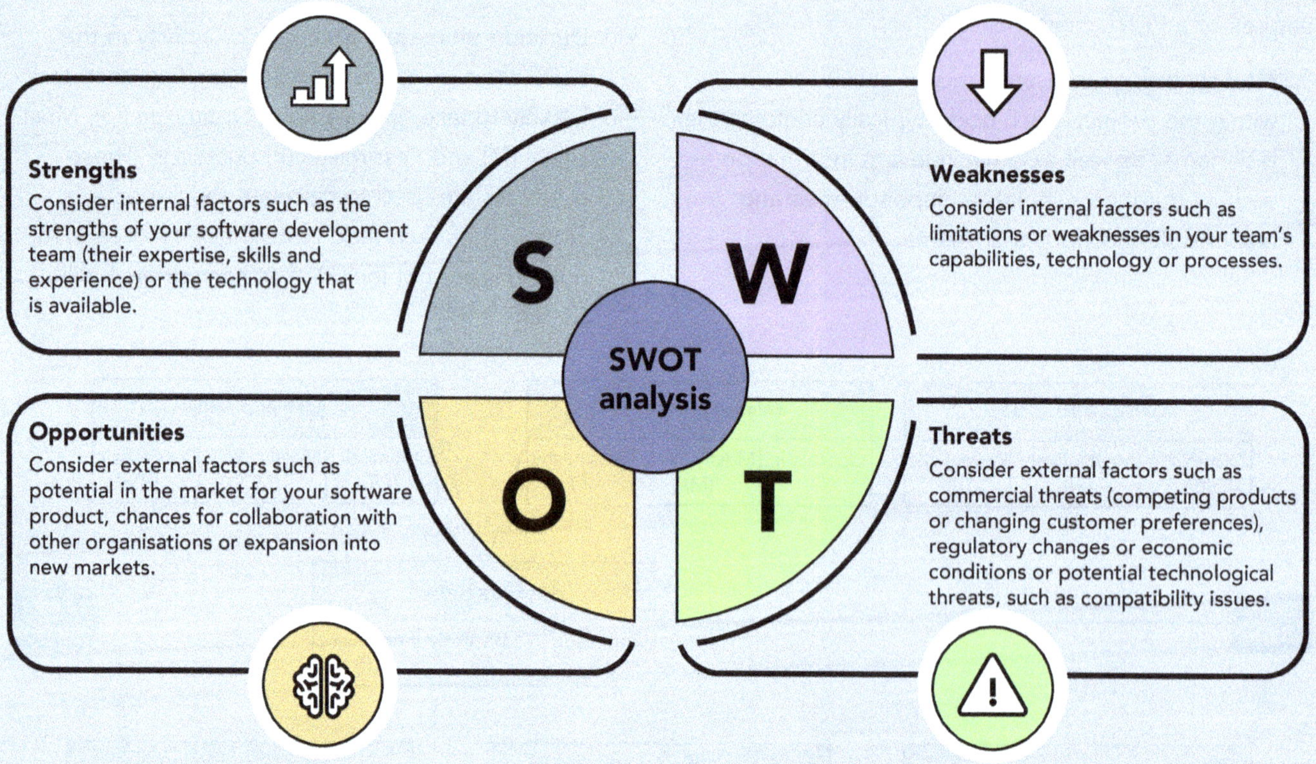
Strengths
Consider internal factors such as the strengths of your software development team (their expertise, skills and experience) or the technology that is available.
S
W
Weaknesses
Consider internal factors such as limitations or weaknesses in your team's capabilities, technology or processes.
SWOT analysis
Opportunities
Consider external factors such as potential in the market for your software product, chances for collaboration with other organisations or expansion into new markets.
O
T
Threats
Consider external factors such as commercial threats (competing products or changing customer preferences), regulatory changes or economic conditions or potential technological threats, such as compatibility issues.

Figure 1.19: A SWOT analysis can help support decision making and develop a business strategy

Once a SWOT analysis has been conducted it can be used to inform project planning in several ways. First, it allows you to develop strategies to address weaknesses and mitigate threats identified in the analysis, for example recruiting additional staff with specific expertise. It can also show you how to make the most of your team's strengths. It can also help set clear project objectives and focus resources and efforts on areas where the project has the greatest potential for success.

Table 1.26: Advantages and disadvantages of SWOT analysis

Advantages	Disadvantages
• Provides a structured approach to identifying internal strengths and weaknesses, as well as external opportunities and threats • Simplifies the analysis of a situation by breaking it down into four key areas • Allows threats to a project to be identified early on • Allows quantitative/ qualitative data to be used to assess a situation.	• Subjective nature may lead to bias • Oversimplification of issues can lead to key aspects being missed • Limited in its ability to prioritise factors identified • Can be difficult to categorise information into the four sections, which can lead to disorganisation.

How defined client requirements affect the selection of project planning tools

Selecting the right project planning tool for the job is important in ensuring success. Defined client requirements play a crucial role in selecting project planning tools as they influence various aspects of project management, including scope, task breakdown, timeline, communication and flexibility.

- **Scope of the project:** the scope of the project, or what needs to be delivered, will influence the selection of an appropriate tool. For example, a large and complex project may be confusing if represented on a flowchart.
- **Task breakdown:** project managers often need to break down a project into manageable tasks that can be easily sequenced. A SWOT analysis or flowchart cannot show tasks and dependencies, whereas a Gantt chart may be more appropriate.
- **Timeline:** client requirements often include deadlines and milestones. Project tools that support the creation of timelines, such as Gantt charts, Critical Path Analysis and PERT charts, allow project managers to allocate resources, set dependencies and establish realistic deadlines based on client requirements.
- **Communication:** client requirements often involve multiple stakeholders with different perspectives and expectations. SWOT analysis and Gantt charts can be useful planning tools to communicate planning and progress to stakeholders whereas some other tools, such as PERT charts, can be more difficult to understand.
- **Flexibility:** client requirements can change over time, so tools that can adapt to reflect these changing requirements can be useful. A Gantt chart or flowchart are easily updated and can flex to changes over time whereas PERT chart are complex and time consuming to make so less able to adapt.

Learning in context 3

Selecting an appropriate planning tool

Amondale Software Solutions, a startup specialising in mobile application development, was getting ready to launch their flagship product: an innovative task management app designed to streamline productivity for users. With a small but dedicated team of developers and designers, they recognised the importance of effective project planning to ensure the successful and timely delivery of their app.

As the project start date approached, the team deliberated on which planning tool would best suit their needs. They considered several options, including Gantt charts, PERT charts and flowcharts. Each tool offered unique features and benefits, but the team needed to choose the one that would provide the most value for their specific project requirements.

They identified several factors that were important in making their decision:

1 Timeline visualisation

2 Resource allocation

3 Stakeholder communication

4 Adaptability.

Timeline visualisation: the Gantt chart provides a clear and visual representation of the project timeline, showing task durations, dependencies and milestones. This allows the team to easily track progress and identify potential bottlenecks or delays. PERT charts can also show a project timeline but require expertise to create them, which the team might not have. A flowchart is limited in its ability to show duration so is not best suited to timeline visualisation.

Resource allocation: with limited resources available, the team needed a planning tool that would help them effectively allocate resources and manage dependencies. The Gantt chart's ability to show task dependencies and resource availability allowed the team to optimise resource allocation and ensure tasks were completed in the most efficient manner. Neither flowcharts or PERT charts show resources so would not be suitable.

Stakeholder communication: the Gantt chart is as a valuable communication tool for the team to share project plans and progress to stakeholders. Its intuitive design and visual layout make it easy for stakeholders to understand the project timeline and milestones. Flowcharts are easy to follow but in a large project are likely to become complicated and harder to navigate. PERT charts can also be complex and difficult to follow, therefore not as suitable for communication as a Gantt chart.

Adaptability: Amondale Software Solutions anticipated that project requirements and priorities might change over time. The flexibility of the Gantt chart allows the team to easily adjust project plans, add or remove tasks, and accommodate changes in scope or timeline as needed. Flowcharts can also be easily updated to reflect changes, although not specifically the timeline of a project. PERT charts can be time consuming to make, so although they can be updated it is not as adaptable as other methods.

Overall, a Gantt chart is the most suitable option for the team. The Gantt chart provides the visibility, control, and flexibility the team needs to navigate the complexities of the project and achieve their goals.

Quick check 7

1 Reflecting on a project that you have been or are going to work on, carry out a SWOT analysis to examine the internal and external factors that might impact the success of your product.

2 Make notes to compare and contrast a Gantt chart and a flowchart as project planning tools. Consider their features and what they may be best used for.

Practice questions 3

When planning an application, relevant legislation should be considered.

1 Explain why considering legislation is important when developing an application. **[2]**

2 A flowchart has been created as part of the development process for a new application.

a Identify **two** advantages of using a flowchart. **[2]**

b Explain **one** disadvantage of using a flowchart. **[2]**

TA4 Application design scoping

Learning intentions

This topic is about how client requirements are determined at the outset of a project and then used to create a specification for development. It will also explore the methods used to decompose or break down the requirements to visualise application designs and when to use them.

It covers:

4.1 Methods of gathering client requirements

4.2 Client requirement specifications

4.3 Decomposition methods

4.1 Methods of gathering client requirements

There are a range of methods that can be used to gather client requirements that vary in the type of information and data that can be collected. These will often be used in combination so that a thorough exploration of the requirements takes place.

Document analysis

Document analysis involves reviewing existing documentation related to the application development project, such as business plans, technical specifications, user manuals or previous project documentation. It helps in understanding the project background, existing requirements, constraints and any other relevant information documented by the client or project stakeholders. The documents help gather data on key requirements, project scope, technical specifications, business goals, constraints and any other relevant information documented in written form. Document analysis is a useful method for gathering clients' requirements if there are similar products on the market or when there is secondary research that shows a gap in client needs.

Table 1.27: Document analysis has its strengths and weaknesses that need to be considered when making choices

Advantages	Disadvantages
• Gives a structured overview of existing requirements, business goals and technical specifications • Can be carried out quickly without needing direct interaction with stakeholders.	• Documents may lack up-to-date information or not cover certain requirements • May not capture the detail around client requirements and preferences.

Focus group

Focus groups involve bringing together a selected group of stakeholders to discuss specific topics related to the application development. This might include members of the target audience for the application, for example. The purpose is to gather insights, opinions and feedback from multiple perspectives simultaneously, fostering discussion and idea generation. Focus groups gather information on the perspectives, preferences and opinions on specific features, functionalities or aspects of the software application. Focus groups are useful when exploring new ideas and there is a need for early feedback on pain points with existing solutions for end users.

Table 1.28: Focus groups have their strengths and weaknesses that need to be considered when making choices

Advantages	Disadvantages
• Gives insights from multiple stakeholders at the same time so a range of perspectives can be given • Facilitates consensus-building (agreement) through group interaction.	• Some participants may dominate the focus group and control the discussion so not everyone is heard • People in the group might conform to the majority and not be willing to give opinions that disagree with this view.

Interviews

Interviews involve conducting one-on-one discussions with individual stakeholders, such as clients, end-users or subject matter experts for the application development project. The purpose is to gather detailed information, preferences, needs and expectations directly from stakeholders in a more personalised and in-depth manner. Through carefully framed questions, the interviewer will gather detailed information on the requirements, specific use cases, potential issues, individual perspectives and any other relevant insights provided by the interviewees. Interviews are useful in the early stages of gathering requirements as they provide an opportunity to clarify or ambiguous or conflicting requirements.

Table 1.29: Interviews have their strengths and weaknesses that need to be considered when making choices

Advantages	Disadvantages
• Provides detailed and personalised understanding of individual stakeholder needs, preferences and concerns • Allows for probing and follow-up questions to clarify responses and explore topics further.	• Requires time and effort to conduct interviews with multiple stakeholders • Interviewer bias or leading questions may influence responses and distort the collected data.

Meetings

Meetings are scheduled sessions involving project stakeholders to discuss various aspects of the application development. These may take place in person or online. The purpose of a meeting is to ask a range of open questions to fully understand the project requirements and support communication and collaboration. Meetings are useful for checking the understanding of requirements and aligning expectations between stakeholders.

Table 1.30: Meetings have their strengths and weaknesses which need to be considered when making choices

Advantages	Disadvantages
• Enables real-time communication, collaboration and alignment of expectations among stakeholders • Allows stakeholders to ask questions and seek clarification if something is not clearly understood.	• Meetings can be time-consuming, especially if not well-structured or focused • Meetings usually have a limited number of attendees so it would not be representative of a wide range of opinions.

Observation

Observations involve directly observing users interacting with existing systems or workflows relevant to the application. The purpose is to understand user behaviours, tasks, workflows, issues and opportunities for improvement by witnessing real-world usage. By observing the use of the existing application or systems, information can be collected on user behaviours, inefficiencies, usage patterns and any other insights gained from observing users in their natural environment. This means that they are useful when developing early ideas on User Experience (UX) and User Interfaces (UI).

Table 1.31: Observation has its strengths and weaknesses that need to be considered when making choices

Advantages	Disadvantages
• Provides first-hand insights into how users interact with existing systems or workflows in real life situations • Reduces chance of bias as observations are based on actual behaviour rather than someone reporting their own activity.	• May not collect information on the thoughts or emotions of users so limited in deeper understanding • Users may change their behaviour when aware of being observed, potentially affecting the observation.

Problem reports

Problem reports are records of issues, bugs or complaints faced by users or stakeholders in existing software applications. The purpose of examining problem reports is to identify and document issues affecting the user experience or functionality of the software, which need to be addressed in the development process. This analysis might help scope client requirements for the development of a new application. Information gathered can include the details of problems encountered, how often they occur, the impact on user experience, potential solutions and any other relevant information related to reported issues. Problem reports are useful in the early stages of development as they highlight existing issues or pain points experienced by users or stakeholders with the current system or process.

Table 1.32: Problem reports have their strengths and weaknesses which need to be considered when making choices

Advantages	Disadvantages
• Helps identify existing issues and bugs experienced by users, guiding improvement efforts • Provides specific feedback on areas needing attention, facilitating targeted solutions for future development.	• Users may only report issues that are particularly frustrating for them, leading to a skewed representation of problems • Problem reports may lack context or detailed information necessary for effective resolution in future development.

Questionnaire

Questionnaires are a series of open and/or closed questions that are used to collect feedback from a large group of stakeholders. These may be conducted online or on paper. They gather both quantitative (numerical) and qualitative (descriptive) data that can be analysed to help in the develop of client requirements. This might include numerical data around application usage, descriptive feedback on specific aspects of the application or demographic information. Questionnaires are useful when for gathering data from a large group or those who are geographically spread. They can also be used in advance of more focussed questioning through interviews, for example.

Table 1.33: Questionnaires have their strengths and weaknesses, which need to be considered when making choices

Advantages	Disadvantages
• Can reach many stakeholders efficiently, gathering feedback from a diverse audience, especially with online questionnaires • Ensures consistency in data collection and allows for quantitative analysis.	• May lack depth or context compared to other methods, as responses are often limited by the questions posed • Response rates may be low, particularly if stakeholders think that the questionnaire as time-consuming or irrelevant.

Shadowing

Shadowing involves observing and accompanying users in their natural environment as they perform tasks relevant to the application. It provides an opportunity to get a first-hand perspective on the client requirements by gaining a deeper insight into the situation. Shadowing can provide a better understanding of user behaviours, workflows and challenges facing users. Information will also be collected on factors influencing behaviour, such as environmental considerations. Shadowing is useful when developing UX and UI as they enable deep insights into user workflows, behaviours and pain points.

Table 1.34: Shadowing has its strengths and weaknesses that need to be considered when making choices

Advantages	Disadvantages
• Provides deep insights into user tasks, workflows and challenges by observing users in their natural environment • Helps develop better understanding of users and their experience by seeing the context first hand.	• Requires large time investment to shadow users effectively, potentially limiting how widely this approach can be used • Interpretation of observed behaviours may vary among observers, so conclusions may be skewed.

Suggestion analysis

Suggestion analysis involves analysing feedback, suggestions or feature requests provided by stakeholders or users. It enables you to evaluate, prioritise and incorporate valuable suggestions or feedback into the development of the client requirements. Information collected includes feature requests, feedback on existing functionality and suggestions for improvement. Suggestion analysis is useful when evaluating potential features as it helps to prioritise and incorporate suggestions from stakeholders and end-users effectively.

Table 1.35: Suggestion analysis has its strengths and weaknesses that need to be considered when making choices

Advantages	Disadvantages
• Includes stakeholders in the development process, making them feel heard and valued • Generates new ideas and feature requests that may enhance the development of future software's functionality or user experience.	• Not all suggestions may be possible or in line with project goals, requiring careful evaluation and prioritisation • Analysing many suggestions can be challenging and potentially overwhelming development teams.

How defined client requirements determine the method used

Understanding what the client wants is key to choosing how to gather information for software projects. If the client's needs are straightforward, talking to stakeholders directly through interviews works well. For more complicated projects, bringing together a focus group to discuss ideas might be better. How much the client and end-users are involved, how much time and money you have, and how risky the project is also affects how you gather information. Picking the right way to get information based on what the client needs ensures you collect the right information for a successful project.

Learning in context 4

Selecting methods for gathering client requirements

XYZ Banking, a leading financial institution, aims to enhance its mobile banking application to improve user experience and increase customer satisfaction. The current app has received mixed feedback, with users reporting issues such as slow performance, confusing navigation and limited features. To address these challenges and align the app with user expectations, XYZ Banking decides to gather client requirements through various methods including focus groups, interviews, problem reports and questionnaires.

1. Focus group: as XYZ Banking has a clearly defined set of end users, they decided that organising a focus group would be beneficial. The focus group enabled customers to discuss their experiences, needs, and preferences regarding mobile banking. The focus group discussions uncovered specific pain points related to complex account management processes, awkward authentication procedures and lack of personalised services. Virtual focus groups were organised for those who could not attend in person due to mobility issues or geographic constraints. In person focus groups were held in venue that were accessible for individuals with disabilities, such as wheelchair ramps and accessible facilities.
2. Interviews: XYZ Banking also conducted one-to-one interviews with selected customers, bank employees, and stakeholders to gain deeper insights into specific pain points and feature requests. This enabled a further understanding of the issues raised that could be explored in more depth through additional questioning. Participants were offered flexible interview formats, such as phone interviews or video calls, to accommodate those with difficulty attending face-to-face interviews due to physical or logistical barriers. Interview questions also used inclusive language and avoided assumptions based on gender, ethnicity or other characteristics.
3. Problem reports: by analysing historical problem reports and customer complaints logged through various channels, XYZ Banking could ensure that the new application did not experience the same issues. These logs identified recurring issues such as transaction errors, login failures and difficulties in navigating certain app sections, which was valuable in scoping out the new application. They also provided support and guidance to users facing barriers in expressing their issues or navigating the reporting process.
4. Questionnaire: XYZ Banking had a large online customer base to which they could send an online questionnaire to collect a large sample of data. Questionnaires were used to collect quantitative and qualitative feedback on their satisfaction levels and feature preferences. The questionnaire data quantified user

Learning in context **Continued**

satisfaction levels and highlighted areas for improvement, such as faster transaction processing, more intuitive navigation and additional account management features. Questions used clear and concise language so they were easy to understand. They also used accessible survey formats, such as online surveys with screen reader compatibility and options for adjusting text size and contrast.

Based on the gathered client requirements and insights obtained from the selected methods, XYZ Banking could prioritise enhancements to the mobile banking application. Key recommendations included streamlining authentication processes, optimising app performance, introducing personalised features and enhancing user interface intuitiveness and accessibility for all users.

Quick check **8**

1 Carry out a survey of the target audience for a project you are working on. In what ways do you find a questionnaire helpful and what are its limitations?

2 If you were developing a new application for your school or college, which method(s) would you use to gather information on client requirements? Tell someone and justify your answer.

4.2 Client requirement specifications

Creating client requirement specifications is important for software development. It ensures a clear understanding of client needs, defines project scope, aligns with client expectations, serves as a basis for agreement, guides development, aids in quality assurance, mitigates risks and provides documentation for future reference. Overall, it ensures efficient project execution, client satisfaction and delivery of a high-quality product. The elements of client requirement specification include:

Purpose of new system

The purpose of the new system is a statement that describes the overarching goal or objective of developing the new software application. It provides clarity and direction for the development team by outlining the main reason for creating the system.

Functional requirements

Functional requirements are detailed descriptions of the specific functionalities or features that the new software application must have. It will specify the actions or tasks the system should do to meet the needs of users and achieve the system's purpose. This can be gathered through interviews, focus groups or surveys with stakeholders to understand what tasks the system needs to perform.

Non-functional requirements

Non-functional requirements are specifications that describe the level of quality or characteristics of the system, such as performance, usability, security and scalability. It defines the elements that are critical for the system's success but are not directly related to specific functionalities, for example the number of users that can be supported or response times. This can be gathered during meetings with stakeholders to identify performance, security, usability and other non-functional aspects required by the system.

Process constraints

Process constraints are limitations or restrictions that must be followed during the software development lifecycle. These will guide the development team in sticking to specific processes, standards or regulations that cover the project. This can be gathered by document analysis for business processes or interviewing stakeholders.

Current system deficiencies

Current **system deficiencies** are of shortcomings, issues or gaps in the existing system that the new software application aims to address or improve on. Identifying deficiencies provides insight into the problems or limitations of the current system, so that these might be addressed in the development of solutions for the new system. This can be gathered through document analysis, user feedback, such as through questionnaires, or suggestion analysis.

Data formats

Data formats are the format for the structure, organisation and standards for representing and exchanging data within the software application. Establishing the data formats to be used ensures consistency and means that the data can be used across different components or modules of the system. This can be gathered through meetings with stakeholders and analysis of existing data sources.

Client-defined constraints

Client-defined constraints are specific limitations, preferences or requirements given by the client that must be considered during the development of the software application. This can be gathered through meetings with stakeholders within the business such as budget holders and network specialists.

Table 1.36: Each of these constraints plays a critical role in shaping the development process and outcomes of the software application

Constraint	Purpose
Budget	This constraint outlines the financial limitations or resources allocated for the development of the software application. It helps guides decisions regarding resource allocation, scope management and prioritisation of features.
Time	This constraint specifies the duration or timeline within which the software application must be developed and delivered. It ensures that the project stays on schedule and meets deadlines, supporting effective project planning, scheduling and resource management.
Integration	This constraint defines requirements related to compatibility with other systems, platforms or technologies. It ensures seamless integration with existing systems or third-party applications, minimising disruptions and enabling data exchange or communication between different software.
Software	This constraint specifies any software dependencies, requirements, or compatibility considerations for the development. It ensures that the software application is developed using compatible technologies, frameworks or platforms, leading to smooth deployment, maintenance and support.
Hardware	This constraint outlines hardware requirements, specifications or compatibility considerations for the deployment environment. It ensures that the software application is compatible with the hardware on which it will run, optimising performance, reliability and scalability.
Data storage location	This constraint specifies the geographical location where data associated with the software application must be stored or processed. This includes whether the data will be stored locally on site, using a cloud-based service or on a physical storage device. This is important because it addresses legal, regulatory or compliance requirements related to data privacy, security and sovereignty, ensuring relevant laws and regulations are followed.

Version and source control

Version control, also known as source control, is a system that manages changes to documents, source code, or any other set of files over time. It helps track changes to files, allowing developers to go back to previous versions, compare changes and work effectively with team members.

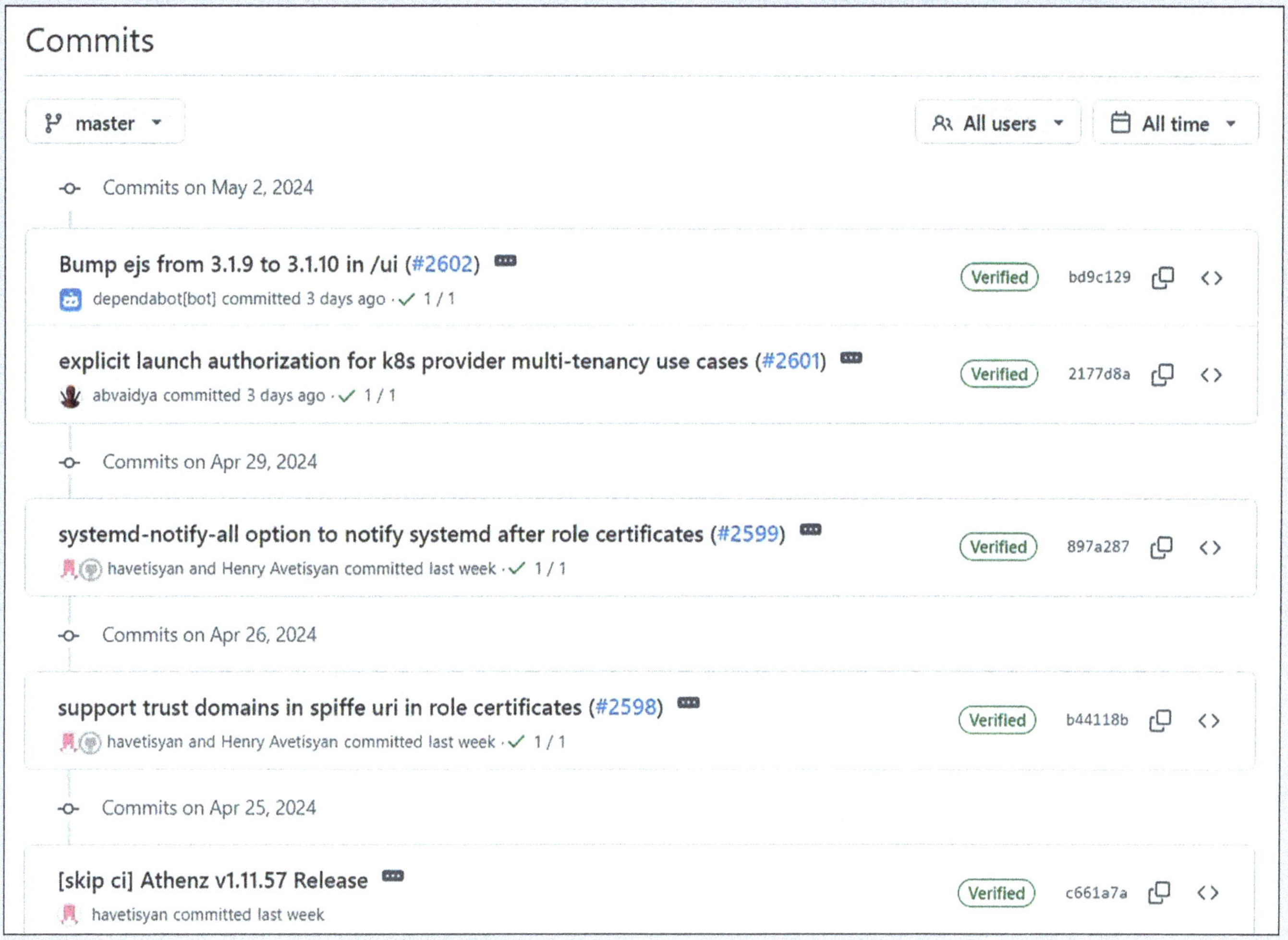
Commits
master
All users
All time
Commits on May 2, 2024
Bump ejs from 3.1.9 to 3.1.10 in /ui (#2602)
dependabot[bot] committed 3 days ago · 1 / 1
Verified
bd9c129
explicit launch authorization for k8s provider multi-tenancy use cases (#2601)
abvaidya committed 3 days ago · 1 / 1
Verified
2177d8a
Commits on Apr 29, 2024
systemd-notify-all option to notify systemd after role certificates (#2599)
havetisyan and Henry Avetisyan committed last week · 1 / 1
Verified
897a287
Commits on Apr 26, 2024
support trust domains in spiffe uri in role certificates (#2598)
havetisyan and Henry Avetisyan committed last week · 1 / 1
Verified
b44118b
Commits on Apr 25, 2024
[skip ci] Athenz v1.11.57 Release
havetisyan committed last week
Verified
c661a7a

Figure 1.20: GitHub enables version control, allowing developers to manage and track changes to their code over time

How to elicit client requirements

Eliciting or finding out about the client requirements is a crucial step in the software development process, as it lays the foundation for understanding what the client needs and expects from the application. A range of the methods identified before could be used to fully understand what the client wants such as interviews, questionnaires and focus groups. By combining these methods and tailoring them to the specific needs and context of the project, you can effectively elicit client requirements and ensure that the resulting application meets the needs and expectations of its intended users.

Quick check 9

1. Make notes on why it is important to create client requirement specifications.
2. Imagine you are creating a new version of an application you are familiar with. Create a client requirement specification document, using the headings above to structure your document.

4.3 Decomposition methods

Abstraction

Abstraction in software development means simplifying complex systems by focusing on the important parts and ignoring unnecessary details. This makes it easier for everyone to understand and communicate about what the software needs to do.

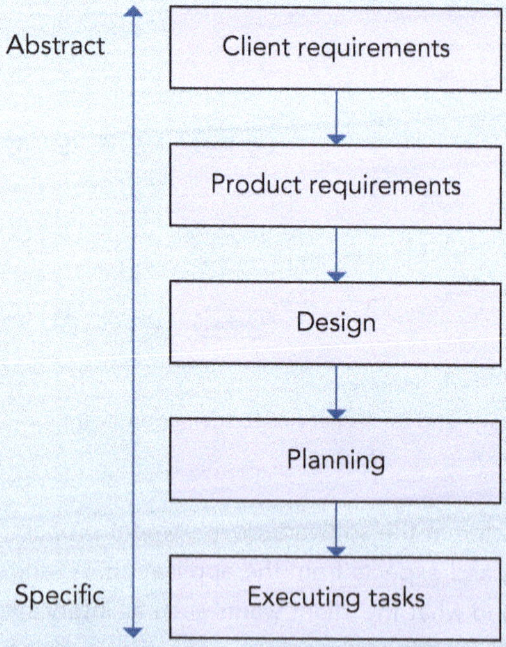
Abstract
Specific
Client requirements
Product requirements
Design
Planning
Executing tasks

Figure 1.21: Abstraction of the software development lifecycle

It is especially useful at the beginning of a project when gathering and analysing requirements. Abstraction helps outline the main structure and key functions of the software.

Depending on how clear the client's requirements are, different levels of abstraction might be needed. Clear requirements allow for more detailed abstraction, while vague requirements need a broader approach. Abstraction helps create diagrams or models that show an overview of the software's structure and functions.

Pattern recognition

Pattern recognition in software development means spotting recurring themes or similarities in what clients want or need. This helps organise and prioritise tasks. For example, if lots of clients request a feature that allows users to save their progress, this recurring theme can be identified and prioritised.

When many people give input, for example with feature requests, pattern recognition finds common ground and aligns expectations. In large projects with hundreds of requirements, for example, recognising patterns can group similar ones together, making it easier to address them efficiently.

Detailed requirements often show patterns that simplify design. These patterns can highlight reusable components or templates. They guide the design of the application's structure, user interfaces and data models. For example, if a pattern of data input forms is identified, a standard template can be created for all forms, ensuring consistency and saving time.

Modularisation

Modularisation where a large amount of information is broken down into smaller, manageable modules or components, can be implemented in a top-down or bottom-up approach.

Top-down modularisation involves starting with a high-level overview of the software application and then breaking it down into smaller modules or components. Each module represents a specific set of functionalities or features, allowing for easier development and maintenance of the software.

This approach works well for:

- making big software easier to handle by breaking it into smaller pieces
- planning for future changes or growth in software needs because it's flexible and can grow with requirements
- handling projects with many teams or people by providing a clear structure and helping everyone work together.

Bottom-up modularisation involves starting with smaller, individual modules or components and then gradually combining them to build larger, more complex structures. Each module is designed to perform a specific function or task, and these modules are then integrated to create the final software application.

This approach works well for:

- Making new software by using parts that are already made or combining them to create new features. This saves time and avoids repeating work.
- Making it easier to change and add to the software later. Each part can be changed without affecting the rest of the software.
- Making the development process smoother by breaking it into smaller steps, making it easier to manage and ensuring a more reliable outcome.

The specificity and granularity of client requirements influence the level of modularisation required. Well-defined and clear requirements lead to clear module boundaries, while vague or overlapping requirements may need to be refined more than once. Modularisation is visualised through architectural diagrams that show the relationships and interactions between different modules.

Parsing of requirements

Parsing of requirements involves breaking down complex requirements into smaller, manageable chunks, identifying key features, functionalities, constraints and dependencies. This process helps ensure that the client's needs and expectations are clearly understood and documented, providing a solid foundation for the software development process.

It is useful when gathering requirements from stakeholders through a range of different methods such as interview and surveys to structure the information. It also helps break down complex requirements into manageable parts, identify dependencies and check again project constraints.

The level of detail and specificity in gathered client requirements determines the granularity of parsing required. Detailed requirements may be parsed into individual features or user stories, while broader requirements may require further detail to identify underlying functional or non-functional aspects. Parsed requirements are visualised through use case diagrams or flowcharts which provide a visual representation of process flows and decision logic within the application.

Table 1.37: The choice of method depends on factors such as project complexity, stakeholder preferences and the nature of the requirements being analysed

Method	Advantages	Disadvantages
Abstraction	• Simplifies complex requirements by focusing on essential parts and ignoring unnecessary details • Flexible and allows for generalisation that can be applied across multiple requirements.	• As it generalises, it may lead to the loss of specific details and overlooking important aspects of the requirements • Generalised requirements may be open to interpretation, leading to misunderstandings or between stakeholders.
Pattern recognition	• Saves time and effort in analysis by identifying recurring themes, similarities or trends • Promotes consistency in requirements by standardising common patterns or solutions for similar problems.	• May lead to oversimplification of requirements, ignoring unique aspects • Subject to bias as patterns may be seen differently by different stakeholders.
Modularisation	• Scalable and flexible by breaking down requirements into smaller, manageable components or modules • Modules can be reused across different projects or components, promoting consistency.	• Makes requirements document more complex, requiring more management • May require additional time and resources, particularly in larger or more complex projects.
Parsing of requirements	• Improves clarity by breaking down complex requirements into smaller, more manageable components • Enables better organisation and prioritisation by allowing for detailed analysis and categorisation of requirements.	• Can be time-consuming, particularly in larger projects with lots of requirements or stakeholders • Can be complicated making requirement documents difficult to manage.

Quick check 10

1 Imagine you are developing a new e-commerce app for a local shop. Explain to a friend the method that you would use to decompose the client requirements and the reasons why.

2 Make notes to summarise the differences between abstraction, pattern recognition, modularisation and parsing of requirements.

Practice questions 4

Kool Kustom Tees, a local clothing business wants to improve its engagement with customers through a new e-commerce app. The application aims to provide customers with easy-to-use access to their online catalogue, account information and order history. The application will store customer data including card details.

1 The client has requested stakeholder interviews take place as part of gathering information for the application requirements.

  a Explain **one** advantage of stakeholder interviews. [2]

  b Explain **one** disadvantage of stakeholder interviews. [2]

2 Stakeholder interviews are one way of gathering information about a client's requirements. State **one** other method. [1]

3 Identify **two** non-functional requirements for the new application. [2]

TA5 Human computer interface and interaction

Learning intentions

This topic is about how users can interact with a software application, for example using audio, gesture, touch or visual methods. It will examine the types of devices used to interact with software applications and their features. It will also explore how visual design is used when developing human computer interfaces. Finally, the topic will introduce the documents and diagrams used to design the human computer interface, examining how to create them and what makes them effective.

It covers:

5.1 Human computer interaction and devices

5.2 Human computer interface visual design considerations

5.3 Human computer interface design documents and diagrams

5.1 Human computer interaction and devices

Human computer interaction is about how people interact with computers and other digital technologies. When designing an application, the human computer interaction should be designed so that the way that the technology is used, such as a smartphone app or software menu is easy, efficient and enjoyable.

5.1.1 Types of human computer interaction

Audio

Audio interfaces allow users to interact with computers using sound, such as voice commands or audio feedback. They are particularly useful for hands-free use and accessibility for visually impaired users. Audio interfaces are commonly used on Smart speakers such as Amazon Echo and Google Home, smartphones, voice-controlled assistants such as Siri and Alexa and voice-enabled applications.

Table 1.38: Advantages and disadvantages of using audio interfaces

Advantages	Disadvantages
• Can use the application software without needing to use your hands, which is useful where manual input is inconvenient or impossible • Accessible for visually impaired users or those with mobility impairments • Voice commands can make it easier for users to explain what they need.	• Privacy concerns around devices always listening to monitor for voice commands • Commands can be misunderstood, especially when there is no visual element to the device • Environmental factors such as background noise or accents can affect accuracy of speech recognition.

Table 1.39: Advantages and disadvantages of using movement interfaces

Advantages	Disadvantages
• Can offer immersive experiences in virtual reality environments or gaming scenarios • Mimics natural human movements, making interaction intuitive and engaging • Allow users to interact without physical contact with a device.	• May struggle to accurately recognise complicated or small movements, so the system doesn't behave as expected • When used for a longer time users may become tired or uncomfortable, especially with repetitive movement • Users need enough space for full-body gestures, which may not be possible in all environments.

Movement/gesture

Movement or gesture interfaces allow users to interact with computers through physical movements or gestures, such as waving a hand or pointing. They are often used in gaming consoles, Virtual Reality (VR) systems and touchless interfaces. This type of interface is commonly found in gaming consoles such as Xbox Kinect, VR headsets such as Oculus Rift and HTC Vive, motion-sensing devices such as Leap Motion (a hand tracking camera) and touchless interfaces such as hand gesture recognition systems.

Touch

A touch interface allows users to interact with computers by directly touching the screen or a touch-sensitive surface. They are intuitive and widely used in smartphones, tablets, and touchscreen computers, offering a physical and responsive interaction experience. A touch interface is used on a wide range of devices including smartphones, tablets, touchscreen laptops, interactive kiosks, ATMs, point-of-sale systems and digital signage.

Table 1.40: Advantages and disadvantages of using touch interfaces

Advantages	Disadvantages
• Easy to understand and use for end users • Can interact directly with on screen elements which gives immediate feedback and a sense of control • A wide range of interactions can be used including tapping, swiping and pinching.	• Touchscreens require cleaning to remove smudges and fingerprints, which can affect use • Repeated use of touch screens over time can cause discomfort and Repetitive Strain Injuries (RSI) • Can be difficult to control by touch alone.

Visual

Visual interfaces provide information for interaction with users through graphical elements such as icons, text, images and animations. One type of visual interface is a **Command-Line Interface (CLI)**.

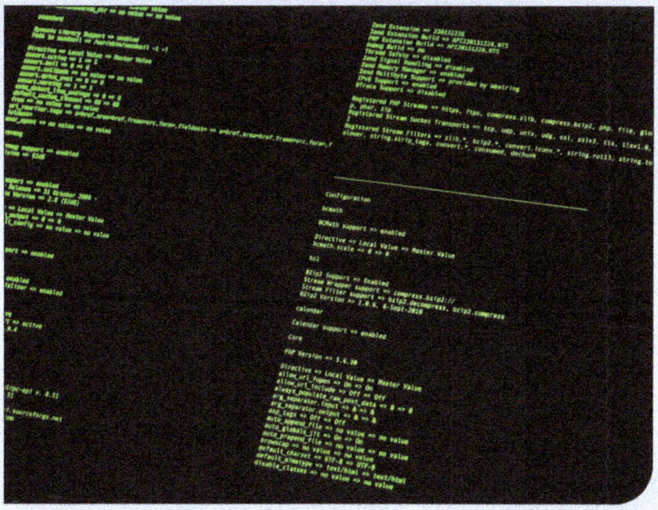

Figure 1.22: Command Line Interface (CLI) uses text commands to control the software functionalities

It allows users to interact with computers by typing commands in a text-based environment. They are efficient for experienced users and automation tasks, allowing precise control over system operations and software functionalities. A CLI is used on desktop computers, servers and laptops that are running command-line operating systems such as Unix/Linux, macOS Terminal or Windows Command Prompt.

Table 1.41: Advantages and disadvantages of using Command Line Interface

Advantages	Disadvantages
• Efficient way for experienced users to quickly enter commands • Can use scripting and automated features which is helpful for repetitive tasks • Can be used to remotely manage servers or other networked devices.	• New users will have to learn commands to use this type of interface • Typing mistakes or incorrect commands will mean that errors may happen, or the system will not behave as expected • Difficult to find out about available commands and options.

Another type of visual interface is a **Graphical User Interface (GUI)**. GUIs provide users with a visual way to interact with computers through graphical elements like windows, buttons, menus, and icons. They offer an intuitive and user-friendly experience, allowing users to carry out tasks by clicking, dragging and dropping visual elements, which is especially helpful for novice users. GUI interfaces are widely used on desktop computers and laptops, smartphones, tablets, smart TVs, wearable devices such as smartwatches, gaming consoles, ATM machines and point-of-sale systems.

Table 1.42: Advantages and disadvantages of using Graphical User Interface

Advantages	Disadvantages
• Intuitive and user friendly • Gives immediate visual feedback so it is easy to understand the consequences of an interaction • Supports multitasking so users can interact with several tasks at once.	• Can use a lot of system resources and slow down less powerful systems • Range of features and options can be confusing for users • May need additional features such as screen reader software to assist with accessibility.

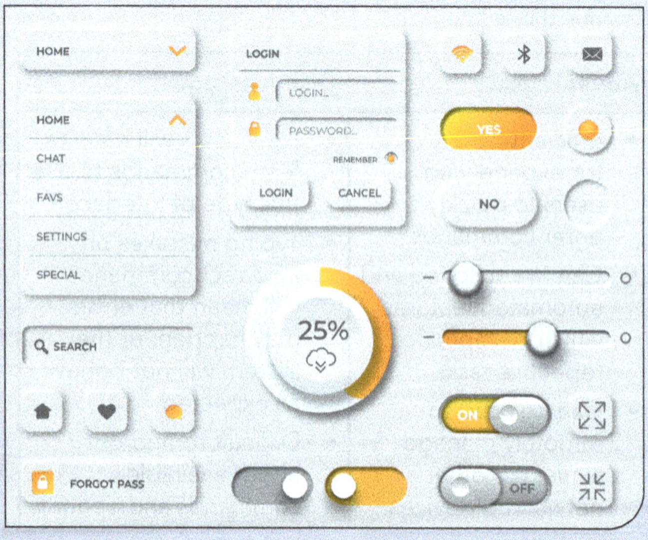
HOME
LOGIN
LOGIN...
PASSWORD...
REMEMBER
LOGIN
CANCEL
YES
NO
HOME
CHAT
FAVS
SETTINGS
SPECIAL
SEARCH
25%
ON
OFF
FORGOT PASS

Figure 1.23: Examples of images used to create a GUI that is intuitive and user-friendly for the target audience

How gathered client requirements affect the selection of the type of human computer interaction

Client requirements play a crucial role in determining the type of human computer interaction that will be selected for a particular project.

First, the user needs should be considered. Client requirements provide insight into the needs and preferences of the users who will be interacting with the system. This understanding helps in choosing an approach that aligns with the users' expectations and goals.

Second, the context is important. Based on client requirements, designers can tailor the interaction design to match the specific way in which the software application will be used. For example, if the client wants to create a highly engaging mobile application, the interaction might focus on using intuitive touch-based interactions and **responsive design** principles. This means that the screen and elements resize and move depending on the screen size of the device used to access them.

Third, the choice of human computer interaction will be affected by technological constraints such as platform compatibility, device capabilities or existing infrastructure. These constraints affect the selection of techniques and technologies that can be realistically used for the project.

Finally, client requirements may also involve considerations for accessibility, ensuring that the design is inclusive and usable by individuals with diverse abilities. This might involve selecting interaction methods that accommodate different sensory, motor or cognitive capabilities of users.

5.1.2 Types of device

There are a range of devices that might be used for human computer interaction with a software application. Each has its own characteristics which need to be considered when planning interaction methods.

Desktop

A desktop computer is a computing device designed for use on a desk or table. It typically consists of a monitor, keyboard, mouse and Central Processing Unit (CPU) in a separate case. Desktops offer high performance, customisation options and are easy to upgrade compared to other computing devices. They are commonly used for tasks requiring significant computational power, such as gaming, video editing and software development.

Games console

A games console is a specialised computing device designed primarily for playing video games. It typically connects to a television or monitor and includes a controller for user input. Games consoles come with pre-installed or downloadable games and often offer online multiplayer capabilities. They are optimised for gaming performance and may include additional features such as media streaming and internet browsing.

Laptop

A laptop is a portable computing device designed for mobile use. It has an integrated display, keyboard, touchpad or trackpad and internal components (such as the CPU, memory and storage) incorporated into a single unit. Laptops offer flexibility and convenience, allowing users to work, browse the internet, watch videos and perform other tasks on the go. They come in various sizes and configurations, ranging from portable models to high-performance gaming laptops.

Smart speaker

A **smart speaker** is a wireless speaker with built-in voice-controlled virtual assistant technology. It can respond to voice commands and perform various tasks, such as playing music, providing weather forecasts, setting reminders and controlling smart home devices. Smart speakers typically connect to the internet via Wi-Fi and rely on cloud-based services to process voice commands and provide information. Examples include Amazon Echo with Alexa, Google Home with Google Assistant and Apple HomePod with Siri.

Figure 1.24: A child using a smart speaker to help with homework

Smart TV

A **smart TV** is a television set with integrated internet connectivity and interactive features, allowing users to access streaming services, apps and online content directly on the TV screen. Smart TVs often include built-in apps for popular streaming platforms like Netflix, Disney+ and YouTube, as well as web browsers and social media apps. They may also support voice control, screen mirroring and home automation integration, making them central hubs for entertainment and digital content consumption.

Smartphone

A smartphone is a handheld mobile device that combines the functionality of a phone with computing capabilities such as those of a computer. It features a touchscreen display for user interaction and typically runs on a mobile operating system (such as iOS or Android). Smartphones offer a wide range of features, including voice calls, text messaging, web browsing, photography, social media access, app installation and mobile payments. They are essential tools for communication, productivity and entertainment on the go.

Tablet

A tablet is a portable computing device with a touchscreen display. It is larger than a smartphone but smaller than a laptop. It is designed for mobile use and offers capabilities such as those of a smartphone or laptop, including web browsing, email, app usage, multimedia consumption and gaming. Tablets are versatile devices suitable for tasks such as reading e-books, watching videos, taking notes and sketching. They come in various sizes and configurations, ranging from budget-friendly options to high-end models with advanced features.

Augmented Reality (AR)/Virtual Reality (VR)/Mixed Reality (MR) devices

Augmented Reality (AR)/Virtual Reality (VR) and **Mixed Reality (MR)** devices are technologies that alter or enhance the user's perception of the physical world by overlaying digital content or creating immersive virtual environments. Augmented Reality (AR) overlays digital information onto the real world, typically viewed through a smartphone or specialised AR glasses. Virtual Reality (VR) creates entirely simulated environments that users can interact with using VR headsets, blocking out the real world entirely. Mixed Reality (MR) blends elements of both AR and VR, allowing digital and physical objects to interact in real-time, often seen through dedicated MR headsets or glasses. These technologies are used for applications in gaming, education, training, healthcare, design and entertainment.

Floor Lamp
Indoor Plant
3 Seater Sofa
$950.00
Coffee Table
Rug

Figure 1.25: Augmented reality on a smartphone used to visualise furniture in a living room

Quick check 11

1 Can you explain the advantages and disadvantages of using touch interaction with application software? Make notes and discuss with a friend.

2 Consider an application you regularly use. Identify the device and method of human computer interaction. Why do you think it was chosen? Is it effective? Makes notes on your thoughts.

5.2 Human computer interface visual design considerations

Human computer interface visual design considerations involve designing the visual elements of a user interface to improve usability, accessibility and user experience.

Colours

Colours play a crucial role in interface design as they can convey meaning, evoke emotions and guide user attention to a specific element on the screen. Colours can represent different actions or states within an interface. For instance, green might signify success or confirmation, while red could indicate errors or warnings. Bright or contrasting colours can draw attention to important elements such as buttons or alerts. Colour schemes are often used to maintain consistency and create a **visual identity** for an interface.

Your computer is now protected

Figure 1.26: The use of colour can give meaning to what is happening on the screen, for example green might be used to show success

The colour scheme, along with other elements such as typography and layout, form the **house style**. The house style is a set of guidelines and standards that the application will follow across all aspects of design and development.

When selecting colours for a human computer interface, there are several strategies that can be used to improve the effectiveness of human computer interfaces. For example, when selecting colours, choices should comply with **accessibility standards**, considering factors such as **contrast ratio** and colour blindness. Using a **consistent** colour scheme throughout the interface establishes familiarity with the application and supports user understanding. It is also important to conduct user testing to assess how colour choices impact user experience and adjust accordingly based on feedback.

Interaction

Interaction design focuses on how users engage with the interface and the feedback they receive from the system. Interfaces should provide immediate and clear feedback to user actions, such as button clicks or form submissions. This might be a sound playing or a pop-up message appearing to indicate success. Interfaces should be responsive to user input, with smooth transitions (when an element is appearing or disappearing from the screen). It also includes animations where appropriate to make the process more visually appealing. Designers should also create navigation that is intuitive so it feels as natural as possible to the end user. They should guide users through the interface to help them accomplish tasks efficiently.

When planning interaction, there are some considerations to ensure effective design.
For example, designers should make sure that interactions are streamlined by taking out unnecessary steps and providing clear pathways for completing tasks. It is also important to provide immediate and informative feedback in response to user actions, reducing uncertainty and errors. Design interactions should also focus on the user's needs and preferences, for example the complexity of navigating the interface.

Location hierarchy

Location hierarchy refers to the organisation of elements within the interface to guide user attention and understanding, for example the position of navigation buttons, logo or title. **Visual hierarchy** is a key element. This says that important elements should be prominent and easily noticeable, while secondary elements can be less prominent. Visual hierarchy can be shown by the position, size, colour or style of the element. For example, more important items of text might be bold or in italics.

When reading content on a visual interface, users naturally consume information in a **Z reading pattern**. Designers often take the Z pattern into account when organising content and placing important elements to ensure that key information is easily noticed and absorbed by users as they scan the interface.

It is also important that related elements should be grouped together visually to indicate their relationship and importance. This makes it easier for the end user to locate relevant information. Navigation menus and buttons should also be placed in easily accessible locations, following common patterns to enhance usability.

To improve the effectiveness of human computer interfaces, designers should consider optimising the visual hierarchy by prioritising important elements, using techniques such as size, colour and placement to guide user attention. It is also important to conduct user research to understand how users find using the interface and navigate interface elements, informing decisions about location hierarchy. It is also important to consider responsive design. Location hierarchy should adapt seamlessly across different devices and screen sizes to maintain usability and consistency.

Messages

Messages, including help and error messages, are essential for providing guidance and feedback to users.

Help

Help messages are designed to assist users in understanding how to use a particular feature or function within the software. They provide additional information or instructions to clarify confusing concepts or processes. Help messages should be informative, concise and relevant to the user's current context. They may include explanations, tips, examples or links to further resources.

Help messages should be placed near the relevant interface elements, such as tooltips, question mark icons or contextual menus. For example, a help message might explain the purpose of a button, provide guidance on filling out a form field or offer instructions on how to navigate a complex feature.

Error

Error messages inform users when something goes wrong or when their action cannot be completed successfully. They help users understand the nature of the problem and provide guidance on how to resolve it. Error messages should be clear, specific and actionable. They should explain what went wrong, why it happened and what steps the user can take to correct the issue. Error messages can vary in severity, ranging from minor warnings to critical errors. They may include messages about invalid input, system failures, connectivity issues or permission errors.

Error messages should be visually distinct, using colour, icons or formatting to draw attention. They should also be placed in prominent locations where users are likely to notice them. For example, an error message might tell the user that their password is incorrect when trying to log in, say that a file cannot be saved due to insufficient disk space or warn about a network connection failure when loading a webpage.

Typography

Typography is the way text looks including the fonts, sizes, spacing and justification, making text easy to read and visually appealing. Typography influences readability, hierarchy and overall visual appeal. It also helps make brands look unique and recognisable.

Style

Style refers to the appearance of the text, such as whether it's bold, italic or normal. Different styles can be used to convey different meanings or emphasise important information. For example, headings might be bold to stand out, while regular text is usually plain.

When looking to improve typography style, it is important to choose the right font so it can be read easily. It should also be used consistently throughout the interface, with a limited number of font variations so that it does not appear cluttered. Text style should also be accessible for all users including those using screen readers.

Size

Size is how big or small the text appears on the screen. Larger text is often used for headings or titles to grab attention, while smaller text is used for paragraphs or less important information. It is important to choose sizes that are easy to read and appropriate for the context. For example, you wouldn't want tiny text on a mobile app where users are viewing content on small screens.

To improve the typography in terms of size, it might be necessary to set a larger default font size for text elements in the design so they can be read. It is also important that fonts are clear and legible at both smaller and larger sizes. Responsive design should also mean that application should adjust font size based on the screen size and resolution.

How gathered client requirements impact visual design

Client requirements play a significant role in shaping the visual design of software applications for the following reasons:

- Understanding user needs: client requirements provide insights into the needs, preferences, and expectations of the end users. Visual design must align with these requirements to ensure that the software meets user expectations and provides a positive user experience.
- Defining design objectives: client requirements help establish design objectives and goals for the software application. Visual design decisions are guided by these objectives, such as creating a modern, minimalist interface or incorporating branding elements to reinforce the client's identity.
- Determining design elements: client requirements influence the selection of design elements such as colours, typography, imagery and layout. For example, if the client's brand colours are specified, the visual design should incorporate these colours to maintain brand consistency.
- Ensuring usability: client requirements often include usability criteria and functional specifications. Visual design must support usability by organising information logically, providing clear navigation and ensuring accessibility for all users.
- Balancing aesthetics and functionality: client requirements often strike a balance between aesthetic appeal and functional requirements. Visual design must balance these factors to create an interface that is visually engaging, user-friendly and aligned with the software's functionality and purpose.

Learning in context 5

Improving human computer interface design

VirtualFitUK is a leading fitness application that offers users personalised workout plans, nutrition tracking and virtual coaching sessions. Despite its popularity, the company has received feedback from users regarding the usability and effectiveness of the design of its smartphone app. Users have reported difficulties navigating the application, understanding features and accessing relevant information. As a result, VirtualFitUK is committed to improving its design to enhance user experience and satisfaction.

Several challenges have been identified that hinder the current HCI design:

- complex navigation structure leading to user confusion and frustration
- inconsistent visual design elements impacting brand identity and user recognition
- lack of intuitive features and guidance for new users
- limited accessibility options for users with disabilities.

To better understand the issues, VirtualFitUK conducts surveys, interviews and usability testing sessions with current users to gather feedback on pain points and areas for improvement. The collected feedback and research findings are analysed to identify common themes, usability issues and user preferences.

Clear requirements and design objectives are defined based on the analysis, focusing on improving navigation, usability and user engagement. VirtualFitUK's design team collaborates to create prototypes that address the identified usability issues and design objectives.

New design features include:

- Accessibility features, such as keyboard navigation, screen reader compatibility and colour contrast adjustments, are integrated into the design to enhance usability for users with disabilities
- New visual design to reflect the brand's identity while maintaining consistency across the application
- Clear visual hierarchy, intuitive icons and consistent typography to improve readability and user comprehension
- In-app tutorials, tooltips and contextual help messages provide users with assistance and guidance as they navigate the application.

Through its human computer interaction design enhancement, VirtualFitUK achieves significant improvements in user experience and satisfaction:

- User feedback shows a noticeable increase in usability, with users expressing appreciation for the streamlined navigation and intuitive features.
- User activity statistics demonstrate higher user interaction rates and increased time spent within the application.
- Accessibility enhancements ensure inclusivity, allowing users of all abilities to access and benefit from VirtualFitUK's features.
- The refreshed visual design reinforces the brand's identity and positions VirtualFitUK as a leader in design within the fitness industry.

Quick check 12

1 Different colours convey different moods and emotions. Carry out research on colour psychology and create an infographic to explore the effect of different colours when used in design.

2 Create a presentation to explore the visual design of an application you use. For each element, reflect on how effective it is in its design.

5.3 Human computer interface design documents and diagrams

Processing and data handling

Data flow diagrams

A Data Flow Diagram (DFD) in application design is a visual representation of the flow of data within a software system. It shows how data moves from one component to another within the system, including processes, data stores and external entities.

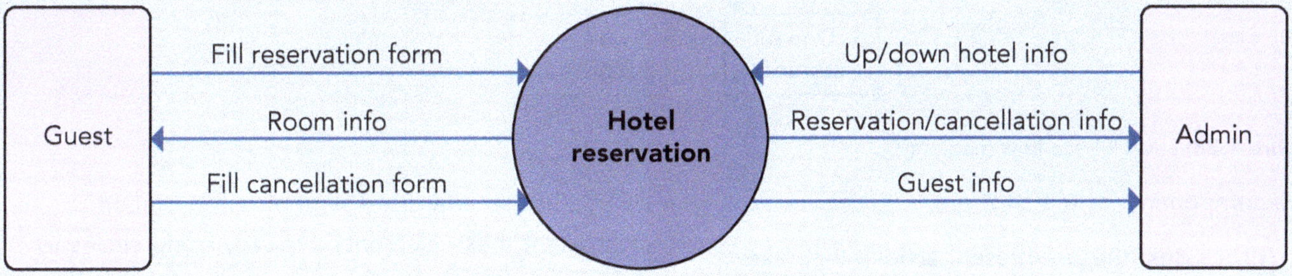
Guest
Fill reservation form
Room info
Fill cancellation form
Hotel reservation
Up/down hotel info
Reservation/cancellation info
Guest info
Admin

Figure 1.27: Level 0 Data flow diagram

There are two levels of data flow diagram: Level 0 and Level 1. The Level 0 DFD, or Context Diagram, gives a big-picture view of the system and how it interacts with outside entities. It shows the system as one unit, with external entities around it. It does not show the details of what happens inside the system but focuses on how data moves between the system and the outside. It is the first step in understanding what the system does and who it interacts with, before getting into more specific details.

The Level 1 DFD goes deeper into the system compared to the Level 0 DFD. It breaks down the system into smaller parts called subprocesses or components. Each part represents a specific job or task in the system. It also shows how data moves between these parts and where data is stored. While the Level 0 DFD focuses on the system's interactions with the outside world, the Level 1 DFD zooms in to show how data moves within the system itself.

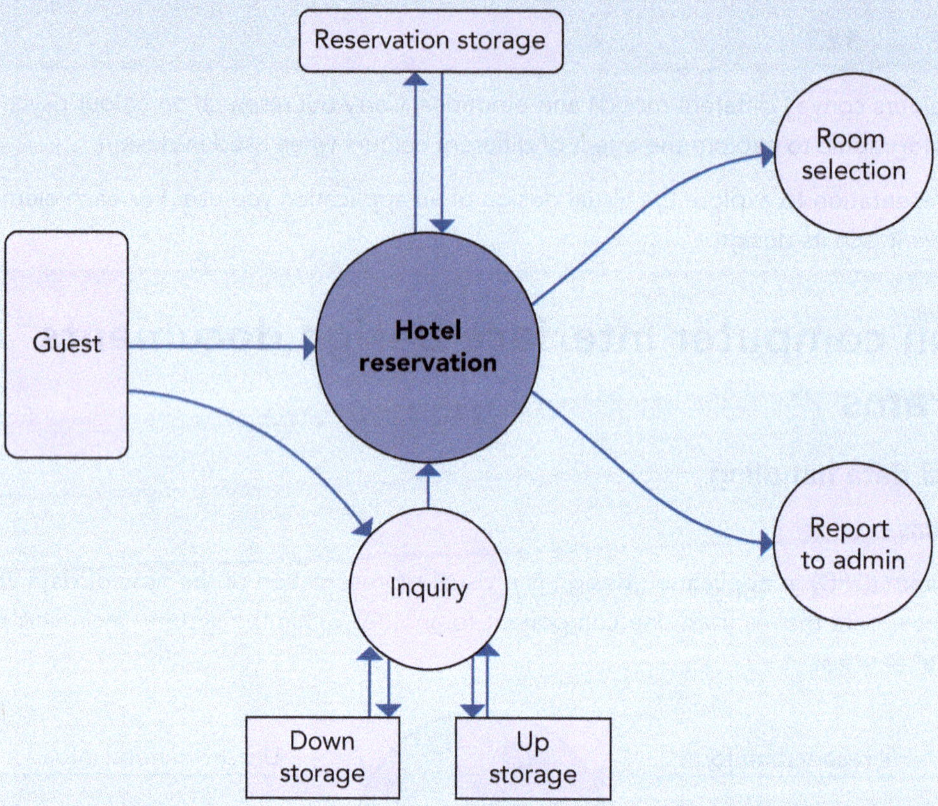
Reservation storage
Room selection
Guest
Hotel reservation
Report to admin
Inquiry
Down storage
Up storage

Figure 1.28: Level 1 Data flow diagram

The components of the DFD are:

- **Processes:** these represent actions that take place within the system. Processes can include tasks such as data input, data processing, data storage and data output.
- **Data flows:** these represent the movement of data between components in the system. Data flows show the path that data takes as it moves from one process to another, between processes and data stores, or between processes and external entities.
- **Data stores:** these represent where data is stored within the system. Data stores can include databases, files or other storage mechanisms where data is kept for later use.
- **External entities:** these represent entities outside the system that interact with it. External entities can include users, other systems, devices or sources of data input.

DFDs use standardised symbols and notation to represent these elements, typically using circles to represent processes, arrows to represent data flows, rectangles to represent data stores and squares to represent external entities.

In application design, DFDs are used during the early stages of system analysis and design to model the flow of data and interactions within the system. They help designers and developers understand how data moves through the system, identify dependencies between components and visualise the overall structure and functionality of the application.

DFDs are particularly useful for communicating complex systems to stakeholders, facilitating discussion and decision-making, and ensuring that all parties have a shared understanding of how the application functions. They serve as a blueprint for the development process, guiding the implementation of software systems and ensuring that they meet the requirements and expectations of users.

When creating a data flow diagram:

- be clear on what the app does and how it works
- identify who or what sends data to or receives data from the app (like users or other systems)
- identify processes, breaking the app into smaller tasks that handle data, such as 'Process Order'
- find where data is kept, like databases or files
- use arrows to show how data moves between entities, processes and stores, labelling them with the data type
- use symbols such as circles for processes, rectangles for external entities, open rectangles for data stores, and arrows for data flows
- create levels, starting with a simple overview (Level 0), then add details in more levels (Level 1, Level 2, etc.)
- check your diagram for accuracy and clarity, and get feedback and make changes if needed.

An effective DFD should:

- be clear and easy to understand, with labels and annotations providing context for each component
- maintain consistency in notation and formatting throughout the diagram
- ensure that all relevant processes, data flows and interactions are represented in the diagram
- ensure that the diagram accurately reflects the current state of the system and its data flows.

They can be improved by simplifying the diagram by focusing on the most essential components and interactions, avoiding unnecessary complexity. It is also important to use software tools specifically designed for creating DFDs to streamline the creation process and improve the visual presentation of the diagram.

Flowcharts

A flowchart, when used for human computer interface design, is a visual representation of the sequential steps and decision points within the software application. It illustrates the flow of user interaction, including navigation pathways, user inputs, system responses and branching logic.

Flowcharts typically consist of various symbols representing different elements such as processes, decisions, inputs/outputs and connectors. Common symbols include rectangles for processes, diamonds for decisions, parallelograms for inputs/outputs and arrows for the flow of control. Conventions include following a top-down or left-to-right flow, using clear labelling for each symbol and maintaining consistency in symbol usage and formatting.

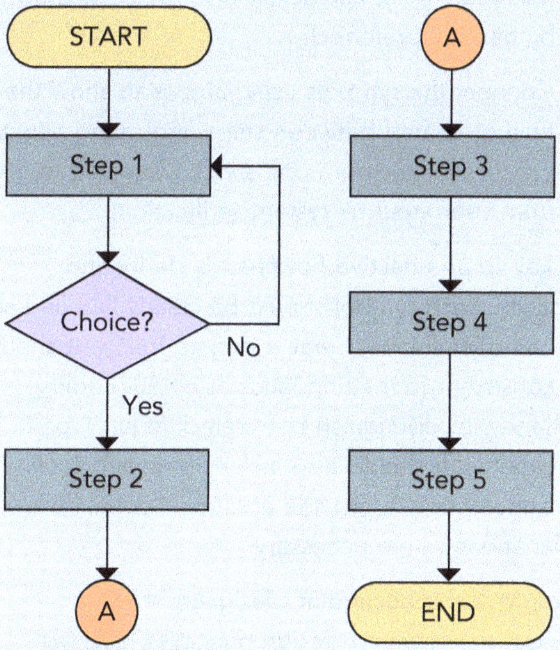
START
Step 1
Choice?
No
Yes
Step 2
A
A
Step 3
Step 4
Step 5
END

Figure 1.29: Typical symbols used when creating a flowchart to show a process

Flowcharts are suitable for illustrating the sequence of steps or processes involved in completing a task within an application. They are used during the design phase to visualise the logical flow of user interactions, data processing or system operations. Flowcharts are particularly useful for documenting complex processes, identifying decision points and understanding system behaviour.

When creating a flowchart:

- Identify the particular function or feature of the application you want to represent in the flowchart (e.g. user login process, data retrieval).
- Decide the sequence of steps involved in the process, including any decision points (e.g. user enters credentials, system verifies credentials).
- Choose appropriate symbols to represent each step, decision, input or output (e.g. rectangles for processes, diamonds for decisions).
- Draw the flowchart using a suitable tool like Microsoft Visio, Lucidchart or draw.io, or draw it by hand, if preferred.
- Connect the symbols using arrows to show the flow of control between steps, indicating how the process moves from one step to the next (e.g. from user input to system verification).

The key to an effective flowchart is clarity and simplicity. Each symbol should be clearly labelled and have an overall layout that is easy to follow. It should use consistent formatting, such as colour coding or shapes, to distinguish between different types of elements. It should also include relevant details and annotations to provide additional context or explanations where necessary.

To improve the document, designers should consider user-centred design principles, such as grouping related steps together or minimising the use of technical jargon. If necessary, additional documentation or supplementary materials can accompany the flowchart, such as written procedures or explanatory notes.

User interface designs

User interface designs are the documents used to plan how the human computer interface will look within software applications. They contain key information such as the layout, visual design, interactivity, navigation and user feedback for each screen. Commonly used diagrams are **visualisation diagrams** and **wireframe diagrams**.

Visualisation diagram

Visualisation diagrams are drawings or sketches of what the human computer interface (HCI) will look like. They show the content and position of various elements of the HCI including images, graphics, text and interactive features such as navigation. They also include annotations to provide information such as font sizes, colours and styles and image colours and colour scheme. This is important in showing the developer what is required when creating the HCI.

A visualisation diagram is appropriate to use during the development of the HCI to:

- plan and organise the structure of the system
- communicate design decisions stakeholders, developers and team members
- identify potential design flaws with the HCI
- provide a reference and guide for designing and testing the software system.

A visualisation diagram may be created by hand or on a computer. When creating the diagram, consideration needs to be given to what elements are required on each screen, when they will go and what they will look like.

To create a visualisation diagram:

- Understand the project requirements and user needs; for example, for a fitness tracking app, identify user needs like tracking workouts, monitoring progress and setting goals.
- Gather design inspiration by looking at other similar products and examining how they design their dashboards and user interfaces.
- Create detailed visual representations of the app screens, either by hand or on a computer.

- Add User Interface (UI) elements such as buttons, icons and navigation bars, ensuring they are intuitive and user-friendly.
- Add annotations to show colours, fonts and images, reflecting the visual identity of the application.
- Include detail about user interactions and animations, for example, how buttons will respond when clicked, how screens will transition, and any animations that enhance the user experience.
- Gather user feedback and make necessary adjustments to the design.

An effective visualisation diagram will provide enough detail that someone else could take the document and use it to create the product. It will also clearly communicate design ideas and rationale to stakeholders, such as the client.

A visualisation diagram focuses on the final design and appearance of the application software. By contrast, a wireframe is a more basic, low-detail sketch which is better used to show structure and the placement of elements.

Figure 1.30: Visualisation diagrams provide information on graphics, colours and fonts as well as justifications for design choices

Wireframe diagram

Wireframes are used to outline the structure and layout of a user interface for the software application. They focus on content organisation and functionality of the HCI without detailing visual design.

Wireframe diagrams typically use:

- Basic shapes such as rectangles, squares, circles and lines to represent interface elements like buttons, input fields, text areas and images
- Placeholder text is used to indicate where actual content will appear in the final interface.
- Labels and annotations provide additional context or descriptions for interface elements.
- Arrows or lines may represent navigation paths, indicating the flow between different screens or pages.
- Grids and alignment guides help maintain consistency and alignment among interface elements.

Wireframe diagrams are appropriate to use during the early stages of software design. They help with planning and conceptualising the layout and structure of the user interface. They are also used for communicating design ideas and concepts to stakeholders, developers and designers. Wireframes are helpful when refining and iterating on interface designs based on feedback from stakeholders.

To create a wireframe, first understand the project requirements and user needs to inform the wireframe design. Start with rough sketches of the interface layout and structure, focusing on key elements and functionality before using wireframing tools or software to create digital versions of the wireframes, refining the design as needed. Detail can be added, including labels, annotations and navigation elements.

To create a wireframe:

- Understand project requirements and user needs, like easy navigation and quick checkout.

- Start with rough sketches of the main screens, such as the home page, product listing and checkout page, highlighting key elements like search bars and product images.
- Focus on key elements and functionality like a shopping cart icon, product filters and user login options.
- Use wireframing tools or software to create digital versions of the wireframes.
- Refine the design as needed, adjusting the layout and structure based on initial feedback, ensuring elements are well-organised and user-friendly.
- Add detail, including labels, annotations and navigation elements like menus and breadcrumbs.
- Review and update based on feedback from stakeholders.

Wireframes can then be reviewed and updated based on feedback until the design meets the project requirements.

Effective wireframes have the following elements:

- Clarity: wireframes should clearly communicate the layout, structure and functionality of the interface
- Simplicity: wireframes should be simple and easy to understand, focusing on essential elements without unnecessary detail.
- Flexibility: wireframes should be flexible enough to accommodate changes and iterations as the design process progresses.
- Alignment with requirements: wireframes should align with project requirements and user needs, serving as a blueprint for the final interface design.

To improve effectiveness, it is important to gather feedback from stakeholders and end-users. Feedback and testing can be used to refine the design to better meet user needs and project requirements. It is also important to encourage collaboration and communication among stakeholders, designers and developers to ensure that wireframes accurately reflect the intended functionality and user experience.

Figure 1.31: Wireframe icons are used to show the layout of screens, for example when developing a website

Quick check 13

1 In your own words, try to summarise the purpose of the four documents and diagrams for designing human computer interface design into a single sentence.

2 For an application of your choice, sketch a visualisation diagram for one of the screens. How would a wireframe be different?

Practice questions 5

With the rise of smartphones and the increasing interest in fitness among young adults, KeepFitNow has identified an opportunity to develop a mobile app that caters to the needs of fitness enthusiasts. The app aims to provide users with a platform to log their workouts, track their progress and share their achievements with friends and followers.

Users can log their workouts, including details such as exercise type, duration, intensity and calories burned. The app offers a variety of pre-defined workout categories and allows users to create custom workouts tailored to their preferences.

This is a visualisation diagram of the workout upload screen.

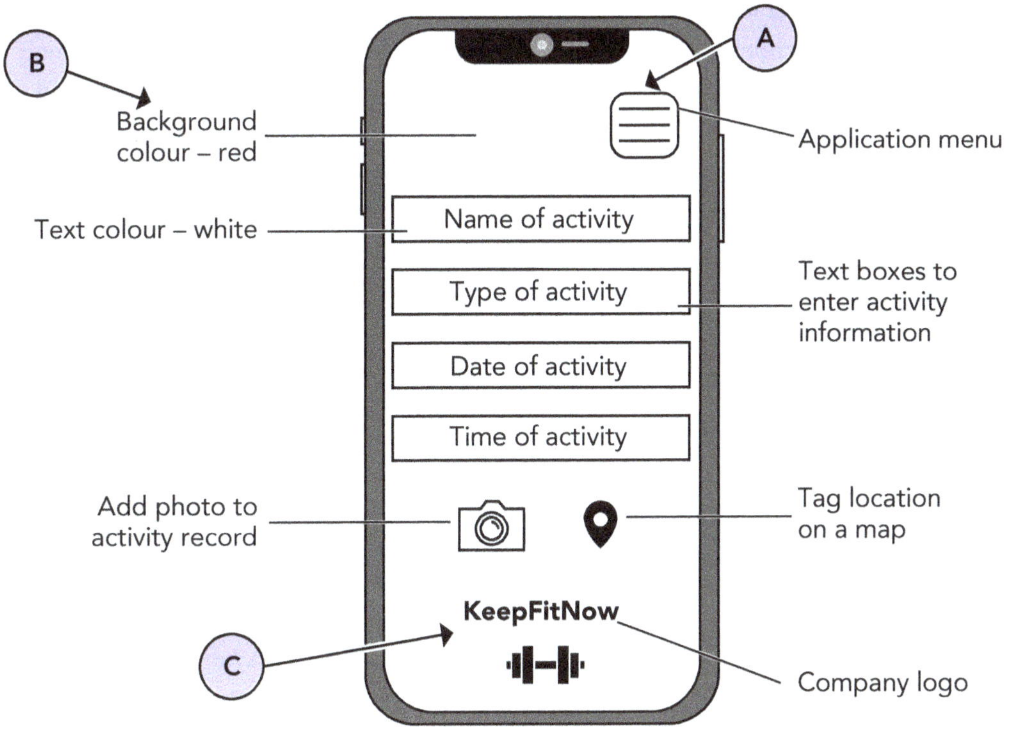
B
Background colour – red
Text colour – white
A
Application menu
Name of activity
Type of activity
Date of activity
Time of activity
Text boxes to enter activity information
Add photo to activity record
Tag location on a map
KeepFitNow
C
Company logo

Figure 1.32: The workout upload screen

1 Copy and complete the table.

Feature	**Letter**
Annotation	
Navigation	
Logo	

[3]

2 KeepFitNow want a touch human computer interface for their application.
Explain **one** advantage and **one** disadvantage of this interface method. [4]

3 Explain **two** ways that the effectiveness of this human computer interface could be improved. [4]

TA6 Job roles and skills

Learning intentions

This topic is about the various job roles and skills required for software application development. It will examine the responsibilities of each role and how they contribute to the development process. It will also explore the use of appropriate language, tailored to the audience, non-verbal cues, questioning techniques and verbal and written communication, required for clear, efficient and productive interactions.

It covers:

6.1 Job roles

6.2 Communication skills required in application development

6.1 Job roles

The software application development process requires several different roles to work together collectively. Understanding these roles and their contributions is crucial for effective collaboration and project success.

Application designer

Application designers are integral to the software development process as they plan how a software application will work and look, making sure it meets both technical requirements and user needs. An application designer is responsible for planning the overall structure and layout of a software application, ensuring it meets technical requirements and user needs. They create detailed technical specifications and develop prototypes and mock-ups to visualise the application's design. Application designers work closely with developers, systems analysts and project managers to ensure the design is practical and meets both technical and business objectives. They also address design issues and refine solutions to help prevent potential problems and ensure the application functions effectively and efficiently.

Mobile application designer

Mobile application designers create apps for smartphones and tablets, ensuring they are easy to use, work well on different devices and meet platform-specific guidelines. Mobile application designers focus on creating user-friendly designs specifically for mobile devices, ensuring the app works well on various screen sizes and orientations. They emphasise touch interfaces and mobile usability, designing with performance limitations such as battery life and processing power in mind. Mobile application designers use tools such as Sketch, Figma or Adobe XD to create wireframes and prototypes tailored for mobile experiences. Their role includes testing these prototypes on mobile devices to ensure optimal performance and user experience.

Mobile application designers play a crucial role in the process of software application development in creating a mobile specific design and ensure that the final product is optimised for mobile use.

Project manager

Project managers plan, organise and oversee software projects to make sure they are completed on time, within budget and to the required quality standards. Project managers play a crucial role in the software development process by developing detailed project plans, schedules and milestones to organise the project and keep it on track. They manage resources such as budget, time and team members, ensuring that tasks are allocated efficiently and that the project stays on schedule and within scope and budget. Project managers identify and mitigate potential risks and facilitate clear communication among stakeholders and team members, providing regular status updates to ensure everyone is informed and aligned. Their oversight helps maintain project momentum and quality standards.

Figure 1.33: A project manager will oversee all elements of the project from start to finish ensuring it is ready on time and on budget

Systems analyst

Systems analysts gather information about what a software application needs to do and then create detailed plans that the software development team will follow. Systems analysts are responsible for gathering and documenting business and technical requirements, translating these into detailed technical specifications for the software development team. They conduct feasibility analyses to assess whether proposed solutions are practical and in line with business goals. Systems analysts also identify system issues and suggest improvements, acting as a bridge between business stakeholders and technical teams to ensure clear communication and mutual understanding, aiding a smooth development process.

Systems designer

Systems designers map out how the different parts of a software system will fit together, ensuring everything works smoothly and efficiently. Systems designers design the overall architecture of information systems, creating detailed **technical blueprints** and diagrams that illustrate how different system components will interact. They ensure that the system is scalable, secure and efficient, planning for seamless integration of various components. Systems designers contribute to software application development by providing thorough documentation to guide **systems administrators**, ensuring the technical aspects of the application are well-understood and correctly implemented and laying the groundwork for a robust and maintainable system.

User Experience Designer (UXD)

User Experience Designers (UXDs) study how people use applications and design them to be as easy and enjoyable to use as possible. They may also review an existing application and evaluate its current user experience, applying this to a new design. User Experience Designers (UXDs) focus on creating seamless and satisfying user journeys through the application. They conduct detailed user research to understand the target audience's needs, behaviours and pain points. UXDs design **interaction flows** that make the software application intuitive and easy to use. They create prototypes and conduct usability testing to gather feedback and refine the user experience.

By collaborating with UI designers and product managers they ensure that the user experience is a central consideration throughout the development process, leading to a product that is both functional and enjoyable to use.

User Interface Designer (UID)

User Interface Designers (UIDs) focus on how an application looks. User Interface Designers (UIDs) focus on the visual elements of the application, ensuring it is both attractive and user-friendly. They design the layout, colour schemes, typography and **iconography** to create a **cohesive** and visually appealing interface. UIDs ensure visual consistency throughout the application, aligning with brand guidelines and design systems.

They design interactive elements such as buttons, forms and menus to be intuitive and engaging. UIDs use design tools such as Sketch, Figma or Adobe XD to create detailed UI designs and prototypes, working closely with UX designers to ensure the visual design supports and enhances the overall user experience.

UIDs enhance the overall aesthetic appeal of the application. Their detailed UI designs and prototypes guide team members in implementing the visual elements effectively. UIDs work closely with UX designers to ensure the visual design supports and enhances the user experience, resulting in a polished and user-friendly final product.

Figure 1.34: User Interface Designers (UIDs) will use wireframe diagrams to gather feedback from stakeholders about interaction of the human computer interface

Quick check 14

1 Choose one of the mentioned job roles and research current job vacancies online. Make a summary of the key responsibilities required for the role from the advert.

2 For the job role you select above, review the responsibilities listed. How would each of these support the software application development process?

6.2 Communication skills required in application development

Appropriate language to meet the needs of the audience

Appropriate language should be clear and straightforward and avoid unnecessary technical jargon or complexity. This ensures that all stakeholders, regardless of their technical expertise, can understand the information being communicated. The language should be relevant to the audience's role and level of involvement in the project. For example, a technical user might be asked to:

'Configure the server settings by accessing the admin panel and updating the IP address field.'

This would be confusing for a non-technical user. Instead, they might be given instructions such as:

'To set up your connection, go to Settings and enter your network details.'

Communication should also be professional and respectful, without using slang or acronyms where they are not required. For example, you might instruct someone by asking:

'Please enter your username and password to log in.'

It would be unprofessional and too casual to phrase it like this:

'Hey, just pop in your username and password to get started!'

When communicating with the client, it might not be appropriate to talk about UAT and UI, but instead User Acceptance Testing and User Interface.

Language should also be tailored to the specific type of communication. This includes considering factors such as the stage of the project, the audience's familiarity with the topic and project, and any previous discussions or decisions related to the project. Information should be communicated concisely, without unnecessary detail. This helps to keep communications focused and prevents the audience from becoming overwhelmed with irrelevant details.

In every stage of the project and within every job role, appropriate language is vital in ensuring ensures effective communication, collaboration, precision and user satisfaction.

- During the requirement gathering and analysis stage, the project manager must understand the client's expertise and communication preferences to help with tailoring language to their level of technical understanding.
- During the design and prototyping stage, the UX/UI designer needs to use language that is understood by stakeholders so they can visualise the final product and provide relevant feedback.
- During the development stage, the team need to use appropriate technical language during code reviews to ensure that feedback is clear and actionable, and to help maintaining code quality and consistency across the project.
- During the testing stage, system developers will need precise descriptions and explanations of issues from the project manager who will collect and aggregate feedback from various stakeholders and users. This allows issues to be fixed efficiently.

Non-verbal

Non-verbal communication is crucial for effective collaboration and project management across the development team. Non-verbal communication includes:

- gestures and facial expressions: convey emotions and intentions, building a deeper understanding among team members
- body language such as posture and eye contact during meetings or presentations can suggest confidence and engagement.

The appropriate use of non-verbal communication varies across job roles and stages of the development cycle. These non-verbal cues not only build interpersonal relationships but also streamline the development process by reducing the chance of misunderstandings and promoting alignment within the team.

For example, a system designer might nod and maintains eye contact while the project manager discusses the goals, showing understanding and agreement. However, a system designer frowning or looking confused can prompt the project manager to clarify the task or requirement immediately, preventing potential misunderstandings.

When presenting a new interface to stakeholders, a UX designer presenting might look for non-verbal feedback, such as nods of approval, smiles or attentive body language, which suggest positive feelings. However, crossed arms or lack of eye contact might suggest resistance or disagreement.

During a meeting with a stakeholder to gather information on client requirements, a systems analyst may nod attentively, maintain eye contact and takes notes, showing active listening and engagement. However, when the client mentions a specific workflow, the systems analyst furrows their brow slightly and tilts their head, indicating confusion or the need for further clarification. Noticing this, the project manager may pause the discussion and ask the client to elaborate on that workflow, gaining clarification.

Overall, integrating non-verbal communication appropriately within each job role and development stage optimises collaboration, builds understanding and ultimately leads to the successful delivery of software applications.

Figure 1.35: Non-verbal cues, such as gestures and facial expressions, can help build rapport with others and gain support for an idea

Questioning techniques to elicit specific information

The use of questions is an important verbal communication in gathering requirements, clarifying any ambiguous areas and checking stakeholders' expectations. These techniques typically involve open-ended questions through interviews, surveys or focus groups, aimed at uncovering user needs, preferences and constraints. By encouraging active participation and seeking feedback iteratively, question techniques allow the identification of potential issues early in the development lifecycle, so reducing risks and enhancing the overall quality of the software product.

Table 1.43: Types of question in software development

Type of question	Explanation	Purpose/reason for use	Examples	Benefits	Limitations
Open-ended	Questions that allow for detailed, expansive answers.	To gather comprehensive insights and detailed feedback.	'What features do you think are missing in the app?'	Encourages detailed responses and creative ideas.	Can lead to lengthy, unfocused answers.
Closed-ended	Questions that can be answered with a simple 'yes' or 'no,' or a specific piece of information.	To obtain clear, concise information.	'Does the app support multi-language features?'	Provides quick, straightforward answers.	Limits the depth of the information gathered.
Leading	Questions that suggest a particular answer or outcome.	To confirm assumptions or guide the respondent towards a specific answer.	'How useful do you find the app's new notification feature?'	Can confirm specific features or ideas.	May bias the responses, leading to skewed data.
Probing	Follow-up questions that delve deeper into initial responses.	To gain more detailed information or clarification.	'Can you explain why you find that feature difficult to use?'	Helps uncover detailed insights and underlying reasons.	Can make respondents feel interrogated if not handled sensitively.
Rhetorical	Questions asked to make a point rather than elicit an answer.	To emphasise a point or idea.	'Isn't it clear that user-friendly design is important?'	Can effectively emphasise key points.	Does not provide new information or insights.

(Continued)

Type of question	Explanation	Purpose/reason for use	Examples	Benefits	Limitations
Hypothetical	Questions based on imagined scenarios.	To explore potential outcomes and encourage creative thinking.	'What would you do if the app crashed during an important task?'	Encourages imaginative and critical thinking.	May not always reflect realistic scenarios or practical solutions.
Reflective	Questions that reflect the respondent's previous statements.	To confirm understanding and show active listening.	'You mentioned that the app is slow. Could you specify where this happens?'	Validates the respondent's input and builds rapport.	Can sometimes seem repetitive or redundant.
Clarifying	Questions asked to ensure understanding of a previous answer.	To clear up any ambiguities or confusion.	'When you say the app is 'slow,' do you mean during startup or navigation?'	Ensures accurate understanding and avoids miscommunication.	Can interrupt the flow of conversation if overused.
Multiple-choice	Questions offering several predefined answers.	To quantify preferences or opinions.	'Which feature do you use most often?' **A** Chat **B** Calendar **C** Notifications.	Simplifies data analysis and comparison.	Limits responses to predefined options, potentially missing other insights.

The appropriate use of question techniques varies based on the job responsibilities and the phase of application development.

- During the requirements gathering phase, project managers may use question techniques to understand stakeholders' needs and preferences effectively. Through interviews, surveys or focus groups, they dig into users' workflows, pain points and desired features, ensuring the business objectives align with the technical solutions.
- Software developers use question techniques during the design phase to check requirements, resolve queries and confirm design decisions. By posing targeted questions to product owners and end-users, developers can refine user stories, prioritise features and ensure the usability and scalability of the application.

Overall, the application of question techniques at each stage of the development process supports teams to deliver software solutions that meet stakeholders' expectations while minimising the need to rework solutions.

Verbal

Verbal communication is characterised by tone of voice, clarity and precision, **active listening** and persuasiveness. Using clear and precise language ensures that ideas and instructions are explained effectively, minimising misunderstandings. Active listening involves understanding and interpreting the messages from others accurately. Persuasiveness is about getting stakeholders to agree on an idea or solution, building consensus to take the project forward.

Verbal communication is vital for requirement gathering by engaging with clients to understand their needs and expectations. It is also important in team meetings for discussing progress, challenges and solutions with team members. Presentations also heavily rely on verbal communication for explaining project milestones, demonstrating prototypes or delivering final product presentations to stakeholders.

Verbal communication is important in the early stages of the project, especially during the requirements analysis and design phase where clear understanding and negotiation of project scope is critical. It is also used throughout development. Agile project management methods, for example, rely on regular quick meetings called stand-ups, where progress is shared using verbal communication.

While all job roles will use verbal communication to some degree, it is particularly important in the following roles:

- Project managers use verbal communication to coordinate tasks, facilitate team meetings, and engage with stakeholders to provide updates and gather feedback.
- System developers will use verbal communication to discuss progress, tackle challenges and collaborate on solutions.
- UX/UI developers will use verbal communication to engage in discussions with clients, users and the development team to understand requirements, present design ideas and gather feedback.

Written

Written communication is the process of conveying messages, information or ideas through written words, numbers and images. It might include emails, reports, manuals and even social media posts. Written communication must be clear and precise so that all team members understand project requirements, specifications and updates accurately. Documentation also plays a crucial role in maintaining a record of decisions made, code changes implemented and issues encountered, helping project management and future reference. Consistency in communication style and terminology builds a shared understanding among team members, preventing misunderstandings and reducing errors. Written communication also allows developers to exchange information and ideas across different time zones and schedules efficiently.

Written communication helps to transfer knowledge and share information with new team members, ensuring continuity in project development even with personnel changes.

Within the job role of application designer and at various stages of application development, written communication serves distinct purposes tailored to specific needs. During the planning and requirements gathering stage, written communication is used to outline project objectives, document user stories and define feature specifications. Throughout the coding and implementation phase, the team rely on written communication through code comments, messages and technical environments.

Learning in context 6

Exploring how each job role contributes to software development

AppVenture is a leading software design company specialising in developing innovative and user-centered mobile applications. Their latest app, TravelEase, is a mobile application designed to streamline travel planning, bookings and itinerary management.

1 **Planning/requirements gathering stage**

During this stage, the project manager, Sarah, defines the project scope, timeline and budget. She conducts a kick-off meeting with all stakeholders to clearly outline the project goals and deliverables and wants to meet in person so she can read non-verbal cues more easily.

Systems analyst, John, conducts interviews with potential users and stakeholders to understand their needs. He asks closed questions to gather data that can be easily analysed. He also uses open questions to explore their experience in more depth, asking them to describe the issues faced when planning travel. He collates this information into a detailed requirements document, including tables and charts to clearly illustrate findings to the client.

2 **Design stage**

Systems designer, Mylo, creates architecture diagrams that outline the system components and their interactions. He shares these diagrams in a meeting with the development team for feedback and approval using clear verbal communication to explain complex technical details and architecture decisions. He also employs active listening to gather feedback from the development team. For visual communication, he creates detailed diagrams and shares these during presentations for better understanding and feedback.

UX designer, Emily, creates wireframes for the TravelEase app's key features. She conducts user testing sessions to validate these designs and iterates based on feedback. Emily employs effective user-centred communication skills during user testing sessions, asking open-ended questions to gather qualitative feedback. She also uses empathy to understand user pain points and integrates this feedback into her designs.

UI designer, Laura, creates high-fidelity mock-ups of the app's screens. She conducts design review meetings where she uses persuasive communication to justify design choices and visual communication to walk through the prototypes interactively. Laura also practices active listening to incorporate the team's feedback into her designs.

Application designer, Steve, uses written communication skills to write detailed functional design documents and use case diagrams that specify how each feature should work. He also uses technical communication skills during meetings to discuss and clarify these documents with other technical team members, ensuring everyone understands the specifications.

Mobile application designer, Nina, creates mobile-specific mock-ups and prototypes ensuring that the design is responsive and user-friendly on various devices. She conducts usability tests with effective verbal communication to guide users through tasks and uses written communication to document findings and suggestions for improvements.

3 **Development stage**

The project manager, Sarah, holds daily meetings to check in with the development

Learning in context **Continued**

team, track progress, and address any issues using active listening skills to understand team members' updates and concerns. She asks clarifying questions to ensure she accurately captures the status of each task and any issues that arise and clear and concise language to communicate project priorities and deadlines. She sends weekly progress reports to stakeholders using professional writing skills to communicate the project's status, milestones achieved and any risks or issues clearly and effectively. She makes sure the reports are well-organised, using bullet points and headings to highlight key information, making it easy for stakeholders to quickly grasp the project's progress and any critical points that need attention.

The systems analyst, John, responds to developers' queries via email using precise and unambiguous language and holds ad hoc clarification meetings to ensure the requirements are well understood. He includes relevant details and examples to illustrate his points, ensuring that his explanations are easily understood. He also manages a support ticket system for tracking requirement-related questions using written communication skills to document responses clearly and concisely, so the information is accessible and understandable for future reference.

4 Testing stage

The project manager, Sarah, uses technical communication skills to effectively use specialist software to manage and prioritise bugs. She writes detailed bug reports that include screenshots, steps to reproduce the error and priority levels, ensuring developers understand the issues clearly. She holds regular status meetings using active listening to understand the team's progress and challenges and uses persuasive communication to motivate them and ensure deadlines are met.

The systems analyst, John, reviews test cases to ensure they cover all requirements and participates in validation sessions to confirm that the application meets the specified needs. He provides written feedback on test cases, highlighting any gaps or improvements needed.

The UX designer, Emily, conducts usability tests with real users and uses interpersonal communication skills to create a comfortable environment for them to provide honest feedback. She uses probing questions to gather in-depth insights and creates a written report of findings, presented in a clear and structured format.

5 Deployment stage

The project manager, Sarah, prepares a detailed deployment checklist, using her verbal communication skills to ensure everyone understands their responsibilities and active listening skills to address any concerns raised by the stakeholders. Throughout the deployment process, she provides regular status updates by email using written communication skills to keep all team members and stakeholders informed about the progress and any potential issues.

The systems analyst, John, coordinates user acceptance testing by scheduling and conducting meetings with key users, where he uses interpersonal communication skills to gather feedback and ensure users are comfortable with the system. He uses his technical writing skills to create detailed reports and summaries that help stakeholders

Learning in context Continued

understand the validation outcomes and any remaining issues.

The systems designer, Mylo, reviews the deployment architecture to ensure it is robust and scalable. He uses his technical communication skills to explain complex architectural concepts and decisions to both technical and non-technical stakeholders and provides technical support to address any architecture-related issues, often through video calls or collaborative tools.

6 **Maintenance stage**

The project manager, Sarah, manages a maintenance schedule and uses issue tracking tools to prioritise and address any bugs or feature requests. She uses her strong verbal and written communication skills to provide regular updates to stakeholders through detailed status reports, email updates and weekly conference calls. During these updates, she clearly explains the status of maintenance activities, any challenges faced and the next steps, ensuring all stakeholders are informed and engaged.

The systems analyst, John, analyses system performance reports and gathers user feedback to identify areas for improvement. He uses his analytical communication skills and active listening to interpret complex data and present it in a clear, understandable manner during regular team sessions to discuss findings with the team and prioritise maintenance tasks.

The UX designer, Emily, uses her communication skills to design user feedback surveys that are clear and easy to understand, ensuring high response rates. She uses her persuasive communication skills to present these findings in meetings with the development team, asking for iterative updates to improve user experience.

The application designer, Steve, documents requests to change the system and updates the functional design specifications. He applies his technical writing skills to ensure the documentation is precise and easily understood by the development team. During update meetings, he uses his verbal communication skills to clearly explain the new features and changes, ensuring everyone is aligned. He encourages questions and feedback, using active listening to address any concerns.

The mobile application designer, Nina, monitors the mobile app's performance and uses her written communication skills to create detailed design documentation that outlines the changes made and their impact on the app's performance. In meetings with the mobile development team, she uses her presentation skills to clearly explain the updates, using visual aids and demonstrations to ensure the team fully understands the changes and their importance.

Through effective communication and collaboration among these roles, AppVenture successfully developed and maintained the TravelEase app, ensuring it met user needs and provided a seamless travel planning experience.

Quick check 15

1 Using examples from your own experience of communicating technical ideas, make note on why the use of appropriate language for the audience is important.

2 Prepare and deliver a presentation about a topic in this unit, for example about a job role described in this Topic Area. Gather feedback on your verbal and non-verbal communication. What went well and what could you improve?

Practice questions 6

1 A project manager has been appointed to oversee development of the application.

a Identify **one** responsibility of the project manager. [1]

b Explain how this responsibility will contribute to the overall software application development. [2]

2 The project manager will require strong verbal communication skills as part of their job role.

Explain **one** way that verbal communication skills will be used by the project manager. [2]

F161 Developing application software

Topic Areas

TA1: Application software considerations
TA2: Data and flow in application software
TA3: API and protocols
TA4: Application software security
TA5: Operational considerations
TA6: Legal considerations

Applications can come in many different forms and there are a wide range of devices that can run them. In this unit, you will learn about the different application platforms that are available and how their different characteristics need to be considered when developing an application. You will also learn how data flows in application software and how API and protocols are used in applications. Finally, you will learn about application security, operational and legal considerations.

TA1 Application software considerations

Learning intentions

This topic is about what needs to be considered when creating software for different platforms and devices.

It covers:

1.1 Application platforms

1.2 Devices

1.3 Storage locations

1.1 Application platforms

There are many different ways to access applications beyond installation to a computer or tablet. Deciding which of these platforms is most suitable for a particular use, such as **Extended Reality (XR)**, requires an understanding of the characteristics, advantages and disadvantages of each platform.

Augmented Reality (AR)/Virtual Reality (VR)/ Mixed Reality (MR)

Augmented reality

AR adds a digital **overlay** on top of the real world. This overlay can contain information in many different forms, for example adding text to describe what the viewer is seeing or adding a cartoon character into the real world. AR applications are generally used on mobile phones or tablet computers.

Educational:
AR can allow the user to be provided with contextually relevant information about the location they are in. For example, imagine walking around a historic city and whenever you look at a site or artefact you point your phone at it. The AR app would show the image from the camera and add text explaining what you are seeing and the historical importance of it. If the historical artefact was only partially preserved the app would also be able to show an overlayed image of what it would originally have looked like.

Instructional:
AR can be used to teach specific skills. For example, a trainee car mechanic could use an AR application on a tablet computer that shows the stages of replacing the brakes. An overlay would show what to do next, what tools are required and provide useful information such as what part number is needed for replacement.

Research:
AR can allow people to visualise something in a different location. For example, AR could be used for market research by allowing consumers to view virtual items in their own home.
A market researcher might want to understand if a new style of TV would sell. The researcher could create a phone app that would show what the new TV would look like in the home. The person taking part in the research would use the app to show what the TV would look like in their home and then be asked questions about whether they prefer the new design and if they would buy it.

Figure 2.1: Example uses of AR

Virtual reality

VR allows the user to step into a **virtual world** where they can explore and interact with their surroundings. VR also allows the user to interact with virtual objects and people. VR requires the use of a VR headset that provides images via a small screen in front of each eye and sound through speakers.

As users move around, the headset senses the direction they are facing and how they are moving. Many also provide handheld controllers that allow the users hands to interact with virtual objects in the VR environment by pressing a button. Controller types can vary with the VR environment, for example using steering wheels in a virtual race.

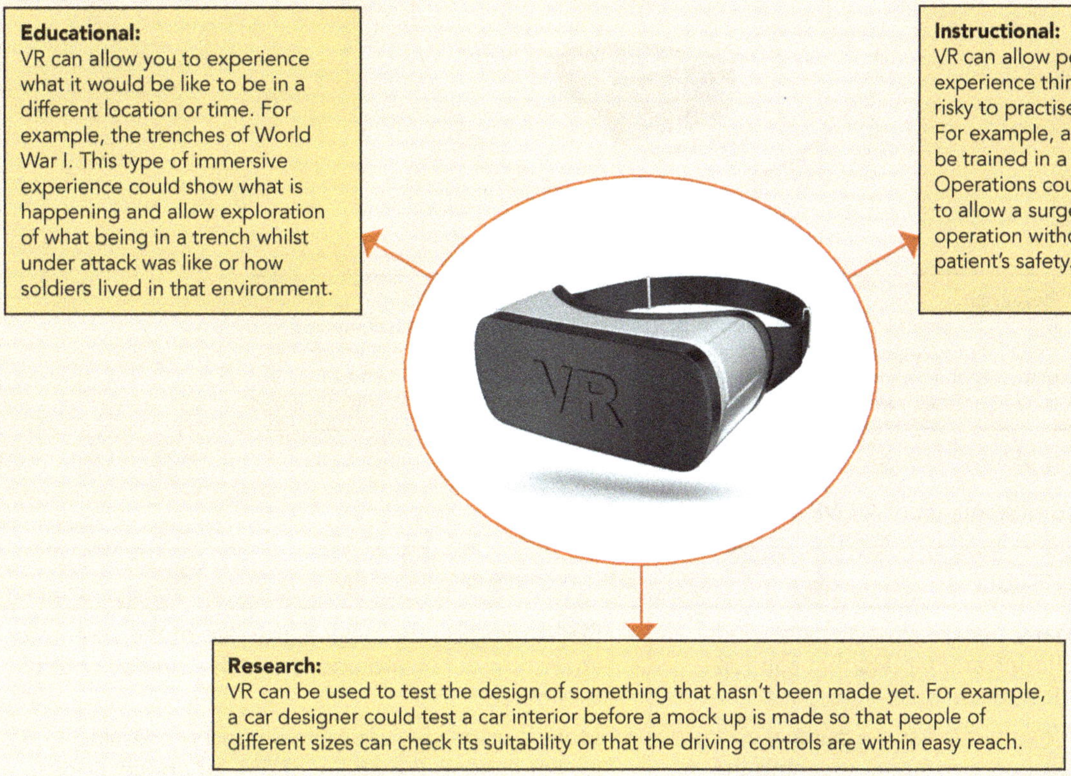
Educational:
VR can allow you to experience what it would be like to be in a different location or time. For example, the trenches of World War I. This type of immersive experience could show what is happening and allow exploration of what being in a trench whilst under attack was like or how soldiers lived in that environment.
Instructional:
VR can allow people to train and experience things that could be risky to practise in the real world. For example, allowing surgeons to be trained in a safe way. Operations could be simulated to allow a surgeon to practice an operation without risking a patient's safety.
VR
Research:
VR can be used to test the design of something that hasn't been made yet. For example, a car designer could test a car interior before a mock up is made so that people of different sizes can check its suitability or that the driving controls are within easy reach.

Figure 2.2: Example uses of VR

Mixed reality

MR combines AR and VR allowing physical and virtual environments to be merged together. An AR headset allows the user to see the environment they are in while also showing digitally generated objects in that environment.

MR is more immersive than AR as the user does not need to hold a device (such as a phone or tablet) to see or interact with the virtual object or other information that is being shown.

Educational:
MR can be used to help people visualise something that doesn't exist yet or no longer exists. For example, when visiting a historical building, MR could be used to view a virtual character from the relevant time period in the building. The user could interact with the virtual character to find out what life was like and how the building would have originally looked.

Instructional:
MR can help provide step by step instructions on how to complete a task. For example, a trainee engineer could use MR to show the steps to service a particular model of generator. As each step is completed the trainee engineer could be shown the next task with an overlay showing how to access the relevant part on the generator they are working on.

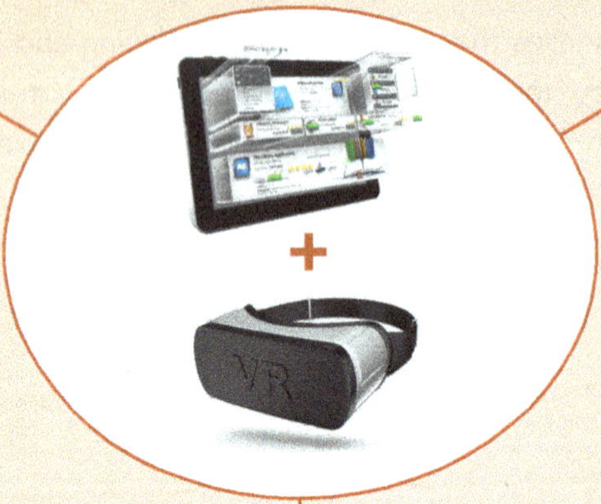

Research:
MR can be used to try experiments out using a visual representation of a computer model. For example, a researcher could use physical blocks to represent chemical elements and they could be combined into virtual compounds. The MR headset could show the virtual compound and allow the simulated chemical reactions to be monitored.

Figure 2.3: Example uses of MR

Table 2.1: Advantages/disadvantages of AR, VR and MR

Platform	Advantages	Disadvantages
Augmented Reality (AR)	• Many people already have phones and tablets that can run AR applications. • AR software can be purchased from existing app stores meaning that a wide audience can access AR.	• Depending on the device, the size of the screen to show the real environment and the overlay could be limited. • Many current devices have limited processing power limiting the ability of the AR application.
Virtual Reality (VR)	• VR headsets are designed to run VR applications and so are likely to have enough processing power and suitable sensors to sense the orientation of the wearer and so on • Much more immersive than AR • Screen size is not a limiting factor.	• Some people have reported issues with using VR for extended periods, such as dizziness or feeling sick • Specialist hardware, such as a VR headset, is required • Ownership is not as widespread as phones/tablets • Headsets are expensive • Current headsets are bulky and relatively heavy and so are not likely to be worn for extended periods • Requires a sufficiently large safe space to move around in and interact with the virtual environment.
Mixed Reality (MR)	MR has the advantages of VR but allows interaction with the user's actual environment.	Not suitable for some applications, such as some types of games, as seeing the current physical location would stop the game being as immersive.

Websites

Creating an application as a website is a popular option as most people have access to a device that can view websites. This means that issues around developing software for different devices (such as Microsoft Windows PCs, Apple Mac computers, iPhones or Android phones) is reduced.

Websites can be used for different purposes:

- Ecommerce websites allow the sale of physical goods, digital products and services. One study showed that nearly 31% of the UK's total retail sales were through ecommerce websites in 2023. An example of an Ecommerce website is Amazon.
- Informative websites provide information to the user. These could be general and cover a wide range of different topics (for example, Wikipedia) or be specialised for a particular topic, area or interest, such as information about a particular model of car.
- Educational websites are used to provide education material or content to people. This isn't just limited to students at a school or college as many professionals access professional development training via websites. Education can also just be for fun, such as websites that teach people how to cook elaborate dishes (for example, BBC Good Food).
- Social media websites allow people to communicate and share information. They can be broad in nature (for example, Facebook), focussed on communication (for example, WhatsApp, Signal or Telegram), focussed on a particular group (for example, LinkedIn for professionals) or for sharing types of media; Video (for example, TikTok), Photos (for example, Instagram) and so on.

Table 2.2: Advantages and disadvantages of websites as an application platform

Advantages	Disadvantages
• Devices capable of accessing websites are widespread. • Users do not need to install specialist software to be able to access the application. This means that the application can be accessed from more than one device (for example home and work computers). This can be very convenient for users. • Understanding of how to access and interact with websites is widespread. • Applications can be completely customised in terms of how they look and operate. This allows for uniqueness and also allows specialist additional hardware such as bank card readers to be used. • Application websites can be found using a search engine. • Websites can be bookmarked.	• Each device can have different specifications, for example different screen sizes and different input and output devices (for example touchscreen, mouse, keyboard, microphone, speakers and so on). • The website needs to work and look attractive across different combinations of screen size, input and output devices. • Each web browser (for example Chrome, Edge, Firefox) might have different capabilities or require the application to be programmed using different methods. • Users expect websites to look and behave in a limited number of ways. This might reduce creativity in terms of application design. • Interaction with additional hardware could be limited. • It is possible to spoof websites meaning users may access a fake if they are not careful to check the URL. • If not optimised for search engines, it may not be found by a user. • If security is not maintained, a user might download a virus.

Computer games

Computer games are a huge part of the applications market, projected to be worth $682 billion by 2030. Games are continually developing in terms of the range of platforms they can be played on and the types of game available. This broadens their appeal and target audience. The games market includes those sold for use on consoles, mobile phones and desktop computers. Many players will buy games on multiple platforms, for example on a games console to play at home and on mobile phones to play while away from home.

While the primary use of computer games is for entertainment, they can also be used for education purposes, such as helping to learn a foreign language or teaching mathematics in a fun way.

Table 2.3: Advantages and disadvantages of computer games as an application platform

Advantages	Disadvantages
• A large percentage of people enjoy playing computer games and are willing to purchase games software. • Most devices that can run games have an application store that makes distribution of the game relatively easy.	• There is a need to develop games for a wide range of different hardware if a company wants to gain large market share. • Highly competitive space potentially requiring large investment to create a popular game. Many games require the services of artists and music producers as well as programmers and project managers.

Quick check 1

1 Write about the differences between Augmented Reality (AR) and Virtual Reality (VR), including what devices would be suitable for each.

2 How do you think AR could be used to help people understand a historic site such as the Acropolis in Athens?

1.2 Devices

Applications can be accessed using a wide range of different devices. Before developing an application, you should be aware of the characteristics of that type of device along with the advantages and disadvantages of it.

Desktop

A desktop computer is designed to be used in one fixed location, usually on a desk. They can have a separate monitor and base unit (that contains the CPU, RAM, storage devices and so on) or have all components built into the monitor.

While desktop computers are no longer as popular as they were, they are still used extensively in business environments, particularly if high-performance CPUs are required. This is because power requirements are not as important when running from mains power rather than battery power. A desktop computer can be linked to a cabled network or Wi-Fi and have a large monitor to allow better usage.

Table 2.4: Advantages and disadvantages of desktop devices

Advantages	Disadvantages
• Can be very powerful as they do not need to be run from a battery • Large screen sizes are available, which is ideal for some tasks such as photo editing • Can connect to a wired network that can provide faster data transfer speeds and are less likely to suffer from interference • Easy to add additional devices or data storage • Includes Wi-Fi capability.	• Need a suitable fixed location • Need to be connected to mains power all the time.

Haptic

A haptic device transmits information by using physical stimulation such as vibrations or resistance. These types of devices are often used as part of a virtual reality system; for example, haptic gloves can give the sensation of picking up a virtual object using resistance so the wearer feels as though they have got hold of an object.

Table 2.5: Advantages and disadvantages of haptic devices

Advantages	Disadvantages
• Helps the wearer to be immersed in VR simulations • No alternative way to simulate touch/feel of objects.	• Expensive and still a niche product • Not widely supported and often manufacturer specific.

Figure 2.4: Haptic glove being used with a VR headset

Laptop

A laptop is designed to be portable. Laptops have a display, keyboard, touchpad and battery all integrated into a single unit. They can be used on the go, for example, on a train or plane, or carried between different places such as school and home.

Many business users of laptops will be able to plug their laptop into a larger screen and an external keyboard/mouse when at the office. This gives the advantages of a laptop while still giving access to the advantages of a desktop.

Table 2.6: Advantages and disadvantages of laptop devices

Advantages	Disadvantages
• Portable and can run off battery or mains power • Widespread and commonly in use • Can be plugged into external peripherals to allow a larger screen/ external keyboard and mouse • Includes Wi-Fi capability.	• Often limited processing power available as need to be able to run off a battery • Screen size tends to be small to allow for portability • Keyboard may have been reduced in size to fit the case • Can be easily stolen.

Server

Servers are powerful computers dedicated to providing some kind of service, such as access to files or websites, via a network. They normally run 24 hours a day, 7 days a week and are likely to be accessed by many people at once, so need to be engineered to be reliable.

Servers tend to run specialised Operating Systems (OS) such as Windows server or Linux as these provide features to make the systems secure, **scalable** and accessible to many users at once.

Table 2.7: Advantages and disadvantages of servers

Advantages	Disadvantages
• Highly reliable, designed to be run 24/7 • Can be accessed by many users at once due to high levels of processing power.	• Expensive compared to many other device types • Uses a specialist operating system and will need to be managed by specialist staff • Could require high levels of power availability and specialist cooling to run reliably.

Smart devices

A smart device is often a pre-existing type of device (such as a washing machine) that has additional capabilities and is connected to a network such as the internet. A smart device can connect to your home Wi-Fi and allow you to:

- access the device from an app on your phone wherever you are and allow you to remotely access functionality, for example starting a wash
- monitor tasks being performed by the device from anywhere and let you know when they are complete.

Table 2.8: Advantages and disadvantages of smart devices

Advantages	Disadvantages
• Widespread and often relatively cheap devices • They do not look like classic computers so they fit into the home environment well.	• Fears over privacy of collected information • Often not updated regularly, so can they be insecure • No common platform, so each manufacturer will often produce their own app to interface with a smart device.

Tablet/hybrid

Tablets are portable computing devices that are larger than mobile phones but usually smaller than laptops. The primary input and output device is a large touchscreen. An on-screen keyboard can be used for text entry but most people find these slower to type on than a physical keyboard.

A hybrid device combines the features of a tablet and a laptop, usually by having a removable keyboard that has an integrated touchpad.

Table 2.9: Advantages and disadvantages of tablet/hybrid devices

Advantages	Disadvantages
• Highly portable • Runs off battery or mains • Can use a stylus to scan from or handwrite information • Hybrid devices can have a physical keyboard attached.	• On-screen keyboards are not as useable as physical keyboards • Often limited processing power due to the thinness of design and need to run from battery • Applications can be limited compared to what is available.

Wearables

A wearable device is one that is worn on the body. A smart watch or fitness tracker is a common type of wearable device. They tend to be optimised to have a small display, be power efficient and have a range of sensors such as heartbeat or step counter as part of the package. Often these devices will be able to communicate with a larger device (such as a mobile phone or tablet) to allow data collected to be analysed and to allow settings to be adjusted easily.

Table 2.10: Advantages and disadvantages of wearables

Advantages	Disadvantages
• Continuous monitoring of health/other data such as activity levels • Hands-free operation • Connects to other devices such as mobile phone.	• Limited functionality compared to mobile phones or other devices • Small screen size can limit usage • Small battery may require frequent charging.

256

Figure 2.5: Smart watch showing heart rate and calories used during exercise

Console

A console is a generic term for any digital device, other than those detailed in this section, that allows a human to interact with it. These kinds of device do not have to have a keyboard and might be used for a specific purpose.

For example, a self-service checkout in a supermarket. It is designed to be easy to use and allow customers to scan items and pay for them. A self-service checkout has a barcode scanner, touch screen, a card reader and a receipt printer built into it.

Table 2.11: Advantage and disadvantage of console devices

Advantage	Disadvantage
Specifically designed for each situation, so hardware is optimised for this.	Each console has different features/capabilities, so applications need to be specifically written for each one.

Quick check 2

1 What advantages might a smart washing machine provide compared to a normal washing machine?

2 What information might be useful to communicate to a runner using a wearable device?

1.3 Storage locations

There are two main categories of storage location: on-site or cloud. On-site storage is located within a building belonging to the company that owns the data. Cloud storage is provided in a remote location rather than on-site. Often cloud storage is owned and managed by someone other than the business who the data belongs to. Access to cloud storage tends to be provided via the internet.

When choosing a suitable storage location, several factors must be considered:

- the amount of data to be stored and whether the amount will change in the future
- how quickly the data will need to be accessed
- whether the data will only need to be accessed by one user or multiple users
- whether the data needs to be stored in one location or be transportable.

1.3.1 On-site

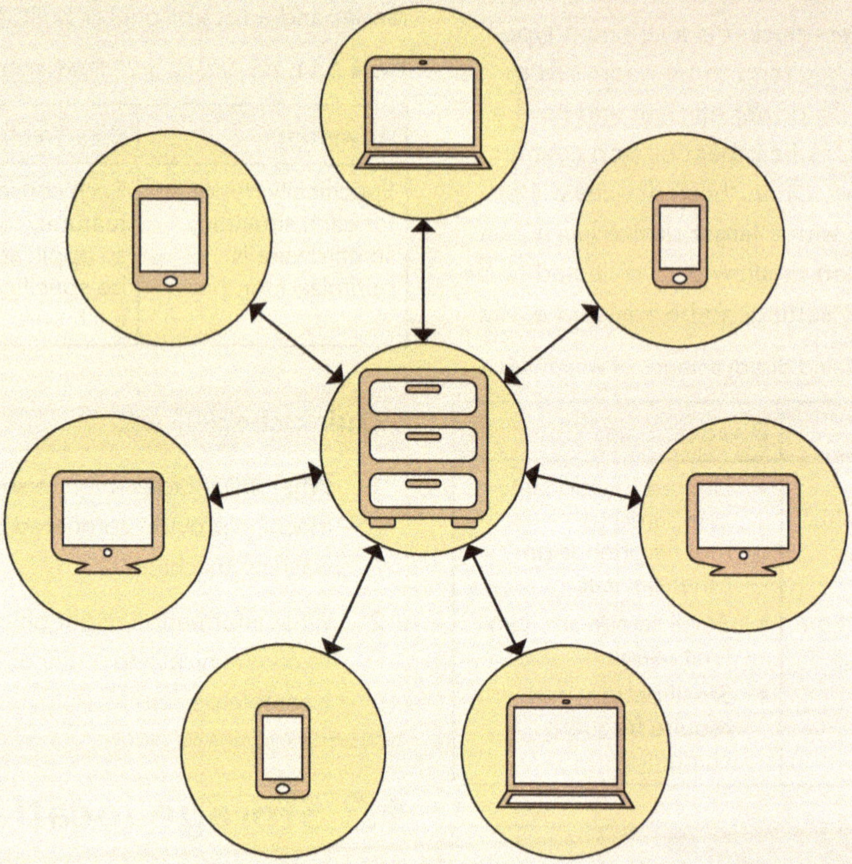

Figure 2.6: File servers are dedicated computers that are used to store and make files available to users connected to a network. Usually, file servers run 24 hours a day, 7 days a week. They are potentially accessed by large numbers of users at the same time and so the hardware is designed to be suitable for this situation. File servers are typically used to allow files to be shared among users to allow for collaboration and to centralise file storage

NAS
Device

Figure 2.7: Network Attached Storage (NAS) devices make files available to users on a network in a similar way to a file server. A NAS tends to be designed to support a small number of users and is ideal for small business use

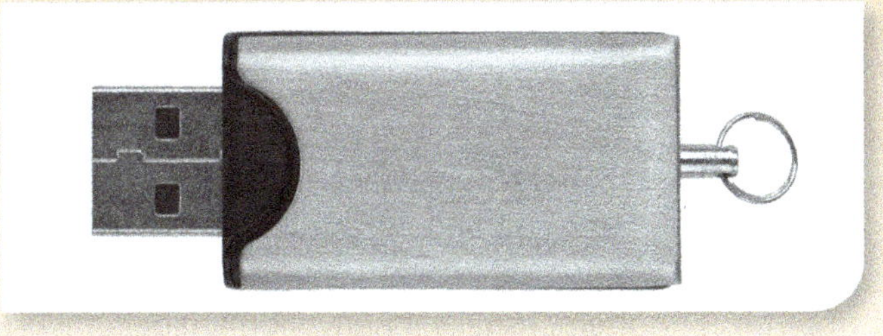

Figure 2.8: Portable storage devices are designed to allow files to be easily transported from one location to another. They will use a common interface standard (such as USB) so they can be easily connected to a range of different devices

Figure 2.9: Solid state drives (SSD) use microchips for storage, usually flash memory. They can be used in computers, servers or portable storage devices

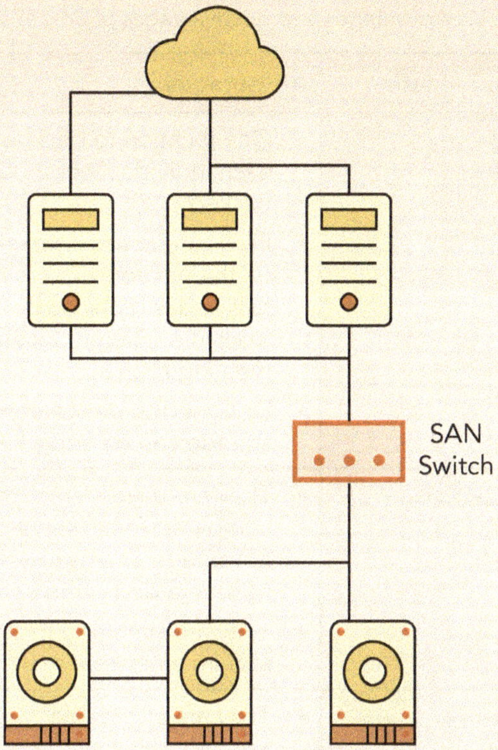
SAN
Switch

Figure 2.10: Storage Area Network (SAN) are independent networks that connect multiple storage devices together to provide a pool of storage to multiple servers. The SAN appears as local storage to each server that is accessing it

Table 2.12: On-site storage locations

Type	File servers	Network Attached Storage (NAS) devices	Portable storage device	Solid State Drive (SSD)	Storage Area Network (SAN)
Users	Large number of users	Small number of users	Single user	Single user	Large number of users
Data	Large amounts of data	Small amounts of data	Small amounts of data	Small amounts of data	Large amounts of data
Scalability	Scalable	Scalable	Not scalable	Not scalable	Scalable
Portability	Not portable	Not portable	Portable	Sometimes portable	Not portable

Table 2.13: Advantages and disadvantages of on-site storage locations

Storage location	Advantages	Disadvantages
File servers	• One location to backup rather than each individual computer needing files backed up. • Files can be accessible from any computer on the network. This is useful if a computer fails and is replaced or if the user needs to work in a different location, for example a meeting room. • Designed to be scalable, meaning more storage can be added if required.	• They are expensive due to the hardware and infrastructure required. • A trained person is required to manage them, usually a network manager.
Network Attached Storage (NAS) devices	• They are usually small, quiet devices compared to file servers. This is an advantage as small businesses are unlikely to have a dedicated server room. • They are simple to manage and do not require a network manager.	• They tend to have smaller storage capacities. • They have limited flexibility in terms of customisation compared to file servers.
Portable storage device	• They are affordable. • They are very easy to transport.	• They generally hold small amounts of data. • They can be easily lost. If lost the data could be accessed by some-one else and have disastrous consequences for a business.
Solid State Drive (SSD)	• They have no moving parts, which makes them reliable. • Compared to hard disk drives they have fast data transfer speeds. • SSDs consume less power than hard disk drives.	• They have smaller storage capacities. • They are usually more expensive per gigabyte compared to hard disk drives. • While SSDs do not have moving parts they still have a finite number of write cycles but this is improving over time.
Storage Area Network (SAN)	• High-speed access to very large amounts of storage. • The storage is scalable, meaning that more storage can be added as necessary. • All the storage devices in a SAN can be centrally managed and backed up.	• They are complex to setup and manage, requiring staff with specialist knowledge. • They can be expensive to install and be a single point of failure unless designed to provided redundancy (replicated storage facilities in case one fails). Redundancy adds additional cost and complexity.

1.3.2 Cloud storage

Cloud storage allows data to be stored on remote storage systems, usually managed by a third party. Access is either via the internet or through private networks. Cloud storage can be located in a range of different places depending on the characteristics needed by the application being developed.

When choosing a suitable cloud storage location, several factors must be considered:

- the amount of data to be stored and how much the amount of data being stored will change along with how frequently this will change
- how sensitive the data is as this will affect how much security is required
- how cost effective the storage needs to be.

Location of cloud storage

Table 2.14: Cloud storage locations

Location	Private	Public	Hybrid	Community
Security	Very secure as dedicated to one business/organisation.	Potentially less secure as infrastructure shared among many users	Very secure as dedicated to one business/organisation	Security is tailored to type of business organisation
Scalability	Scalable but not instantly	Easy to scale	Usually easy to scale	Limited scalability
Cost	Expensive	Cost effective	Depends on implementation	Fairly cost effective
Description	Private cloud storage is dedicated to a single business or organisation. Normally, private cloud storage is managed by a third-party provider who owns the hardware and provides cloud storage to the business or organisation for a fee. Access could be via the public internet or other, more secure methods such as a Virtual Private Network.	Public cloud storage is provided by a third-party provider who owns and manages the hardware. The cloud infrastructure is shared among multiple customers/businesses. Access tends to be via the public internet and requires users to authenticate themselves before being able to access files or data.	Hybrid cloud storage combines elements of public and private cloud storage. There are many variations of hybrid cloud storage, but a common example is allowing an organisation to seamlessly integrate on-site data storage with cloud storage. This can provide flexibility when large amounts of data need to be stored or if some data needs to be accessible externally.	Community cloud storage is cloud storage that is shared by multiple businesses or organisations that have similar requirements. For example, multiple healthcare providers could use a community cloud storage environment as the requirements for features like data security and backups are likely to be the same.

Table 2.15: Advantages and disadvantages of cloud storage locations

Location	Advantages	Disadvantages
Private	• Security is higher than when hardware is shared among multiple customers • The cloud setup can be customised to the businesses requirements and can offer better performance and reliability as resources aren't shared with other businesses • Increased reliability.	• Higher cost as the hardware is dedicated to the single business • Scalability is not as easy as the private cloud would require additional hardware to be installed.
Public	• Cost effective as the business can set the amount of storage needed easily and increase this on demand • Maintenance of the required hardware and software is the responsibility of the third-party supplier • Smaller businesses can find public cloud storage beneficial as technical.	• There are potential security concerns as the businesses data is stored on shared infrastructure. • There are unlikely to be any customisation options as the service is provided with the same features to all customers.
Hybrid	• Flexible as organisations can decide what data should be stored on-site or in the cloud, for example more sensitive data could be kept on-site • As the amount of data stored in the cloud can be managed this can make hybrid cloud storage cost effective • Can be used to help ensure data is backed up off site in case of problems.	• Complex to manage data in different types of location requiring each organisation to employ specialist staff to setup and manage them • Potential security concerns as complex to ensure that security decisions are maintained on-site and in the cloud • Access speeds to data can be different depending on whether the required data is stored on-site or in the cloud.
Community	• Cost effective as community cloud storage can share infrastructure among multiple organisations or businesses, so cheaper than a private cloud but more secure than a public cloud • Service can be specifically customised for particular community requirements • Potential for collaboration between users in a secure way.	• Cannot be customised for one particular business or organisation as a cloud needs to serve multiple businesses/organisations • Limited scalability as infrastructure isn't as flexible as a public cloud provider due to limited number of customers • Potential governance issues as changes cannot be made by one business/ organisation because features are shared among the community.

Learning in context 1

Cloud storage

Cloud storage consists of large numbers of servers and storage devices connected together and located in a data centre. The average data centre has around 100 000 servers.

Each server generates heat, and the data centre needs to be cooled to keep the servers running. Cooling is often provided by running a large air conditioning system. It isn't environmentally friendly or cheap to run such large air conditioning systems.

Businesses are looking at a range of different ways to reduce the environmental impact and cost of running data centres. Some businesses have started to look at novel ways of providing cooling without using air conditioning.

In 2018 IBM created an underwater mini data centre (864 servers) and lowered it to the sea floor off Scotland's Orkney islands. It was raised two years later to check on the state of the servers. The experiment was declared a success, and it used less energy than its land-based equivalent.

Another approach has been to build data centres in Iceland where the annual average temperature doesn't rise above 5 °C. These data centres use natural cooling, allowing the cool outside air into them to provide cooling. Invest in Iceland uses a promotional slogan stating that it is the 'coolest location for data centres'.

Amazon is taking a different approach with its Dublin data centre. It is using the heat generated to heat university and council buildings, replacing boilers in those buildings. It is estimated that this project will save 1400 tons of CO_2 emissions each year.

Figure 2.11: An underwater data centre

Types of cloud storage

There are five main types of cloud storage. Each of these has advantages and disadvantages that are dependent on the use case and type of data to be stored.

When choosing a suitable type of cloud storage, several factors must be considered:

- Will end users expect to be able to store files organised into folders and subfolders?
- Will the cloud storage be used with existing applications that will only work with files, folders and subfolders?
- How important is speed of access to the data?
- How scalable does the storage need to be?

File storage

File storage allows users to store files as they would with a local file system, using a hierarchy of folders and files.

As end users of computers are used to this type of storage, they find it intuitive to use. Additionally, files can be shared with other users, making collaboration easy.

However, file storage isn't always efficient or easy to organise and scalability depends on how it is implemented. Accessing files can be slower than other types of cloud storage when access to large amounts of data is required.

Object storage

Object storage takes each piece of data needing to be stored, adds metadata and a unique identifier and bundles it into an object. These objects are then stored without the use of files or folders; instead, the unique identifier and/or the metadata can be used to locate and access each object.

Object storage is ideal for storing unstructured data (data that isn't stored in predefined organised format) such as videos, images and backups. It is highly scalable, meaning that if more storage space is required this can be added easily. Objects can be stored across multiple servers and data centres. Copies of objects can be stored and made available in different international locations, providing resilience if a server fails and increasing access speed to the data.

However, object storage can be slower to update data than other storage systems, so it is not always useful for frequently updated data. It can also be more difficult to provide hierarchical structure to data than with files/folders in file storage.

Block storage

Block storage stores data in fixed sized blocks and allows data of any type to be stored, for example database entries or individual files. The block storage system splits the data up into fixed sized blocks and adds a unique identifier to each before writing the data to the storage device.

Advantages of block storage include its high performance in terms of reading and writing of data and high levels of scalability. Block storage enables finely tuned control of where different types of data is stored. For example, frequently required data could be stored on an SSD whereas less frequently needed data could be stored on hard disk drives. The application accessing the data would be unaware of the different locations and would just request the data as normal.

Disadvantages include potentially more complex set up than other types of storage and this can increase management and overall cost. Also, less metadata is stored compared to other storage methods.

Elastic/scalable storage

Elastic or scalable storage is cloud-based storage that can automatically scale up or down depending on need.

The scalability is designed to be seamless, so the end user or application won't notice that the amount of storage available is being changed. Elastic storage is cost effective as the organisation doesn't need to pay for unused capacity. The automatic nature of the scaling simplifies management, particularly in applications where the storage requirements change frequently.

However, it isn't suitable for all application types. For example, if the amount of storage space need changes infrequently, then elastic storage isn't always the cheapest option.

Cloud-based database services

Cloud-based database services provide managed database services in the cloud.

Positive aspects of this type of storage include the freedom it gives to organisation to focus on using the database, rather than managing tasks such as creating databases, keeping the database management system up to date and running regular backups. Management of backups and replication is handled by the cloud database provider. Additionally, databases can be easily and rapidly scaled up or down depending on requirements.

On the other hand, costs are usually higher than in-house databases, particularly for very large databases but can depend on number of transactions (items being added to, removed from or modified in the database). There may be limited configuration options of the database, which might impact speed of access to data. Another downside for organisations is the possibility of being tied to the cloud database provider as moving large amounts of data can be complex and costly.

Quick check 3

1 What are the differences between a file server and a NAS device?

2 Write about what SANs are and why they are useful.

Practice questions 1

A holiday company is developing an application to allow the user to find out about different destinations before booking a holiday.

1 One option being considered is to provide access to the application through a website.

Explain **two** advantages to the holiday company in providing the application through a website. **[4]**

2 Another option being considered is to allow the user to virtually explore the destination from the comfort of their own home.

Explain what type of device would be most suitable for this. **[2]**

3 The holiday company is considering moving its on-site file storage to the cloud.

Explain **one** advantage and **one** disadvantage to the holiday company of moving its file storage to the cloud. **[4]**

TA2 Data and flow in application software

Learning intentions

This topic is about how data flows though application software. It also covers what types of data an application might get as an input, how that data could be formatted and the different types of output that can be expected from a software application. It covers:

2.1 Data format and types

2.2 Data flow

2.3 Data states

2.1 Data formats and types

2.1.1 Data formats

There are several different ways to format data for storage or **transmission** by an application. The choice of which one is most suitable will depend on the types of data that need to be stored or transmitted, the quantity of data and the complexity of how that data is structured.

American Standard Code for Information Interchange (ASCII)

Characteristics: ASCII is a standard encoding system format that uses eight binary digits (a byte) per character to represent Roman letters, numerals, punctuation marks and other characters such as control codes.

Use: ASCII is widely used for encoding plain-text data in files and communication protocols.

Example: the capital letter 'A' is 65

Table 2.16: Table of ASCII characters

Dec	Hx	Oct	Char		Dec	Hx	Oct	Html	Chr	Dec	Hx	Oct	Html	Chr	Dec	Hx	Oct	Html	Chr
0	0	000	NUL	(null)	32	20	040		Space	64	40	100	&#64′	@	96	60	140	%#96;	`
1	1	001	SOH	(start of heading)	33	21	041	!	!	65	41	101	&#65′	A	97	61	141	%#97;	a
2	2	002	STX	(start of text)	34	22	042	&#32	"	66	42	102	&#66′	B	98	62	142	%#98;	b
3	3	003	ETX	(end of text)	35	23	043	#;	#	67	43	103	&#67′	C	99	63	143	%#99;	c
4	4	004	EOT	(end of transmission)	36	24	044	$	$	68	44	104	&#68′	D	100	64	144	%#100;	d
5	5	005	ENQ	(enquiry)	37	25	045	%	%	69	45	105	&#69′	E	101	65	145	%#101;	e
6	6	006	ACK	(acknowledge)	38	26	046	&	&	70	46	106	&#70′	F	102	66	146	%#102;	f
7	7	007	BEL	(bell)	39	27	047	'	'	71	47	107	&#71′	G	103	67	147	%#103;	g
8	8	010	BS	(backspace)	40	28	050	(	(	72	48	110	&#72′	H	104	68	150	%#104;	h
9	9	011	TAB	(horizontal tab)	41	29	051	,	)	73	49	111	&#73′	I	105	69	151	%#105;	i
10	A	012	LF	(NL line feed, new line)	42	2A	052	*	*	74	4A	112	&#74′	J	106	6A	152	%#106;	j
11	B	013	VT	(vertical tab)	43	2B	053	+	+	75	4B	113	&#75′	K	107	6B	153	%#107;	k
12	C	014	FF	(NP form feed, new page)	44	2C	054	,	,	76	4C	114	&#76′	L	108	6C	154	%#108	l
13	D	015	CR	(carriage return)	45	2D	055	-	-	77	4D	115	&#77′	M	109	6D	155	%#109;	m
14	E	016	SO	(shift out)	46	2E	056	.	.	78	4E	116	&#78′	N	110	6E	156	%#110;	n
15	F	017	SI	(shift in)	47	2F	057	/	/	79	4F	117	&#79′	O	111	6F	157	%#111;	o
16	10	020	DLE	(data link escape)	48	30	060	0	0	80	50	120	&#80′	P	112	70	160	%#112;	p
17	11	021	DC2	(device control 1)	49	31	061	1	1	81	51	121	&#81′	Q	113	71	161	%#113;	q
18	12	022	DC2	(device control 2)	50	32	062	2	2	82	52	122	&#82′	R	114	72	162	%#114;	r
19	13	023	DC3	(device control 3)	51	33	063	3	3	83	53	123	&#83′	S	115	73	163	%#115;	s
20	14	024	DC4	(device control 4)	52	34	064	4	4	84	51	124	&#84′	T	116	74	164	%#116;	t
21	15	025	NAK	(negative acknowledge)	53	35	065	5	5	85	55	125	&#85′	U	117	75	165	%#117;	u
22	16	026	SYN	(synchronous idle)	54	36	066	6	6	86	56	126	&#86′	V	118	76	166	%#118;	v
23	17	027	ETB	(end of trans. block)	55	37	067	7	7	87	57	127	&#87′	W	119	77	167	%#119;	w
24	18	030	CAN	(cancel)	56	38	070	8	8	88	58	130	&#88′	X	120	78	170	%#120;	x
25	19	031	EM	(end of medium)	57	39	071	9	9	89	59	131	&#89′	Y	121	79	171	%#121;	y
26	1A	032	SUB	(substitute)	58	3A	072	:	:	90	5A	132	&#90′	Z	122	7A	172	%#122;	z
27	1B	033	ESC	(escape)	59	3B	073	;	;	91	5B	133	&#91′	[	123	7B	173	%#123;	{
28	1C	034	FS	(file separator)	60	3C	074	<	<	92	5C	134	&#92′	\	124	7C	174	%#124;	|
28	1D	035	GS	(group separator)	61	3D	075	=	=	93	5D	135	&#93′	]	125	7D	175	%#125;	}
30	1E	036	RS	(record separator)	62	3E	076	>	>	94	5E	136	&#94′	^	126	7E	176	%#126;	~
31	1F	037	US	(unit separator)	63	3F	077	?	?	95	5F	137	&#95′	_	127	7F	177	%#127;	DEL

In the following example:

Name: Mo Hussein

Address: 123 Any Road Anywhere BR11 1PQ

would read as below:

78 97 109 101 58 32 77 111 32 72 117 115 115 101 105 110 10 65 100 100 114 101 115 115 58 32 49 50 51 32 65 110 121 32 82 111 97 100 32 65 110 121 119 104 101 114 101 32 66 82 49 49 32 49 80 81 10

Table 2.17: Advantages and disadvantages of ASCII characters

Advantages	Disadvantages
• ASCII can be used to represent most European languages. • It is simple, readable by a human and has broad support across different systems.	• ASCII is limited to 256 characters as there are 256 possible combinations of eight 0s and 1s. • ASCII is not able to represent enough characters to be useable for all written languages, as some languages require thousands of characters.

Unicode

Characteristics: Unicode is a standard encoding system format like ASCII but is designed to be able to represent all of the world's printable characters.

Use: Unicode is designed to replace other systems like ASCII as it has a much larger range of characters available. This allows support of many more languages, for example Chinese and Japanese characters, along with many other symbols, including over 3,000 emoji.

Example: Code U+1F600 is 😀.

Table 2.18: Advantages and disadvantages of Unicode

Advantages	Disadvantages
• Unicode supports almost all characters used in modern written languages, making it useful globally. This can help to enable software internationalisation. • Unicode has expanded to include emojis, symbols and technical characters, supporting modern communication patterns.	• Unicode requires more storage space compared to encoding standards like ASCII. • Unicode is large and complex, with over 140,000 characters, which can make it difficult to fully understand. • As Unicode is a complex standard, some systems may not fully implement it or may implement it incorrectly, leading to issues in displaying or processing text.

Comma-Separated Values (CSV)

Characteristics: CSV is a plain-text format for tabular data, where each line denotes a record (data about one thing or person) with fields (a single data item, such as a name or ID number) separated by commas or other delimiters.

Use: CSV format is frequently utilised to exchange data between applications and spreadsheet software where further analysis can be done.

Example:

Name, Address

Mo Hussein, 123 Any Road Anywhere BR11 1PQ

When viewed in a spreadsheet will look like:

Name	Address
Mo Hussein	123 Any Road Anywhere BR11 1PQ

Table 2.19: Advantage and disadvantage of CSV

Advantage	Disadvantage
CSV is human readable and efficient for handling large data sets.	CSV is not a good choice for complex data structures and can have problems with special characters in fields, especially if the character being stored is the same as the delimiter in use

Fixed width

Characteristics: Fixed width format is a plain-text format where each different piece of data or field has a predefined width, this means that each record (data about one thing or person) has the same length.

Use: This data format is not normally used in modern systems as having variable sizes for data is much more efficient. Data may need to be put into this format to support legacy systems.

Example:

M	o													
H	u	s	s	e	i	n								

Fixed width of 15 characters for first name and second name. Notice the wasted space for each name and that a name of more than 15 characters wouldn't be able to be stored.

Table 2.20: Advantage and disadvantage of fixed width format

Advantage	Disadvantage
It is simple to read and write data in fixed width format.	If the data to be stored in a field is shorter than then predefined width, then the rest of the space available is padded with spaces or another character. If the data to be stored is longer than the available space, then it will be truncated.

JavaScript Object Notation (JSON)

Characteristics: JavaScript Object Notation (JSON) is a text based, human-readable data interchange or storage format.

Use: It is widely used for exchanging data between web applications and servers, configuration files and when using APIs (you will learn more about these in TA3).

Example:

JSON files can contain two types of data structure:

- A collection of name/value pairs, for example

```
{"Name":"Ellie", "Breed":"Labradoodle",
  "Age":4}
```

- An ordered list of values, for example

```
["January", "February", "March", "April"]
```

Example:

```
{
    "person": {
        "name": "Mo Hussein",
        "address": {
        "street": "123 Any Road",
        "city": "Anywhere",
        "postcode": "BR11 1PQ"
        }
    }
}
```

Table 2.21: Advantages and disadvantages of JSON

Advantages	Disadvantages
• It is easy to organise data into a format that can efficiently import or export data between different systems • Scalable • Lightweight • Simple to read/write • Text based human-readable format • Language independent.	JSON can be verbose, particularly for large data sets.

eXtensible Markup Language (XML)

Characteristics: eXtensible Markup Language (XML) uses tags to define the meaning and structure of data in a hierarchical format.

Use: It is commonly used for configuration files and exchanging data between different systems.

Example:

```
<person>
  <name>
  Mo Hussein
  </name>
  <address>
    <street>
    123 Any Road
    </street>
  <city>
  Anywhere
  </city>
    <postcode>
    BR11 1PQ
    </postcode>
  </address>
</person>
```

Table 2.22: Advantage and disadvantage of XML

Advantage	Disadvantage
XML is a flexible and highly customisable format.	XML often generates much larger file sizes compared to other formats as it is verbose and contains redundant data, causing more storage space to be used or time to transmit from one system to another.

2.1.2 Data types

Data comes in different types depending on what needs to be stored and how it might need to be used. Choosing the correct data type is an important part of designing a software application.

Table 2.23: Advantages and disadvantages of data types

Data type	Description	Examples	Advantages	Disadvantages
Boolean	• The Boolean data type can only store two possible values, true or false. • Booleans are commonly used in programming for conditional statements and logic gates.	In a program, a Boolean variable 'is_weekday' could be true if it's a weekday or false if it is a weekend day.	• Efficient for logical operations • Can help to make code easier to understand due to its simplicity.	Can be restrictive, as can only store two values; true or false.
Character	• The character data type represents an individual letter, number, or symbol from a character set (for example ASCII). • Characters are used for representing textual data, such as in strings or for input/output operations.	In the string 'Hello, world!', each letter ('H', 'e', 'l', 'l', 'o', and so on.) is a character.	Represents single characters, allowing for control over text data.	Only represents one character at a time, making it inefficient for storing or manipulating longer pieces of text.
Date	• The date data type represents a specific date, typically including day, month and year in a numeric format. • Dates are used in a wide range of applications including time management, scheduling, data analysis and so on.	• '03/05/2024' represents 5th March 2024. • The order of days, month and year depends on the country or ISO standard in use.	• Allows for uniform representation of dates and follows international date standards • Can help to simplify date calculations.	Can be more difficult to manipulate than simple data types.
Integer	• An integer data type represents whole numbers (positive, negative, or zero) without any fractional or decimal part. • Integers are used for counting and arithmetic operations.	The numbers 10, –5, or 0 are examples of integers.	• Efficient use of storage space for whole numbers compared to real data type • Good performance for arithmetic operations.	Cannot represent fractions, limiting its use in applications requiring floating point numbers.
Real	• The real data type stores floating point numbers, that is numbers with both integer and fractional parts. • Reals are used for storing measurements, calculations involving precision, and so on.	The numbers 3.14 or –0.001 are examples of real numbers.	Can represent fractional numbers, allowing for precision in calculations.	• Precision can vary, leading to potential calculation errors. • Requires more storage than integers.

(Continued)

Data type	Description	Examples	Advantages	Disadvantages
String	• String data type represents a sequence of characters (letters, numbers, symbols). Data to be stored as a string is normally enclosed within quotation marks inside the application. • Strings are used for storing and manipulating text data, such as names, addresses, messages, and so on.	'Hello, world!' is a string.	Flexible as can represent text of varying lengths.	Large amounts of text can require a lot of storage space.

Learning in context 2

Scenario

Tickets4U sell concert tickets online using an ecommerce website. When a user books tickets they must enter their name, email address, date of birth and number of tickets required. The cost of the booking would be calculated, displayed and stored with the other details. Booking details are stored in a database and tickets will be emailed out to the purchaser.

Data types

The data types chosen would be:

- Name and email address will be stored as a string as it consists of a sequence of characters.
- Date of birth will be stored as a date as this is the best format to allow calculations with a date to be done. The date of birth will be checked to see that the person booking the concert is over 18.
- Number of tickets required will be stored as an integer as only whole tickets are purchasable.
- Cost of booking would be stored as real as this is the best format to represent money as it allows for a decimal value, such as £95.75, to be stored.

Each concert venue runs its own computer systems and different software applications are used to manage bookings and to allow staff to check tickets when people arrive for the concert.

The data from Tickets4U's ecommerce website needs to be sent to the venue that the concert is at. This is done using XML as this is a common format that can be understood by a range of different systems and is also human readable should any booking need to be checked manually.

Quick check 4

1 Write down an example of data that could be stored in each of the following data types: character, integer, real, string.

2 Write about the differences between CSV and XML data formats.

2.2 Data flow

Data refers to raw facts and figures that on their own have little or no meaning. For example, '583281' is data as we do not know what it refers to; it has no context.

Data can be converted to information by organising it or presenting it in a meaningful context. If I say 'My phone number is 583281' then it becomes information.

One way to help remember this is data + context = information.

Application software will need to have data inputted into it, then process that data to produce output data. The data may also need to be stored.

2.2.1 Input

The data being inputted to an application can be in many different forms:

- Number: numerical data can include data inputted by the user entered into a form or the application. It can also include data from sensors such as temperature sensors or distance sensors.
- Text: textual data includes alphanumeric characters, words and sentences. These could be entered directly into the application or obtained from sources such as documents, emails or web pages.
- Movement: movement data represents physical movements captured from motion sensors, GPS devices or accelerometers.
- Audio: audio data including voice commands, sound recordings or other sound. These sounds are likely to be captured by microphones.
- Image: image data can include photographs (static images) or video (moving images). The images might be captured by cameras or a scanner.

2.2.2 Storage

Applications may need to store data for a number of reasons, including:

- Persistence: allowing applications to store data even when they have been shut down. This could be for settings, data that might want to be reviewed at a later date or to allow data to be processed, analysed or viewed again.
- Reporting: allowing data to be stored means that results can be used for historical analysis, trend analysis and other forms of reports.
- Legal requirements: some industries or businesses might be required to store data for a specified time period to show how decisions were made or to allow for later analysis.
- Collaboration: some data may need to be stored so that other people can contribute to the work being done. For example, a report may need details from all parts of the company to be entered before any calculations could happen.

The data being stored by an application could be on-site or in the cloud (see Section 1.3 for further details). The decision of where to store the data will depend on various factors including:

- how much data needs to be stored
- how long the data needs to be retained for
- who needs access to the data.

2.2.3 Output information

The information being outputted from a software application needs to be suitable for the purpose the software is designed for. Output might be in a range of different formats to help the user quickly and accurately understand the information provided.

Possible forms of information outputted from a software application includes:

- Number: numeric output includes calculated values such as mathematical results and summaries of data.

- Text: textual output can include text indicating the status of something, structured reports or summarised content.
- Movement: this could be represented by visual representations of movement or by actual movement using motors or devices such as a robotic arm.
- Audio: audio output can include warning sounds, notification alerts, music or synthetised speech.
- Image: processed image output includes visualisations, graphics or augmented reality overlays. These outputs might be static (for example a single graphic) or moving images, such as an animated visualisation.

Different types of output can be combined, for example an image could be annotated and have detected objects tagged with text describing what has been recognised.

How data flows through application software

Data flow refers to the movement of data through an application. It incorporates the input, processing and output of data and includes storage and retrieval of data.

There are three main components to consider when thinking about data flowing through an application; data sources, processing and data destinations.

Data sources refers to where data comes from. This includes inputs to the application as well as external sources such as data from databases or APIs.

Input data can come from a wide range of sources including:

- user input, for example a user of the application types something or chooses an option from a menu
- sensors, for example a temperature sensor, accelerometer or barcode reader
- file upload, for example a user of the application uploads a spreadsheet containing details of stock for a business.

External sources include:

- a database, for example an ecommerce website will keep details of items for sale, descriptions of these items and stock levels in a database
- Application Programming Interface (API): An API allows an application to access data or make changes to another system. This is discussed in detail in Section 3.1. An example API might be for a weather forecast service. The application would use an API to request a weather forecast for a particular location and the API would send this data to the application.

Processing components will manipulate the data. This processing will be done by following an algorithm that states what should be done to the data.

Once processing is complete then the data will be sent to a data destination. A data destination is a place where data is used or stored. For example, data might be sent to a database or saved as a file. It might also be displayed to a user of the application or sent to another application for further processing.

Figure 2.12 shows a simplified data flow that occurs when a customer visits an ecommerce website and makes a purchase.

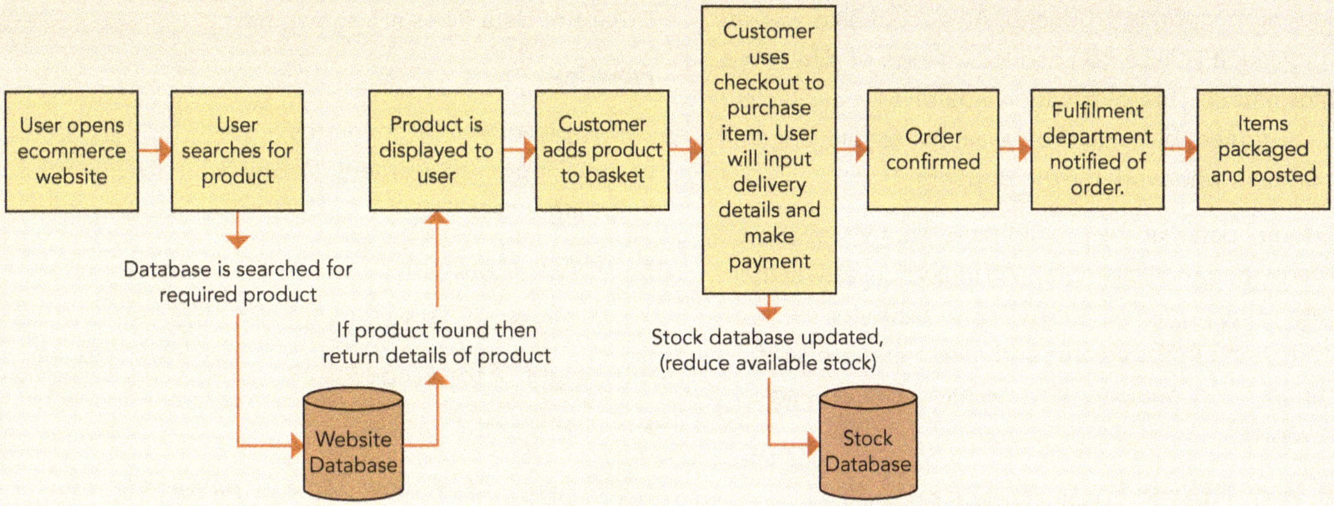
User opens ecommerce website
User searches for product
Database is searched for required product
Website Database
If product found then return details of product
Product is displayed to user
Customer adds product to basket
Customer uses checkout to purchase item. User will input delivery details and make payment
Stock database updated, (reduce available stock)
Stock Database
Order confirmed
Fulfilment department notified of order.
Items packaged and posted

Figure 2.12: Example data flow

How information flows from application software

Information is data with context, for example raw sales figures would be data but when provided with context, such as quantity sold on each date and type of products sold it would become information. Information can be used to help a business plan how much of each product to buy in the future or what ranges of products should be expanded.

In an ecommerce system, information flows from a range of sources such as databases, external data such as weather forecast data and forecasting algorithms.

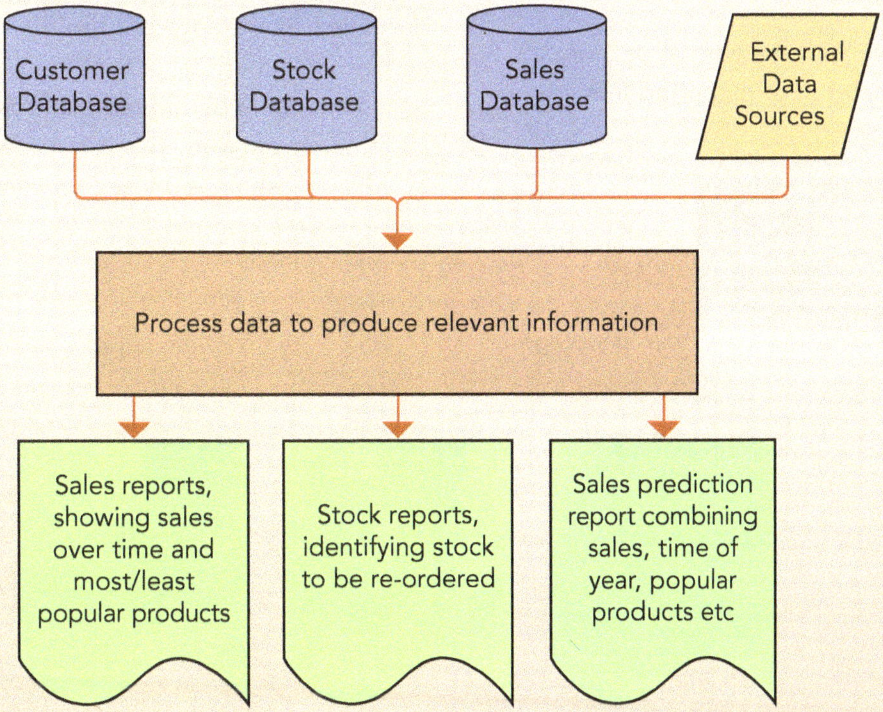
Customer Database
Stock Database
Sales Database
External Data Sources
Process data to produce relevant information
Sales reports, showing sales over time and most/least popular products
Stock reports, identifying stock to be re-ordered
Sales prediction report combining sales, time of year, popular products etc

Figure 2.13: Example data flow

In Figure 2.13, data flows from the databases and external data sources. This data is then processed, and information is produced. An ecommerce website application is likely to produce a range of different information. This information wouldn't be available to customers but would be available to relevant staff members who work for the business.

External data can help build more comprehensive information. For example, McDonald's uses weather data to help predict what stock to order for each store as more ice creams and milkshakes are sold during warm weather, whereas more coffee is sold in winter.

2.2.4 Black box concept

The black box concept simplifies the representation of data flow through application software by focusing on the inputs and outputs without needing to consider the internal workings.

It involves representing the application software as a black box with input arrows indicating data flow in, output arrows indicating data flow out, and a central black box representing the processing being done within the application.

Each arrow is labelled with the type of data or information being inputted or outputted from the application.

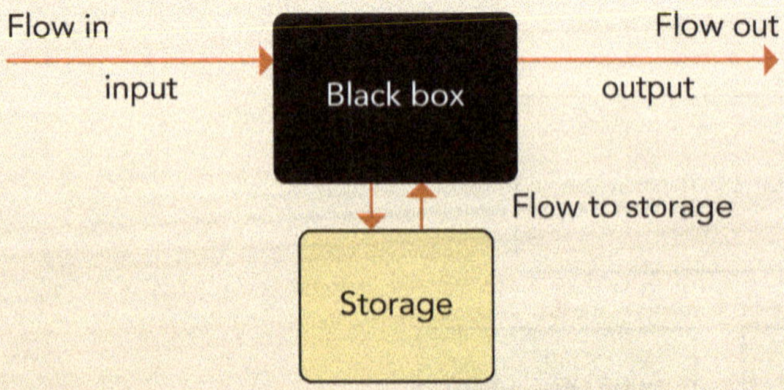
Flow in
input
Black box
Flow out
output
Flow to storage
Storage

Figure 2.14: Example of the black box concept

An application to generate quotes for the cost of making a replacement window is being designed. Details of data flows are shown next.

Flow in

The application that generates a quote for the cost of a making a replacement window would require the following inputs:

- Name of customer
- Address of customer
- Height of the window
- Width of the window
- Material the window frame is to be made from
- The type of glass for the window.

Flow to storage

The application would save a copy of the quote to storage, so it could be retrieved if the customer wants to order the replacement window or wants to modify any details.

Flow out

The output from this application would be a document that is addressed to the customer and includes the total cost of the window. This document could be printed and posted to the customer or emailed. This is outside of the scope of the application as it just calculates the price and generates the quote.

Learning in context 3

Scenario

Tickets4U sell concert tickets online using an ecommerce website. When a user books tickets they must enter their name, email address, date of birth and number of tickets required. The cost of the booking would be calculated, displayed and stored with the other details. Booking details are stored in a database and tickets will be emailed out to the purchaser.

Flow of data

Tickets4U's ecommerce website has inputs that are processed, generating various outputs. Data would also need to be stored.

Input

Data inputted to the booking system includes name, address, email address, date of birth and number of tickets required. Inputted data is then processed.

Processing

The ecommerce website application then processes this data and works out a total cost, reserves the seats so no one else can book them. Once processing is complete then the required information would be outputted and stored.

Output information

The booking system would output tickets (sent via email) and update the venue about bookings (this might only be done once a day or when the bookings are finished).

Storage

Details of the concert booking would be stored to allow details of tickets to be checked and to allow any updates to be emailed to the person who booked the tickets. The database would be updated to show that the seats have been reserved, meaning that no one else can purchase them.

Quick check 5

1 Write about the differences between data and information.

2 List the inputs and outputs that a car park ticket machine might require.

2.3 Data states

There are three different states that data can be described as being in: at rest, in transit and in use. Knowing what state data is in can allow for appropriate security measures to be in place and ensuring that data access can be optimised.

At rest

Data 'at rest' is data that is being stored, not actively in use or being transmitted. Data in this state is stored in file systems or databases. For example, data stored on a computer's solid state drive, data in database system or stored in cloud service like Dropbox or Microsoft OneDrive can be described as 'at rest' if it is not in use.

In transit (motion)

This refers to data that is actively being transmitted from one device to another device or from a device to one or more authorised users. It can be described as in motion from one device or system to another device, person or system. Data in transit is more susceptible to interception than in the other states. For example, an email being sent, or files being uploaded to a server can be described as 'in transit'.

In use

Data that is 'in use' is being actively processed by a system, program or user. For example, a spreadsheet that is being edited or querying a database are situations where the data can be described as 'in use'.

Learning in context 4

Scenario

Tickets4U sell concert tickets online using an ecommerce website. When a user books tickets they must enter their name, email address, date of birth, number of tickets required. The cost of the booking would be calculated, displayed and stored with the other details. Booking details are stored in a database and tickets will be emailed out to the purchaser.

Data states

The ecommerce website application would have data in all three possible data states:

At rest

- Once the booking had been made the data about booking would be stored in case the booking needs to be changed or updates about the concert need to be sent out. This data would be stored in a database on a server's secondary storage and would be described as 'at rest' as it isn't currently being used.

In transit

- The booked concert tickets are emailed to the person who booked them. The data contained within the email is 'in transit' until it arrives at the destination email address.
- Also, data is transmitted to the concert venue and while this data is being transferred from one computer to another it is 'in transit'.

In use

- While the booking is being made the data is 'in use'. The person booking the tickets may have entered their details and then choose the seats they want, while this is happening the data is 'in use' until the booking is completed.

Quick check 6

1 Write about the three different states that data can be described as being in.

2 Give an example of data in each state.

Practice questions 2

A car park allows the user to pay for a parking space using a mobile phone application. The user must enter their car number plate, the number of hours (whole hours only) and the application will show the cost in pounds and pence.

1 Copy and complete the table. Choose the correct data type by ticking the relevant box. Only **one** tick per row.

	Integer	Real	String
Number plate			
Number of hours parking required			
Cost			

[3]

2 Once the booking has been made the details are uploaded to a server using the JSON data format. Describe **two** advantages of using JSON in this situation. [4]

TA3 API and protocols

Learning intentions

This topic is about what APIs are and how they are used within software applications. This topic also discusses what protocols are and explains some of the most common protocols used within different software applications.

It covers:

3.1 Application Programming Interfaces (API)

3.2 Protocols

3.1 Application Programming Interfaces (API)

Role

An **Application Programming Interface** (API) is a method to allow two or more software applications to communicate with each other. These applications could be on the same computer system but are more likely to be on different systems and connected via a network, for example the internet. The API allows data to be communicated between systems in a predefined format.

Learning in context 5

API use

Mobile phone weather applications use an API to collect weather data from a weather forecasting organisation such as the Met Office or Open-Meteo.

The weather application would request forecast data for a specific area, probably based on the user's current location, The forecast would be returned in a standard format, probably using a format such as JSON or XML. The weather app would then format and display the data to the user in an appropriate format.

As well as general purpose weather applications, weather data is important in many industries too. For example:

- The aviation industry uses weather data to inform pilots of the best flight path to take to avoid bad weather. This helps to ensure the safety of passengers and air crew.
- Farmers will use weather data to help decide when to use fertiliser, whether additional watering will be necessary if a lack of rain is forecast and to plan when crops should be harvested.
- Shipping companies will use weather forecasts to ensure that container ships will avoid bad weather as this can delay deliveries and pose a risk to the crew of the ship.

Some weather forecasting organisations allow free access to their API for non-commercial use. Investigate Open-Meteo's website. Find out more information on the Open-Meteo's website about:

- the kinds of data that are available with or without subscription
- what data is available without cost
- the different APIs they offer
- how data is requested and received.

Types

There are several different types of API. When they are used depends on the type of software application in use, where the different systems that need to communicate are located and the type of data being send/received.

Internal

Internal APIs are used within a business to allow different departments and systems to communicate and share data.

For example, in an ecommerce business an internal API would be used to allow the sales departments systems to check stock in the warehouse system.

Table 2.24: Advantages and disadvantages of internal APIs

Advantages	Disadvantages
• As internal APIs are not publicly available this reduces security risks. • As the business maintains the API for its own use it can be customised to work well with internal systems and requirements.	Developing, creating and documenting APIs takes technical knowledge and time. This could be difficult for smaller businesses to manage.

Private

Private APIs are designed for specific use cases outside the business. They allow access to the businesses internal systems by external systems or applications in a tightly controlled way.

For example, an ecommerce business might have a mobile application developed to allow for easy ordering via a smart phone. The application would place orders via a private API.

Table 2.25: Advantages and disadvantages of private APIs

Advantages	Disadvantages
• A private API can be created that meets all the requirements of the specific use case. • Security risks are reduced as access to the API is not public.	Can take time to develop a private API, especially is multiple different private APIs are required for different use cases.

Public

Public APIs are open to external businesses and developers.

They are used when a business wants to allow wide access to its data. This is often for commercial purposes as the business that owns the API can charge for its use.

For example, many weather forecaster businesses allow access to their forecast data using an API. They charge for commercial use of the forecast.

Table 2.26: Advantages and disadvantages of public APIs

Advantages	Disadvantages
• Can allow for a wide range of people and business to access data from the business, potentially increasing profits. • Using a public API can allow you to integrate data into your application without having to collect the data yourself.	• Publicly accessible APIs can be a security risk. For example, a DDoS attack might make the API unavailable. • Time consuming for the owning business to setup, manage, document and support other users. • A public API can be withdrawn or have details of how to access changed requiring the users' application to be updated.

Partner

Partner APIs are shared with business partners and are used to allow for data to be transferred between the businesses.

For example, a business might allow a partner business to place orders directly into the ordering system. This could simplify and speed up ordering of regularly used items.

Table 2.27: Advantages and disadvantages of partner APIs

Advantages	Disadvantages
• Allow for efficient collaboration between partner businesses. • Stops the general public accessing the API while allowing specific partners access to certain data or systems.	• Requires the business to have technical staff who can manage access and maintain the API. • Using a partner API can introduce risk as the owning business might change how the API works or stop its use.

Composite

Composite APIs combine multiple other APIs, so the user of the composite API can request data or services that require data from different systems.

For example, a weather forecaster might have an API for historic weather measurements and a different API for forecasts. A developer of an application might want to display past days weather and future forecasts. Using a composite API would allow this to be done without needing to access each API separately.

Table 2.28: Advantages and disadvantages of composite APIs

Advantages	Disadvantages
• A composite API can simplify how an application requests data by only needed to make one request rather than a request to several different APIs. • Only needing to deal with one request could be more efficient for the business that owns the APIs that are available as a composite API.	• Requesting data from a composite API is more complex that accessing a regular API. • If errors occur, then it can be more difficult to debug due to the complexity of requesting data from multiple APIs in one go.

Architecture

An API's **architecture** describes how requests to an API should be made and how the response will be structured. The type of architecture being used will depend on what the application does, how complex its actions are and whether **encryption** or **authentication** are needed.

Representational State Transfer (REST)

Representational State Transfer (REST) is often used by relatively simple applications that involve sending, receiving or modifying a resource on a server.
A resource is a piece of data, for example, details of a product, user or a file.

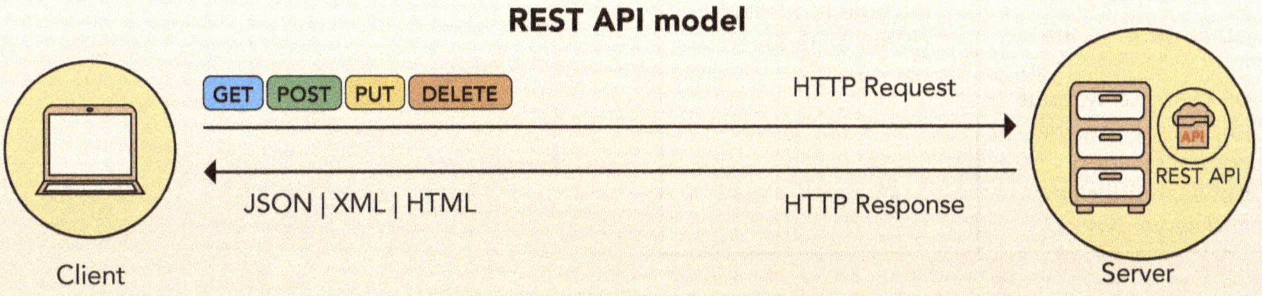
REST API model
GET
POST
PUT
DELETE
HTTP Request
JSON | XML | HTML
HTTP Response
Client
API
REST API
Server

Figure 2.15: Overview of how a REST API works

REST architecture allows a client to make a request to a server, usually across the internet. This request will retrieve, modify or create a resource on a server. The server will respond to the request and that response will depend on the operation requested.

When using REST the client makes a request to retrieve, create or modify a resource (data) from a server. REST has four standard types of request:

- GET: retrieve a resource from the server
- POST: create a new resource on the server
- PUT: update a resource on the server
- DELETE: remove a resource from the server.

Table 2.29: Advantages and disadvantages of REST

Advantages	Disadvantages
• REST is **stateless**, meaning the client and server do not need to know about what state each other are in. This means that any messages sent between them do not require knowledge or understanding of prior messages. This simplifies implementing the communications between an application and server. • REST separates the client and server – the client and server do not need to know how each other work, so the implementation can be changed without impacting how the communication between the client and server works.	• As REST is stateless this means that each request must contain all details required to understand the request. This can mean having to send large quantities of data in each request. • REST has limited standard types of request. This can make implementing applications that do not fit into these standard types of request very complex. • REST can have performance issues due to having to make multiple requests to gather all required data.

Simple Object Access Protocol (SOAP)

SOAP is often used for corporate systems such financial applications and booking systems as it provides authentication and security.

SOAP allows messages to be sent between clients and servers and is based on the XML format. The messages contain data that the server or client requires.

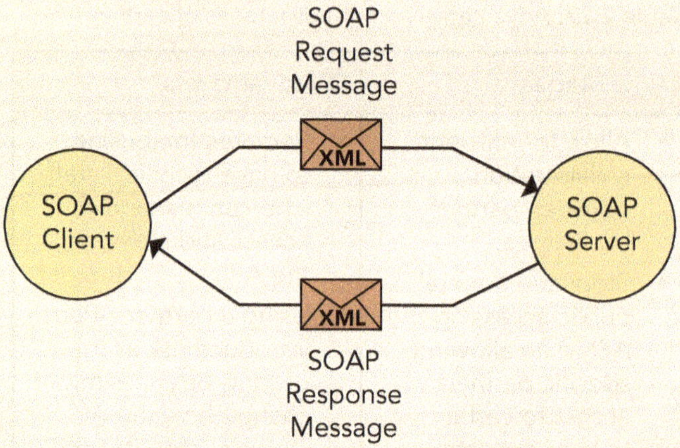

SOAP Request Message
XML
SOAP Client
SOAP Server
XML
SOAP Response Message

Figure 2.16: Overview of how SOAP works

SOAP has three components:

- Envelope, which describes the structure of the message and how processing should take place.
- Encoding rules, which allow applications to define data types to be used in message exchange.
- Description of acceptable formats for requests and responses.

SOAP is a highly reliable and can be extended to allow for complex operations to take place.

Table 2.30: Advantages and disadvantages of SOAP

Advantages	Disadvantages
• As with REST, SOAP is stateless. • SOAP provides end-to-end security of messages, provides integrity checking and authentication. This makes it a good choice for data that needs to be kept secure, for example, financial data.	• SOAP can be complex as it relies on XML and can be extended. This can lead to increased time/cost during development. • SOAP messages can be larger than other protocols due to the use of XML. This could reduce the speed at which messages can be exchanged.

Remote Procedure Call (RPC)

RPC is often used in applications that require high-performance, particularly when the API only connects to a single **provider**, rather than multiple sources of data.

RPC is a protocol that allows an application to call (run) a procedure or **function** that is on a remote server as though it was running in the local application. RPC abstracts the complexity of connecting and transferring data through the network, which could be the internet. If the call is to a function, then data can be passed into the remote function and then a response will be returned.

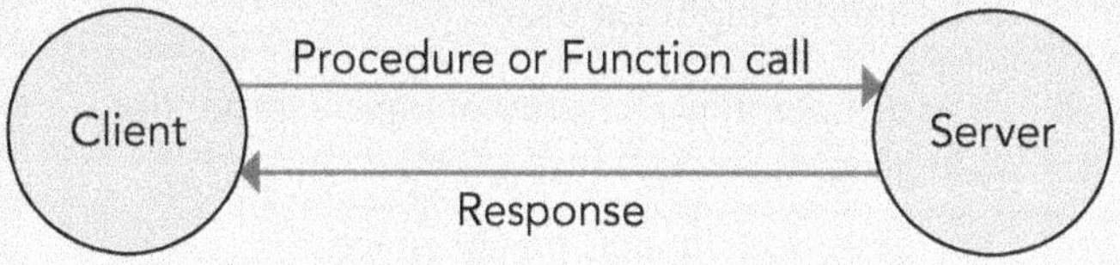
Client
Procedure or Function call
Response
Server

Figure 2.17: Overview of how RPC works

Table 2.31: Advantages and disadvantages of RPC

Advantages	Disadvantages
Using RPC is simple as the developer of the application just calls the required procedure or function in the same way as a local procedure or function. This can speed up and simplify development of applications.	• As the connection is abstracted any delay or problem with connecting to the remote system can cause issues with the application as the developer won't necessarily be able to mitigate against these issues. • RPC can be vulnerable to security issues as it does not natively provide security options.

Learning in context 6

API architecture

A new bank, SmartBank, is being launched. SmartBank doesn't have any physical branches and all transactions will be managed using a smartphone application.

As SmartBank is setting up its own internal systems it is having the smartphone banking application written specifically for its systems.

SmartBank are going to use an API to transfer data between the application and the bank's servers. The application will use a private API as the application will be used outside the business (by the bank's customers) and SmartBank will benefit from being able to customise the API to provide exactly the information and facilities required by the banking application. As the application and internal system are owned and managed by the same business this is an appropriate choice, any changes required can be made without involving a third party.

The API architecture must support authentication, so the bank can be sure that the authorised user is viewing or making changes to their bank account and must also support encryption as the data being sent across the network is sensitive financial information. These requirements mean that the developers choose the SOAP architecture. While SOAP messages tend to be larger than other architectures, this is acceptable as authentication and security are more important and a small delay while sending messages is acceptable for this situation.

Quick check 7

1 Summarise the different types of API and when they might be used.

2 You are planning to write an application that will allow users to book a stay in a holiday cottage. Specify and justify which API architecture you would use.

3.2 Protocols

A **protocol** is a set of rules for transmitting data between different devices, usually via a network. There are many different protocols that are used in different situations. Some protocols govern the sending data such as files or emails, whereas other protocols are used to send data across networks and include rules about how the data should be structured and how different devices on a network will be identified.

TCP/IP stack

The TCP/IP stack is a set of networking protocols that govern how devices on a network communicate with each other and with other devices connected via the internet. It is named after the two most important protocols in the stack, Transport Control Protocol (TCP) and Internet Protocol (IP). The TCP/IP stack is split into four layers that work in a hierarchical set, where each layer collaborates with layers either side. Data passes down the stack when sending data and up the stack when receiving data.

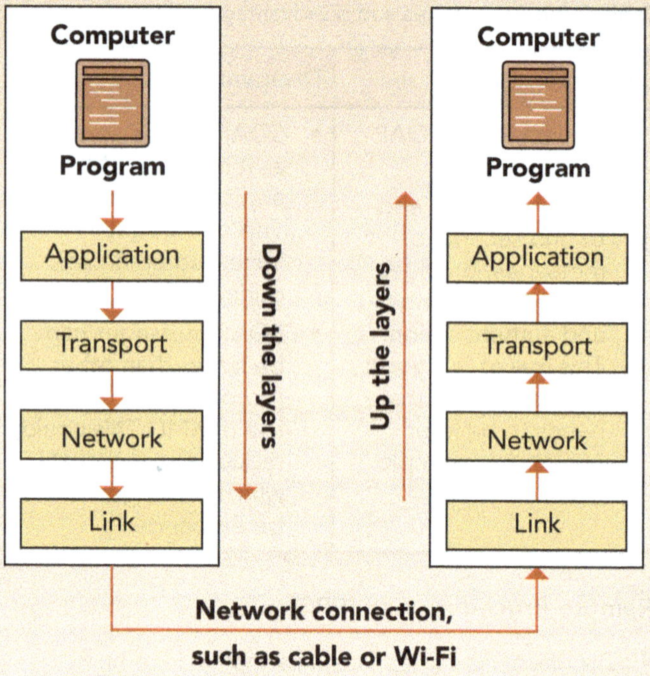
Computer
Program
Application
Transport
Network
Link
Down the layers
Up the layers
Computer
Program
Application
Transport
Network
Link
Network connection,
such as cable or Wi-Fi

Figure 2.18: Layers within the TCP/IP stack. Data is sent down the layers when sending and up the layers when receiving

Each layer in the TCP/IP stack is independent but must communicate with the layer above and below using a standard method. This is useful as a layer can be replaced without affecting the rest of the stack. For example, if an alternative method of communication at the link layer was to be used, perhaps swapping a wired connection for a Wi-Fi connection, then the rest of the layers do not have to be modified. This makes updating layers or adding additional features easier.

Application – this is the top layer of the stack and consists of protocols that interact with applications that are used by end users of a device.

Example protocols that work at this layer are: FTP, HTTP, POP3, SMTP, SNMP.

Transport layer – the transport layer is responsible for end-to-end communication over a network. User Datagram Protocol (UDP) and TCP are both at this layer. Which one of these protocols is used depends on whether guaranteed delivery or speed of delivery is the most important factor.

Example protocols that work at this layer are: TCP, UDP.

Network layer – this layer is responsible for addressing, routing and transferring packets between devices on interconnected networks. The internet protocol is at this layer. The interconnected networks are usually part of the internet, so this layer is sometimes known as the internet layer.

Example protocols that work at this layer are: ICMP, IP.

Link layer – the link layer controls the transmission and reception of packets from the network. This layer hides the complexity of connecting to a wired or wireless network.

File Transfer Protocol (FTP)

File Transfer Protocol (FTP) is a protocol that is used to transfer files between a client and a server on a computer network. FTP is insecure as it doesn't encrypt the data it sends but is simple to use and most operating systems support it.

FTP is generally used when transferring one or more files to a web server once development has been completed on a local computer but can be used whenever transferring files is necessary.

Hyper Text Transfer Protocol (HTTP)

HTTP provides a standard way for web browsers to communicate with web servers. It defines how messages between web browsers and servers should be formatted and how each should respond to a range of commands.

When a user enters a **URL** into a web browser a HTTP request is made to the relevant server and the server will send back the requested page using a HTTP response.

HTTP does not encrypt the data being sent or received. This means it is unsuitable for use when data includes personal or sensitive data (for example, passwords, banking information and so on). Instead, HTTPS (Hyper Text Transfer Protocol Secure) is used as this does encrypt data.

Post Office Protocol (POP)

POP is used to download email from a mail server to an email client on a local computer. Usually once the email has been downloaded from the server it is deleted to free up space for future emails. POP is an old protocol from when most people only had access to one device. It has now been superseded by IMAP as people want to access their email on multiple devices, for example a computer and a smart phone.

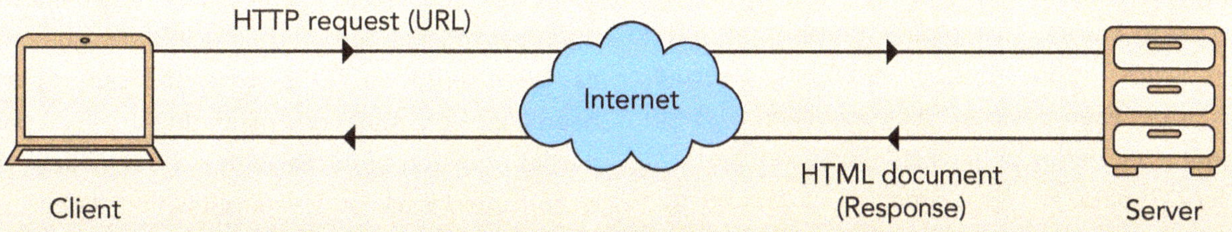
HTTP request (URL)
Internet
Client
HTML document
(Response)
Server

Figure 2.19: Overview of how HTTP works

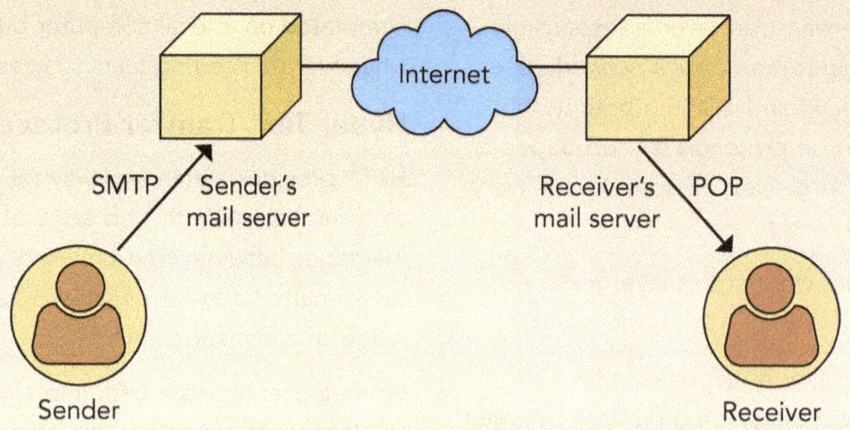
Internet
SMTP
Sender's
mail server
Receiver's
mail server
POP
Sender
Receiver

Figure 2.20: This diagram shows SMTP being used to send an email from one mail server to another to another and the receiver downloading emails from a mail server using POP

Simple Mail Transport Protocol (SMTP)

SMTP is used when sending email using the internet. It is primarily used to send email from the senders' mail server to the recipients' mail server. SMTP specifies the format of email being sent and what should be done if the recipients' mail server isn't responding.

Simple Network Management Protocol (SNMP)

SNMP is used for monitoring and managing devices connected to an IP based network. It is used to allow network managers to monitor the status of devices such as PCs, servers and networked printers. SNMP can also be used to modify the settings of these devices to allow for centralised management.

Transport Control Protocol (TCP)

TCP is used to ensure reliable data transmission between devices. It does this by establishing a secure connection between devices. This connection is used to transmit a sequence of 'packets'. A packet is a small block of data, any large amounts of data being sent is split into multiple packets.

TCP provides facilities for:

- error detection
- acknowledgement of receipt of packets
- retransmission of lost or corrupt packets
- sequencing packets into the correct order.

Sequencing packets into the correct order is necessary as different packets can take different routes through the network, so may arrive in a different order from how they were sent. As TCP puts the packets back into order before an application receives them it can be said that TCP guarantees that data will be received in the order it was sent.

TCP keeps a log of all packets sent and maintains a timer from when each packet was sent. If packets aren't received correctly or at all, they aren't acknowledged by the recipient device. Similarly, if the timer reaches zero and no acknowledgement has been sent then TCP assumes the packet has been lost. Both situations mean that TCP will pause the transmission of further data to resend any lost or corrupted packets. This ensures that data is guaranteed to arrive.

TCP is used to transmit data for actions such as web browsing, file transfer and remote access. TCP utilises IP to route packets from one device to another.

User Datagram Protocol (UDP)

UDP is a simple and lightweight protocol that uses IP to routes packets from a source device to a destination device. UDP sends packets of information without establishing a connection which means that it does not guarantee delivery of packets and cannot reorder packets that arrive out of order. UDP is an alternative protocol to TCP in the TCP/IP protocol stack.

UDP is often used in scenarios where timely delivery of data is more important than guaranteed delivery, for example live streaming or online gaming. These uses are likely to prioritise speed of delivery and can tolerate some packet loss. UDP is also used for multicast communication (the same packet sent to multiple recipients), for example, a live stream being shared with lots of viewers. SNMP uses UDP to communicate with the devices being managed or monitored.

Internet Protocol (IP)

IP is used to route packets from a source device to a destination device. This routing occurs when sending data across one or multiple networks (such as the internet). To allow this to happen IP has an addressing system, where every device has an IP address to identify it

When data is split into packets, IP adds information to the packets including:

- Source address: when sending a packet, the source address is added to the packet
- Destination address: the IP address the packet should be sent to.

IP is a 'best effort delivery' protocol meaning that it doesn't guarantee the delivery of packets or have facilities for resending lost or corrupted packets. TCP is a higher-level protocol than IP and TCP provides these additional features if they are required.

Internet Control Message Protocol (ICMP)

ICMP is a supporting protocol in the TCP/IP stack. It is used to send error messages when a network device has issues with the transmission of an IP packet. For example, if a device is unavailable the **router** would send an error message using ICMP. ICMP isn't generally used by end-user applications and isn't used to send data between devices.

Quick check 8

1 Write down a definition of the term protocol.

2 State the benefit of the TCP/IP stack being split into layers.

Practice questions 3

You are writing a weather forecast application that will run on a smartphone. The application will use the current location of the phone and access the appropriate forecast data from a server using an API.

1 Describe what an API is. [2]

2 You have decided to use the REST architecture when implementing the weather application.

Explain why the REST architecture is appropriate for this use case. [2]

TA4 Application software security

Learning intentions

This topic is about current threats to application security and what risks these pose to applications. It also covers physical and digital security mitigations and how these help to protect application software.

It covers:

4.1 Security considerations

4.1 Security considerations

Threats

There are a wide range of different threats that can impact a software application or the system it runs on.

Botnets

A botnet is a network of internet connected computers that have been infected with malware. This malware allows the infected computers to be used without the owner's knowledge to perform some form of task. The type of tasks that a botnet can be used for are:

- send spam emails
- perform DDoS attacks
- stealing data.

Once computers have been infected, they are controlled using command and control software. Sometimes botnets are rented out by criminals to allow other criminals to perform the tasks mentioned previously.

Table 2.32: Many threats rely on other threats to gain access or to do whatever they're designed to do

Threat	Definition
Botnets	A botnet is a network of internet connected computers that have been infected with malware. This malware allows the infected computers to be used without the owner's knowledge to perform some form of task.
Denial of Service (DoS)/Distributed Denial of Service (DDoS)	A DoS attack is designed to make a computer system, application or network unusable or inaccessible. A Distributed Denial of Service (DDoS) attack is a form of DoS attack where the target system or network is flooded with requests from many computer systems, often using a botnet to send the requests.
Hacking	Hacking is a term used to describe someone gaining unauthorised access to a computer system and the data stored within that system.
Lack of supplier support	Once a supplier stops supporting a software application or piece of hardware then this increases the risk of other threats being able to affect a system.
Malicious spam	Spam is unwanted emails that are sent to many people. Malicious spam is designed to get malware onto a computer system.
Malware	Malware is a blended word made from malicious software. Malware is a broad term that can be used to describe a wide range of different software that will cause problems for a computer system or network.
Out of date software, hardware or firmware	Out of date software, hardware or firmware increases the risk of other threats being able to affect a system.

Denial of Service (DoS)/Distributed Denial of Service (DDoS)

A DoS attack is designed to make a computer system, application or network unuseable or inaccessible. This can be achieved in several different ways, usually flooding the network or computer system with requests to connect from a single computer system. These requests overload the system making it unuseable, meaning that any application that runs on that system would be unavailable for use.

If the system being attacked was a web server, then the website hosted on that server would not work. If the attack was aimed at an ecommerce website, then the lack of access could cost the business a lot of money through lost orders. The reputation of the business might also be damaged.

Often these attacks are motivated by profit, for example, the attackers might hope that the business being attacked would pay a ransom to end the attack.

A Distributed Denial of Service (DDoS) attack is a form of DoS attack where the target system or network is flooded with requests from many computer systems, often using a botnet to send the requests. The computer systems sending the requests are managed by a command and control server.

It is far more difficult to deal with a DDoS attack compared to a DoS attack due to the request coming from many different locations and the number of requests that can be made at any one time.

Hacking

Hacking is a term used to describe someone gaining unauthorised access to a computer system and the data stored within that system.

Once a hacker has access to a computer system, the risks to application security include:

- the stealing or **corruption** of data
- preventing the use of the system or software application
- preventing accessing the data within the system or software application
- installation of malware
- using the computer system as part of a botnet.

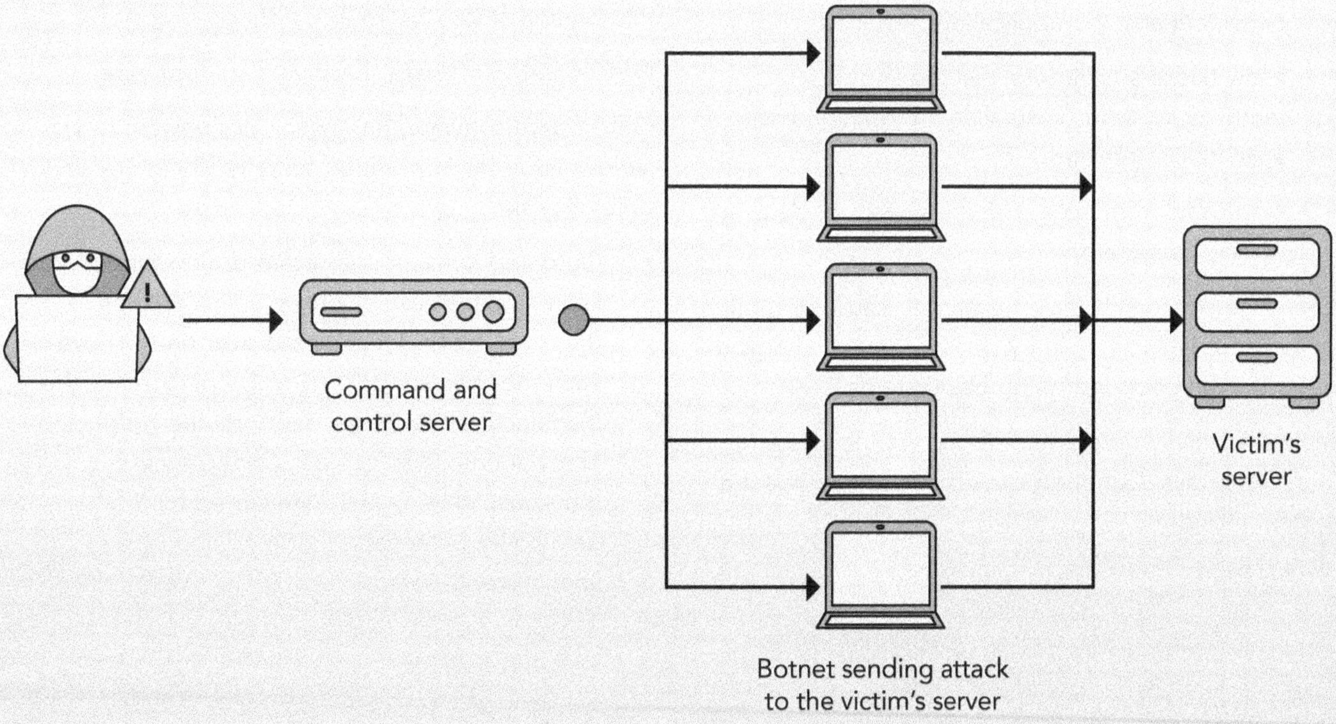
Command and control server
Botnet sending attack to the victim's server
Victim's server

Figure 2.21: Overview of how a DDoS attack happens

Lack of supplier support

If a supplier stops supporting a software application this raises a number of security risks. These include:

- Vulnerabilities will not be patched. See 'Out of date software, hardware or firmware' for further details.
- No updates will be available for the software, so new security threats will not be mitigated against.
- No technical support will be available, which could lead to security being compromised.

These risks could allow hackers to more easily gain unauthorised access to software applications or the data they store.

Malware

Malware is a blended word made from malicious software. Malware is a broad term that can be used to describe a wide range of different software that will cause problems for a computer system or network.

Examples of what malware can be used for:

- stealing information from the infected computers or servers and the applications installed
- allow hackers to access infected systems remotely, potentially stealing information from application software
- stop users from accessing the system or data within the system.

Often the creators of malware want to cause disruption or allow for financial gain by stealing data or charging users to gain back control of their systems.

Malware initially gets access to a computer system in several ways. Common ways that malware infect a system include:

- users inadvertently allow access (for example, by clicking on a link in a **phishing** email)
- out of date software, hardware or **firmware**
- downloads from a website that has been infected with malware.

Malicious spam

Spam is unwanted emails that are sent to many people. Spam is often used to advertise a product or service.

Malicious spam is designed to get malware onto a computer system. The malware might be attached to the email and be designed to look like a document. The unsuspecting user might open the document and infect their computer. The content of these emails is designed to make the user think they need to urgently deal with a request or that they may have won some money, so that they will open the attachment without thinking about their actions.

The malware installed by clicking on a link in a malicious spam email could stop access to software applications or might allow hackers to steal the information stored by an application.

Out of date software, hardware or firmware

Out of date software, **hardware** or firmware is a serious issue for application security. There are several different risks:

- Outdated software, hardware or firmware is likely to have several known vulnerabilities that have been documented over time. These vulnerabilities are unlikely to be patched as the manufacturer no longer supports the product. The vulnerabilities can be used to access the application, or the data stored by it. The data could be accessed or modified by an unauthorised person.

- Lack of updates could mean that newer versions of protocols or encryption may not be used which would reduce the overall security of the application. This may give hackers a way to gain unauthorised access to a software application or the data it stores.
- Applications often use libraries of code supplied by third parties. Out of date software, hardware or firmware will not receive updated versions of these libraries which may result in known vulnerabilities being introduced, again allowing access to the application or the data it stores.

Physical security mitigations

Physical security is the way that computer systems and networks are protected against physical attacks. It is much easier to access or damage data when a hacker can gain physical access to the computer or server it is running on.

There are a range of different physical security mitigations that can be useful, depending on the type of equipment being protected. Often many different physical security mitigations are combined to further decrease the risks.

Physical security mitigations protect software applications by preventing attackers from accessing the hardware where the application is running. This makes it more difficult to gain access to the application or the data it contains.

Biometrics

Biometrics have been defined as 'The automated recognition of individuals based on their biological and behavioural characteristics' by the **ISO standards body**.

The biological and behavioural characteristics that can be used for recognition include:

- fingerprints
- face recognition
- speech recognition
- keystroke dynamics (recognising the way someone types).

Once someone has been recognised using biometrics, they can be allowed access to a computer system or software application.

The advantages of biometrics over more traditional methods such as passwords or a PIN are that the person can't lose them, it is difficult to steal them and they can be much quicker to use, for example, using a fingerprint to access a mobile phone is much quicker than typing a password.

This protects software applications and the data they contain by only allowing people who should have access to be able to use them.

Cable locks

Cable locks consist of a metal cable that is anchored to an immoveable object and then locked to a device. They are designed to stop devices being stolen by an opportunistic thief.

Figure 2.22: Cable lock secured to a laptop

This helps protect software applications by reducing the risk of a device being stolen. The device could contain sensitive data and it is easier to access applications and data when a device can be worked on over a period of time or dismantled to access a storage device.

Cameras

Cameras are used as additional physical security mitigations as they help to reduce the risk of hackers physically accessing computer systems as the live feed from the cameras might be being watched by security staff or they can allow the hacker to be identified after the attack has taken place.

This protects software applications as cameras act as a deterrent to physically accessing the hardware that the application runs on.

Locks

Locks are often an overlooked physical security mitigation. Locks can be used to secure doors, rooms or storage areas from unauthorised access. If a computer system is stored in a locked location, then it is more difficult for a device to be stolen or other vulnerabilities to be used to access the applications or data stored on a device.

Locks can be opened by using a key, code, biometrics, Radio Frequency Identification (RFID) or swipe card.

RFID

RFID is a technology that can be used to identify a person and allow them to access a building or application.

RFID has two parts:

- A tag is a small transponder that can be part of a plastic card or small keyring device. The tag contains an antenna and a microchip. The microchip contains an identification number, and the antenna allows an RFID reader to communicate with the microchip.
- An RFID reader is a device that sends out radio waves that are received by the tag. The tag then transmits the identification number back to the RFID reader.

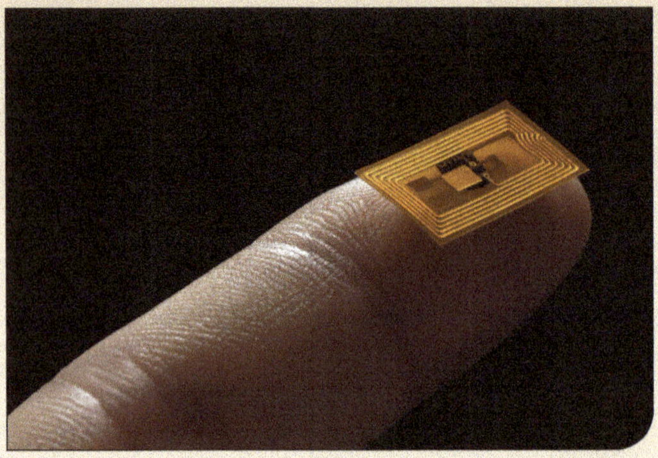

Figure 2.23: An RFID tag. Normally tags are part of a plastic card or keyring

Each person who needs access to a building or application can be issued with a RFID tag. Each tag has a unique identification number, and this will be linked to the person who should have access. Tags can be set to only allow access to certain parts of a building or application and have set times that access will be granted.

Using RFID helps to secure a software application by reducing the possibility of unauthorised access and it is easy to revoke access when a person no longer should have access to that application.

RFID can also be used to track items within shops or warehouses as the tag does not need to physically touch a reader.

Safe

A safe can be used to store portable devices that aren't in use or backups. Having the devices or backups in a safe reduces the chances of them being easily stolen which helps to keep the software application and associated data secure.

Swipe cards

A swipe card is a plastic card with a magnetic strip on one side. This stripe can be used to store an identification number that can allow the person who has possession of the card to access a device, building or room. This can help to secure an application by restricting who has access.

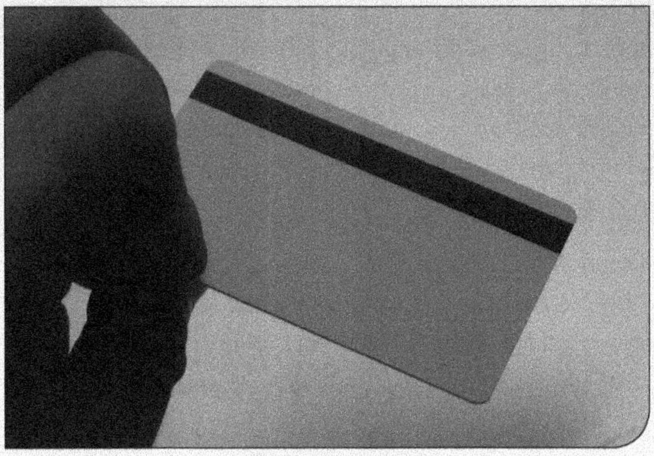

Figure 2.24: A magnetic swipe card

Many bank and credit cards have a magnetic strip on the rear side. Swipe cards are simple to use but have been replaced with alternative methods of identifying a person in many situations as they can be easy to copy.

If access to software application requires the use of a swipe card this helps to reduce the change of unauthorised access as the hacker would need to acquire an authorised swipe card.

Digital security mitigations

Protecting computer systems, the applications they run, and the data stored using physical security methods isn't enough, digital security mitigations are also needed.

Access rights

Access rights are the permissions that a user or particular application has. These permissions can allow or deny access to individual applications, files or entire drives. Permissions can also allow different levels of access, some users might be able to read information or files but not modify or they might allow full control (read, write and delete). Different systems use different terminology for levels of access.

Access rights can also be applied within some software applications. An application used to manage a

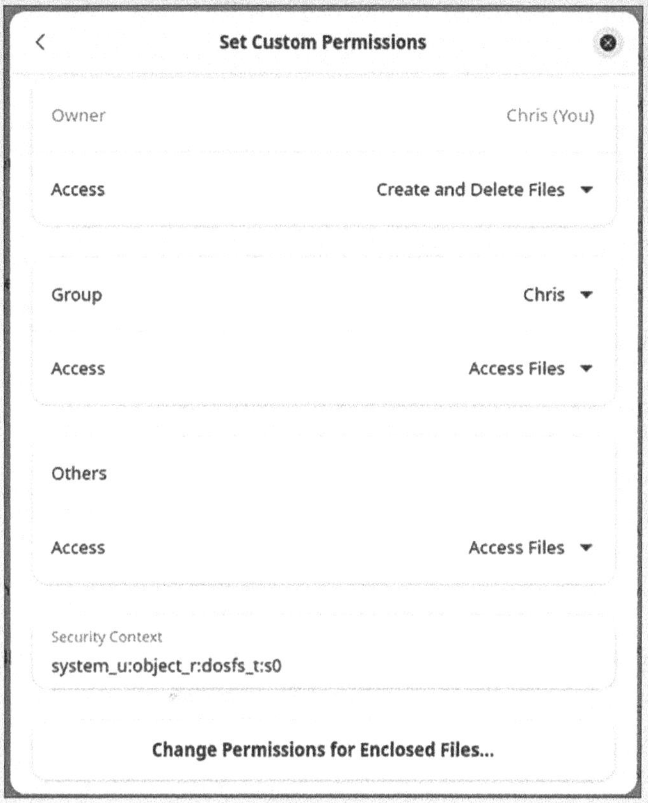
Set Custom Permissions
Owner
Chris (You)
Access
Create and Delete Files
Group
Chris
Access
Access Files
Others
Access
Access Files
Security Context
system_u:object_r:dosfs_t:s0
Change Permissions for Enclosed Files...

Figure 2.25: Example of a permissions window

business might consist of different modules, for example, sales, finance, stock ordering and so on. Users might only be able to access the module relevant to them, for example a salesperson would need access to the sales module but not to the others. A manager within the business might need access to all modules to be able to get an understanding of how the business is running.

Restricting access rights to only give the required access to information can help minimise the impact of hacking or other threats. If a hacker gained access to a user account that only had access to the sales details of a business, they could still cause damage, but this would be less than if they had access to the financial details or all data.

Anti-malware

Anti-malware is a type of software that is installed to a computer or server that will help to protect against malware.

Anti-malware software will scan all files on a computer or server to detect any malware that has been able to gain access. It acts as a barrier and scans files flowing from out of the system into the system. Once malware has been found the user will be alerted, and the malware will either be removed or quarantined. These actions should stop the malware from deleting, corrupting or stealing data.

Backup

A backup is the process of creating a copy of data from a computer system or application to another storage location. This copy would be used in case of hardware failure, loss of data from user error or from a threat (as detailed previously).

Backups should be done regularly, usually at least once per day. Being able to restore data from a recent backup helps to minimise the data loss or downtime of an application that could prove catastrophic for a business.

Cryptography

Cryptography is the science of securing information so that it cannot be understood by unauthorised people. There are several different ways this can be implemented but the most common is by using encryption.

Encryption

Encryption is the process of scrambling electronic data into a form that is 'unreadable', or meaningless, without knowing the key. Data needs to be decrypted using the key to make it 'readable', or understandable, again.

Data can be:

- at rest: data that is being stored, not actively in use or being transmitted
- in transit: data that is actively being transmitted from one device to another.

Data at rest can be encrypted. This means that data stored on a secondary storage device such as an SSD would be encrypted. This protects the data if a device, such as a laptop, is stolen as the data would be unreadable without knowing the key.

At rest, encryption can be made automatic, so the user doesn't need to do anything other than logon to access the data. Making all data at rest encrypted automatically means that users are unable to forget to encrypt sensitive data and this increases security.

Data in transit can also be encrypted. How this is done depends on how the data is being transmitted. For example, transferring data to a website can be protected by using HTTPS. Encrypting data in transit protects the data in case it is intercepted.

Learning in context 7

Encryption of information

Laptops and other devices frequently contain sensitive information and are regularly forgotten, lost or stolen.

For example, in 2023 parliamentary staff reported 38 laptops, 21 tablets, 16 smartphones missing. These devices went missing from a range of different locations including offices, trains, taxis, cars and pubs. Only about 33% of these devices were later found.

These devices could contain personal information, details of upcoming policy changes or information relating to national security. The implications of this data being leaked could range from embarrassment to unfriendly foreign powers knowing more than we'd like about our defence capabilities.

Parliamentary Digital Services (PDS), the department that manages the UK parliament network, states that if data is being moved outside of the Parliamentary Estate then mitigations must be in place, for example only encrypted laptops may be used. This should reduce the chance of anyone gaining access to the data stored on these missing devices. Further security precautions may also allow many of these devices to be remotely wiped by PDS.

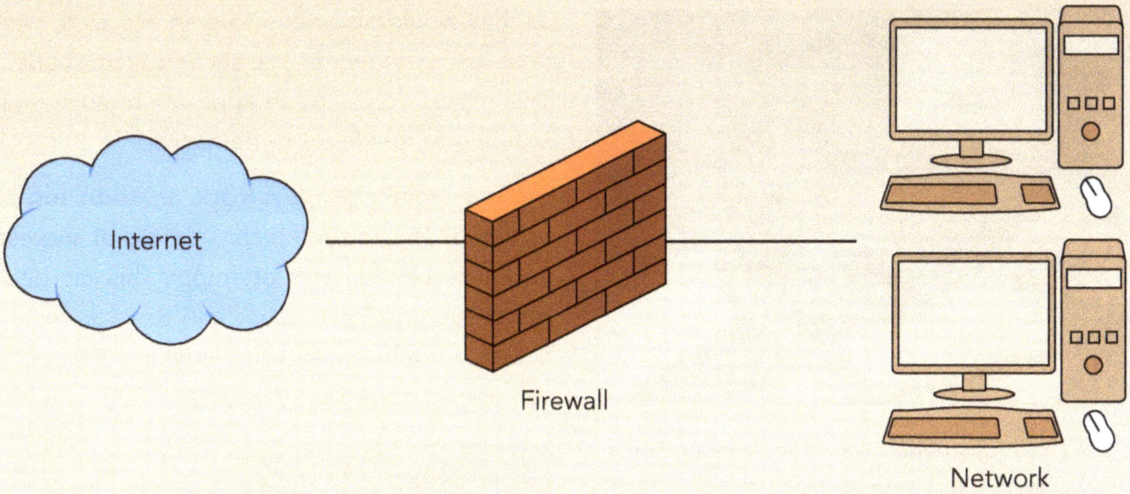
Internet
Firewall
Network

Figure 2.26: Diagram showing a firewall is located between a network and the internet

Firewalls

A **firewall** is a system that monitors incoming and outgoing traffic (in the form of **packets** of data) from a computer, server or network. It will allow or block traffic by comparing it to a set of predefined security rules.

These rules can reduce the chance of digital threats impacting a computer system, including making it more difficult for hackers to gain access. More advanced firewalls will record details of any attacks in a firewall log. This log will contain details of source and destination addresses, protocols and what security rule was triggered. This information is useful to check that the rules have been implemented correctly and to identify if additional security measures are needed.

Firewalls can be implemented in either hardware or software.

A hardware firewall is a device that usually sits between a network and the internet. Hardware firewalls are able to handle large amounts of network traffic and are highly configurable. They are expensive to purchase and require specialist knowledge to manage, so they are usually used by businesses rather than home users.

A software firewall is an application that is installed on a computer. Many operating systems come with a built-in software firewall that is configured in a way that will help to protect against the most common threats.

Firewalls can use whitelists or blacklists to restrict access to certain IP addresses. A whitelist only allows access to pre-approved IP addresses and blocks access to all other IP addresses. A blacklist will block certain IP addresses (usually from a downloadable list of known malicious sources) and allow access to all others.

Two-Factor Authentication (2FA)

2FA is a security method that requires a user to use two methods (factors) of authentication before access to an application is granted.

One factor is something you know (usually username and password) and the second factor is often something you have, as in you have access to your email account or your smart phone. A code is either sent to or generated by the second factor.

The code could be:

- sent to the registered email address of the user
- sent in a text message to the registered phone number of the user
- generated using a 2FA application on the user's mobile phone.

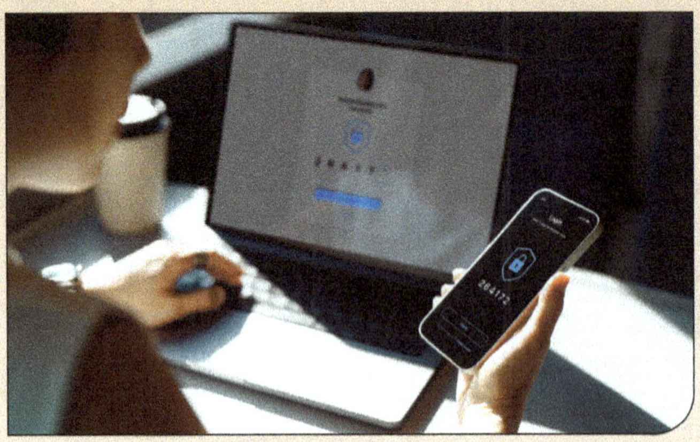

Figure 2.27: Two-factor authentication code generated on a mobile phone being inputted to an application

The code is only valid for a limited amount of time and needs to be inputted to the application to allow access.

Having two factors stops access if a hacker manages to find out the username and password of a user, as they would also need to gain access to whatever receives or generates the second factor code. This makes access to an application much more secure and less likely to be hacked.

When a login attempt is made an **audit log** can be updated. This log will record details of successful and unsuccessful login attempts. This can be useful for debugging login issues and to track unauthorised access. Regularly reviewing logs and fixing any issues can help protect sensitive data.

Quick check 9

1 What are factors in 2FA?

2 Write about how out of date software, hardware or firmware can make a software application more vulnerable.

Practice questions 4

1 A website owner is concerned about digital threats to her ecommerce website. Describe how a Distributed Denial of Service (DDoS) attack differs from Denial of Service (DoS) attack. [2]

2 A business has decided to improve its physical security by securing access to the building by adding cameras and using RFID locks rather than traditional keys.

Explain how RFID cards and cameras will improve security. [4]

TA5 Operational considerations

Learning intentions

This topic is about how software is tested before coming into widespread use, how completed software can be installed or updated in different situations and how policies will impact the creation and use of software.

It covers:

5.1 Testing

5.2 Types of application software installation

5.3 Policies

5.1 Testing

The purpose of testing is to:

- check that the application works and looks as expected
- identify and remove errors and bugs within the developed system.

Testing is important because without testing it is not possible to know that the system operates as expected. This could lead to issues including:

- software that **crashes** frequently
- software that provides incorrect outputs
- legal issues
- reputation damage to either the business using the software or the company that developed the software.

Testing should take place throughout the development of a system and once the system is complete. Testing during development will test each feature as it is implemented. This is helpful as the source of the problem is easier to locate which means that time and effort to fix is reduced. Testing during development can also involve the end users of the application and this will help to check that the application being developed will meet the needs of the actual users.

Testing during development allows issues to be identified and resolved quickly.

Testing once the system is complete allows the whole system to be checked as even though each individual part should have been checked during development, sometimes integrating the individual parts of a system may lead to unexpected issues.

Test plan structure

A test plan is created that covers all the requirements of the system. There are lots of variations around what is included in a test plan. A typical design is as shown in Table 2.33.

Table 2.33: A typical test plan design

Test Number	Test Type	Test Description	Test Procedure	Test Data	Expected Result	Actual Result	Remedial Action Required	Retest Result
1	Normal	Test that user can login using correct username and password	Open application, choose login from menu. Type username and password in. Press login.	Username: jsmith Password: Testdogcat4	User is logged in correctly	User is logged in correctly.	N/A	N/A

The columns in the table are:

Test number – this is useful for identifying the test when discussing with other people involved with the project.

Test type – there are three main types of test data, normal, extreme and erroneous. These are discussed next.

Test description – this provides an overview of the reason for the test.

Test procedure – this is a description of how the test should be carried out.

Test data – this is the data to be used in the test. Having the test data specified here allow the test to be redone should further investigation or remedial action needed.

Expected result – this is what the system should do when the test procedure is followed with the specified test data.

Actual result – this is what the system actually does when the test procedure is followed using the specified test data.

Remedial action required – if the expected result and the actual result differ then the issue needs to be fixed. This details what is required to be done. If a test fails and the issue isn't fixed, then the end user of the software could experience the same issue. Remedial action must be taken to ensure a fully working system is delivered.

Retest result – once the remedial action has taken place the test will need to be re-run. The result of the retest should be recorded here. It is important to retest to ensure that the remedial action has been successful otherwise the user could end up experiencing the same issue. Remedial action must continue to happen until the issue is fixed.

Types of test data

Table 2.34: There are three types of test data that should be included in all test plans

Type of test data	Description
Normal	• This is typical, sensible data that should be accepted by the system. • If the purchase quantity of an item must be between 0 and 10 then 5 could be used as normal data. • This type of data is used to ensure that the system works as intended and that output is correct for normal data.
Extreme	• Extreme test data should cover the minimum and maximum values of normal test data that should be accepted by the system. • If the purchase quantity of an item must be between 0 and 10 then extreme data would be 0 and 10 for this system. • This type of data is used to check that the system operates at the extremes of normal data. This is an area where errors frequently occur as it is easy for a programmer to inadvertently make a mistake such as using greater than 0 rather than greater than or equal to 0 in a conditional statement.
Erroneous	• This is data that should not be accepted by the system. • If the purchase quantity of an item must be between 0 and 10 then 11 or 'abc' could be used as erroneous data. • This type of data is used to ensure that the system doesn't accept data that is inappropriate. Accepting inappropriate data may lead to the system crashing or any calculations/decisions made on the entered data being incorrect. • Applications should provide feedback to users that the data isn't acceptable to allow them to correct it.

Types of testing

There are two main types of testing; technical and user.

Technical testing

Technical testing is done by a developer or by a specialist in testing, often called a quality assurance engineer.

Technical testing is a time consuming and therefore costly process as lots of different tests need to be performed that cover all of the possible ways of using the software. It can also lead to a false sense of security as it usually is not possible to test every single scenario of usage, device and operating system that the software application might be run on.

Technical testing can be manual or automated. Manual testing involved someone actually using the application and entering test data by hand, simulating a real user doing work with the application. This has some benefits such as finding poorly worded instructions or bad organisation of inputs but is slow, potentially tedious work. Whenever humans are involved in tedious work the possibility of mistakes increases, meaning that test data may be inputted incorrectly or accidentally missed.

Table 2.35: Checks made in technical testing

Functionality of the software	Does the application do what it is supposed to and produce the correct output?
Performance	Does the application respond to inputs within a suitable timeframe and not crash when being used?
Hardware requirements	Does the application work correctly on a range of different makes/models of hardware?
Operating system requirements	Does the application work on different versions of operating systems?
Security issues	Are there any security issues or vulnerabilities with the application?

Table 2.36: Automated testing has a number of advantages

Speed	Automated tests can be completed more quickly than a human could do the same tests.
Repeatability	Once the tests have been setup they can be used repeatedly, this is useful as the tests can be re-run when any changed to the application have been implemented.
Coverage	It is possible to run more tests using automation than with manual testing alone, meaning that a wider range of inputs can be tested.

It can be time consuming to setup automated testing and is likely to require expensive software to run the automated testing. Most testing will be a mixture of manual and automated testing to ensure that the application works as intended.

Table 2.37: There are a range of different technical testing methods that are likely to be used during the development of an application

Type of technical test	Details
Fuzz testing	Fuzz testing, also known as fuzzing, is an automated testing method that generates random data, including extreme and invalid data that is input into the application. This type of testing is used to detect crashes and other weaknesses in software.
Load/stress testing	Load or stress testing will help evaluate how software behaves when being used under a normal amount of load and when subjected to extreme workloads. This allows the developers to be confident that the software will work as expected under a range of different conditions.
Migration testing	If the application being developed is designed to replace an existing system, then migration testing is used. This type of testing checks that the data in the existing system can be imported into the new application without causing issues such as data loss.

Technical testing will occur throughout the development of the application and once the application appears to be complete. Once technical testing has been completed the test process could move on to user testing.

Table 2.38: Advantages and disadvantages of technical testing

Advantages	Disadvantages
Early detection of bugs is possible, which will stop them becoming larger issues.	Unclear messages to users could be missed if automated technical testing is used on its own.
Automation of technical tests can provide a speedy way of consistently testing an application and potentially removes the risk of human error.	Automated technical testing can be time consuming to setup. Manual testing can have human error issues.
Technical testing can allow the whole application to be tested, particularly if a combination of manual and automated technical testing is used. This can help to ensure that the application produces accurate output. This can help improve the overall quality of the application.	Time consuming and costly to test every possible use and feature of an application.
The application can be tested on a range of different devices and (if appropriate) different operating systems.	Limited scope as tests the functionality of the application but doesn't look at user experience or customer satisfaction.
Performance can be tested to ensure that performance issues are fixed before release.	Might give a false sense of security if tests aren't comprehensive as some issues may go undetected.

User

User testing involves using real **end users** of the software to test the application. This type of testing will help to identify issues with the user interface, problems with navigating around the application and any missing functionality from the point of view of the users.

User testing is likely to be one of the final steps before the application is released. There are different methods of user testing that include:

- Beta testing – a version of the software is released to a limited audience outside of the company that developed the software. The real end users would be expected to provide regular feedback that will help the developers make final adjustments to the application.
- Useability testing – this involves observing real end users trying to complete a range of tasks using the software. This can help find useability issues and get feedback from the user on how they expect the software to operate.

Table 2.39: Advantages and disadvantages of user testing

Advantages	Disadvantages
Feedback will be from actual end users and this is more likely than technical testing to identify issues with messages the application generates and other user interface issues.	Getting this kind of feedback can be time consuming and will only be able to ask a small number of users.
Improved user satisfaction as users will be able to point out any issues that will make the software useable in real life situations.	Different users might not agree about how well the application works. This might be down to different expectations or different uses of the software.
If a wide range of users are involved, then the application is likely to be tested on a wide range of different hardware and operating systems.	User testing can be time consuming as each tester will need to get access to the application and be provided instructions on what they should be testing.
Performance of the application will be tested in real world situations.	Individual users might not test all features of an application.

Learning in context 8

User testing

McDonald's UK, one of the largest fast-food businesses, conducted user testing of its mobile app by asking customers who hadn't used the app before to try it out in-store while consultants watched the process and got the customer to explain what they were trying to do.

The testing identified several issues with the app including with the user interface design, how the ordering process worked and what customers expected to be able to do with the app.

The results of the user testing fed into a new version of the application that had an improved user interface, allowed customers to order from any location at any time and choose different collection methods.

Quick check 10

1 Write down the purpose of testing.

2 Write about the difference between technical testing and user testing.

5.2 Types of application software installation

There are a wide range of different ways to install or update software. The choice of installation method will depend on a number of factors including:

- the number of computers the software needs to be installed on
- whether having a consistent version of software installed on each computer is necessary
- the type of device the software is being installed on
- if the software is being upgraded, installed for the first time or needs to be repaired.

Create ghost/image and deployment

This method involves setting up one computer with the operating system and any required software. Then a complete disk image (a 'ghost' image) of a system configuration is created and saved to a server. This image can then be used to setup a single computer or multiple computers at once by using software that connects the computer to the network and installs the disk image.

This method is ideal for organisations where multiple computers need to have the same software configuration, for example schools or offices.

Table 2.40: Advantages and disadvantages of creating and deploying ghost/images

Advantages	Disadvantages
• It is very efficient for setting up large numbers of computers in an identical way. • It ensures consistency across the systems and is more time efficient than having to install software on a large number of computers.	• If the hardware is not identical then compatibility issues may arise. • It does not allow for personalised setups per computer.

Upgrade

Upgrading involves installing a newer version of the software over an existing installation, retaining user settings and data when possible.

This is ideal when a new version of a piece of software needs to be installed as upgrade installations are relatively quick. Upgrades may have new features and/or provide security updates. Users appreciate settings and data being retained.

Table 2.41: Advantages and disadvantages of upgrading

Advantages	Disadvantages
• They keep the system up to date with the latest features and security patches while maintaining user preferences and data. • Relatively quick to upgrade compared to other methods.	• Sometimes, upgrades can introduce bugs or performance issues. • Backups need to be done before upgrading in case the upgrade goes wrong, potentially losing data.

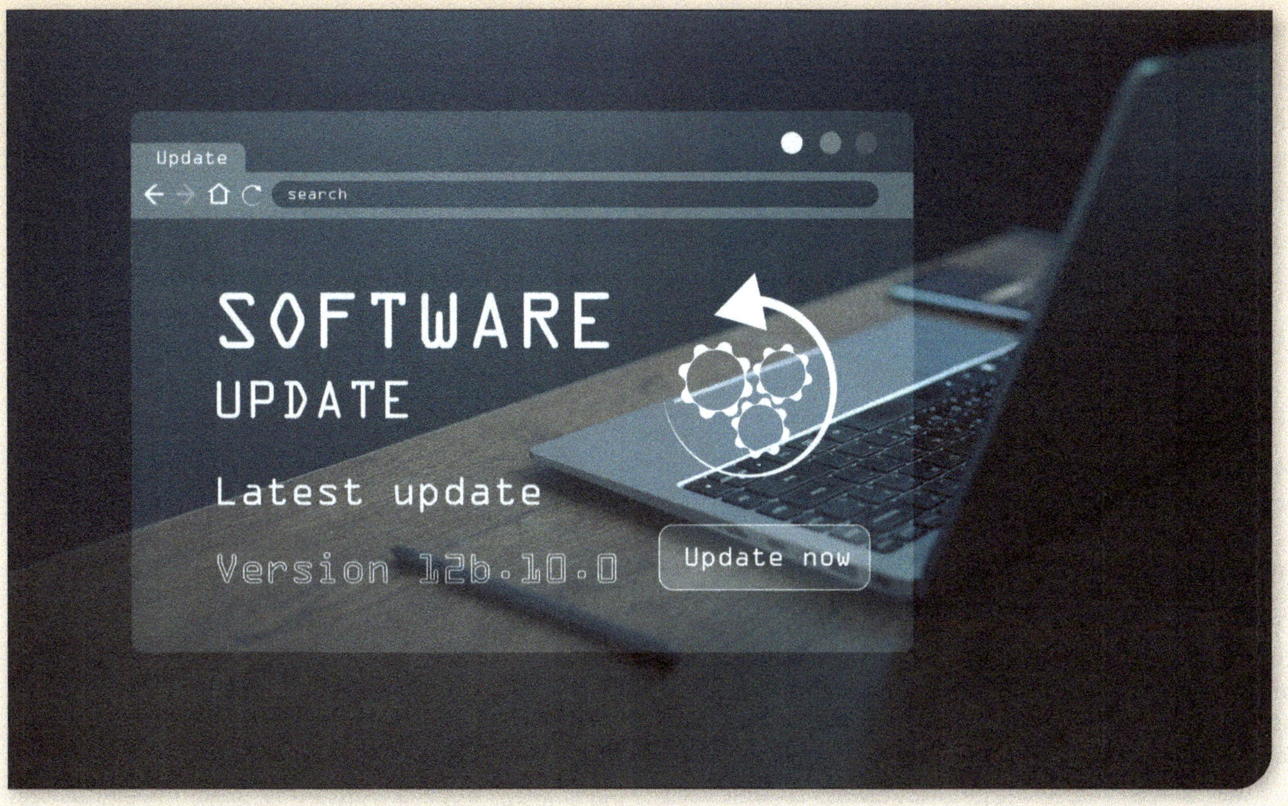
Update
search
SOFTWARE
UPDATE
Latest update
Version 12b.10.0
Update now

Figure 2.28: Upgrades can deliver new features and security patches to existing applications

Clean install

A clean install involves removing the current software and installing it from scratch. It is likely this method would also involve erasing all existing data on the computer.

This type of install can be useful if a computer or application has become corrupted. It can also help to avoid issues when upgrading to a significantly different version of software, which can happen if upgrades have not been done regularly.

Table 2.42: Advantages and disadvantages of clean installing

Advantages	Disadvantages
This can improve system performance and help to resolve persistent software issues.	• Data will need to be backed up and restored. • User settings can be lost. • A clean install is a time-consuming process.

Repair/modify installs

This method allows the repair of an existing software installation that is not working correctly or modify its features without having to fully reinstall.

This can be a quick method to fix minor software issues or when a user needs additional optional features installing.

Table 2.43: Advantages and disadvantages of repairing/modifying installs

Advantages	Disadvantages
• It is possible to quickly fix minor issues or allow additional features to be installed. This saves time. • Data and settings will not need restoring.	• This may not fix serious software issues. • Backups would need to be taken in case of data loss.

Remote install

Software is installed on one or many computers from a remote location via a network. Management tools allow the install to be started by an IT technician and reports that confirm the successful installation or any issues can be viewed.

This method is ideal in an organisation that might require software to be installed to multiple computers or where having a technician visit each computer would be impractical or too time consuming.

Table 2.44: Advantages and disadvantages of remote installing

Advantages	Disadvantages
This enables efficient centralised management of software installations, especially useful for IT departments managing large numbers of computers.	• This requires suitable management software to be purchased and technicians trained to use it. • Not always suitable for all software installs. • Allowing remote software installation can present security risks.

Unattended installation

Installation of software is done automatically without requiring any user interaction. This often uses preconfigured settings that are chosen before the software installations starts.

This method is ideal for installing software to large numbers of computers where the settings or installation options will be consistent across the computers.

Table 2.45: Advantages and disadvantages of unattended installation

Advantages	Disadvantages
This saves time and ensures consistency in software setups, especially useful when large numbers of identical installations are required.	• It is not possible to customise individual computers with different settings or options. • Initial setup of the unattended installation process can be complex, time consuming and requires testing before use.

Cloud download/install

Software is downloaded and installed directly from the cloud, rather than from physical media such as USB flash drives or a local network. This may require initial installation of software to allow the cloud download/install to work.

This method can be convenient when having the latest version of software is important or if the business does not want to have large amounts of server storage dedicated to storing software packages for installation on individual computers.

Table 2.46: Advantages and disadvantages of cloud downloading/installing

Advantages	Disadvantages
• The version of software being installed will automatically be the latest version. • Reduces the need for large amounts of server storage or depending on physical media. • This method may also keep the software up to date automatically.	• The installation speed will be dependent on internet connectivity and bandwidth. Should the internet connection fail during an installation then the whole process may need to be restarted. • There are potential security and privacy concerns over accessing the software installer online. • Problems may arise if the business wants to use a consistent version of the software on all its computers.

Mobile install

Mobile installation is allowing the installation of software to mobile devices, such as mobile phones or tablet computers, through the app store provided by the device manufacturer.

This method is ideal when a business provides mobile devices to its employees. The installation could be managed centrally by the IT department or allow for self-service, where users are allowed to install approved applications on company owned devices.

Table 2.47: Advantages and disadvantages of mobile installing

Advantages	Disadvantages
This method provides a simplified installation process and if self-service installation is allowed then the app store provides centralised discovery through the app store interface. Update management is must also done through the app store.	• App store policies must be followed, and internet connectivity is required. • It is unlikely that users can customise the installation process.

Network install

This method allows software applications to be installed over a local network. This allows a single source, usually a server, to serve multiple installations.

This method is ideal for businesses when the computers are connected to a network and can ensure that the same version of a software application is used consistently throughout the business.

Table 2.48: Advantages and disadvantages of network installing

Advantages	Disadvantages
This is an efficient method for installing software on multiple computers within the same network. It removes the need for physical media to be stored. The version of software being installed can be made consistent.	The performance of the network can be affected by network traffic generated by the install.

Quick check 11

1 List the different types of installation with a concise description of each.

2 Write about the difference between a clean install and an upgrade.

5.3 Policies

A policy is a document that details how a business or person within a business should behave. A business is likely to have a range of policies that cover different parts of the business. This section detail policies that may have an impact on the requirements an application that is being developed might have to meet.

Application user guide

An application user guide is designed to provide end users with instructions on how to effectively and efficiently use an application. It will explain the application's features, functionalities and how to troubleshoot common issues.

Application user guides typically include an overview of the application, installation procedures, step-by-step guides on how to use each feature, troubleshooting tips and answers to Frequently Asked Questions (FAQs). The manual might also detail how to get support from the developers.

Some user guides will have a technical requirements section. This section would detail the minimum hardware requirements and details of operating systems (including version numbers) that the software would run on. This section is used to allow the end user to check that the computer system they have or are considering buying would work with the software application.

The user guide is often written alongside the software development process. The developers work with technical writers to create a comprehensive and easy to understand manual.

Acceptable Use Policy (AUP)

The Acceptable Use Policy (AUP) outlines how a business's IT resources, including computers, network, internet connection and applications, may be used. This is to ensure they are used ethically, legally and without compromising security.

The AUP is likely to include details of acceptable and unacceptable use, potential consequences for breaking the rules in the policy, guidelines for keeping data safe and what to do if a problem occurs.

When developing applications for a specific business, developers will ensure the software complies with the AUP by incorporating features that prevent misuse, by providing features such as:

- encryption of sensitive data
- logs of user activity
- a permissions system where different types of user (for example, employee or manager) have different levels of access to data or features.

Backup(s)

A backup policy ensures that data is regularly copied and stored securely away from the main system so that it can be recovered in case of data loss, corruption or a cyber-attack.

This policy will outline what data needs to be backed up, how frequently the backups should be run, where the backups should be stored and how long the backups should be kept for.

When an application is being developed for a specific business, the developers will need to consider how the data from the application will be backed up. The business will already have a backup system in place, so the new application will need to be designed to work with whatever backup system is being used. The developers will also need to test restoration processes to ensure data can be successfully restored.

Codes of practice

Codes of practice provide details of standards of professional conduct within a business.

These codes might cover topics such as who is allowed access to certain types of information, confidentiality, integrity, user privacy and compliance with legal requirements.

While developing an application, adherence to codes of practice involves implementing security measures, ensuring accessibility, protecting user data, meeting legal requirements and regularly auditing the adherence to these standards.

Staying safe online

This policy aims to educate employees about the risks associated with online activities and how to avoid common cyber security threats like phishing, malware and identity theft.

Guidelines are likely to include safe browsing practices, how to create secure passwords along with security guidance such as recognising phishing attempts and how to report them.

Developers can incorporate security features that help users stay safe online, such as secure authentication methods, warnings about unsecured connections and tools for managing privacy settings.

Use of information

The purpose of a use of information policy is to manage how information is used within the organisation, ensuring it is handled responsibly, fairly and in compliance with data protection laws.

This policy might detail the classification of data, authorisation levels for accessing different types of information, guidelines for sharing and storing information and how the organisation complies with data protection laws.

When developing an application this policy might require developers to implement access controls, encrypt sensitive data and log who accesses data.

Quick check 12

1 Write about what details a backup policy will contain.

2 List the topics that an application user guide might contain.

Practice questions 5

1 Explain **one** advantage and **one** disadvantage of user testing. [4]

2 Describe what an Acceptable Use Policy (AUP) is likely to contain. [2]

TA6 Legal considerations

Learning intentions

This topic is about what legal considerations need to be thought about when creating software applications. There are a number of different laws and regulations that must be considered depending on what the application does.

It covers:

6.1 Legal considerations

6.1 Legal considerations

When developing a software application there are a number of legal considerations that have to be complied with. The main regulations and laws are detailed next.

Legislation and regulations

Computer Misuse Act (CMA)

The CMA is designed to protect computer systems and the data they contain from unauthorised access or modification by criminalising these actions. It also covers making, supplying or obtaining of tools that could be used to gain unauthorised access to computer systems.

Should someone be convicted of breaking the CMA then they could face criminal charges, potentially being fined or imprisoned.

To ensure a software application meets the requirements of the CMA, the developers should ensure that the application is secure, likely by implementing strong authentication methods and where appropriate different levels of permission and an audit log.

The latest version of this Act at the time of publishing is the Computer Misuse Act 1990.

Learning in context 9

The Computer Misuse Act (CMA)

The CMA was introduced after hackers obtained the username and password belonging to an engineer who worked for a telecoms company. When the hackers used the stolen login details, they found they could access Prince Phillip's email.

The hackers were caught and then convicted under the Forgery and Counterfeiting Act. However, the convictions were overturned on appeal as the hackers hadn't committed forgery. The CMA was created to deal with people who accessed or modified data without permission.

The CMA started to be reviewed in 2023 but as of the time of publication no changes have been made. Technology has moved on a great deal since 1990. What do you think needs to be covered in a new version of the Act?

Freedom of Information Act (FOIA)

The FOIA is designed to provide public access to information held by public authorities, such as government departments, police forces, health trusts or state schools. This should help to promote transparency and accountability.

The act also makes public authorities proactively publish certain types of information and to respond to requests for information within specified timelines. The act does not allow access to all information as it includes exemptions to protect sensitive information from disclosure, balancing public interest and privacy.

Should a public authority not meet the requirements of the FOIA then this could result in legal challenges that could force the organisation to respond as well as being fined.

Developers need to make sure that the application allows easy access to information that could be part of a FOIA request. This will require the stored data to be efficiently searched and relevant results extracted to an easy to access format.

For example, if a request was made to a health authority, they would want to be able to be able to search for any records held under that person's name and be able to also have the option for using other names that the person may have used (for example, shortened versions of first names or maiden names). The output from this search would need to be in a format where the contents could be checked for any irrelevant information (for example, data about a different person with the same name), and in a format that the requester could easily access themselves.

The latest version of this Act at the time of publishing is the Freedom of Information Act 2000.

Data Protection Act (DPA)

Data protection is governed by the Data Protection Act and the UK General Data Protection Regulation. The Act provides the legal framework, and the Regulation provides requirements and procedures that must be followed to implement the Act. Together they designed to protect personal information and ensure that it is processed in a fair, secure and lawful manner.

The DPA controls how your personal information is used by organisations and the government. The DPA provides six data protection requirements (see Figure 2.29).

The latest version of this Act at the time of publishing is Data Protection Act 2018.

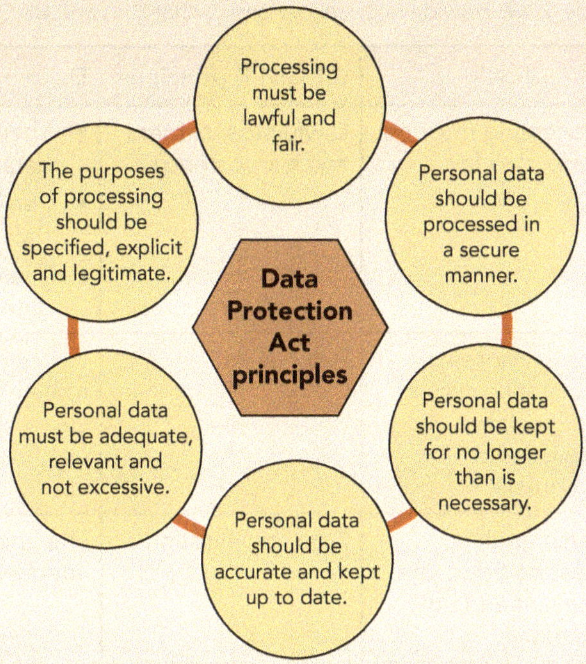
Data Protection Act principles
Processing must be lawful and fair.
Personal data should be processed in a secure manner.
Personal data should be kept for no longer than is necessary.
Personal data should be accurate and kept up to date.
Personal data must be adequate, relevant and not excessive.
The purposes of processing should be specified, explicit and legitimate.

Figure 2.29: Principles of the Data Protection Act

UK General Data Protection Regulation (UK GDPR)

The UK GDPR is designed to protect individuals' personal data and ensure that organisations process this data in a secure, fair and lawful manner by creating rules and procedures for how data should be treated.

UK GDPR has seven key principles that are based on the requirements listed previously. These principles must be taken into account when designing and implementing a software application.

The principles are:

- lawfulness, fairness and transparency
- purpose limitation
- data minimisation
- accuracy
- storage limitation
- integrity and confidentiality
- accountability.

Table 2.49: How developers can ensure that DPA and UK GDPR Principles are met

DPA principles	UK GDPR principles	Developer actions
Processing must be lawful and fair	Lawfulness, fairness and transparency	• There must be valid reasons for collecting and using personal data that is going to be used within the application. • Personal data must be used in a fair manner, meaning that the data cannot be used in a detrimental or misleading way. • The use of data must be transparent, meaning that uses of the data must be honestly.
The purposes of processing should be specified, explicit and legitimate	Purpose limitation	If data is going to be used in a new way, then permission will need to be got from the people the data is about.
Personal data must be adequate, relevant and not excessive	Data minimisation	The application must only collect data that is needed for the intended purpose.
Personal data should be accurate and kept up to date	Accuracy	• The application may need to provide a method of checking that the data is being kept up to date. This could be done by asking the users to check and update the data stored on an annual basis. • There needs to be a system created that allows individual people to challenge and, if necessary, correct any inaccurate data that is stored.
Personal data should be kept for no longer than is necessary	Storage limitation	• Personal data must not be kept for longer than it is needed. • The designer of the application will need to be able to justify how long data is to be kept for and why it is needed for that long. Stored data must be regularly reviewed and erase it when no longer needed. • Have a system that allows people to challenge storage of their data, and where necessary, allow for that data to be erased.
Personal data should be processed in a secure manner	Integrity and confidentiality	The application will need to have security measures in place to ensure that data is stored in a secure way and can only be accessed by authorised people.
N/A	Accountability	The people or business that run an application must take responsibility for what is done with personal data. Records are kept to show that all principles are being met.

All this will need to be considered when developing an application that collects personal data. Decisions around how the application will work, store and allow access to data will need to be considered. As well as implementing requirements into the application, processes to ensure that the data is managed in line with the principles will need to be developed.

If a data breach (where confidential or personal data or information is exposed or stolen) occurs, then the business must have a procedure in place to notify affected people and inform the Information Commissioner's Office (details follow in the next section).

Consequences of not following DPA or UK GDPR Rules

If the rules within the DPA or UK GDPR are not followed, then the Information Commissioner's Office has a range of options that are used depending on the severity and risk to people's data. These include:

- warnings that require the problems to be fixed
- bans on processing data
- fines of up to £17.5 million or 4% of the business's annual worldwide turnover, whichever is higher.

At the time of publishing UK GDPR was last updated in 2020.

Privacy and Electronic Communications Regulations (PECR)

These regulations are designed to give people privacy rights when using electronic communication systems. The latest update was in 2019. PECR contains specific regulations about:

- marketing communications
- cookies and similar technologies
- security and privacy of public communication services.

Marketing communications

A business must not send unsolicited marketing by email, text, phone, fax or other electronic messages without permission. To comply with this requirement the business wanting to send marketing messages must seek permission, a common way to do this is to get people to tick opt-in boxes when signing up to use an application or service.

Cookies and similar technologies

A cookie is a very small text file that is downloaded to a computer when accessing a website. The cookie allows the website to store user preferences and to identify the device being used.

If cookies are going to be used, then the website must inform the user that cookies are being used and what they are being used for. Normally the user must accept the use of cookies. There are exceptions to this for essential cookies being used for a service a user has requested, for example to allow an ecommerce site to remember what has been added to a basket.

These requirements apply if a different technology to cookies is being used for the same purpose.

Cookie settings
ACCEPT

Figure 2.30: Information on how a site uses cookies is often held separately from the action needed to accept or reject them

Security and privacy of public communication services

Telecoms providers (such as mobile phone networks) or internet service providers have to ensure the security of personal data stored by them or transmitted across the service.

They also have to ensure the privacy of people using the service. This is done by restricting the use of traffic data (data about the routing, duration or timing of messages sent) and the use of location data to not allow this to be used for marketing or other services without permission.

People using a public communication service also have the right to getting bills that are not itemised and to allow calls to be made that don't show the number the call is coming from.

PECR works alongside the DPA and UK GDPR, adding specific rules about privacy and electronic communications, including the use of personal data in marketing. PECR rules take priority over UK GDPR and the DPA but the rules within all these acts and regulations must be met.

An online service can meet PECR and UK GDPR by following this guidance taken from the ICO:

- if your online service stores information, or accesses information stored on user devices then you should ensure that comply with PECR first, including the requirements to provide information and obtain consent; and
- the UK GDPR applies to any processing of personal data outside of this storage or access.

PECR also states that data protection legislation (DPA and UK GDPR) rules must also be met.

If the regulations within PECR are not complied with then the ICO has a range of actions that can be taken including:

- criminal prosecution
- non-criminal enforcement and audit
- fine of up to £500 000 issued against the organisation or its directors.

Independent bodies

Information Commissioner's Office (ICO) in the UK

The ICO is the UK's independent authority set up to uphold information rights in the public interest, protect data privacy for individuals and promote openness of information stored by public bodies.

The ICO oversees and enforces a number of different acts and regulations including:

- DPA
- UK GDPR
- PECR
- FOIA.

The ICO has the power to issue warnings, guidance, serve enforcement notices, and impose fines on businesses that fail to comply with the law.

Quick check 13

1 What is the main purpose of each act or regulation? Produce a brief summary in a table.

2 What must a company do if they want to use cookies when a user accesses a website? How might they do this?

Practice questions 6

A business is considering launching a new application that is designed to help students revise for exams.

1 The business already has the contact details of hundreds of customers that bought a game they created, and they would like to use the details to send marketing emails about the new application.

a State the legislation or regulation that controls this behaviour. **[1]**

b State **one** way the business could seek consent to send marketing emails to existing customers. **[1]**

2 Outline whether the Freedom of Information Act applies to this business. **[2]**

SCAN
- RESPONSIVE
- STRATEGY
- Analysis
- Experience
- BRAND
- FRAMWORK
- DESIGN
UX DESIGN
WEBSITE
DEVELOPER
USER EXPERIENCE

F162 Designing and communicating UX/UI solutions

Topic Areas

TA1: Principles of UX and UI design

TA2: Plan UX/UI solutions

TA3: Design UX/UI solutions

TA4: Communicate UX/UI solutions

TA5: Review and improve UX/UI solutions

Designing and communicating UX/UI solutions is crucial across computing, job roles and daily life. Effortless experiences boost productivity and satisfaction in software, websites and digital platforms. Intuitive interfaces reduce cognitive load, aiding task completion across various industries such as marketing, finance, healthcare and education.

In everyday life, from apps to smart devices, well-designed UX/UI simplifies tasks, enriching lives with easy access to information and services. This clarity helps users understand what the product does and how to use it. As a result, users' expectations align with what the product delivers, leading to positive experiences.

In this unit, you will discover the role and importance of UX and UI design in our lives and develop foundation knowledge and skills in these areas.

TA1 Principles of UX and UI design

Learning intentions

This topic is about the principles of UX and UI design.

It covers:

1.1 Basics of UX and UI

1.2 Application end user considerations

1.3 UX/UI design principles

1.4 UX/UI design psychology

1.5 UX/UI experience

1.6 UX/UI interface design standardisation

1.1 Basics of UX and UI

User Experience (UX) and **User Interface (UI)** are two aspects of product design that contribute to the overall user experience. UX is focused on the overall experience and satisfaction of users, encompassing factors such as usability, **accessibility** and desirability. UI, on the other hand, is concerned with the visual presentation and interactive components of the user **interface**, including elements such as layout, **typography**, colours and interactive controls.

User Experience (UX) design

UX design is the process of creating and enhancing the user experience to make the product more user-friendly, efficient and enjoyable. The role of UX design in application development is crucial because:

- A well-designed user experience facilitates easy navigation, task completion and satisfaction, contributing to positive reviews and increased user retention.
- UX design centres on design principles that help create **intuitive**, user-friendly interfaces that correlate with customers' needs, behaviours and preferences.
- UX design can reduce the learning curve, enabling new users to quickly grasp the application, leading to a positive initial experience and encouraging continued usage.

The role of UX design

The primary role of UX design is to understand the needs, goals, preferences and pain points of the users who will interact with a product or service. This involves conducting user research, gathering insights and empathising with users to inform design decisions.

Why is UX design important?

UX design is importance because:

- A well-designed user experience can lead to higher user satisfaction, as users find it easy and enjoyable to accomplish their tasks and achieve their goals.
- Companies that prioritise UX design can gain a competitive edge by offering superior experiences that stand out from the competition and attract users.
- A positive user experience can enhance brand trust, credibility and loyalty, while a poor user experience can damage brand reputation and lead to negative word-of-mouth.

User Interface (UI) design

User Interface (UI) design is the process of creating visually appealing and intuitive interfaces for digital products such as websites, mobile apps and software applications. It involves designing the layout, typography, colours and interactive elements to ensure that users can easily navigate and interact with the product.

The role of UI design is to create an effortless and enjoyable user experience that meets the needs and expectations of the target audience. It aims to achieve this through various means.

Learning in context 1

HSBC mobile app

HSBC offers a mobile banking application.

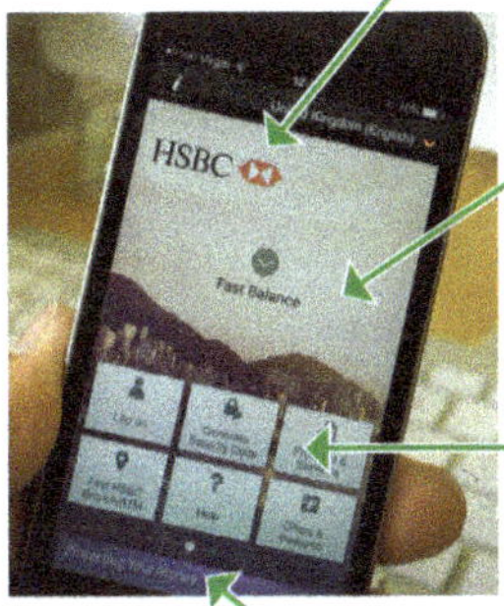
HSBC

Brand identity: UI design helps to communicate the brand identity and personality of a product or company using consistent visual elements such as colours, typography, and imagery. The choice of typography in the HSBC banking app is aligned with their brand identity. The use of clean, modern fonts conveys a sense of professionalism and sophistication, reflecting the bank's commitment to providing high-quality financial services.

Engagement: UI design creates intuitive and responsive interactive elements like buttons, menus, and forms, facilitating user tasks and goals. The app uses intuitive interactions to streamline the user experience. For instance, users can easily navigate through the app by swiping between different screens or tapping on clearly labelled icons and buttons.

Usability: Organising information, designing clear navigation pathways, and optimising interactive elements to make interactions intuitive and efficient. The app has an intuitive layout and recognisable icons and buttons, making the app easy to navigate and use for customers and providing quick and efficient access to banking services and transactions.

Accessibility: UI design includes considerations for accessibility to ensure that interfaces are usable by people with disabilities. This may involve providing alternative text for images, ensuring sufficient colour contrast, and implementing keyboard navigation options, HSBC's mobile app offers high-contrast options to enhance visibility for users with low vision or colour blindness. The use of bolder text and contrasting colours makes content stand out more clearly against the background. This feature ensures that users with visual impairments can easily distinguish between different elements on the screen.

Figure 3.1: The HSBC mobile banking app allows customers to access their accounts, perform various banking transactions and manage their finances directly from their smartphones or tablets

Top of form

UX and UI designers often collaborate closely throughout the design process. UX designers conduct user research and create **wireframes** and prototypes to ensure that the product meets user needs and solves their problems effectively, while UI designers focus on visual design, typography, colour schemes and interactive elements to ensure that the interface is visually appealing and easy to use.

UI
UX

Figure 3.2: Interfaces are a combination of UI and UX design

Quick check 1

1 What is the significance of user feedback in the iterative process of UX design. Provide specific examples of how user feedback can influence the improvement of a digital product.

2 Using the example of the Spotify mobile app, how does User Experience (UX) design and User Interface (UI) design collaborate to create a seamless music streaming experience for users. Provide specific examples to support your explanation.

1.2 Application end user considerations

UX/UI design should consider experience, accessibility and hardware to create digital products that are intuitive, inclusive and compatible across various devices. By prioritising user experience, designing with accessibility in mind and optimising for hardware compatibility, designers can create interfaces that meet the needs of a diverse range of users and provide a positive user experience.

Experience

Table 3.1: Users have varying levels of competence with technology. UX/UI designers need to consider this variability and tailor the complexity of the user interface accordingly

Novice/beginner	Occasional	Regular	Expert
• Design interfaces that are intuitive and easy to navigate, with clear labels and instructions. • Provide guided tours or tutorials to help novice users familiarise themselves with the product. • Minimise **cognitive load**. Cognitive load refers to the total amount of mental effort or 'load' that a person's working memory is under while processing information. By simplifying workflows will avoid overwhelming users with too many options. • Use clear error messages and provide guidance on how to recover from mistakes.	• Design interfaces that allow occasional users to quickly access key features and perform common tasks. • Ensure that the navigation is intuitive and consistent, making it easy for occasional users to find what they need. • Provide contextual help resources or **tooltips** to assist occasional users when needed. • Offer flexible options for customisation and personalisation, allowing occasional users to tailor the interface to their needs.	• Design interfaces that prioritise efficiency and productivity for regular users, with **streamlined** workflows and shortcuts. • Allow regular users to customise their experience, such as saving preferences or creating shortcuts for frequent actions. • Introduce advanced features or power-user options for regular users who are familiar with the product. • Collect feedback from regular users to help designers address their evolving needs and preferences.	• Provide expert users with access to advanced functionality and customisation options to support their expertise. • Offer keyboard shortcuts and other power-user features to enable expert users to navigate quickly and efficiently. • Allow expert users to adjust settings to improve their work. • Optimise performance for expert users who may be working with large data collections or complex tasks.

Available hardware

UX and UI designers need to understand the purpose and role of user hardware so that the experience is optimised for performance, accessibility and usability across a range of devices and platforms.

Input devices

- Different input devices, such as touchscreens, keyboards, mice, styluses, voice commands and gestures, require different interaction patterns.
- Different input devices vary in terms of precision and speed. For example, touchscreens are more suitable for quick, direct interactions, while mice and keyboards offer greater precision and control.
- Users have specific expectations regarding how they interact with **digital interfaces** based on the input device they're using. For example, touchscreen users expect gestures like swiping and tapping to navigate through content, while keyboard users expect keyboard shortcuts and tab navigation.

Screen sizes

- Smaller screens require concise and prioritised content to ensure clarity and avoid clutter.
- Screen size influences navigation and interaction patterns. For example, larger screens can accommodate more extensive navigation menus and sidebars while smaller screens may include a condensed navigational structure and touch gestures, such as swiping, tapping and pinching, as primary navigation methods.
- Screen size affects typography choices and readability. Designers need to select fonts, font sizes and spacing that ensure readability across different screen sizes, viewing distances and resolutions.

Types of device

- Different types of devices, such as smartphones, tablets, laptops, desktops and wearable devices, vary in form factor and screen size.
- Each type of device supports specific input methods, such as touchscreens, keyboards, mice, styluses, voice commands and gestures.
- The performance and hardware capabilities of different devices vary, influencing the design of interfaces in terms of responsiveness, animation effects, media playback and resource consumption.

Learning in context 2

The launch of the Nintendo Wii

The Nintendo Wii introduced motion-sensing controllers that allowed players to interact with games through physical gestures and movements.

Figure 3.3: The input device was known as a Wii Remote (or Wiimote) and featured accelerometers and infrared sensors that could detect motion and position in three-dimensional space

The unique input method of the Wii Remote had an impact on UX/UI design in gaming for several reasons:

- The Wii Remote enabled gesture-based interaction, allowing players to control games by performing physical movements such as swinging, pointing and tilting the controller.
- The capabilities of the Wii Remote inspired game developers to create innovative gameplay mechanics that made use of motion controls in unique ways.
- The intuitive nature of motion controls made gaming more accessible to a broader audience, including casual gamers and people with disabilities.
- The tactile feedback provided by the Wii Remote, such as vibrations and audio cues, enhanced the sense of immersion and engagement for players.

Accessibility needs

Understanding how accessibility needs impact UX/UI design is crucial for creating digital experiences that are inclusive and user-friendly. Below are some examples of how UX/UI designers can address specific needs:

- **Visual impairments**: alternative text for images, using descriptive headings and labels, and ensuring sufficient colour contrast for text, interactive elements and compatibility with a screen reader that can convert digitised text into speech or a braille output.
- **Motor difficulties**: large, interactive targets, minimising the need for precise gestures and offering alternative input methods such as voice commands or keyboard shortcuts.
- **Cognitive impairments** or learning disabilities: Use plain language, providing clear instructions and feedback and avoiding complex layouts or jargon.
- **Hearing impairments**: visual alternatives to auditory content, such as captions for videos, transcripts for audio recordings and visual alerts for important notifications.

Learning in context 3

New York City subway MetroCard

The New York City subway system operates 24 hours a day, 7 days a week, providing transportation for millions of passengers each day.

The MetroCard vending machines were redesigned as they posed significant challenges for individuals with disabilities, including those with visual impairments or mobility limitations. The interface was not user-friendly and it lacked features such as audio feedback or tactile elements that could assist users with disabilities in navigating the system independently.

Improved visual contrast: The interface was redesigned to have high contrast colours and clear typography, making it easier for users with low vision to read the information displayed on the screen.

Audio instructions: The machines were equipped with audio instructions and feedback, providing spoken guidance to users with visual impairments or literacy challenges.

AUDIO

Tactile buttons: The redesigned machines featured tactile buttons with Braille labels, allowing users with visual impairments to navigate the interface by touch.

Accessible payment options: The new design included multiple payment options, including contactless payment methods and compatibility with accessibility features on mobile devices, making it easier for users with mobility limitations to complete.

Figure 3.4: The new NYC Metro card design incorporated several accessibility features

Quick check 2

1 What are the end-user considerations that need to be addressed for novice users, occasional users, regular users and expert users of Facebook.

2 How does responsive design accommodate the varying screen sizes of devices, and how does this adaptation impact UX/UI design, using a news website as an example?

1.3 UX/UI design principles

User Experience (UX) and User Interface (UI) design are crucial components in the development of digital products and platforms. This section will focus on the fundamental principles of UX/UI design. By understanding these principles, designers can create interfaces that prioritise the user experience, resulting in products that are intuitive, efficient and enjoyable to use.

Perception

User perception plays a crucial role in UX/UI design because it directly influences how users interact with digital products and platforms. User perception affects UX/UI design because:

- Users form initial impressions of a digital product or interface within seconds of encountering it, and this can impact their overall satisfaction and how they engage with the product.
- Users prefer an intuitive and easy-to-use interface, so it is important for designers to understand the layout, navigation and organisation of content to enhance its usability.
- Users' perception of complexity affects their ability to navigate interfaces. Designers can enhance comprehension and efficiency by minimising cognitive load through clear hierarchy, intuitive navigation and streamlined interactions.

Navigation design principles

Navigation design principles, including hierarchy, menu selection and recognition versus recall, can impact UX/UI design and dictate how users interact with digital interfaces, influencing usability, comprehension and overall user satisfaction.

Hierarchy

In UX/UI design, hierarchy is an essential principle that is used to logically group and organise information and features in a way that prioritises importance and improves user navigation.

Hierarchy can affect UX/UI design because:

- A clear hierarchy ensures that users can easily prioritise and locate information or features within the interface.
- Visual content such as size, colour, typography and placement can be used to establish hierarchy and emphasise important elements.
- Designers can streamline navigation and reduce cognitive load to enhance the overall user experience.

Menu selection

Menu selection involves the presentation and interaction of navigation menus within the interface. Users rely on menus to access different sections or functionalities of the application or website. Menu selection can impact UX/UI design because:

- Designers must ensure that navigation menus are intuitive and easy to use, allowing users to find what they are looking for quickly and efficiently.
- Considerations such as menu labels, placement and responsiveness are essential for providing a seamless navigation experience across different devices and screen sizes.
- Dropdown menus, **hamburger menus**, tabbed navigation and other menu styles should be carefully chosen based on the content and user needs to optimise navigation usability.

Recognition vs recall

Recognition involves users' ability to identify or recognise options when presented with them, while recall requires users to remember options from memory without visual cues. This can affect UX/UI design because:

- Designers should prioritise recognition over recall by presenting navigation options in a clear, visually prominent manner.
- Using familiar icons, symbols and labels helps users recognise navigation elements more quickly and reduces the cognitive load associated with recall.
- Consistent design patterns and placement of navigation elements across different pages or screens aid in recognition and reduce the need to recall.

Learning in context 4

Menu selection design in the Amazon Store mobile app

The **hamburger menu**, typically represented by three horizontal lines stacked on top of each other, is commonly used in the Amazon store app for secondary navigation options and settings.

Navigation links are commonly used in the Amazon store app to provide users with access to additional options or categories within a specific section of the app. For example, time-limited deals.

Black Friday Deals Week
Shop new deals daily
amazon
Sign in

Tabbed navigation is often employed in the Amazon store app to allow users to switch between different sections or views within the app quickly.

Figure 3.5: The menu selection style of the Amazon Store mobile app is a fundamental aspect of its user interface, dictating how users navigate and access various features and functionalities within the app

Schneiderman's 8 Golden Rules of interface design

Schneiderman's 8 Golden Rules of interface design, proposed by Ben Schneiderman, a pioneer in the field of human computer interaction, provide essential principles and valuable guidelines for creating effective, intuitive, efficient, user-friendly interfaces that are enjoyable for users to interact with. These rules are widely recognised and applied in UX/UI design. They provide designers with guidelines to ensure that interfaces meet users' needs and expectations and enhance usability and user satisfaction and experience.

Table 3.2: How Schneiderman's 8 Golden Rules of interface design impacts UX/UI design

Rule	Impact on UX/UI design
Consistency	Consistency in design elements, terminology and interactions helps users predict how the interface will behave and reduces cognitive load. UX/UI designers would be consistent in their use of design patterns, navigation structures and visual styles throughout the interface.
Enable shortcuts	Providing shortcuts allows experienced users to perform tasks more quickly and efficiently. UX/UI designers would include keyboard shortcuts and gesture-based interactions.
Include informative feedback	Providing timely and relevant feedback informs users about the outcome of their actions and helps them understand the system's state. UX/UI designers could use visual cues, progress indicators or error messages to provide feedback.
Dialogue yields closure	Dialogs and confirmation messages should provide clear and concise information to users, allowing them to make informed decisions and proceed with confidence. UX/UI designers design dialogs with clear titles, descriptive messages and intuitive button labels to minimise user confusion.
Simple error handling	Error messages and recovery methods should be designed to help users understand and recover from errors easily. UX/UI designers use informative error messages and suggestive prompts to guide users towards resolving errors and preventing future mistakes.
Easy reversal of actions	Users should be able to undo or redo actions easily to recover from mistakes or explore alternative paths. UX/UI designers would include undo/redo functionalities, clear navigation paths and confirmation dialogs to provide users with control over their actions and reduce anxiety about making irreversible changes.
Support internal locus of control	Users should feel a sense of control over the interface and their interactions with it. UX/UI designers design interfaces with intuitive navigation structures and customisable settings to empower users.
Reduce short-term memory load	Minimising cognitive load by presenting information in a clear, organised and easily accessible manner improves the users understanding and retention. UX/UI designers prioritise content hierarchy, minimise distractions and provide contextual cues to help users focus on relevant information and tasks.

Interface layout design principles

Above and below the fold

Above-the-fold and below-the-fold layout design principles determine how content is positioned on a screen and aims to optimise user engagement and usability based on initial visibility and scrolling interactions.

Above the fold: content placed above the fold is immediately visible to users without the need for scrolling because it captures users' attention right away. This can impact UX/UI design because:

- Designers must prioritise important content, such as key messages, calls-to-action and primary navigation elements, to be placed above the fold. This ensures that users can quickly access essential information without effort.
- Above-the-fold content should effectively communicate the purpose of the interface and

entice users to explore further, encouraging engagement and interaction.

- Designers should avoid cluttering the above-the-fold area with excessive content or distractions, as it can overwhelm users.

Below the fold: content placed below the fold requires users to scroll down to access it. This area provides additional space for presenting more detailed or secondary content. This can affect UX/UI design because:

- Designers should plan the layout of below-the-fold content to maintain user interest and encourage continued scrolling. Content should be organised logically, with clear visual hierarchy and meaningful grouping.
- Below-the-fold content can provide supplementary information, product details, additional navigation options or related content to support users' needs and enhance their browsing experience.
- Designers should ensure that below-the-fold content is visually engaging and relevant to users' interests, encouraging them to explore further and spend more time interacting with the interface.

Learning in context 5

Simply Teach

Simply Teach is an educational platform designed for teachers to collect resources that support teaching and learning.

The Key Stage 4 section can be considered below-the-fold, as users can explore additional content by selecting one of the sub-menu options that weren't initially visible.

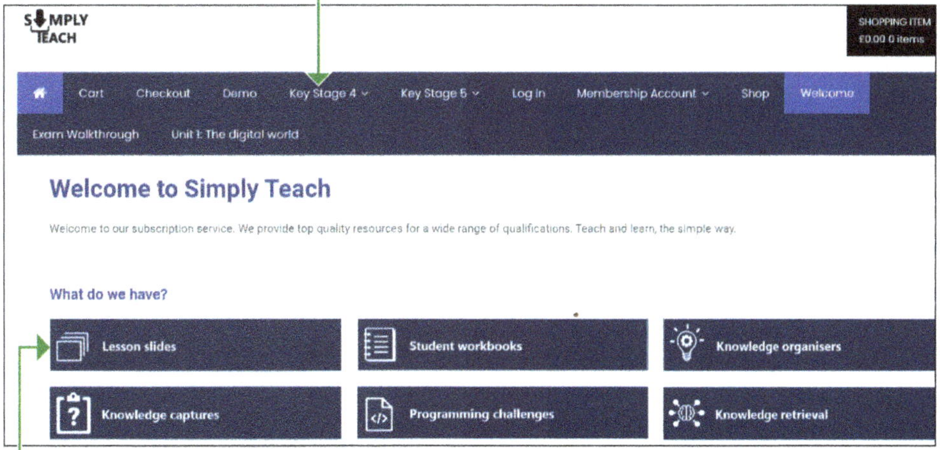
SIMPLY TEACH
SHOPPING ITEM
£0.00 0 items
Cart
Checkout
Demo
Key Stage 4
Key Stage 5
Log In
Membership Account
Shop
Welcome
Exam Walkthrough
Unit 1: The digital world
Welcome to Simply Teach
Welcome to our subscription service. We provide top quality resources for a wide range of qualifications. Teach and learn, the simple way.
What do we have?
Lesson slides
Student workbooks
Knowledge organisers
Knowledge captures
Programming challenges
Knowledge retrieval

The tiles above the fold are instantly visible and provide users with quick access to different pages within the website. This section aims to capture the user's attention and provide essential information and navigation options without requiring any scrolling.

Figure 3.6: Immediately visible content on a webpage is above the fold

Learning in context **Continued**

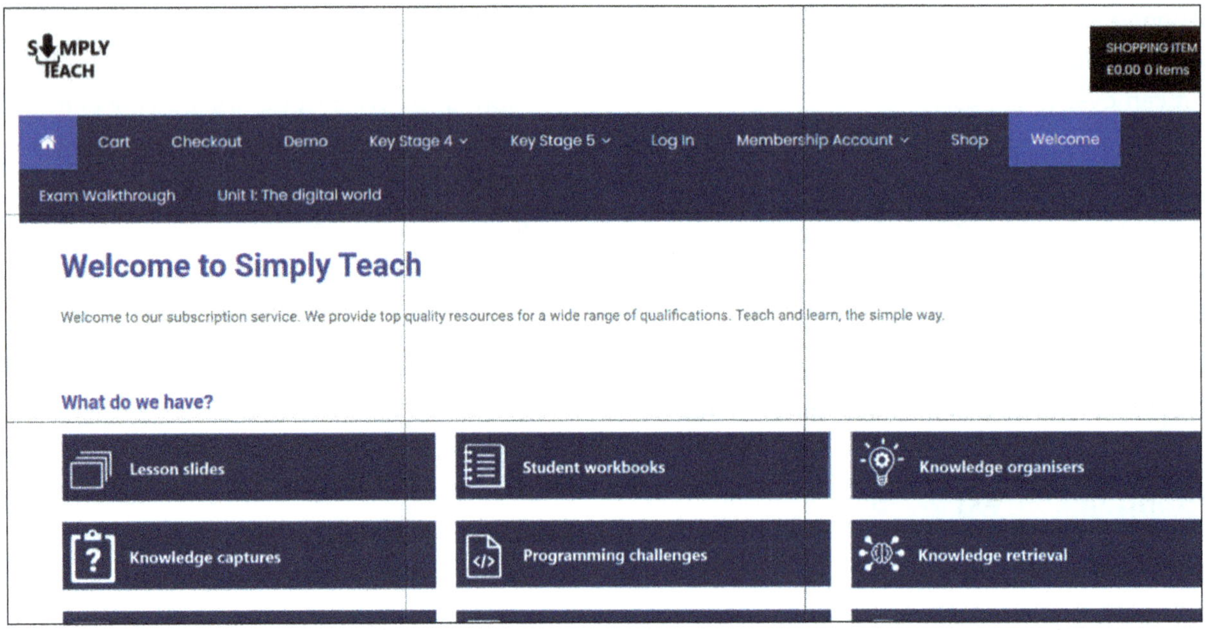
SIMPLY TEACH
SHOPPING ITEM
£0.00 0 items
Cart
Checkout
Demo
Key Stage 4
Key Stage 5
Log in
Membership Account
Shop
Welcome
Exam Walkthrough
Unit 1: The digital world
Welcome to Simply Teach
Welcome to our subscription service. We provide top quality resources for a wide range of qualifications. Teach and learn, the simple way.
What do we have?
Lesson slides
Student workbooks
Knowledge organisers
Knowledge captures
Programming challenges
Knowledge retrieval

Figure 3.7: A web page can be divided into thirds horizontally and vertically to help balance layout

Colour theory

Colour theory plays a significant role in UX/UI design as it influences user perception, emotions and behaviour. The choice of colours can convey brand identity, evoke certain moods and assist in visual hierarchy. For example, using contrasting colours for important elements such as buttons or **call-to-action** prompts helps them stand out, guiding user interaction, improving readability and navigation with the interface.

Information visualisation

In UX/UI design, Information visualisation involves representing complex data or information in a visual format that is easy to understand and interpret. Using charts, graphs, diagrams and infographics can help users grasp large data collections or complex concepts at a glance. For example, in a finance app, interactive charts can enhance usability by helping users understand their spending habits and allows them to track their expenses more efficiently.

Principle of thirds

The principle of thirds is a compositional guideline used in design and photography, dividing an image or layout into nine equal parts using two equally spaced horizontal and vertical lines. In UX/UI design, applying the principle of thirds helps create balanced and visually appealing layouts. For example, in a website layout, positioning the logo or main navigation menu at one of the intersection points can create a visually pleasing composition that guides user attention effectively.

Typography

In UX/UI design, typography significantly influences readability, hierarchy and the overall visual appearance. Choosing appropriate fonts, sizes and spacing ensures text content is legible across various devices and screen sizes. For example, in a mobile app, using a larger and bolder font for headings and a smaller, lighter font for body text helps users quickly scan and understand content, enhancing the usability of the interface.

Quick check 3

1 How do the following rules of Schneiderman's interface design influence UX/UI design, and can you provide examples illustrating their impact?
   - strive for consistency
   - enable frequent users to use shortcuts
   - offer informative feedback
   - design dialogue yields closure.

2 How does recognition versus recall as a design principle impact the UX/UI design of a mobile banking application?

1.4 UX/UI design psychology

Understanding the principles of psychology plays a significant role in creating intuitive, user-friendly interfaces that effectively meet the needs and expectations of users. Designers will consider three key psychological principles: Cognitive load, Hicks Law and the Law of Proximity to gain a better understanding of how users perceive, process and interact with digital interfaces.

Cognitive load

Cognitive load refers to the mental effort required to process information and perform tasks. In UX/UI design, understanding cognitive load and designing interfaces to minimise it is crucial for creating user-friendly experiences.

Features and characteristics of cognitive load

- **Intrinsic** load: this is the inherent complexity of the task or information being presented. UX/UI designers aim to reduce intrinsic load by simplifying tasks, breaking information into manageable chunks and presenting it in a clear and organised manner.
- **Extrinsic** load: this refers to unnecessary cognitive load imposed by the design itself, such as confusing layouts, cluttered interfaces or irrelevant information. UX/UI designers strive to minimise **extraneous** load by removing distractions, maintaining visual hierarchy and providing clear and concise instructions.
- Germane load: refers to the mental effort required for learning, understanding and problem-solving. It is associated with the process of acquiring and integrating new knowledge or skills.

Importance to UX/UI design

- Usability: minimising cognitive load is essential for creating usable interfaces that are intuitive and easy to learn and use. High cognitive load can lead to user frustration, errors and abandonment of the interface.
- Learning curve: interfaces with high cognitive load can have steep learning curves, deterring new users from engaging with the product. Designing interfaces with low cognitive load reduces the learning curve.
- Accessibility: high cognitive load can present barriers to users with cognitive impairments or disabilities. Designing interfaces with low cognitive load improves accessibility and inclusivity for all users.

Impact on UX/UI design

- Simplicity and clarity: UX/UI designers will simplify interfaces and present information clearly to reduce cognitive load. This involves minimising unnecessary complexity, clutter and visual distractions.
- Consistency and familiarity: consistent design patterns and familiar interface elements reduce cognitive load. Users should be able to predict how to interact with the interface based on past experiences.

- Progressive disclosure: progressive disclosure techniques, such as hiding advanced options until needed, help manage cognitive load by presenting information gradually and reduces the risk of the user becoming overwhelmed by the amount or complexity of information presented to them.

Hick's Law

Hick's Law states that the time it takes for an individual to make a decision will increase with the number of choices available.

Importance to UX/UI design:

- Simplicity and clarity: Hick's Law outlines the importance of simplicity and clarity in interface design. By minimising the number of choices presented to users, designers can streamline decision-making processes and enhance usability.
- Reduced cognitive load: interfaces with fewer choices help reduce cognitive load on users, making it easier for them to navigate and interact with the interface.
- Focused user attention: designing interfaces with fewer choices helps focus user attention on the most relevant options or actions, guiding users towards desired outcomes.

Impact on UX/UI design

- Simplified navigation: designers apply Hick's Law by simplifying navigation structures and minimising the number of options presented to users at any given time.
- Prioritisation of content: designers prioritise content and features based on user needs and goals, ensuring that the most important choices are prominent and easily accessible while less critical options are hidden.

Law of proximity

The law of proximity states that objects that are close to each other tend to be perceived as a group. Importance to UX/UI design:

- Visual hierarchy: the law of proximity is crucial for establishing visual hierarchy within interfaces. By grouping related elements together and spacing them apart from unrelated ones, designers can guide users' attention and prioritise content effectively.
- Clarity and organisation: proximity helps create visual order and organisation within interfaces, reducing cognitive load and making it easier for users to navigate and understand the content.
- Consistency and familiarity: consistent application of proximity principles allow users to predict how elements are organised and behave based on past experiences.

Impact on UX/UI design

- By placing related elements closer together, designers can create visual groupings that help users understand the relationship between different parts of the interface. For example, buttons, icons or text fields that are grouped together are perceived as being related and serving a similar purpose.
- The law of proximity helps establish a visual hierarchy within the interface by indicating which elements are more closely related or more important than others. Elements that are closer together are perceived as being more closely related and therefore are given more visual importance.
- When elements are properly grouped based on their proximity, users are less likely to be confused or make errors when interacting with the interface. Clear visual groupings help users understand the structure of the interface and how different elements are organised.

Other examples of UX/UI design psychology

The 'Von Restorff Effect' is a principle that predicts that an item that stands out from its surroundings is more likely to be remembered. In UX/UI design, using the Von Restorff effect can help designers draw attention to important elements within an interface, such as call-to-action buttons or critical messages.

The 'Serial Position Effect' describes how people tend to remember items presented at the beginning and the end of a list better than those in the middle. In UX/UI design, understanding the serial position effect can help designers optimise the presentation of content and information to enhance user recall and comprehension.

Learning in context 6

Netflix

The Netflix website serves as a platform for streaming a wide variety of movies, TV shows, documentaries and original content.

Search and filtering: To help users narrow down their choices more efficiently, the website allows users to quickly find specific shows to watch.

Visual cues and feedback: Design elements such as clear labels, icons, and visual indicators help users understand their options and navigate the menu more easily. For example, notifications.

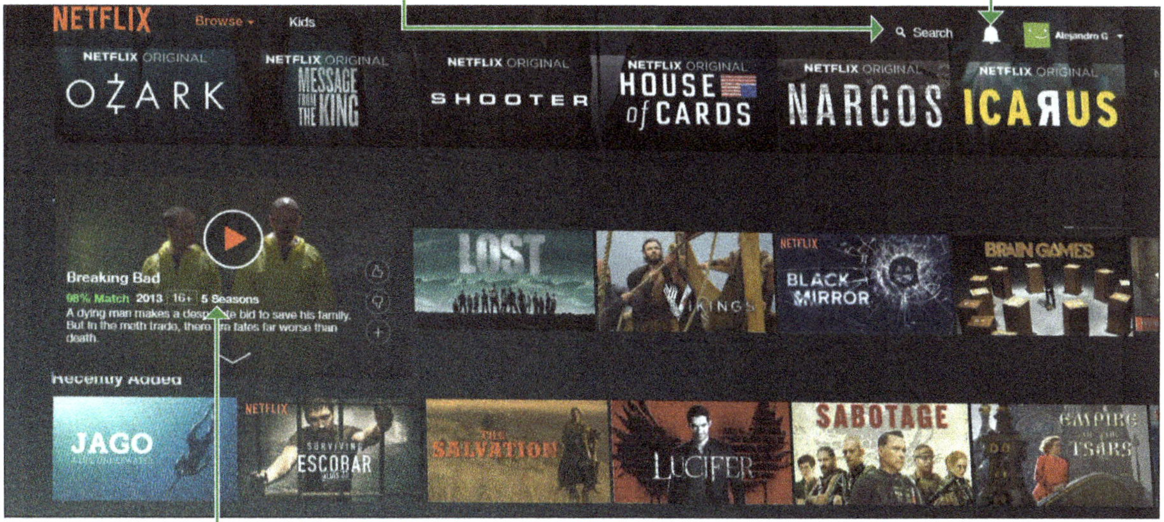
NETFLIX
Browse
Kids
Search
NETFLIX ORIGINAL
OZARK
MESSAGE FROM THE KING
SHOOTER
HOUSE of CARDS
NARCOS
ICARUS
Breaking Bad
98% Match 2013 16+ 5 Seasons
LOST
VIKINGS
BLACK MIRROR
BRAIN GAMES
Recently Added
JAGO
SURVIVING ESCOBAR
THE SALVATION
LUCIFER
SABOTAGE
EMPIRE OF THE TSARS

Progressive disclosure: Within each category, the menu items could be further organised hierarchically, with only a few options initially visible.

Figure 3.8: The layout and design of Netflix helps users find content

Quick check 4

1 How do UX/UI designers address the different types of cognitive load, particularly intrinsic and extrinsic, to optimise user experience?

2 How can UX/UI design principles such as simplicity, clarity, reducing cognitive load and focused user attention be applied to enhance the user experience on the Steam gaming platform?

1.5 UX/UI experience

1.5.1 Factors that impact UX

In UX design, success can depend on a wide range of factors that collectively shape the usability, appeal and effectiveness of digital products and services. Each factor plays a pivotal role in influencing user perception, satisfaction and, ultimately, the success of a design.

Table 3.3: How each factor can impact UX design

Factor	Description	Impact on UX/UI design
Accessible	The design of products or services that can be used by people with disabilities, including visual, auditory, motor or cognitive impairments.	Use of colour contrast, keyboard navigation, screen reader compatibility and alternative text for images to ensure that all users can access and interact with the interface effectively.
Creditable	The perceived trustworthiness, reliability and expertise of a product or service. A credible design encourages users to engage with the product or service.	Use clear and accurate information, providing evidence to support claims, including testimonials or user reviews and maintaining a professional and consistent visual design.
Desirable	The emotional appeal and attractiveness of a product or service. A desirable design engages users and makes them want to interact with the product or service.	Incorporate visually appealing aesthetics, engaging interactions and intuitive design elements that resonate with users' preferences.
Findable	The ease with which users can locate information or features within a product or service. A findable design ensures that users can quickly and intuitively find what they're looking for without frustration or confusion.	Organise content logically, using clear navigation structures, providing search functionality and employing consistent labelling and terminology.
Usable	The ease of use and efficiency with which users can accomplish tasks within a product or service. A usable design minimises friction and cognitive load, allowing users to complete tasks effectively and without errors.	Design intuitive interfaces, minimising cognitive load, streamlining workflows and conducting user testing to identify and address usability issues.
Useful	The extent to which a product or service fulfils the needs and goals of users. A useful design provides value to users, addressing their pain points and solving their problems effectively.	Focus on solving user problems, prioritising essential features and arranging design decisions with user requirements and objectives.
Valuable	The perceived benefit or worth that users get from using a product or service. A valuable design delivers tangible benefits and outcomes to users, such as saving time, saving money or improving productivity.	Deliver meaningful experiences that meet users' needs, exceed their expectations and align with their goals and priorities.

1.5.2 Features of UI

Types of UI

In UI design, the interface through which users interact with digital products plays a critical role in shaping their overall experience. UI design encompasses different approaches and styles, each tailored to meet the needs and preferences of users across various platforms and devices.

Command Line Interface (CLI)

A CLI allows users to interact with a computer system by entering commands as text. Users type commands into a terminal or command prompt, and the system executes them accordingly.

Table 3.4: Advantages and disadvantages of CLI

Advantages	Disadvantages
• CLI applications require fewer system resources compared to graphical interfaces. • CLI provides access to a wide range of system commands and utilities.	• Difficult to use as there is a requirement to memorise the commands. • Novice users may find it challenging to navigate and understand without prior experience or technical knowledge.

Form-based user interface

A form-based UI presents users with a series of input fields or controls arranged in a structured format. Users input data into the form fields, such as textboxes, dropdown menus, checkboxes or radio buttons.

Table 3.5: Advantages and disadvantages of forms-based user interfaces

Advantages	Disadvantages
• Provides a standardised method for collecting user input, making it easier for users to understand and complete. • Input validation and error feedback in forms help prevent common input errors.	• Complex forms with numerous input fields or options may become cluttered and overwhelming for users, leading to cognitive overload and decreased usability. • Form-based interfaces rely heavily on user input for data entry, which can be time-consuming and error-prone.

Graphical User Interface (GUI)

A GUI uses graphical elements, such as windows, icons, buttons and menus, to facilitate user interaction. Users interact with the interface by clicking, dragging and dropping visual elements using a mouse or touchpad.

Table 3.6: Advantages and disadvantages of a GUI

Advantages	Disadvantages
• GUIs are designed to be intuitive and user-friendly, making them accessible to users of all skill levels. • GUIs use visual cues to represent digital content and functionality, making it easier for users to understand and navigate complex interfaces.	• GUIs can be resource-intensive in terms of memory and processing power, particularly when rendering complex graphical elements or animations. • GUIs with excessive visual elements or cluttered layouts can overwhelm users and detract from usability, particularly on small screens or low-resolution displays.

Menu-driven user interface

A menu-driven UI presents users with a hierarchical menu structure containing options and commands. Users navigate through the menus using arrow keys, mouse clicks or touch gestures to select desired actions.

Table 3.7: Advantages and disadvantages of a menu driven interface

Advantages	Disadvantages
• Menu-driven interfaces are designed to be intuitive and user-friendly, requiring minimal training or technical expertise to navigate and use effectively. • Menu-driven interfaces provide a structured approach to navigation, with options organised into logical categories and hierarchies, reducing cognitive load and decision-making effort for users.	• Users must navigate through multiple menus and submenus to access desired options or functionalities, which can be time-consuming for tasks requiring frequent navigation. • Experienced users may find menu-driven interfaces inefficient for performing tasks quickly, especially for repetitive or advanced tasks that require frequent navigation or complex input.

Natural language user interface

A natural language UI allows users to interact with a system using natural language commands or queries. Users input text or voice commands in natural language, and the system interprets and processes the input to perform actions or provide responses.

Table 3.8: Advantages and disadvantages of a natural language interface

Advantages	Disadvantages
• Accessible to users with disabilities, including those with visual or motor impairments, as they support spoken and written communication. • Allowing users to communicate tasks and queries using natural language, potentially reducing the cognitive load.	• They can lack feedback mechanisms to confirm user intent or provide guidance on how to correct errors or misunderstandings. • It raises privacy and security concerns related to the collection and processing of user data.

Touch user interface

A touch UI enables users to interact with a device by touching the screen directly with their fingers or a stylus. Users perform gestures, such as tapping, swiping, pinching and rotating, to navigate through content, manipulate objects and input commands.

Table 3.9: Advantages and disadvantages of a touch user interface

Advantages	Disadvantages
• Using familiar touch gestures that require minimal training or technical expertise to use effectively. • Provides direct access to on-screen elements and actions, potentially reducing the cognitive load.	• The 'fat finger problem,' where users accidentally tap or interact with unintended on-screen elements due to the imprecision of touch input. • Limited input precision compared to traditional input methods such as mouse and keyboard.

Voice User Interface (VUI)

A VUI allows users to interact with a system using voice commands or speech recognition technology. Users speak commands or queries aloud, and the system interprets and processes the speech input to perform actions or provide responses.

Table 3.10: Advantages and disadvantages of a VUI

Advantages	Disadvantages
• Offer hands-free interaction for users, allowing them to communicate with digital systems using voice commands without the need for manual input devices. • Accessible to users with disabilities, including those with visual or motor impairments.	• A risk of a misinterpretation of user speech, particularly for complex queries, leading to errors or misunderstandings in system responses. • Reliance on language models and natural language processing **algorithms** to interpret user speech, which may be limited by the quality and coverage of available language data and algorithms.

The reasons why a user might select one type of UI over another can vary. For example, a software developer needs to automate a series of repetitive tasks involving file manipulation and text processing for large amounts of data.

- The developer is confident in using command-line tools and scripting languages, so they can perform tasks more quickly and efficiently using a CLI compared to navigating through a GUI.
- With a CLI, the developer can easily create and execute scripts to automate complex tasks without the need for manual intervention.
- The CLI provides greater flexibility and control over the execution of commands, allowing the developer to customise workflows.
- The developer may be working with large data or running resource-intensive operations, and using a CLI allows them to optimise resource usage and monitor system performance more closely compared to a GUI.

Learning in context 7

Smart TVs

Smart TVs integrate various interfaces to provide users with a versatile viewing experience.

Graphical User Interface (GUI):

- When you turn on a smart TV, you're greeted with a graphical user interface displayed on the screen. This interface typically consists of a home screen or dashboard featuring app icons, menus and widgets arranged in a grid or list format.
- Each app available on a smart TV, such as Netflix, YouTube or Hulu, has its own graphical interface designed for navigating content, selecting options and controlling playback. These interfaces often feature thumbnail images, text descriptions and navigation menus for browsing through available content.

Voice User Interface (VUI):

- Smart TVs equipped with voice recognition technology enable users to control the TV, search for content and access features using voice commands. Users can activate the voice interface by pressing a dedicated button on the remote control or by using wake words, such as 'Hey, TV' or 'OK, Google.'
- Once activated, users can speak commands or queries and the TV's voice assistant, such as Google Assistant or Amazon Alexa, processes the voice input and responds accordingly. This interface provides a convenient hands-free way to interact with the TV, especially when the remote control is out of reach.

Interaction types

Function keys

Users interact with function keys by pressing the corresponding key on the keyboard to invoke the assigned function or command. Function keys are often used in combination with other keys, such as modifier keys (for example, Ctrl, Alt) or other function keys, to execute keyboard shortcuts or perform specific actions.

Use

Function keys are commonly used in computer applications to provide quick access to specific functions or commands. They serve as keyboard shortcuts for tasks such as saving files (F2), opening help menus (F1) or refreshing a webpage (F5).

Features

- Function keys are typically located at the top row of computer keyboards and labelled F1 to F12.
- Function keys often require modifier keys (for example, Ctrl, Alt) to execute specific commands or functions.

Characteristics

- Function keys provide efficient and convenient access to commonly used commands, improving user productivity.
- They are versatile and can be adapted to different software applications or user preferences.
- Function keys offer a keyboard-focussed interaction method suitable for users who prefer keyboard shortcuts over mouse-based interactions.

Table 3.11: Advantages and disadvantages of function keys

Advantages	Disadvantages
• Function keys provide quick access to commonly used commands or functions, allowing users to perform tasks efficiently without navigating through menus or using mouse input. • Function keys enable keyboard-only operation, allowing users to perform tasks without the need for mouse input or on-screen navigation.	• Function key assignments can vary between software applications and operating systems, leading to inconsistency in usage and requiring users to learn and remember different key assignments. • Function keys can be activated accidentally, especially if users are not careful with their keyboard input or if they inadvertently press the wrong key, leading to unintended actions or disruptions.

Gestures

Users interact with gestures by performing specific physical movements or gestures in front of a compatible input device or sensor, such as a touchscreen, motion sensor or camera-based input system.

Use

Gesture interaction allows users to control devices or applications using physical gestures or movements. It is commonly used in touchscreen devices, Virtual Reality (VR), Augmented Reality (AR) and gaming systems.

Features

- Gesture recognition technology detects and interprets users' gestures, such as tapping, swiping, pinching or waving.
- Users can interact with digital content by performing gestures on touchscreens, touchpads or motion sensors.
- Gesture interfaces may support a variety of gestures to trigger actions, navigate through content or manipulate objects.

Characteristics

- Gesture interaction provides a tangible and intuitive interaction experience, allowing users to interact with digital content in a manner similar to physical objects.

- It offers a high degree of interactivity which enhances user engagement and enjoyment.
- Gesture interfaces require precise detection and interpretation of user gestures to ensure accurate and responsive interactions.

Table 3.12: Advantages and disadvantages of gestures

Advantages	Disadvantages
• Gestures offer intuitive interaction for users, using familiar physical movements that require minimal training or technical expertise to use effectively. • Gestures enable hands-free operation of digital devices or interfaces, allowing users to interact with devices without the need for physical input devices such as keyboards or mice.	• Prolonged use of gestures may lead to physical fatigue or discomfort, particularly for repetitive or complex gestures that require sustained or precise movements, which can affect user experience. • Gestures rely on hardware components such as touchscreens, motion sensors or camera-based input systems, which may be prone to wear and tear over time or susceptible to environmental factors such as moisture or dust.

Voice

Users interact with voice input by speaking commands, queries or prompts to a voice-enabled device or interface, such as a smartphone, smart speaker or virtual assistant. The system then analyses the spoken input using speech recognition algorithms, converting it into text and interpreting the user's intent or request.

Use

Voice interaction allows users to interact with devices or applications using spoken commands or queries. It is commonly used in virtual assistants (for example, Siri, Alexa), automotive systems and smart home devices.

Features

- Voice interaction uses speech recognition technology to interpret and process the user's spoken input.
- Users can perform tasks such as making calls, sending messages, setting reminders or controlling smart devices using voice commands.
- Voice interfaces may incorporate natural language processing to understand and respond to user queries in a conversational manner.

Characteristics

- Voice interaction offers hands-free operation and accessibility, enabling users to interact with devices without using their hands or vision. It provides a natural and intuitive interaction experience, resembling human-tohuman communication.
- Voice interfaces require accurate speech recognition and strong natural language understanding to deliver effective and satisfying user experiences to ensure accurate and responsive interactions.

Table 3.13: Advantages and disadvantages of voice input

Advantages	Disadvantages
• Voice input offers natural and intuitive interaction for users, using familiar spoken language communication methods that require minimal training or technical expertise to use effectively. • Voice input can be accessible to users with disabilities, including those with visual or motor impairments.	• Voice input may be at risk of misinterpretation, particularly for complex queries, leading to errors or misunderstandings in system responses. • Voice input may raise privacy concerns related to the collection and processing of user speech data, including concerns about data security, unauthorised access and potential misuse of sensitive information.

WIMP (Windows, Icons, Menus and Pointers)

Use

WIMP is a Graphical User Interface (GUI) model commonly used in desktop operating systems, productivity software and web applications.

Features

- WIMP interfaces consist of windows, icons, menus and a pointing device (for example, mouse or touchpad).
- Windows provide visual representations of applications or documents and can be resized, moved or overlapped on the screen.
- Icons serve as visual shortcuts for accessing files, folders or applications.
- Menus offer hierarchical lists of commands or options that users can select using a pointing device.

Characteristics

- WIMP interfaces provide a familiar and intuitive interaction experience, mirroring the layout and functionality of a traditional physical desktop, but in a digital environment with virtual objects and controls.
- They provide visual feedback and functions that help users understand how to interact with graphical elements and navigate through content.

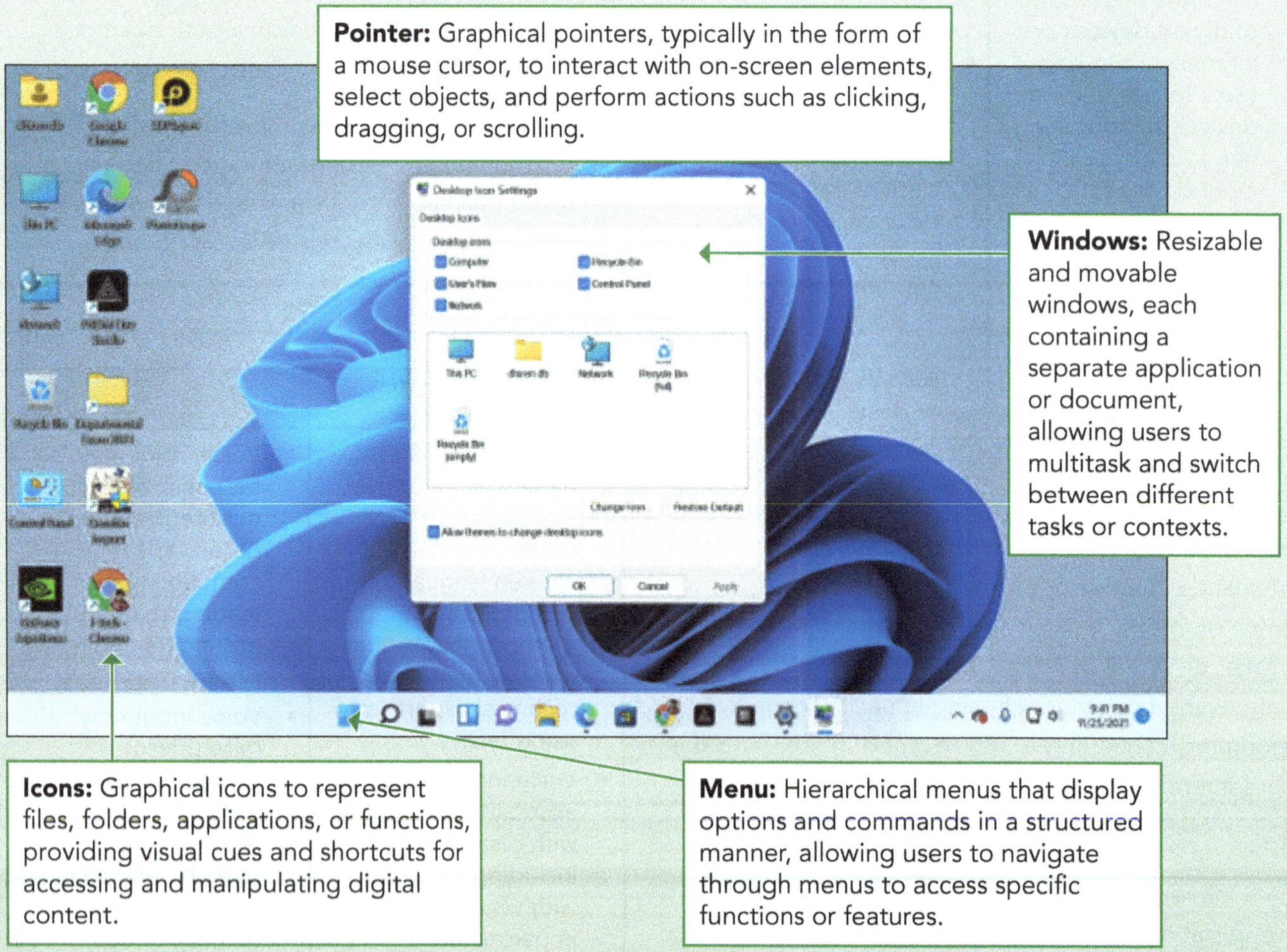
Pointer: Graphical pointers, typically in the form of a mouse cursor, to interact with on-screen elements, select objects, and perform actions such as clicking, dragging, or scrolling.
Windows: Resizable and movable windows, each containing a separate application or document, allowing users to multitask and switch between different tasks or contexts.
Icons: Graphical icons to represent files, folders, applications, or functions, providing visual cues and shortcuts for accessing and manipulating digital content.
Menu: Hierarchical menus that display options and commands in a structured manner, allowing users to navigate through menus to access specific functions or features.

Figure 3.9: Users interact with WIMP interfaces using a combination of mouse input, keyboard shortcuts and gestures

- WIMP interfaces are versatile and flexible, supporting various tasks and workflows in desktop and web-based environments.

Table 3.14: Advantages and disadvantages of WIMP

Advantages	Disadvantages
• Familiar to most users, as they have become the standard interface for desktop and laptop computers. • WIMP interfaces support multi-tasking, allowing users to work with multiple windows and applications simultaneously, switching between tasks or contexts with ease.	• WIMP interfaces rely heavily on mouse input for interaction, which may not be suitable for users with mobility impairments or those who prefer alternative input methods such as touch or keyboard shortcuts. • Can become cluttered and visually overwhelming, especially when working with multiple windows or a large number of icons, menus and shortcuts, potentially leading to reduced productivity and user frustration.

Quick check 5

1 What are the primary differences between a Graphical User Interface (GUI) and a Command Line Interface (CLI)?

2 How does a Voice User Interface (VUI) differ from a Touch-based User Interface (TUI)?

1.6 UX/UI interface design standardisation

Interface standards

Standardisation in UX/UI interface design refers to the establishment of consistent principles, patterns and guidelines to ensure that digital interfaces are user-friendly, accessible and consistent across different platforms and devices. It involves defining best practices, design patterns and specifications that simplify the design process, enhance usability and maintain brand identity.

Common user interface layouts, icons and labels throughout the application

Interface standards refers to the consistent design elements and patterns employed across different screens and sections of a digital interface. These include:

- Layouts: the arrangement of visual elements such as buttons, menus, content areas and navigation bars within the interface. Consistent layouts ensure that users can easily navigate the application and find information intuitively, regardless of the screen they are on.
- Icons: graphic symbols used to represent actions, features or concepts within the interface. Icons serve as visual cues that help users quickly identify functionality and navigate the application. Consistent use of icons enhances usability and reduces cognitive load by providing users with familiar visual language.
- Labels: textual descriptors used to accompany icons or provide information about interface elements such as buttons, fields or menu items. Consistent labelling ensures clarity and comprehension, enabling users to understand the purpose and function of each element without confusion.
- Impact on UX/UI design: common user interface layouts provide consistency and familiarity for users across different screens and interactions within an application.
- They help users understand where to find specific features or content, reducing cognitive load and improving usability.
- Designing with common layouts also enables faster learning curves for new users and enhances overall user satisfaction.

- Consistent use of icons and labels throughout the application helps establish visual patterns and cues that users can quickly recognise and interpret.
- Icons and labels should be intuitive and aligned with user expectations, making it easier for users to understand their meaning and purpose.
- Proper use of icons and labels enhances navigation, communication and overall user engagement within the application.

Cross-platform standards

Cross-platform standards in interface design standardisation refer to guidelines, patterns and principles aimed at ensuring consistency and usability across multiple platforms, such as web, mobile and desktop applications. Some of their features and characteristics include:

- Consistency: consistent design elements and interactions across platforms enhance familiarity and usability for users who switch between devices or operating systems.
- Adaptability: cross-platform standards prioritise adaptability to accommodate the unique characteristics and constraints of each platform. For example, WhatsApp allows users can start a conversation on their smartphone and continue it on their desktop computer without any disruption.
- Responsive design: cross-platform standards promote responsive design practices to ensure that interfaces adapt to various screen sizes and resolutions with relative ease. Interfaces should be optimised for both small mobile screens and larger desktop displays, providing an optimal viewing and interaction experience on any device.

Impact on UX/UI design

- Cross-platform standards ensure consistency in design and functionality across different devices and platforms (for example, web, mobile, desktop).
- Following cross-platform standards improves user experience by providing a smooth transition for users switching between devices or platforms.
- Designing with cross-platform standards in mind allows for scalability and adaptability, catering to a wider range of users and devices.

Standard interface widgets

Standard interface widgets are pre-designed components or controls that are commonly used across various digital interfaces to facilitate interaction and enhance usability.

- Familiarity: standard interface widgets are familiar to users due to their widespread use across digital platforms. Examples include buttons, checkboxes, radio buttons, dropdown menus, sliders, input fields and icons.
- Accessibility: standard interface widgets are designed with accessibility in mind, ensuring that they are usable by people with diverse abilities. Widgets often comply with accessibility standards, such as providing alternative text for images, keyboard navigation support and sufficient colour contrast for readability, to ensure inclusivity.
- Responsiveness: standard interface widgets are designed to be responsive, meaning they adapt to different screen sizes and orientations. They scale appropriately and reflow content to ensure optimal display on various devices, including desktops, laptops, tablets and smartphones, enhancing user experience across platforms.

Designers use standard interface widgets to provide users with familiar and predictable interaction patterns. Consistent use of widgets aids users as they can apply their existing knowledge of how these components function across different applications.

15
TUESDAY
Buy a birthday gift
11:20
James' Birthday
18:00
Pick up my sister
20:30
2021
MARCH
SU MO TU WE TH FR SA
1 2 3 4 5
6 7 8 9 10 11 12
13 14 15 16 17 18 19
20 21 22 23 24 25 26
27 28 29 30 31

Figure 3.10: A calendar is a common widget

Impact on UX/UI design

- Standard interface widgets, such as buttons, checkboxes, sliders and dropdown menus, provide users with familiar interaction patterns that are easy to understand and use.
- Using standard interface widgets reduces the need for users to learn new interaction behaviours, leading to improved efficiency and satisfaction.
- Consistent use of standard interface widgets enhances accessibility and ensures compatibility with assistive technologies, benefiting users with disabilities.

Standard protocols

Standard protocols in interface design standardisation refer to established rules, guidelines and specifications that govern the communication and interaction between different components, systems or devices.

- Interoperability: standard protocols facilitate interoperability by enabling different systems, platforms or devices to communicate and exchange data seamlessly.
- Scalability: standard protocols support scalability by providing a framework for connecting multiple components or systems within a network.
- Security: standard protocols often include provisions for security measures such as authentication, encryption and data integrity verification to mitigate risks associated with unauthorised access, data breaches and malicious attacks.

Impact on UX/UI design

- Standard protocols define rules and guidelines for communication and interaction between different components or systems within an application.
- Adhering to standard protocols ensures compatibility with other software and services, enhancing the overall user experience.
- Compliance with standard protocols also facilitates integration with third-party APIs, enabling developers to leverage external resources and functionalities.

Learning in context 8

GitHub website

GitHub is a platform used by developers for hosting and reviewing code, managing projects and building software alongside millions of other developers. GitHub uses various standard interface widgets such as buttons, input fields, dropdown menus, checkboxes, radio buttons, tabs and more throughout its interface.

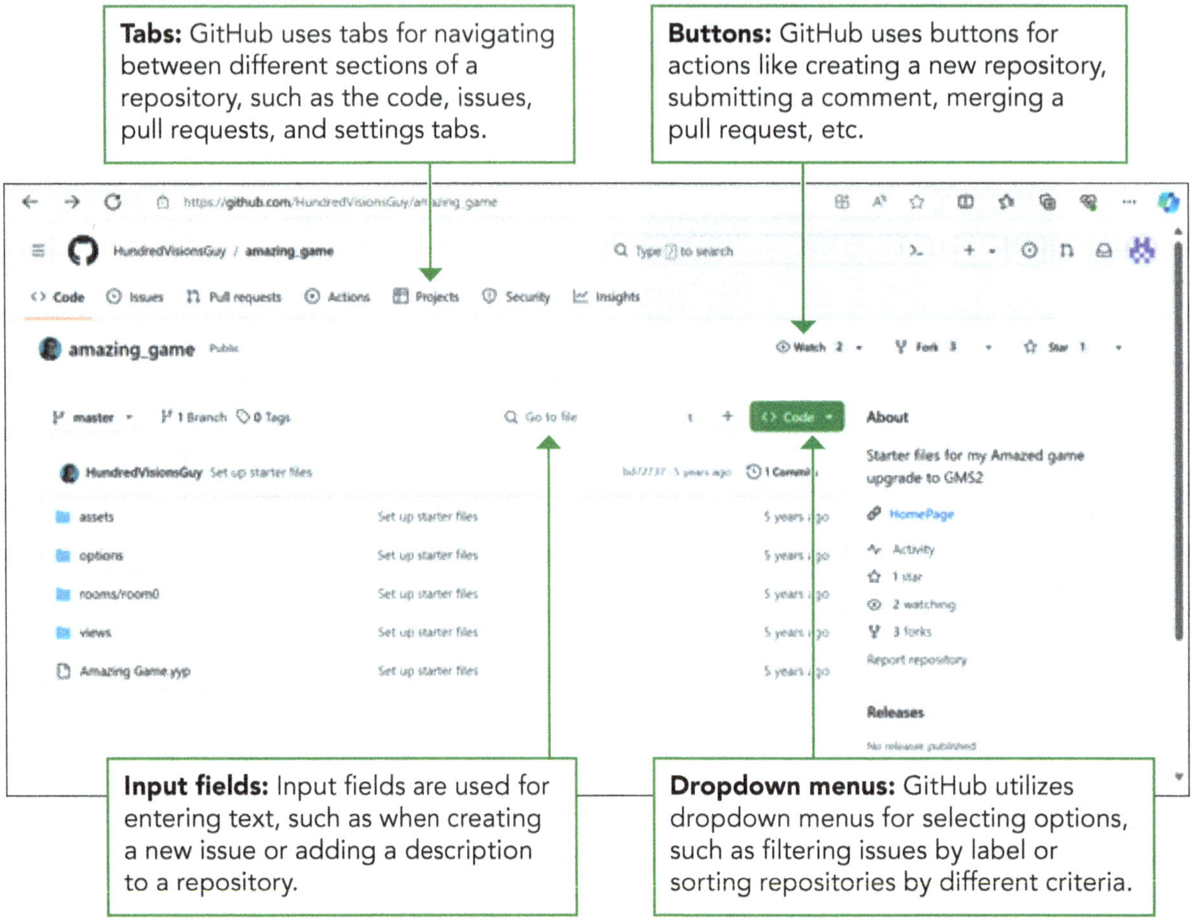
Tabs: GitHub uses tabs for navigating between different sections of a repository, such as the code, issues, pull requests, and settings tabs.
Buttons: GitHub uses buttons for actions like creating a new repository, submitting a comment, merging a pull request, etc.
Input fields: Input fields are used for entering text, such as when creating a new issue or adding a description to a repository.
Dropdown menus: GitHub utilizes dropdown menus for selecting options, such as filtering issues by label or sorting repositories by different criteria.

Figure 3.11: GitHub uses standard interface widgets

Quick check 6

1 Why is standardisation important in UX/UI interface design?

2 How do widgets impact UX/UI design?

TA2 Plan UX/UI solutions

Learning intentions

This topic is about how to Plan UX/UI solutions.

It covers:

2.1 Requirements of UX/UI solutions

2.2 Tools and techniques to document UX/UI ideas and design concepts

2.1 Requirements of UX/UI solutions

In the context of User Experience (UX) and User Interface (UI) design, the success of a digital product will depend on understanding and meeting the needs of its users. This process begins with identifying and documenting requirements, which serve as the foundation for creating intuitive, engaging and effective user experiences. Understanding the types of requirements, their sources and the tools used to document them is crucial for crafting solutions that meet the needs of the user and achieve business objectives.

Types of requirements

Client requirements

Client requirements refer to the specific needs, goals and expectations of the client or **stakeholders** responsible for the UX/UI project. These requirements include business objectives, target audience considerations, branding guidelines and any other preferences or **constraints** specified by the client. This can affect planning and design of UX/UI solutions because:

- Understanding these requirements ensures that the design solution contributes directly to achieving the client's strategic goals.
- Incorporating client requirements into the design process, UX/UI designers can create a tailored user experience that reflects the unique identity of the client's brand.
- It enables regular feedback from the client and allows for continuous improvements, ensuring that the final UX/UI solution meets or exceeds their expectations.
- Design decisions need to be made while considering any budget and time constraints to ensure that the final solution is realistic.

User requirements

User requirements are the specific needs, preferences and expectations of the end users of a product or system. These requirements are crucial for designing solutions that effectively address user needs and provide a satisfying experience. User requirements include aspects such as functionality, usability, accessibility and emotional satisfaction. This can affect planning and design of UX/UI solutions because:

- Understanding the needs and preferences of users, UX/UI designers can create interfaces that are intuitive, easy to use and align with user expectations.
- It helps in enhancing the usability of the product. For example, more intuitive navigation, clear information presentation and efficient task completion.
- By addressing user needs effectively, UX/UI solutions can provide users with a positive experience and, as a result, lead to higher user retention rates and positive **word-of-mouth** referrals.

Solution requirements

Solution requirements include different criteria such as: functional requirements, interface requirements and non-functional requirements.

Table 3.15: How solution requirements can impact the planning and design of UX/UI solutions

Criteria	Description	Examples	Impact on planning and design of UX/UI solutions
Functional requirements	Outline what the system should do and how users should interact with it to achieve their goals.	User authentication, search capabilities, data input forms, navigation menus and interactive elements such as buttons or sliders.	• Determine the layout, structure and functionality of the interface elements. • Define the logical flow of the interface to ensure users can navigate the system effectively.
Interface requirements	Specify the visual and interactive aspects of the UX/UI solution.	Layout, typography, colour scheme, visual hierarchy and interactive elements.	• Ensure consistency in the visual design across different screens and components of the interface. • Consider factors such as readability, contrast and accessibility standards to ensure that the interface is usable by all users, including those with disabilities.
Non-functional requirements	Specify the features of the UX/UI solution that are not directly related to its functional behaviour.	Performance, security, scalability, reliability and usability.	• Minimising loading times, optimising responsiveness and ensuring smooth interactions. • Apply security measures and safeguards to protect user data and ensure confidentiality.

Learning in context 9

Solution requirements for a mobile banking application

In the planning and design of a mobile banking application, various solution requirements significantly influence the design decisions made to ensure an effortless user experience.

Functional requirement: users should be able to transfer funds between accounts easily. This requirement guides the design of a simple and intuitive transfer feature within the app. Designers carry out a straightforward process with clear instructions and minimal steps to ensure that users could transfer funds quickly and securely.

Interface requirement: the interface should be accessible and easy to navigate for users with disabilities. Designers incorporate accessibility features such as screen reader compatibility, high contrast options and large clickable areas to accommodate users with visual impairments or motor disabilities. The interface design should prioritise clarity, simplicity and consistency to enhance usability for all users.

Non-functional requirement: the app should load quickly and perform reliably, even on slower network connections. Designers optimise the app's performance by minimising unnecessary animations and optimising image sizes. They would also conduct performance testing to ensure that the app remained responsive and functional under various network conditions, such as low bandwidth or **intermittent** connectivity.

Sources of UX/UI solution requirements

Sourcing and identifying UX/UI solution requirements involves the process of gathering, analysing and defining the specific needs, objectives, constraints and preferences that will guide the design and development of a User Experience (UX) and User Interface (UI) solution.

Table 3.16: How to source and identify UX/UI solution requirements

Source	Description	How does this source identify UX/UI solution requirements?
Client brief	Documents or communications provided by the client outlining their objectives, expectations, preferences and constraints for the UX/UI design project.	Includes information about the target audience, business goals, branding guidelines, technical requirements and any specific features or functionalities desired for the solution.
Current systems	Current systems refer to the existing products, interfaces or processes that the UX/UI solution aims to improve, replace or integrate with.	UX/UI designers can analyse the strengths, weaknesses and **pain points** of an existing solution, which helps to identify how it could be improved or used to create new solutions that address gaps and meet user needs.
Existing documents	Existing documents include any relevant documentation, such as design specifications, style guides, user manuals or technical documentation, associated with the project or related systems.	Reviewing existing documents helps designers gain a valuable insight into design requirements, branding guidelines, technical constraints and user expectations.
Users/User profiles	Users, or user profiles, represent the individuals who will interact with the UX/UI solution.	User research methods, such as interviews, surveys and observations, are used to gather insights into user demographics, behaviours, needs, preferences and pain points.

Decomposing UX/UI solution requirements into logical components involves breaking down complex requirements into smaller, more manageable parts or modules such as:

- Review the UX/UI solution requirements gathered from various sources such as user research, stakeholder input and existing documentation.
- Identify the key features, functionalities and interactions that the UX/UI solution needs to include to meet user needs and business goals. These could include tasks such as user authentication, data input forms, search functionality, navigation menus and interactive elements.
- Group related requirements together based on common themes, functionalities or user tasks. This helps in organising the requirements into logical categories and ensures that each component serves a specific purpose within the overall solution.

- Define the logical components or modules based on the grouped requirements. Each component should represent a set of features or functionalities that work together to fulfil a specific aspect of the user experience. For example, a 'User Profile' component may include features related to user authentication, profile management and account settings.
- Identify and establish relationships between the components to define how they interact with each other within the overall solution.
- Continuously refine and iterate on the decomposition process to gain a deeper understanding of the requirements and design implications. This could be done by collecting feedback from stakeholders and carrying out usability testing.
- Document the decomposed components and their relationships using diagrams, flowcharts or other visual aids to communicate the design structure effectively to stakeholders, developers and other project team members.

Identifying the required inputs and outputs when planning UX/UI solutions involves understanding the information and actions needed to create an effortless user experience. This could be achieved by:

- Understanding user intentions helping to determine the inputs required to aid their tasks and actions.
- Gathering insights through user research methods such as interviews, surveys and usability testing.
- Mapping out the sequence of steps users will take to complete their tasks within the UX/UI solution.
- Identifying any specific inputs or outputs stakeholders require to meet business goals or regulatory requirements.
- Analysing inputs and outputs from existing systems to identify any gaps or inefficiencies in the current process and determining how the new UX/UI solution can improve on them.
- Understanding the technical considerations such as data sources, **Application Programming Interfaces (APIs)**, integrations and system capabilities.
- Creating documentation or visual diagrams to clearly outline the identified inputs and outputs.

Tools to document UX/UI solution requirements

The components and **conventions** of tools used to document UX/UI solution requirements can vary depending on the specific tool and the preferences of the designers and stakeholders involved. However, here are some common components and conventions:

Requirements specification

A comprehensive document that outlines all the requirements for the UX/UI solution. This includes sections such as purpose/**scope**, business/client requirements, user requirements, functional requirements, interface requirements and non-functional requirements.

- **Purpose/scope**: clearly defines the objectives, goals and scope of the UX/UI solution, providing context for the requirements outlined in the document.
- **Business/client requirements**: describes the high-level business goals, objectives and constraints that the UX/UI solution needs to address. This may include information about target audience, market analysis, branding guidelines and business priorities.

- **User requirements**: specifies the needs, preferences, behaviours and goals of the target users. This section may include user stories, user scenarios or other user-centred design objects.
- **Functional requirements**: describes the specific features, functionalities and interactions that the UX/UI solution must support to meet user needs and business objectives. This may include use case diagrams, user flow diagrams or functional specifications.
- **Interface requirements**: specifies the visual and interactive elements of the user interface, including layout, navigation, typography, colour schemes, **iconography** and interactive components. Wireframes, **mock-ups** and **prototypes** that may be used to visualise interface designs.
- **Non-functional requirements**: defines features of the UX/UI solution that are not directly related to its functional behaviour. This may include requirements related to usability, accessibility, performance, security, scalability and maintainability.

Figure 3.12: A wireframe can be used to document UX/UI solution requirements

Use case diagrams

This is a visual representation of the interactions between users and the system, illustrating how users interact with the solution to achieve specific goals or tasks. This can be achieved through the use of actors and system interactions.

- **Actors**: identifies the different types of users or system components that interact with the UX/UI solution, specifying their roles, responsibilities and permissions.
- **System interactions**: describes the interactions and dependencies between different system components, including external systems, databases, APIs or third-party services.

Learning in context 10

Actors and cases in a use case diagram for a bank ATM

A bank ATM, or Automated Teller Machine, is an electronic banking device that allows customers to perform basic financial transactions without the need for human assistance.

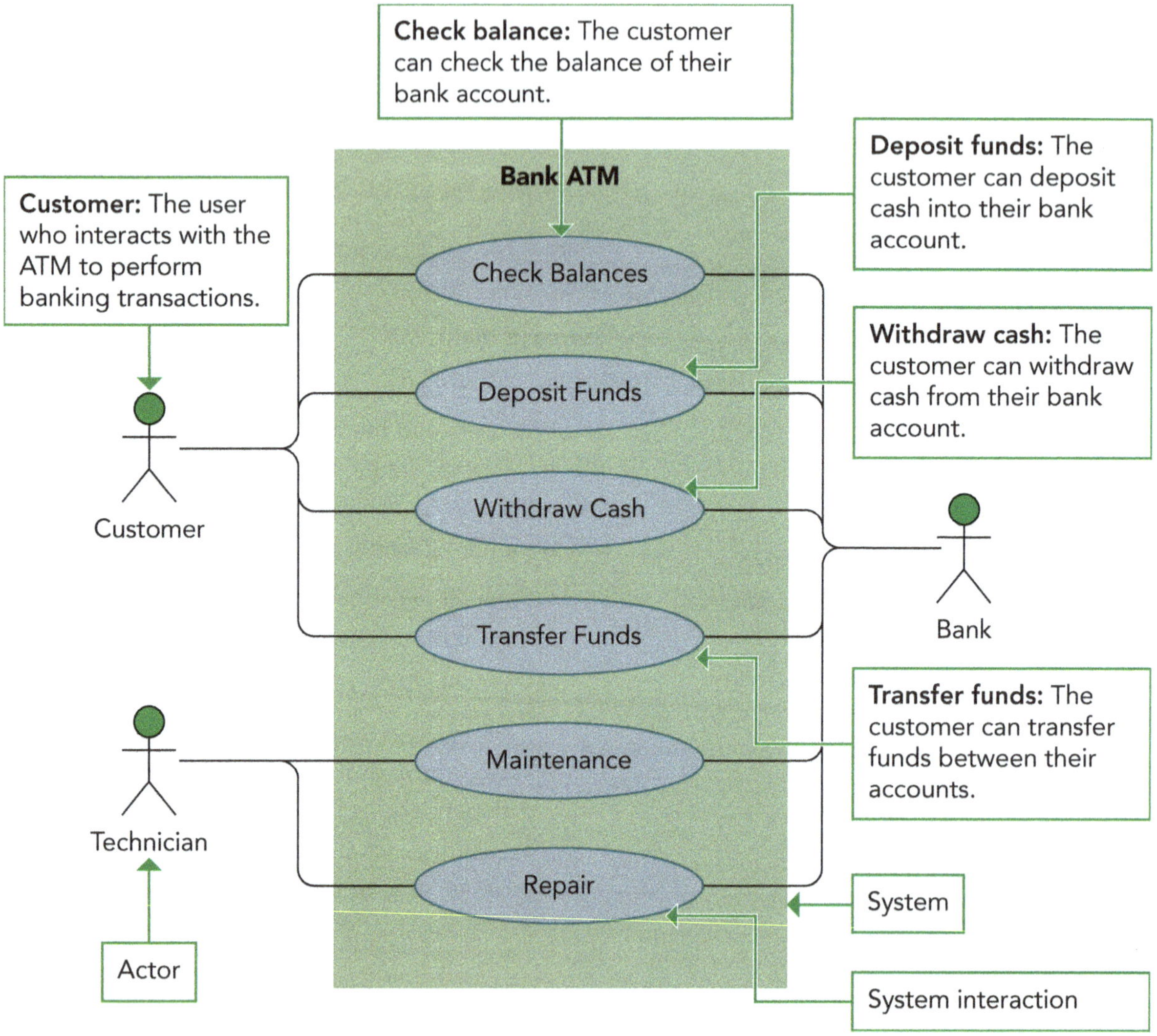
Check balance: The customer can check the balance of their bank account.
Bank ATM
Customer: The user who interacts with the ATM to perform banking transactions.
Check Balances
Deposit Funds
Withdraw Cash
Transfer Funds
Maintenance
Repair
Deposit funds: The customer can deposit cash into their bank account.
Withdraw cash: The customer can withdraw cash from their bank account.
Customer
Bank
Technician
Transfer funds: The customer can transfer funds between their accounts.
System
Actor
System interaction

Figure 3.13: A use case diagram to show interactions with an ATM

Actors

- The customer cannot interact with maintenance and repair functionality
- The technician can only interact with maintenance and repair functionality
- The bank can interact with all functionality.

Systems interaction with the bank ATM

- The 'Withdraw Cash' use case includes authentication and authorisation processes.
- The 'Deposit Cash' use case includes authentication and validation of deposited cash.
- The 'Transfer Funds' use case includes authentication and authorisation processes.

Using tools to document UX/UI solution requirements involves selecting appropriate software or platforms to capture, organise and communicate the requirements effectively.

- Define a clear and organised structure for the requirements documentation.
- Use the selected tools to capture and document the UX/UI solution requirements.
- Encourage collaboration among team members by allowing them to contribute to the requirement documentation.
- Use prototyping and diagramming tools to visualise concepts and ideas. Create wireframes, mock-ups, user flows and interactive prototypes to illustrate the proposed design solutions and demonstrate how users will interact with the system.
- Use clear and concise language, consistent formatting and terminology to ensure that all stakeholders can easily understand and interpret the requirements.
- Review the requirement documentation with key stakeholders, including clients, developers and end users.
- Keep track of changes and updates to the requirement documentation over time.

Learning in context 11

E-commerce website checkout process

E-commerce, short for electronic commerce, refers to the buying and selling of goods and services conducted over the internet or other electronic networks.

A UX/UI designer is tasked with designing the checkout process for an online store. To ensure an effortless user experience, the designer creates a flow diagram to document the steps involved in the checkout process.

- Start: the flow diagram begins with the user clicking on the 'Checkout' button from the shopping cart page.
- Login/registration: if the user is not logged in, the flow branches to include a step for logging in or registering for a new account.
- Billing and shipping information: once logged in, the user is directed to enter their billing and shipping information. The flow diagram includes steps for entering the user's name, address, contact information and shipping method.
- Payment method: next, the user selects their preferred payment method. The flow diagram includes steps for entering credit card details, selecting a saved payment method or choosing alternative payment options.
- Order review: after entering payment information, the user is directed to a summary page where they can review their order details, including itemised costs, shipping options and billing information.
- Confirmation: finally, the user is presented with a confirmation page confirming that their order has been successfully placed. The flow diagram includes a step for displaying a confirmation message and order number, as well as options to print or email the order receipt.

Quick check 7

1 What are the types of requirement that significantly affect the planning and design of UX/UI solution requirements?

2 How can UX/UI solution requirements be sourced and identified effectively?

3 What are some tools commonly used to document UX/UI solution requirements?

2.2 Tools and techniques to document UX/UI ideas and design concepts

Tools and techniques used to document ideas

Mind map

A mind map is a visual tool used to organise, represent and generate ideas or concepts. Its purpose is to help individuals brainstorm, analyse, plan and visualise information in a hierarchical or interconnected manner.

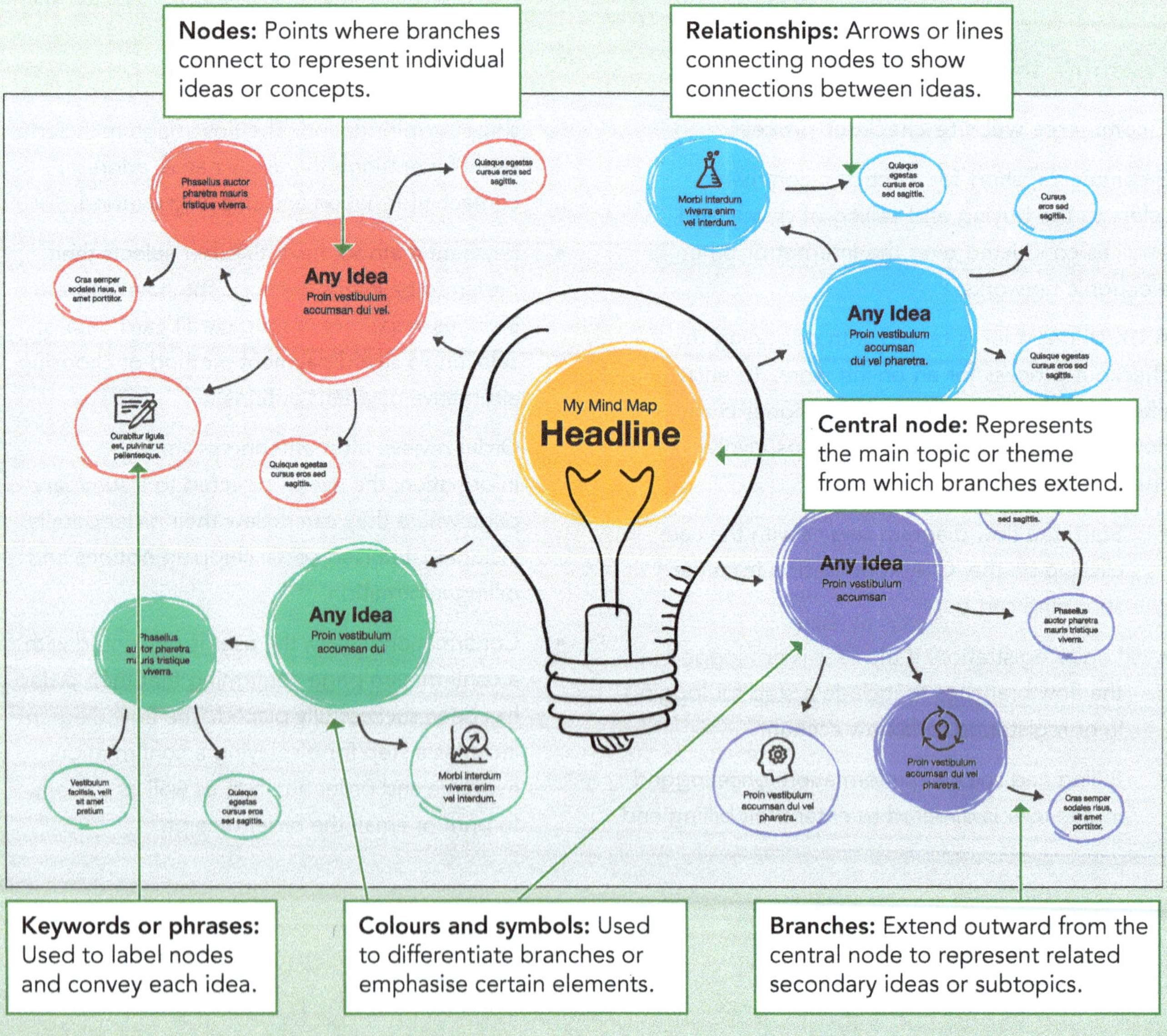

Nodes: Points where branches connect to represent individual ideas or concepts.
Relationships: Arrows or lines connecting nodes to show connections between ideas.
Any Idea
Proin vestibulum accumsan dui vel.
Any Idea
Proin vestibulum accumsan dui vel pharetra.
My Mind Map
Headline
Central node: Represents the main topic or theme from which branches extend.
Any Idea
Proin vestibulum accumsan dui
Any Idea
Proin vestibulum accumsan
Keywords or phrases: Used to label nodes and convey each idea.
Colours and symbols: Used to differentiate branches or emphasise certain elements.
Branches: Extend outward from the central node to represent related secondary ideas or subtopics.

Figure 3.14: A mind map helps to develop ideas into concepts

How a mind map can develop ideas into concepts

- Mind maps provide a structure for brainstorming ideas related to a specific topic or problem.
- As ideas are generated, they can be organised and categorised within the mind map based on their relevance, similarity or relationship to each other.
- As ideas are developed and explored within the mind map, participants can iterate and refine the concepts based on feedback, insights or additional research.

How to use a mind map to document ideas for UX/UI solutions

- Create a central theme: Start with a central theme, such as the problem designers are to solve or the main objective of the UX/UI project.
- Branch out ideas: From the central theme, branch out into sub-themes or related concepts. These could include user journeys, features, functionalities and so on.
- Visualise connections: Use lines or arrows to show connections between different ideas. This helps in understanding the relationships between various components.
- Iterate and refine: Continuously iterate on the mind map as you gather more ideas or insights. Refine it based on feedback and new information.

Mood boards

A mood board is a visual tool used by designers to convey the overall look, feel and artistic direction of a project. It typically consists of a collage of images, textures, colours, patterns and other visual elements that represent the desired mood, style or theme of the design.

How a mood board can develop ideas into concepts

- Mood boards serve as a source of inspiration for designers by collecting and curating visual references related to the project's theme, concept or target audience.
- Mood boards help designers visualise and communicate **abstract** concepts or ideas in a tangible and concrete form.
- Mood boards help designers make informed design decisions by comparing and evaluating different artistic options and stylistic choices.

How to use a mood board to document ideas for UX/UI solutions

- Gather visual inspirations: Collect images, colours, typography and other visual elements that link to the theme of the project.
- Organise visual elements: Arrange the collected visuals on a digital or physical board in a way that communicates the overall design.
- Create variations: Experiment with different combinations of visuals to explore various design directions.
- Share and gather feedback: Share the mood board with stakeholders, clients or team members to gather feedback.

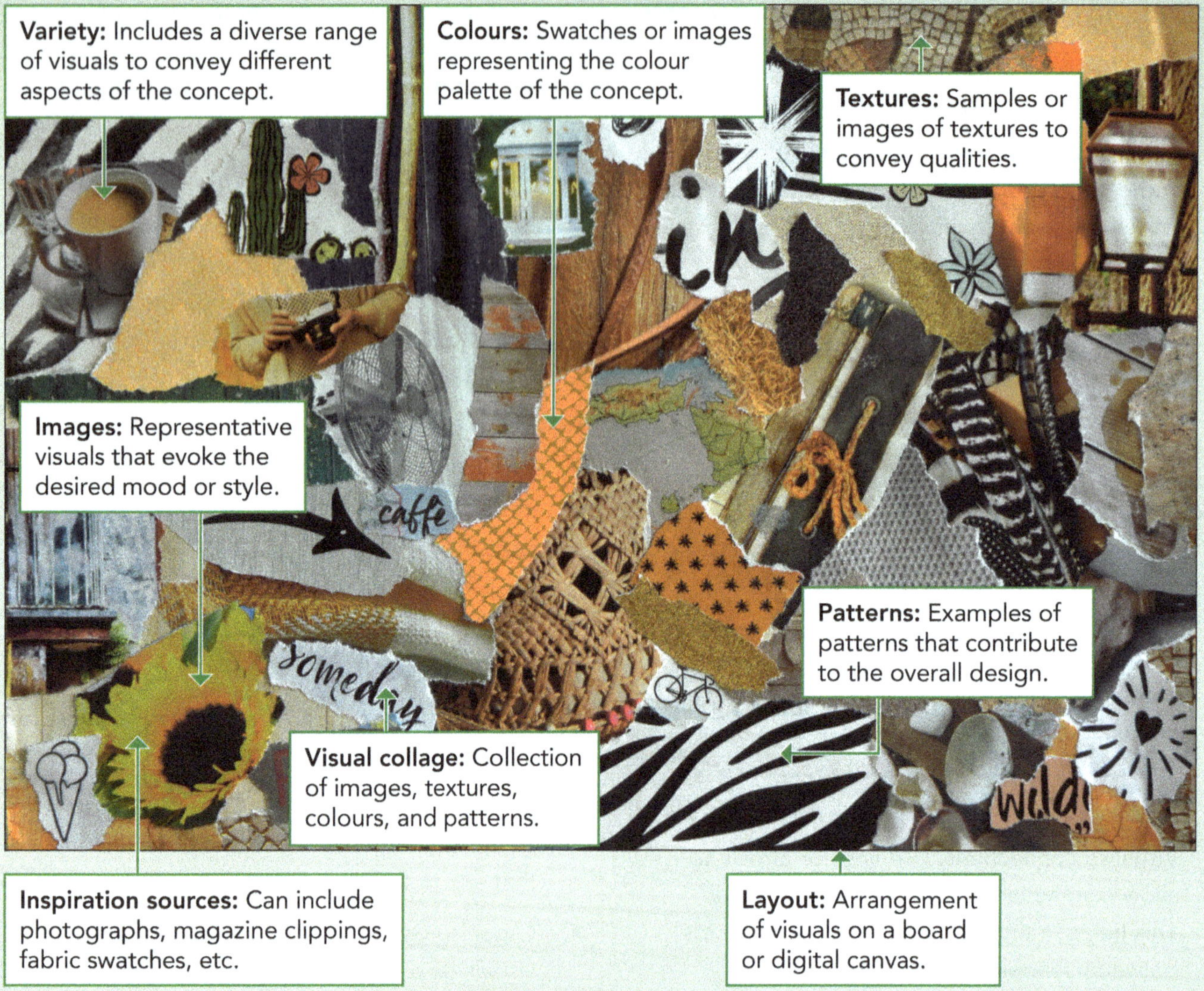
Variety: Includes a diverse range of visuals to convey different aspects of the concept.
Colours: Swatches or images representing the colour palette of the concept.
Textures: Samples or images of textures to convey qualities.
Images: Representative visuals that evoke the desired mood or style.
Patterns: Examples of patterns that contribute to the overall design.
Visual collage: Collection of images, textures, colours, and patterns.
Inspiration sources: Can include photographs, magazine clippings, fabric swatches, etc.
Layout: Arrangement of visuals on a board or digital canvas.

Figure 3.15: A mood board helps to develop the look and feel of a project

Spider diagrams

A spider diagram is a simplified version of a mind map, focusing on central concepts or ideas and their interconnected relationships. Its purpose is to visually organise information around a central topic or theme, with branches moving outward to represent related subtopics or concepts.

How a spider diagram can develop ideas into concepts

- Spider diagrams enable comparison between different concepts, ideas or alternatives by plotting them on the same chart.
- Spider diagrams help designers identify the strengths and weaknesses of different design concepts or solutions by visually highlighting areas of excellence and areas for improvement.
- Spider diagrams provide a clear and concise way to communicate complex design concepts or ideas to stakeholders, clients and team members.

How to use a spider diagram to document ideas for UX/UI solutions

- Identify key criteria: define the key criteria that are important for evaluating the UX/UI solution. This could include factors like usability, accessibility, visual appeal and so on.

- Plot data points: for each criterion, plot data points representing different design ideas or solutions on the spider diagram.
- Analyse strengths and weaknesses: analyse the resulting shape of the spider diagram to identify areas of strength and weakness for each design solution.
- Iterate and optimise: use the insights gained from the spider diagram to iterate on and optimise the design solutions, focusing on improving areas of weakness and leveraging strengths.

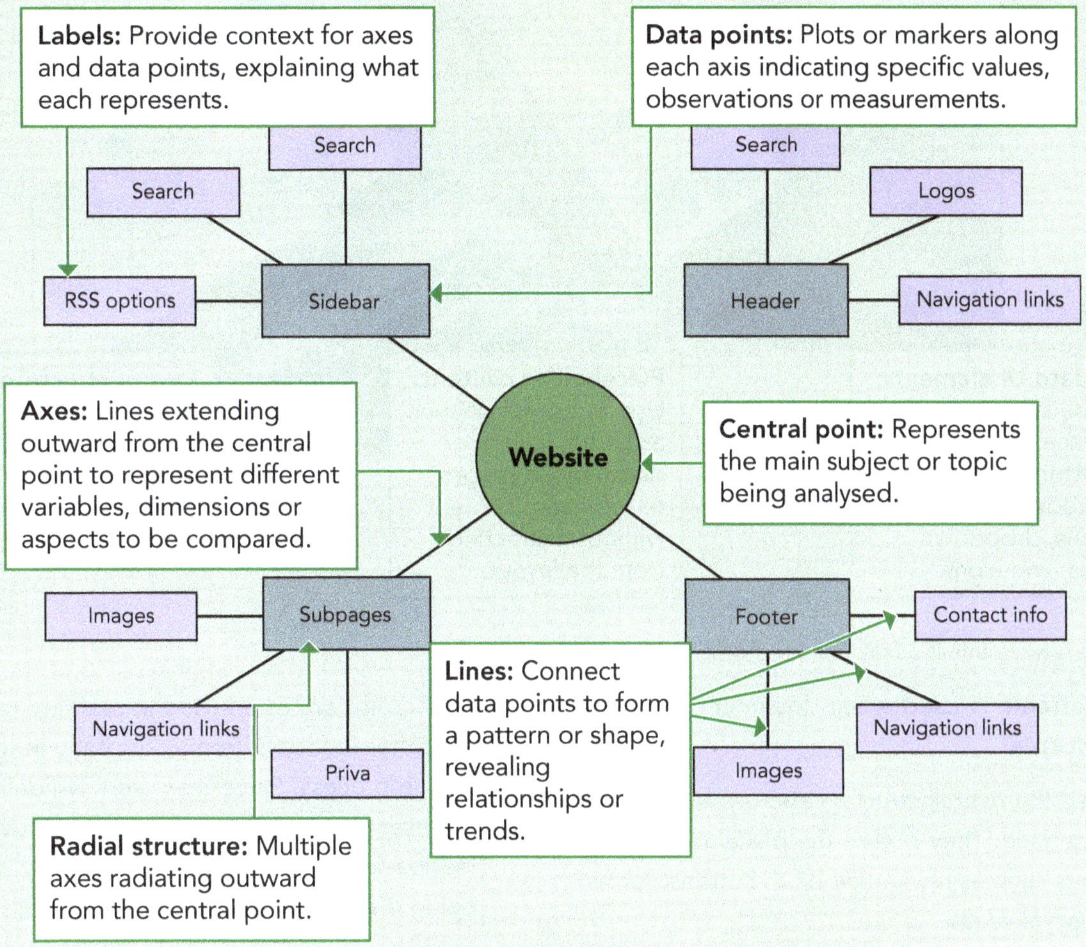
Labels: Provide context for axes and data points, explaining what each represents.
Data points: Plots or markers along each axis indicating specific values, observations or measurements.
Search
Search
RSS options
Sidebar
Search
Logos
Header
Navigation links
Axes: Lines extending outward from the central point to represent different variables, dimensions or aspects to be compared.
Website
Central point: Represents the main subject or topic being analysed.
Images
Subpages
Footer
Contact info
Navigation links
Priva
Lines: Connect data points to form a pattern or shape, revealing relationships or trends.
Images
Navigation links
Radial structure: Multiple axes radiating outward from the central point.

Figure 3.16: A spider diagram shows ideas connected to a central theme

Tools and techniques used to document design concepts

Low-fidelity prototypes

One common tool used for 'low-fidelity prototypes' is a wireframe. The purpose of a wireframe in UX/UI design is to provide a skeletal outline of a digital product, focusing on layout, functionality and user interactions without getting into visual design details such as colours and graphics.

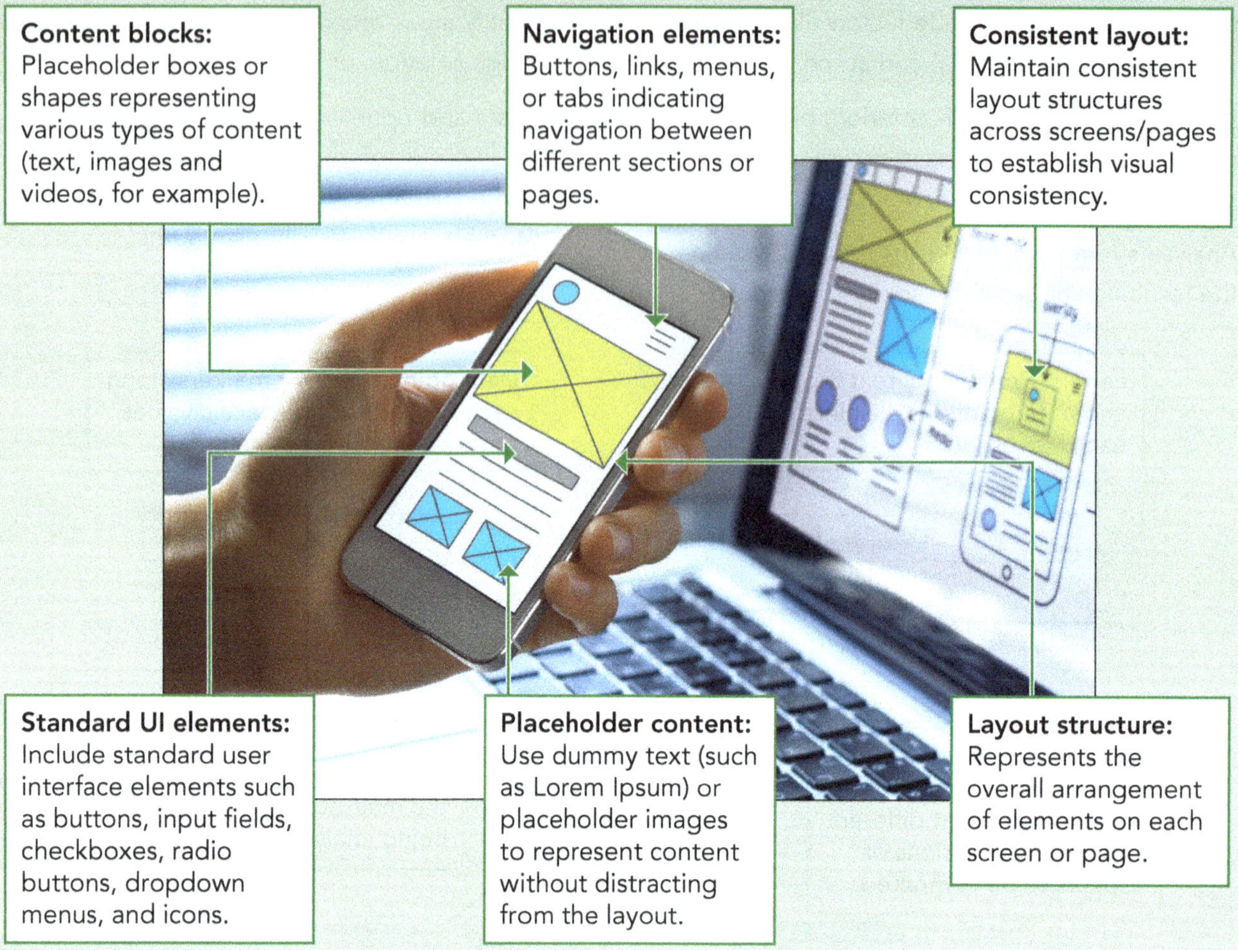
Content blocks: Placeholder boxes or shapes representing various types of content (text, images and videos, for example).
Navigation elements: Buttons, links, menus, or tabs indicating navigation between different sections or pages.
Consistent layout: Maintain consistent layout structures across screens/pages to establish visual consistency.
Standard UI elements: Include standard user interface elements such as buttons, input fields, checkboxes, radio buttons, dropdown menus, and icons.
Placeholder content: Use dummy text (such as Lorem Ipsum) or placeholder images to represent content without distracting from the layout.
Layout structure: Represents the overall arrangement of elements on each screen or page.

Figure 3.17: A wireframe is a common low-fidelity prototype

How a wireframe is used when documenting UX/UI design concepts

- Visualise the overall structure and layout of the user interface. They outline the placement of key elements such as navigation bars, buttons, forms and content areas.
- Map out the functionality and flow of the user interface. They show how users will interact with the interface, including navigation paths, user actions and system responses.
- They provide a clear representation of the content hierarchy, showing what content will be displayed prominently and how it will be organised within the interface.
- Wireframes are often used in usability testing to gather feedback from users early in the design process. Since they are low-fidelity representations, users can focus on providing feedback on functionality and usability without being distracted by visual design details.

Paper prototyping

Paper prototyping is a technique used in UX/UI design to create low-fidelity representations of digital interfaces using pen and paper or other physical materials. The primary purpose of paper prototyping is to explore and iterate on design ideas, gather feedback from stakeholders or users and refine the user experience quickly and inexpensively.

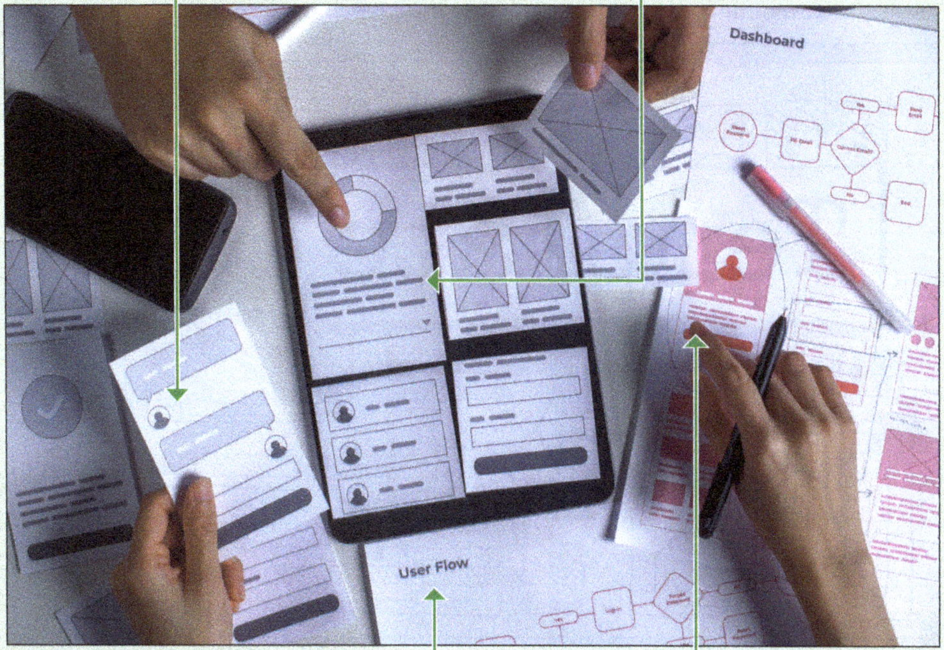
Physical interactive representation/Interactive elements: Physical cut-outs, sticky notes, moveable elements or drawn elements representing interactive components such as buttons, menus, and form fields.
Hand-drawn elements or screens: Sketches or drawings representing individual screens, interface components, interactions or pages of the interface.
Dashboard
User Flow
User pathways: Arrows, lines, or written instructions indicating the flow and sequence of user interactions through the prototype.
Simple navigation indicators: Use arrows or written instructions to indicate navigation pathways and interaction sequences.

Figure 3.18: Paper prototyping can be used to provide simple representation of various interface elements

How paper prototyping is used when documenting UX/UI design concepts

- Generating ideas by brainstorming designs and concepts for the user interface.
- Sketch out rough representations of different layouts, features and interactions on paper.
- Use paper, index cards, sticky notes or other physical materials to create simple representations of interface elements such as screens, buttons, menus and content.
- Act out user interactions with the paper prototype. This could involve manually moving and rearranging elements to simulate navigation, button clicks, form submissions and so on.
- Convert to digital prototyping once the paper prototype has been successfully tested.

Sketches and diagrams

Sketches and diagrams are effective tools for visualisation, communication and problem-solving.

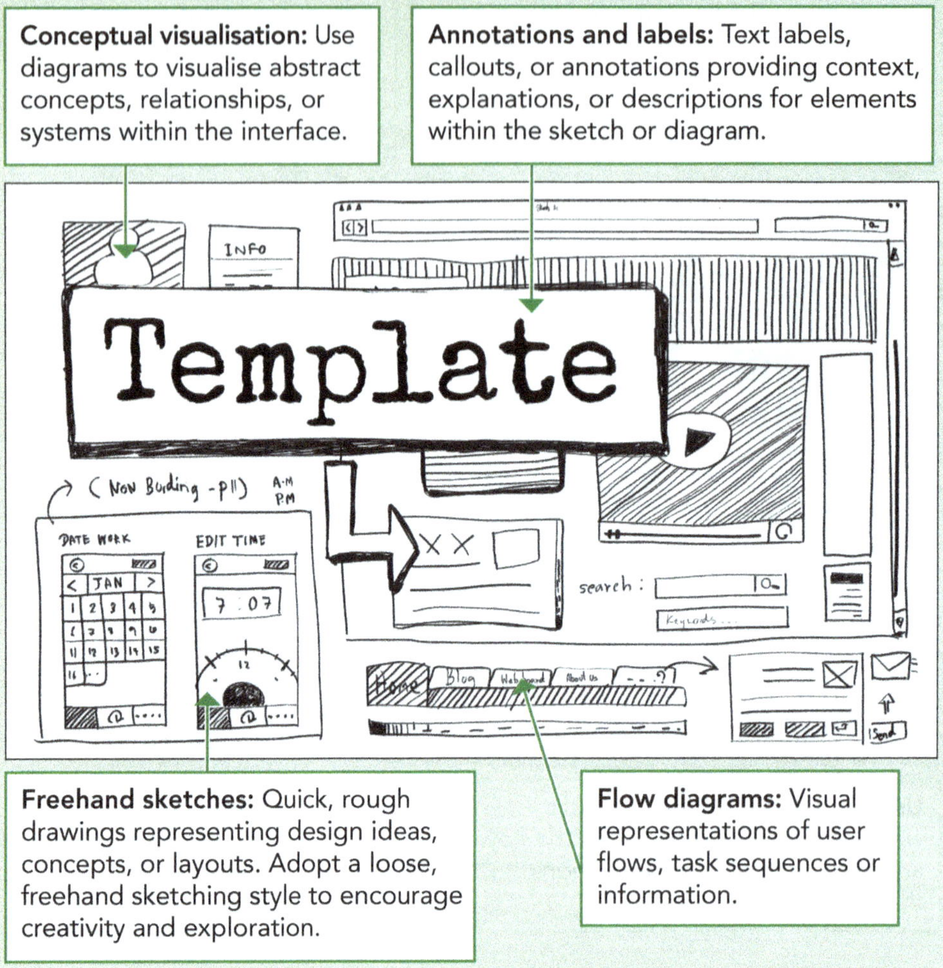

Conceptual visualisation: Use diagrams to visualise abstract concepts, relationships, or systems within the interface.
Annotations and labels: Text labels, callouts, or annotations providing context, explanations, or descriptions for elements within the sketch or diagram.
INFO
Template
DATE WORK
EDIT TIME
JAN
search :
Freehand sketches: Quick, rough drawings representing design ideas, concepts, or layouts. Adopt a loose, freehand sketching style to encourage creativity and exploration.
Flow diagrams: Visual representations of user flows, task sequences or information.

Figure 3.19: Sketches and diagrams can be used to document UX/UI design concepts

How sketches and diagrams are used when documenting UX/UI design concepts

- Use sketches to quickly generate and explore design ideas during brainstorming sessions.
- Sketching allows designers to freely experiment with different layout arrangements, interface elements and interaction patterns.
- They provide a visual representation of design concepts, making it easier for designers to convey their ideas to stakeholders and team members.
- Use flow diagrams or user journey maps that illustrate the steps, interactions and experiences a user goes through when interacting with a product, service or system.
- Detailed diagrams can serve as blueprints for developers, providing clear guidance on how the interface should be implemented.

Learning in context 12

Mobile application for a food delivery service

Consider a scenario where a team of UX/UI designers are working on developing a mobile application for a food delivery service. They use various tools and techniques to document their ideas and design concepts throughout the project:

Wireframes

- They sketch out the layout structure of each screen, including elements such as home screen, menu, restaurant listings, order details and checkout process.
- Annotations are added to describe the functionality of each element, such as buttons for navigation or form fields for entering delivery addresses.

Mood boards

- They gather images related to food, restaurants, delivery and other relevant themes to evoke the desired mood and feel for the app.
- The mood board serves as a reference point for colour schemes, typography and visual styles to be used in the UI design.

Paper prototyping

- They create hand-drawn sketches of key screens and interface elements on paper.
- Interactive components such as buttons and menus are represented using physical cut-outs or sticky notes, allowing testers to simulate user interactions.

Flow diagrams

- They map out the various pathway's users can take, from browsing restaurants to placing an order and tracking delivery.
- Arrows and annotations indicate the sequence of screens and interactions, helping to identify potential problems or areas for improvement.

Sketches/diagrams

- Throughout the design process, designers create sketches and diagrams to explore alternative design concepts and solutions.
- They sketch out rough ideas for new features, interface layouts or interaction patterns on paper.

Quick check 8

1 How do designers use various tools and techniques to effectively document UX/UI ideas and design concepts?

2 How do UX/UI ideas evolve into concrete design concepts during the development process?

TA3 Design UX/UI solutions

Learning intentions

This topic is about how to Design UX/UI solutions.

It covers:

3.1 Tools to represent UX/UI solutions

3.2 Tools and techniques to check UX/UI solution designs

3.1 Tools to represent UX/UI solutions

In User Experience (UX) and User Interface (UI) design, effective representation of design solutions is important. To achieve this, designers use a variety of visual tools and techniques that help in the communication of complex ideas and concepts in a clear and understandable manner. These provide visual representations that help designers analyse, communicate and refine the user experience.

3.1.1 Design tools

Diagrams

Types

Flowchart: a flowchart is a graphical representation of a process or system. Each step is represented as boxes of different types and the order and path is shown by connecting these with arrows. It helps visualise the flow of information or activities within a system, making complex processes easier to understand.

How flowcharts are used to design UX/UI solutions

- Understand the goals of the system or interface and the needs of its users. This forms the basis of the flowchart.
- Create a flowchart that outlines the various pathways users can take to accomplish their goals within the interface.
- Associate each step in the flowchart with the corresponding screen or interface element. This helps in designing the layout and content of each screen.
- Use the flowchart as a reference to prototype and test the interface. Gather feedback from users and stakeholder and iterate on the design to improve usability and effectiveness.
- Flowcharts serve as documentation for the design process, helping to communicate the intended user experience to developers and other stakeholders.

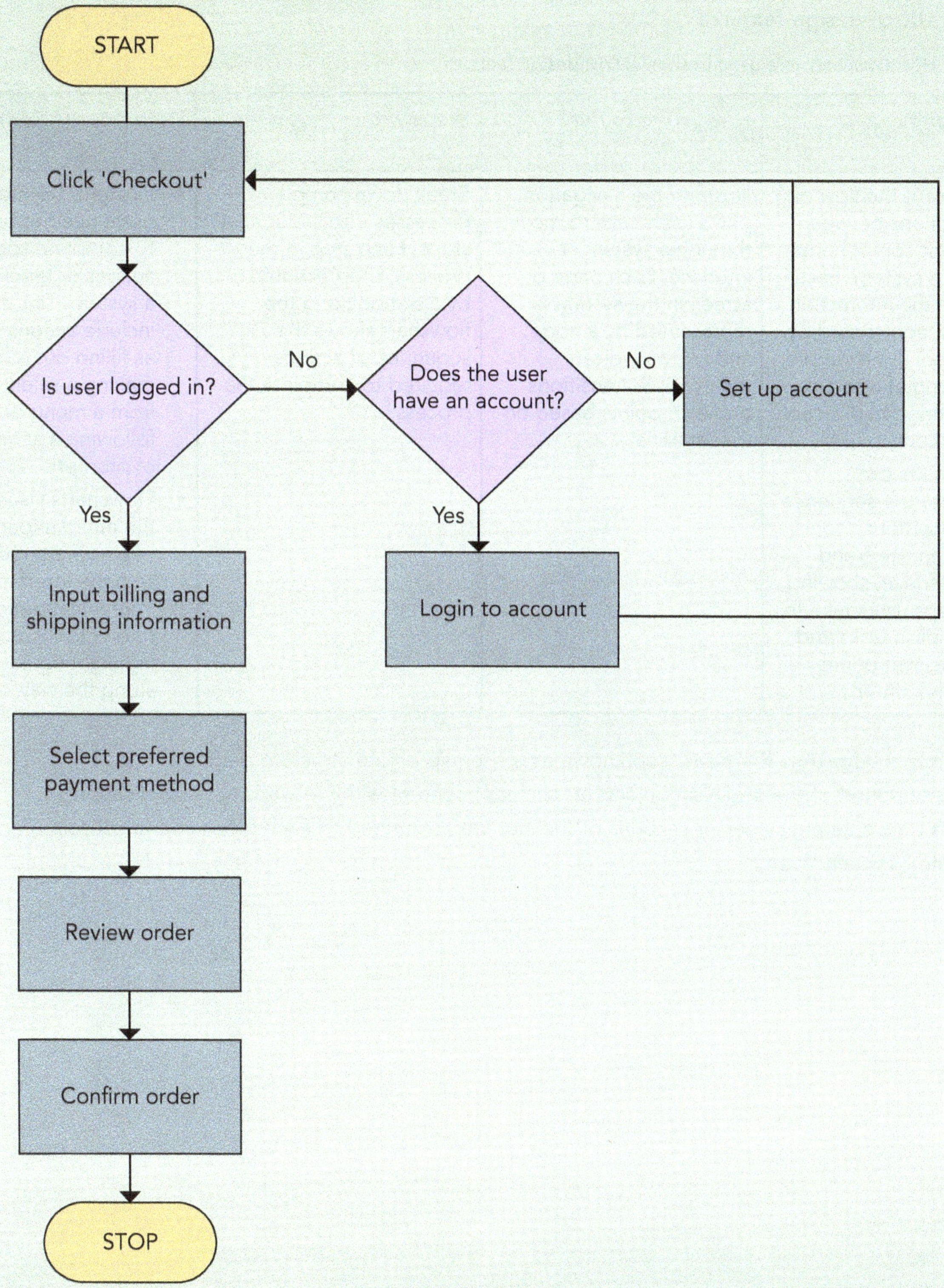
START
Click 'Checkout'
Is user logged in?
No
Does the user have an account?
No
Set up account
Yes
Yes
Input billing and shipping information
Login to account
Select preferred payment method
Review order
Confirm order
STOP

Figure 3.20: A flowchart of an ecommerce checkout process

Flowchart UX/UI design features

Table 3.17: How flowcharts are used to show UX/UI design features

Interaction flows	Navigation routes	Steps within processes	User steps to complete actions
• Represent the flow of interactions between different components within a system. Each step in the interaction flow is represented by a symbol (for example, a rectangle) with arrows indicating the direction of the flow. • Flowcharts can illustrate the sequence of interactions between users and the interface, showing the steps users take to accomplish tasks and the decision points they encounter.	Illustrate the navigation paths users take to move through a system or interface. Each page or screen in the system is represented by a node, and arrows indicate the possible transitions between points based on user actions.	Break down complex processes into sequential steps. Each step in the process is represented by a symbol, and the flowchart shows the sequence of actions required to complete the process.	• Illustrate the steps users need to take to complete specific actions or tasks within a system. This can include actions such as filling out a form, making a selection from a menu or following a series of prompts. • Flowcharts visualise the entire experience of a user interacting with the interface, from initial discovery to task completion, highlighting each step along the way.

Navigation: a **navigation diagram**, also known as a sitemap or site structure diagram, is a visual representation of the organisation and hierarchy of content within a website or application. It illustrates how different pages or sections of the site are connected to each other and how users can navigate between them.

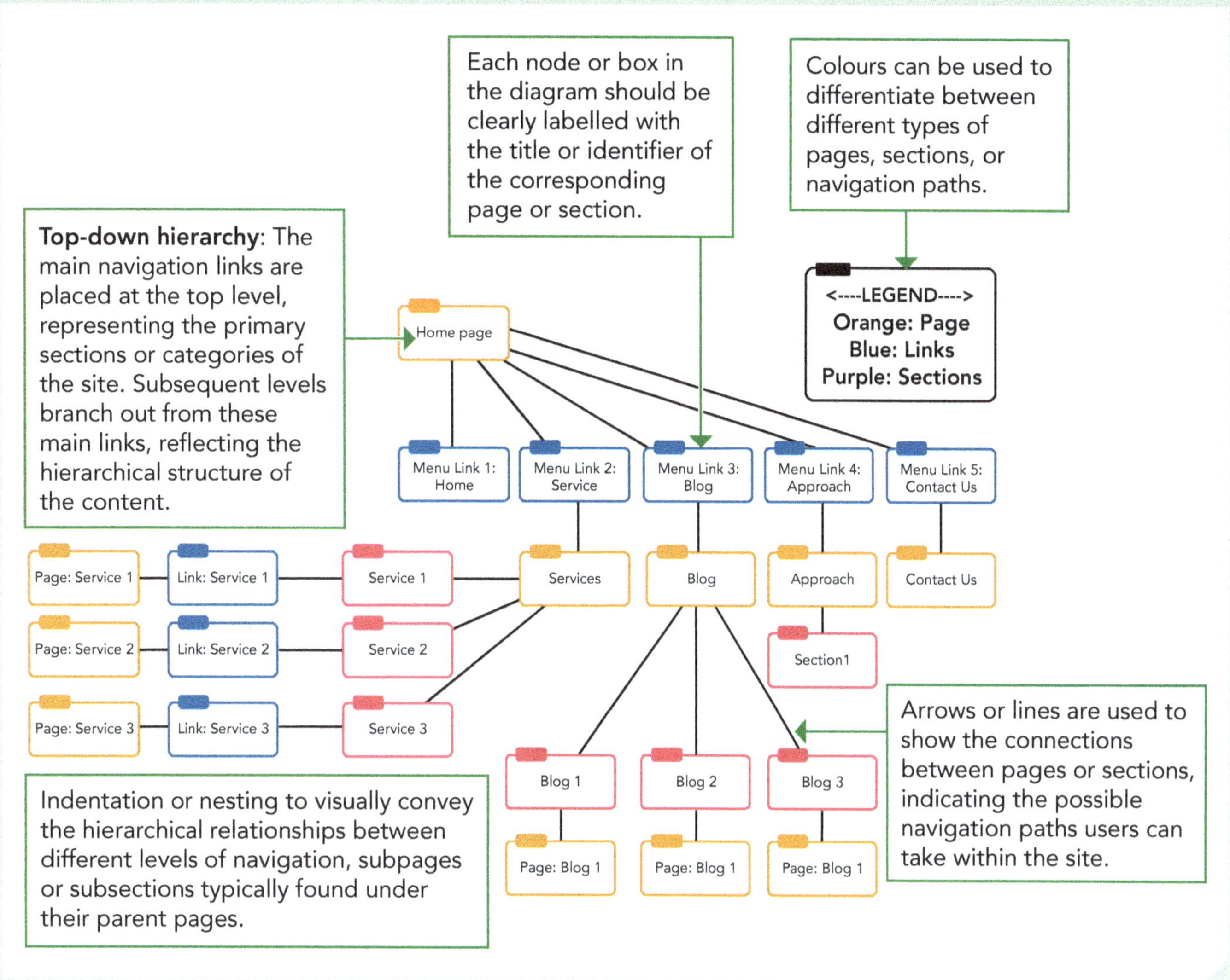
Each node or box in the diagram should be clearly labelled with the title or identifier of the corresponding page or section.
Colours can be used to differentiate between different types of pages, sections, or navigation paths.
Top-down hierarchy: The main navigation links are placed at the top level, representing the primary sections or categories of the site. Subsequent levels branch out from these main links, reflecting the hierarchical structure of the content.
<----LEGEND---->
Orange: Page
Blue: Links
Purple: Sections
Home page
Menu Link 1: Home
Menu Link 2: Service
Menu Link 3: Blog
Menu Link 4: Approach
Menu Link 5: Contact Us
Page: Service 1
Link: Service 1
Service 1
Services
Blog
Approach
Contact Us
Page: Service 2
Link: Service 2
Service 2
Section1
Page: Service 3
Link: Service 3
Service 3
Arrows or lines are used to show the connections between pages or sections, indicating the possible navigation paths users can take within the site.
Blog 1
Blog 2
Blog 3
Indentation or nesting to visually convey the hierarchical relationships between different levels of navigation, subpages or subsections typically found under their parent pages.
Page: Blog 1
Page: Blog 1
Page: Blog 1

Figure 3.21: Conventions and layout of a navigation diagram

How navigation diagrams used to design UX/UI solutions

- Understand the goals and tasks that users need to accomplish within the interface. This forms the basis for designing the navigation structure.
- Determine the main pages, screens or sections that make up the interface and how they are interconnected.
- Use the navigation diagram to map out the various navigation paths that users can take to move between different pages/screens/sections.
- Evaluate the navigation flow to ensure that it is intuitive and efficient, minimising the number of steps required for users to reach their desired destination.
- Prototype the interface based on the navigation diagram and conduct usability testing to gather feedback from users. Use the insights gained to iterate on the design and improve the user experience.

Navigation diagram UX/UI design features

Table 3.18: How navigation diagrams are used to show UX/UI design features

Interaction flows	Navigation routes	Steps within processes	User steps to complete actions
• Show how users engage with the interface elements to accomplish tasks or goals within the system. • Show the sequence of screens or interface states users encounter as they progress through the interaction flow. • By visually connecting different screens and indicating the transitions between them, navigation diagrams effectively communicate the flow of user interactions within the interface.	• Visually represent the pathways users can take to navigate through the website or application. • Show the links or connections between different pages or sections, indicating the possible routes users can follow to access content or features. • Mapping out navigation routes, navigation diagrams can help designers ensure that users can easily find and navigate to the desired information or functionality within the interface.	• Can also illustrate the steps involved in completing specific processes or tasks within the system. • Breaking down complex processes into individual steps and visually connecting them in the diagram, navigation diagrams provide a clear overview of the process flow. • Help designers and stakeholders understand the sequence of actions required to accomplish a task and identify any potential **bottlenecks** or points of confusion in the user journey.	• Show the user steps required to complete specific actions or tasks within the interface. • Outlining the sequence of screens or interface states users encounter while performing an action, navigation diagrams help designers identify the necessary steps and interactions involved in the process. • Allow designers to optimise the user experience by streamlining the workflow, reducing friction and ensuring that users can easily accomplish their goals.

Task flows: a **task flow** is a sequential representation of the steps a user takes to accomplish a specific goal or task within a digital interface, such as a website or application. Task flows focus on the actions users perform and the decisions they make as they move through the interface to achieve their objectives.

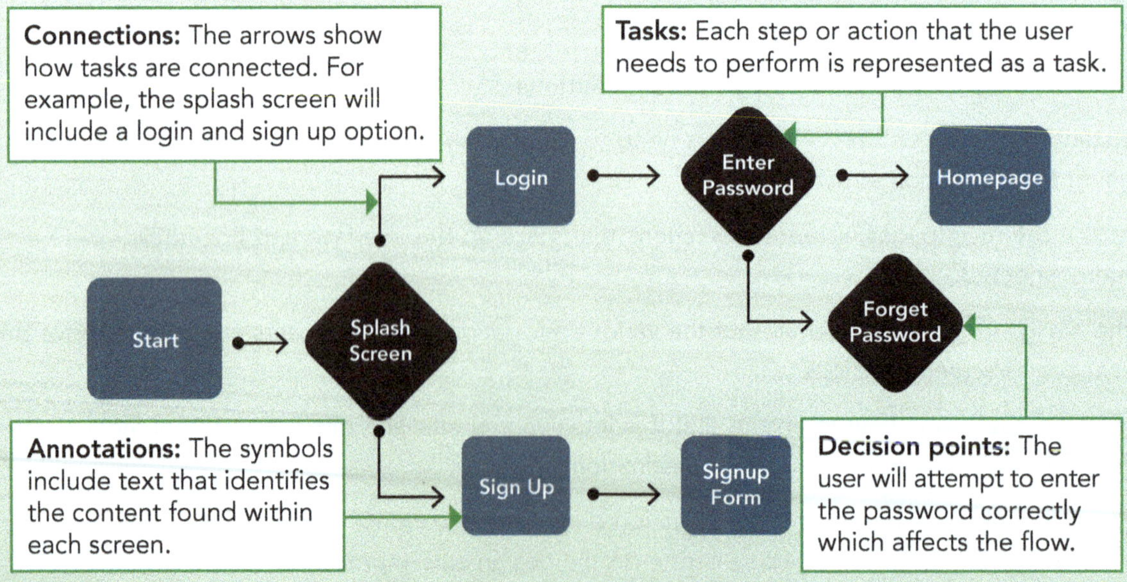

Connections: The arrows show how tasks are connected. For example, the splash screen will include a login and sign up option.
Tasks: Each step or action that the user needs to perform is represented as a task.
Login
Enter Password
Homepage
Start
Splash Screen
Forget Password
Annotations: The symbols include text that identifies the content found within each screen.
Sign Up
Signup Form
Decision points: The user will attempt to enter the password correctly which affects the flow.

Figure 3.22: Conventions and layout of a task flow diagram in designing a UX/UI solution

How task flows are used to design UX/UI solutions

- Clearly define the task or goal that users need to accomplish within the interface.
- Break down the task into individual steps or actions that users must perform to achieve their goal.
- Create a visual representation of the task flow, showing the sequence of steps and the connections between them.
- Evaluate the task flow to identify opportunities for simplifying the user experience. Consider how the interface can guide users through the task more efficiently.
- Prototype the interface based on the task flow and conduct usability testing to validate the design. Use feedback from users to iterate on the design and improve the user experience further.

Task flow UX/UI design features

Table 3.19: How task flows are used to show UX/UI design features

Interaction flows	Navigation routes	Steps within processes	User steps to complete actions
Outlining the high-level interactions users have with a system. They map out the user's journey from the starting point (for example, landing page or home screen) to the final goal (for example, completing a purchase or submitting a form).	Provide detail of the specific navigation paths users follow as they progress through the system. This includes the sequence of screens, pages or sections they visit, as well as any decision points or branching paths they encounter.	Break down complex processes into a series of distinct steps that users must complete to achieve their objectives. Each step in the task flow represents a specific action or interaction, such as entering information into a form, selecting options from a menu or confirming a decision.	Focusing on the user's perspective, highlighting the steps they need to take to accomplish their goals within the system. This includes not only the actions users perform directly but also any feedback or guidance they receive from the system in response to their actions.

Wireflow: a **wireflow** is a hybrid design that combines elements of wireframes and flowcharts. It provides a visual representation of both the layout and the flow of a user interface, showing how screens are connected and how users navigate through them. Wireflows are especially useful for illustrating the interaction design of a digital product or service.

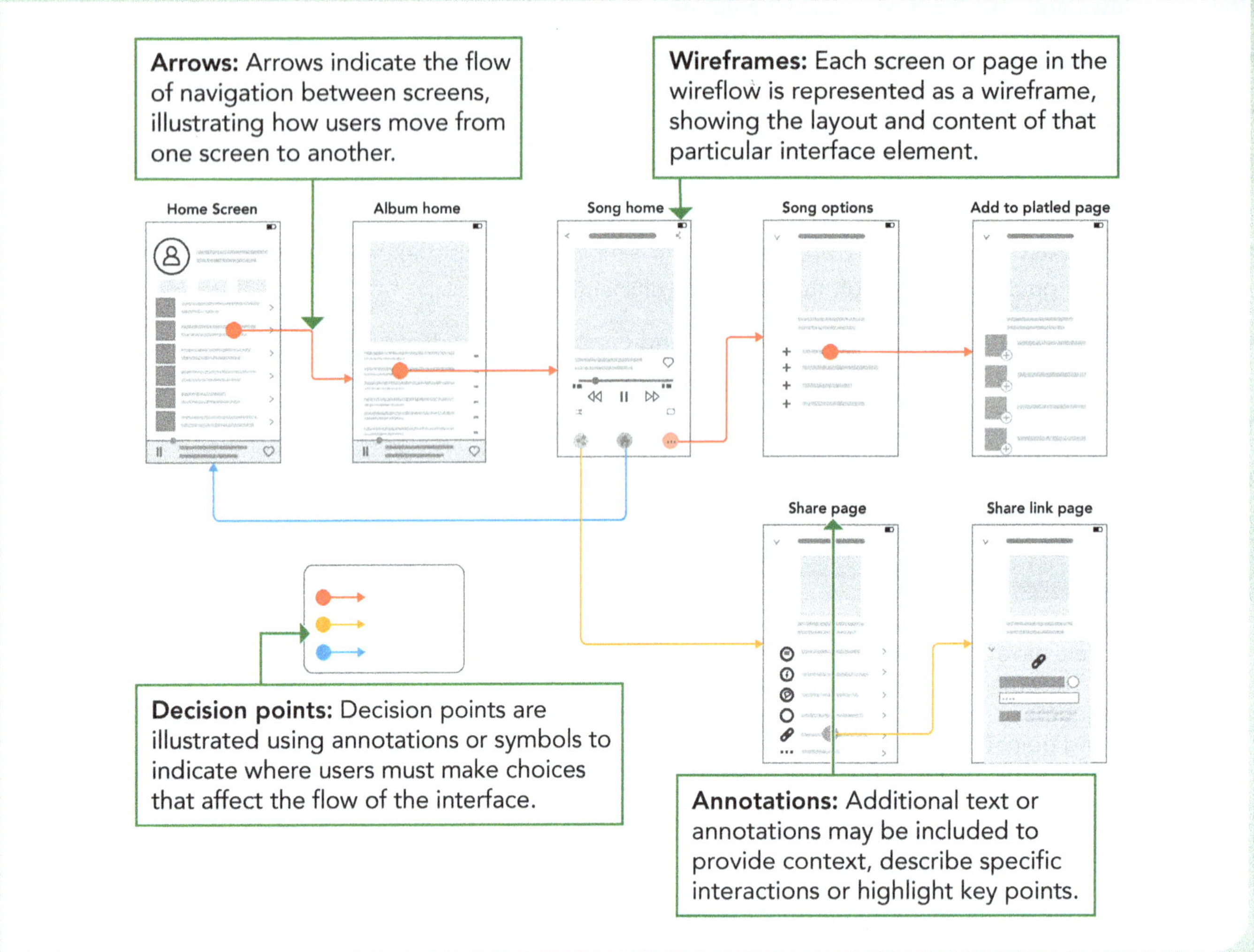
Arrows: Arrows indicate the flow of navigation between screens, illustrating how users move from one screen to another.
Wireframes: Each screen or page in the wireflow is represented as a wireframe, showing the layout and content of that particular interface element.
Home Screen
Album home
Song home
Song options
Add to platled page
Share page
Share link page
Decision points: Decision points are illustrated using annotations or symbols to indicate where users must make choices that affect the flow of the interface.
Annotations: Additional text or annotations may be included to provide context, describe specific interactions or highlight key points.

Figure 3.23: A wireflow is a combination of a wireframe and a flowchart

How wireflows are used to design UX/UI solutions

- Identify the key user flows or pathways through the interface that need to be represented in the wireflow.
- Design wireframes for each screen or page in the interface, focusing on layout, content and functionality.
- Use arrows to connect the wireframes, illustrating the flow of navigation between screens and how users move through the interface.
- Add annotations or symbols to indicate interactions, decision points or other important elements of the interface.
- Review the wireflow with stakeholders, gather feedback and iterate on the design as needed to improve usability and effectiveness.

Wireflow UX/UI design features

Table 3.20: How wireflows are used to show UX/UI design features

Interaction flows	Navigation routes	Steps within processes	User steps to complete actions
To represent the visual design of each screen or page in the user interface. By connecting these wireframes with arrows or lines, designers can illustrate the flow of interactions between different screens or components.	Show the navigation paths users follow as they move through the system. By connecting wireframes with directional arrows, designers can indicate the sequence of screens or pages users visit and the transitions between them.	Break down complex processes into a series of steps represented by individual wireframes. Each wireframe shows a specific screen or interaction within the process, such as entering information into a form or making a selection from a menu.	Highlight the user's perspective by showing the steps they need to take to accomplish their objectives within the system. Each wireframe represents a specific action or interaction, such as clicking a button or entering text into a field.

High-fidelity prototypes

A high-fidelity prototype is a detailed representation of a digital product or interface that closely resembles the final product in terms of appearance, functionality and interactivity. High-fidelity prototypes are typically created using specialised design tools or software and often include realistic visuals, interactive elements, animations and transitions. They aim to **simulate** the user experience as closely as possible to gather accurate feedback and test usability before it reaches the end-user. Graphical mock-ups and screen flows are two methods used to design high-fidelity UX/UI solutions.

Types

Graphical mock-ups: a **graphical mock-up** is a visual representation of a digital interface or product design created using graphic design software. It showcases the visual aspects, layout and design elements of the user interface. Graphical mock-ups provide a realistic preview of how the final product will look, allowing stakeholders to visualise the design and provide feedback before development begins.

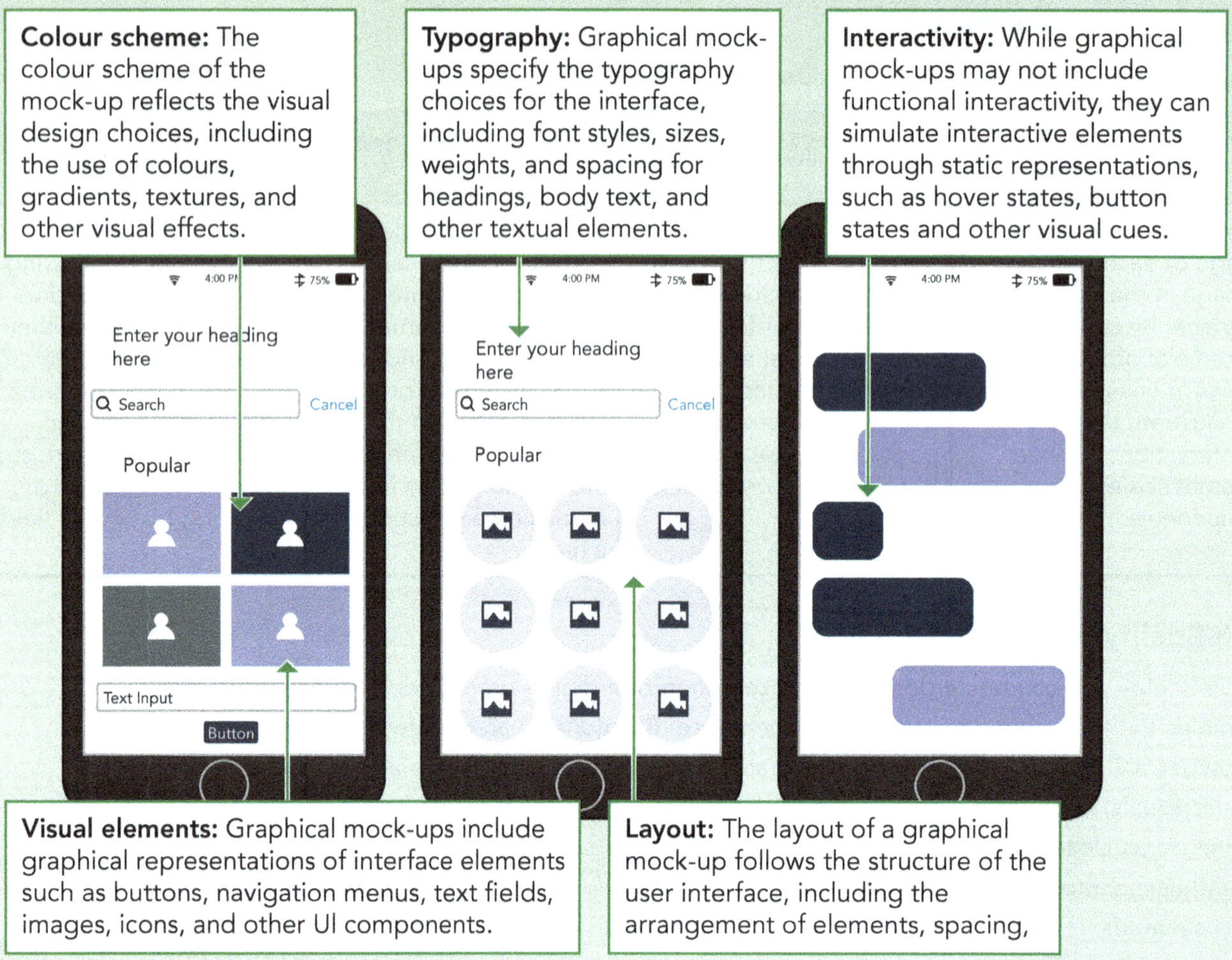
Colour scheme: The colour scheme of the mock-up reflects the visual design choices, including the use of colours, gradients, textures, and other visual effects.
Typography: Graphical mock-ups specify the typography choices for the interface, including font styles, sizes, weights, and spacing for headings, body text, and other textual elements.
Interactivity: While graphical mock-ups may not include functional interactivity, they can simulate interactive elements through static representations, such as hover states, button states and other visual cues.
Enter your heading here
Search
Cancel
Popular
Text Input
Button
Enter your heading here
Search
Cancel
Popular
Visual elements: Graphical mock-ups include graphical representations of interface elements such as buttons, navigation menus, text fields, images, icons, and other UI components.
Layout: The layout of a graphical mock-up follows the structure of the user interface, including the arrangement of elements, spacing,

Figure 3.24: Conventions and layout of a graphical mock-up

How graphical mock-ups are used to design UX/UI solutions

- To help translate design concepts and ideas into visual representations, allowing designers to visualise the intended look and feel of the interface.
- Designers can use graphical mock-ups to explore different design variations, experiment with layout options, colour schemes and typography choices, and iterate on the design until they achieve the desired outcome.
- As a communication tool for gathering feedback from stakeholders, clients or users. Designers can present the mock-ups to stakeholders for review and incorporate their feedback into the design process.
- Provides developers with a clear **blueprint** for building the interface. By following the design specifications outlined in the mock-up, developers can ensure that the final product aligns with the intended design vision.
- Designers can use graphical mock-ups to conduct user testing. By presenting the mock-ups to users and observing their interactions, designers can gather insights into the user experience and identify areas for improvement.

Screen flow: a **screen flow** is a visual representation that illustrates the sequence of screens or pages within a digital interface, showing how users navigate through the interface to accomplish tasks or access information. Screen flows are commonly used in UX/UI design to map out the user journey and understand the interaction patterns within an interface.

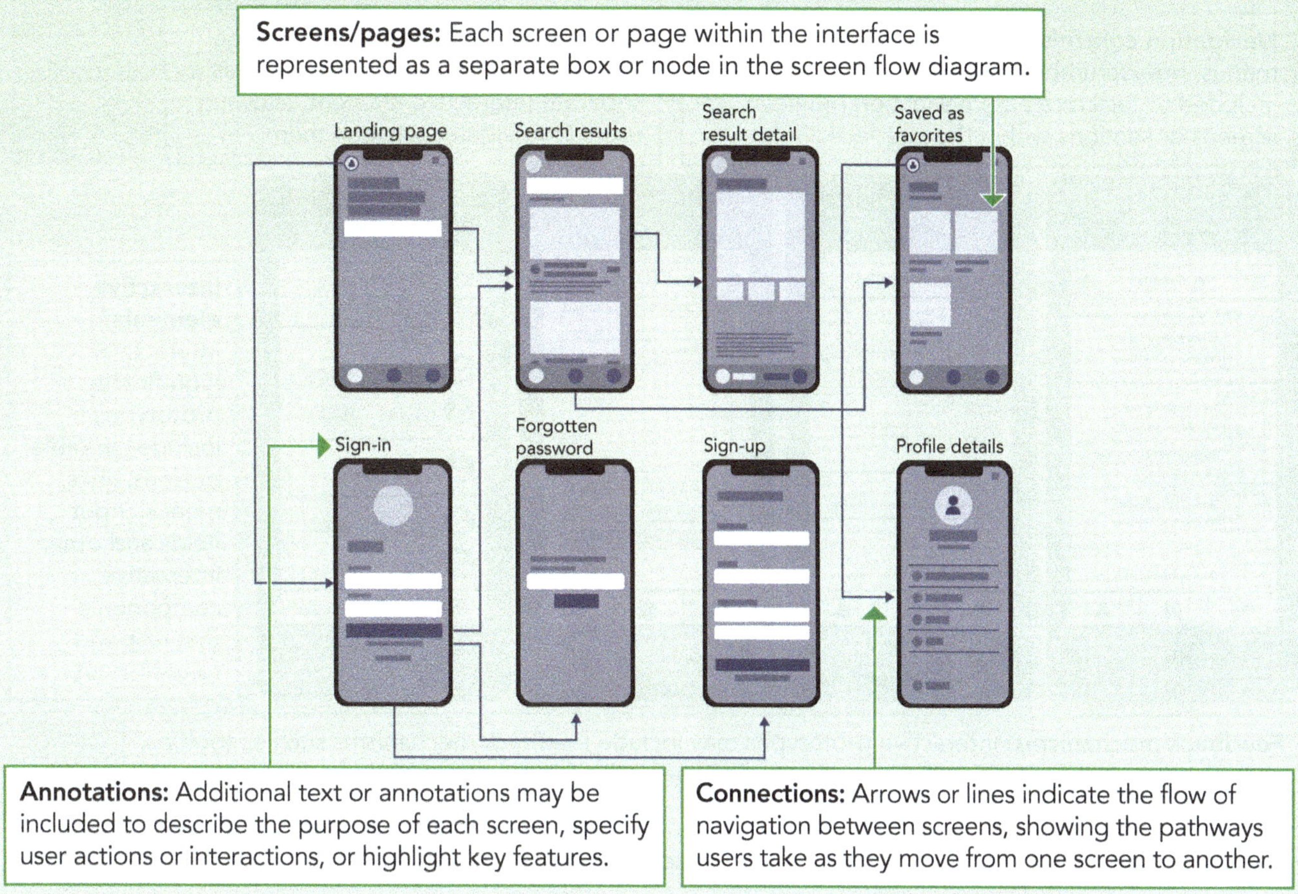
Screens/pages: Each screen or page within the interface is represented as a separate box or node in the screen flow diagram.
Landing page
Search results
Search result detail
Saved as favorites
Sign-in
Forgotten password
Sign-up
Profile details
Annotations: Additional text or annotations may be included to describe the purpose of each screen, specify user actions or interactions, or highlight key features.
Connections: Arrows or lines indicate the flow of navigation between screens, showing the pathways users take as they move from one screen to another.

Figure 3.25: Conventions and layout of a screen flow

How screen flows are used to design UX/UI solutions

- Identify the key user flows or pathways within the interface that need to be represented in the screen flow diagram. This could include tasks such as logging in, browsing products, completing a purchase and so on.
- Create a visual representation of the screens or pages involved in each user flow, arranging them in sequential order to illustrate the navigation flow.
- Use arrows or lines to connect the screens and indicate the direction of navigation between them. Include annotations to describe the user actions or interactions required at each step.
- Identify decision points or branches within the user flows where users make choices that affect the direction of navigation. Use conditional logic or annotations to illustrate
- Review the screen flow diagram with stakeholders, usability experts or end users to gather feedback and identify areas for improvement. Iterate on the design based on feedback to optimise the user experience.

Interactive: an interactive high-fidelity prototype is a digital representation of a user interface that closely resembles the final product in terms of appearance, functionality and interactivity. It allows users to interact with the interface in a realistic manner, simulating the actual user experience. Interactive high-fidelity prototypes often include interactive elements, animations, transitions and other dynamic features.

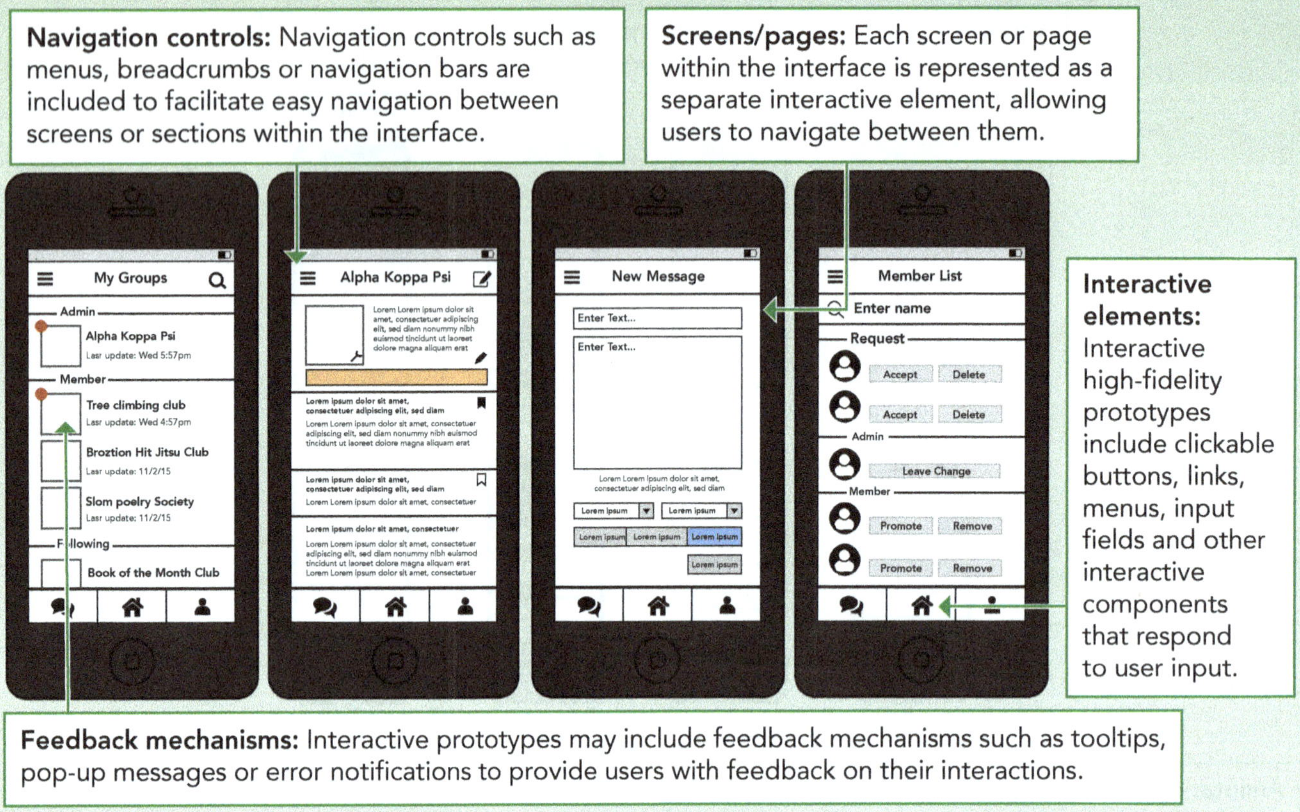
Navigation controls: Navigation controls such as menus, breadcrumbs or navigation bars are included to facilitate easy navigation between screens or sections within the interface.
Screens/pages: Each screen or page within the interface is represented as a separate interactive element, allowing users to navigate between them.
Interactive elements: Interactive high-fidelity prototypes include clickable buttons, links, menus, input fields and other interactive components that respond to user input.
Feedback mechanisms: Interactive prototypes may include feedback mechanisms such as tooltips, pop-up messages or error notifications to provide users with feedback on their interactions.
My Groups
Admin
Alpha Koppa Psi
Member
Tree climbing club
Broztion Hit Jitsu Club
Slom poelry Society
Following
Book of the Month Club
Alpha Koppa Psi
New Message
Enter Text...
Enter Text...
Member List
Enter name
Request
Accept
Delete
Admin
Leave Change
Member
Promote
Remove

Figure 3.26: Conventions and layout of an interactive high-fidelity prototype

UX/UI design features

How interactive high-fidelity prototypes are used to design a UX/UI solution

- Use the interactive high-fidelity prototype to validate design concepts, test usability and gather feedback from stakeholders, clients or end users.
- Conduct user testing sessions with the interactive prototype to observe how users interact with the interface, identify usability issues and gather insights into the user experience.
- Iterate on the design based on feedback from user testing sessions, making refinements and improvements to the interface to enhance usability and effectiveness.
- Use the interactive prototype as a communication tool to collaborate with team members, share design ideas and communicate design decisions effectively.
- Present the interactive prototype to stakeholders or clients for final design approval, allowing them to interact with the interface and provide feedback before moving on to development.

How high-fidelity prototypes are used to show UX/UI design features

High-fidelity prototypes are all used to show UX/UI design features in the following ways.

- Navigation aides: consistent and intuitive across screens, following established UX/UI patterns to make navigation easy for users.
- Layout: prioritise content hierarchy and readability, ensuring that important information is prominently displayed and easily accessible.
- House style: apply the brand's visual identity consistently throughout the screen flow, including colours, typography, logos and imagery. Use design elements from the brand's style guide or design system to maintain visual

consistency and reinforce brand recognition. Incorporate brand-specific design elements, such as custom icons or patterns, to reflect the brand's personality and values.

- Content: populate each screen with realistic content, including text, image and multimedia elements, to provide a clear understanding of the intended user experience. Use placeholder content where necessary to indicate where actual content will be displayed and maintain focus on layout and design elements. Ensure that content is concise, relevant and aligned with the target audience's needs and expectations.
- System interaction and event handling: include event triggers and states to simulate dynamic interactions, such as dropdown menus or collapsible panels, allowing users to interact with the prototype in a realistic manner. Incorporate interactive elements such as buttons, links, form fields and sliders to simulate user interaction with the mock-up. Design interactive components with appropriate feedback mechanisms, such as hover effects, click states or animations, to provide visual cues to users.
- Error handling and feedback: design error states and validation messages for form fields to provide feedback to users when input errors occur. Include error messages or tooltips near the affected fields to explain the nature of the error and suggest actions to correct the error. Use visual cues such as colour, icons or animation to draw attention to errors and guide users toward resolving them. Include confirmation messages or success indicators to provide feedback to users when actions are completed successfully.

Table 3.21: How particular high-fidelity prototypes are used to show UX/UI design features

High-fidelity prototype	Graphical mock-ups	Screen flow	Interactive
Navigation aides	• Include navigation elements such as menus, **breadcrumbs** or navigation bars to help users orient themselves within the interface. • Highlight active or selected navigation items to provide feedback on the user's current location within the interface.	• Each step in the screen flow should clearly indicate the navigation path users will take through the interface. • Include navigation elements such as arrows, buttons or annotations to guide users from one screen to the next.	• Include interactive navigation elements such as menus, breadcrumbs or navigation bars to guide users through the prototype. • Use interactive components such as buttons or links to simulate navigation interactions, allowing users to move between screens or sections of the prototype.
Layout	• Use grid systems and alignment guides to create visually balanced and effective layouts. • Consider responsive design principles to ensure that layouts adapt to different screen sizes and devices.	• Use alignment guides, white space and visual hierarchy effectively to create visually appealing and easy-to-navigate screens. • Consider the flow of information and user interactions when arranging elements on each screen, ensuring logical progression and intuitive navigation.	• Use alignment guides, white space and visual hierarchy effectively to create visually appealing and easy-to-navigate screens. • Consider responsive design principles to ensure that layouts adapt to different screen sizes and devices.

Learning in context 13

Fidelity continuum of a satellite navigation (sat nav) mobile app for smartphones

A fidelity continuum refers to a spectrum or range of fidelity levels in design, particularly in prototyping. The progression is from sketch to low fidelity (lo-fi) to a high-fidelity (hi-fi) prototype.

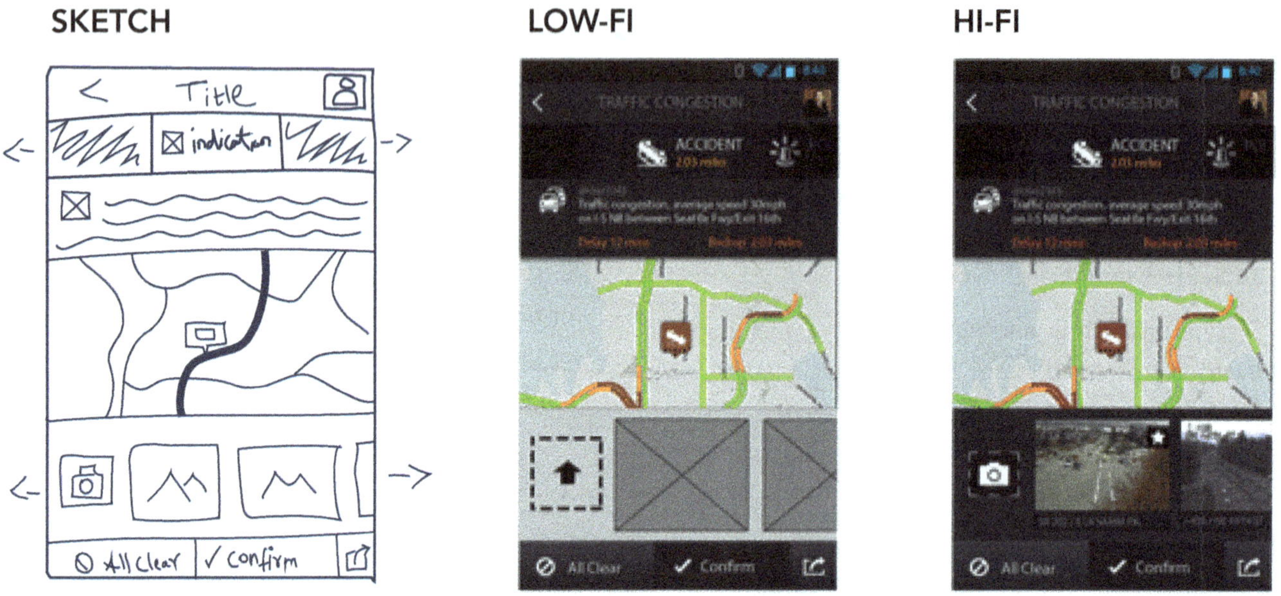
SKETCH
LOW-FI
HI-FI
Title
indicator
All clear
confirm
ACCIDENT
All Clear
Confirm
ACCIDENT
All Clear
Confirm

Figure 3.27: The diagram illustrates the progression using the example of designing a satellite navigation (sat nav) mobile app for smartphones

Sketching phase:

- In the sketching phase, designers start by brainstorming ideas and sketching rough drafts of the app interface on paper or using digital sketching tools.
- They might sketch out basic layouts for key screens such as the home screen, search destination screen, map view and turn-by-turn navigation interface.
- The sketches focus on the core functionalities and user flow, with simple annotations to indicate interactions and navigation paths.

Lo-fi prototyping:

- After selecting promising sketches, designers move on to create lo-fi prototypes using prototyping tools.
- Lo-fi prototypes translate the sketches into digital wireframes with more detail but still lacking in visual polish.
- The lo-fi prototypes focus on refining the user flow, interactions and basic visual elements such as buttons, text fields and navigation menus.
- Interactive features such as tapping to set a destination or zooming in/out on the map may be included in the lo-fi prototype to demonstrate basic functionality.

Hi-fi prototyping:

- Once the lo-fi prototype has been validated through user testing and feedback, designers proceed to create hi-fi prototypes.

Learning in context **Continued**

- Hi-fi prototypes involve adding detailed visual elements such as colours, typography, icons and graphics to create a polished and realistic representation of the final product.
- The hi-fi prototypes closely resemble the final app, with refined map visuals including terrain, landmarks and road details, as well as polished UI elements and animations.
- Interactive features are fully implemented, allowing users to simulate real-world interactions like entering destinations, getting directions and navigating through different views seamlessly.

3.1.2 Software tools

Software types

Standard software

Standard software tools offer basic capabilities for creating diagrams and prototypes, though they are not specifically designed for UX/UI design. It can:

- Use slides to create wireframes or mock-ups of different screens or pages in your UX/UI solution.
- Arrange shapes, text boxes and images to represent the layout and structure of the interface.
- Add annotations or notes to provide context or explain design decisions.
- Create transitions or animations between slides to simulate user interactions and demonstrate the flow of the interface.

Vector drawing

Vector drawing software provides more advanced tools for creating detailed illustrations and graphics, making them suitable for creating high-fidelity prototypes. It can:

- Use vector shapes, lines and curves to design precise wireframes or mock-ups of UI elements.
- Use layers and artboards to organise your designs and iterate on different versions.
- Incorporate typography, icons and other design assets to enhance the visual appeal of your prototypes.

Diagramming

Diagramming software offers specialised tools for creating diagrams, flowcharts and other visual representations of processes or systems. It can:

- Use predefined shapes and symbols to create flowcharts, user flows, sitemaps or other diagrams to illustrate UX/UI solutions.
- Connect shapes with lines or arrows to represent relationships or connections between different elements.
- Add annotations or labels to provide context or explanations for different parts of the diagram.

Interface prototyping software

Interface prototyping software is specifically designed for creating interactive prototypes of UX/UI solutions. It can:

- Use design tools to create wireframes or mock-ups of individual screens or components in your interface.
- Incorporate interactive elements such as buttons, links and form fields to simulate user interactions and navigation.
- Define transitions and animations to create a realistic and engaging user experience.
- To test prototypes with users to gather feedback and iterate on design improvements.

Software tools and techniques

Image/canvas size – image/canvas size refers to the dimensions of the digital workspace or area where design elements are created and arranged. It determines the width and height of the design space, which can vary based on the intended platform or output medium, such as mobile devices, desktop screens or print materials. UX/UI designers will use standard dimensions for common screen sizes or customise the canvas size to match specific requirements. Another alternative is to resize or crop images as needed to fit the canvas dimensions.

Layout tools – layout tools are software features that assist in arranging and organising design elements within a digital workspace. They include tools for aligning, distributing and spacing elements, as well as features for creating grids, guides and templates to maintain consistency and structure in the layout. UX/UI designers can experiment with different layout options to find the most effective arrangement for presenting information and guiding user interactions.

Drawing tools – drawing tools are software features that enable users to create and manipulate graphical elements, shapes and lines within a digital workspace. They include tools for drawing freehand, creating geometric shapes, editing paths and applying strokes and fills to shapes.

Layers and grouping – layers and grouping are organisational features used in graphic design software to manage and organise design elements within a digital workspace. Layers allow users to stack and order elements, while grouping enables users to organise related elements together for easier editing and manipulation.

Typography – typography refers to the art and technique of arranging fonts to make written language readable and visually appealing. It involves selecting appropriate fonts, adjusting font size, weight, spacing and alignment, and incorporating typographic hierarchy to convey meaning and emphasis. This helps UX/UI designers maintain consistency in typography across the design to create a cohesive and professional look.

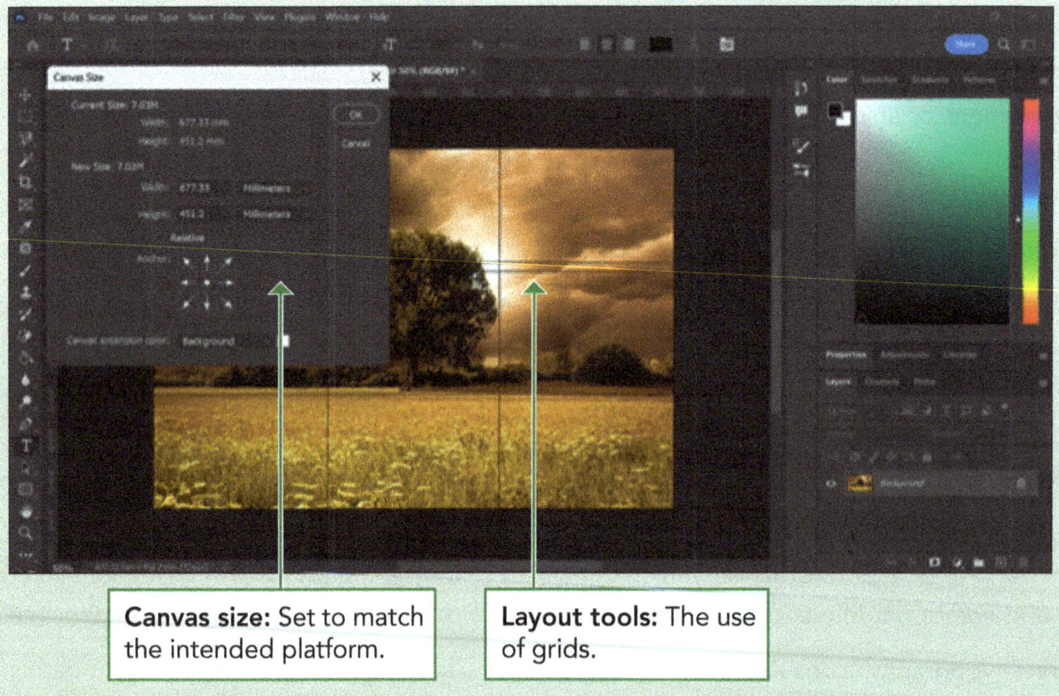
Canvas size: Set to match the intended platform.
Layout tools: The use of grids.

Figure 3.28: Grid and canvas sizes in a visual editing application

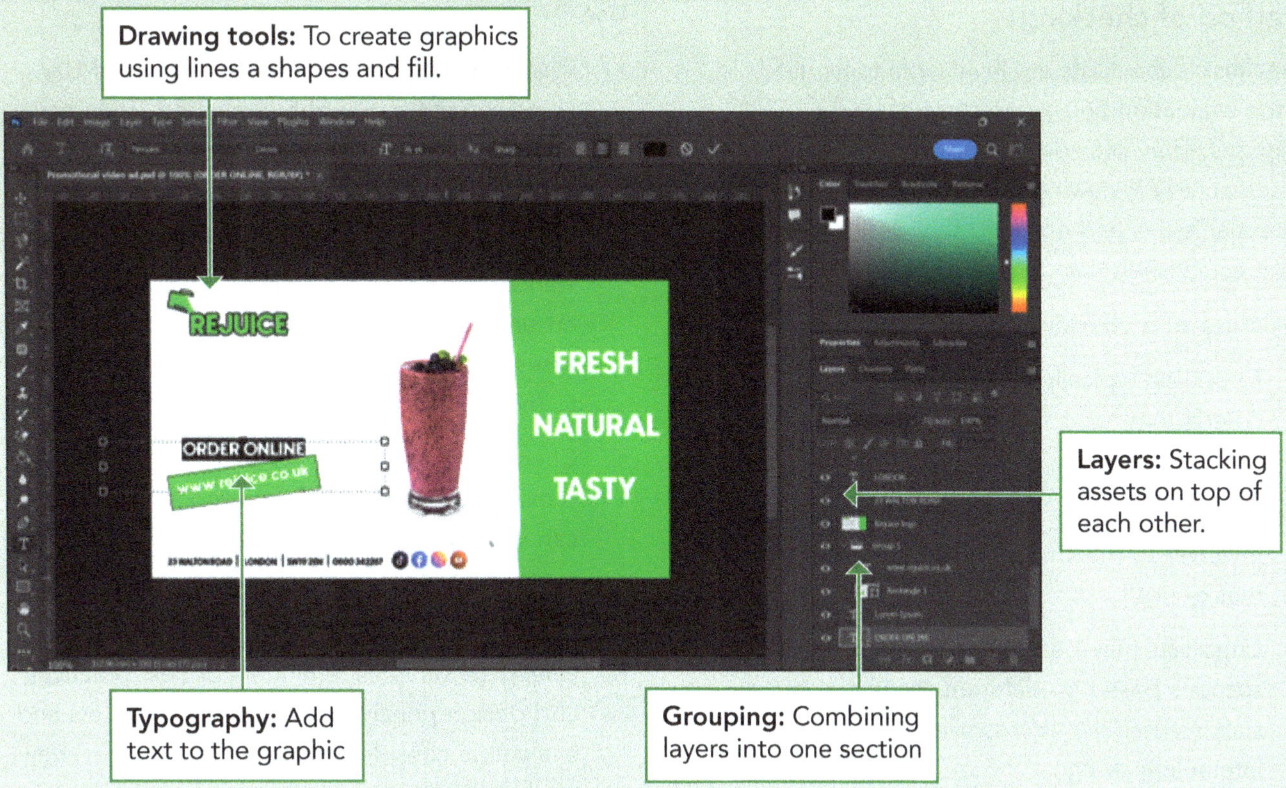
Drawing tools: To create graphics using lines a shapes and fill.
REJUICE
ORDER ONLINE
FRESH
NATURAL
TASTY
Layers: Stacking assets on top of each other.
Typography: Add text to the graphic
Grouping: Combining layers into one section

Figure 3.29: Typography, layers, drawing tools and grouping in a visual editing application

Image library objects – image library objects are pre-made graphical elements, icons, illustrations or symbols that can be imported into a digital design workspace. They provide designers with a library of ready-to-use assets that can be customised and incorporated into their designs.

Interactivity – interactivity refers to the ability of a digital design or prototype to respond to user input and simulate real-world user interactions. In UX/UI design, interactivity is achieved through features such as clickable buttons, links, menus and interactive elements that enable users to navigate, explore and engage with the design. Interactivity is essential for creating realistic and engaging user experiences in digital products and prototypes. UX/UI designers can define interactive behaviours, transitions and animations to simulate user flows and demonstrate the functionality of the design.

Quick check 9

1. How can diagrams be used to effectively communicate UX/UI design features such as interaction flows and navigation structures?
2. How can graphical mock-ups effectively illustrate various features of UX/UI design?

3.2 Tools and techniques to check UX/UI solution designs

Creating designs that are both aesthetically pleasing and functionally effective is crucial. However, ensuring the quality and effectiveness of UX/UI solution designs requires systematic evaluation and assessment. Therefore, designers use a variety of tools and techniques, including checklists, UI audit metrics and interface metrics, to thoroughly evaluate and validate their designs.

Method of checking

Checklist – checklists are invaluable tools used in the evaluation and assessment of UX/UI solutions. They provide a structured framework for systematically reviewing design elements, identifying potential issues and ensuring that design solutions meet established standards and best practices.

Structure of a checklist

- Checklists typically consist of a list of items or criteria that need to be evaluated.
- Each item on the checklist is accompanied by a checkbox or some other indicator that allows the reviewer to mark whether the criteria has been met or not.
- Checklists may be organised into categories or sections based on different aspects of the design, such as usability, accessibility, visual design and interaction design.

Content

- The content of a checklist is tailored to the specific goals and requirements of the design project.
- Examples of checklist items may include:
  - Usability criteria (for example, clear navigation, intuitive interface)
  - Accessibility guidelines (for example, sufficient colour contrast, keyboard accessibility)
  - Visual design elements (for example, consistent typography, appropriate use of white space)
  - Interaction design patterns (for example, responsive design, error handling)
  - Content guidelines (for example, concise and informative text, use of imagery)
  - Compliance with design standards or brand guidelines.

Use

- Checklists help ensure that all aspects of UX/UI design are thoroughly evaluated. They cover a wide range of criteria, including usability, accessibility, visual design and interaction design.
- They promote consistency by providing a standardised set of criteria for evaluation. This ensures that different designers or evaluators are assessing designs using the same criteria, leading to more consistent feedback.
- Checklists simplify the evaluation process by providing a structured framework. Evaluators can quickly scan through the checklist to identify areas of concern or improvement, saving time and effort.
- Checklists serve as reminders of best practices and design principles. They help designers and evaluators consider important factors that they might otherwise overlook.
- Checklists provide a record of the evaluation process, documenting what aspects of the design were assessed and any issues identified. This documentation can be valuable for tracking changes over time and for future reference.

UI audit metrics to check

UI audit metric checks refer to specific criteria used to evaluate UI designs to identify strengths, weaknesses and areas for improvement. The criteria explained below help designers identify usability issues, accessibility barriers, design inconsistencies and other areas for improvement in UI designs to enhance the overall user experience.

Branding and messaging – in assessing branding and messaging within UX/UI design solutions, it is crucial to ensure consistency with brand guidelines across elements like logos, colours, typography and tone of voice. This includes verifying that messaging effectively communicates the brand's values, mission and unique selling points. Additionally, evaluating visual elements and text composition with the intended brand image and target audience is essential.

Customer journey bottlenecks and roadblocks – to enhance user experience, it is essential to thoroughly map the customer journey, making use of user behaviour data like a visual representation of data that shows where users are clicking, tapping or looking on a web page or application known as a heatmap In addition to this, flow analytics to detect any bottlenecks or friction points, this could be achieved by tracking the paths that users take as they navigate through different pages or screens, as well as the actions they perform at each stage of the journey.

Design inconsistencies – conducting a comprehensive review of the UI design is essential to pinpoint any inconsistencies in visual elements such as colours, typography, spacing and alignment. By examining these aspects, designers can ensure that the interface maintains a cohesive aesthetic and user experience. It is crucial to strive for consistency not only within individual screens but also across different modules and components throughout the interface.

Layout and hierarchy inconsistencies – in the process of UX/UI design evaluation, it is important to assess the layout and hierarchy of elements present on each screen or page. This involves analysing whether the layout follows the established design principles such as visual hierarchy, grid systems and proximity. By ensuring alignment with these principles, designers can optimise the organisation of content and elements to enhance user understanding of the interface. Additionally, it is vital to prioritise important content and actions, ensuring they are readily accessible, while appropriately de-emphasising less critical elements.

Legal compliance – when evaluating a design, it is crucial to ensure laws and regulations are followed, such as safeguarding data privacy or ensuring web accessibility. This involves thoroughly reviewing the design to confirm the presence of necessary legal disclaimers, terms of service and privacy policies, making sure they are prominently displayed and easily accessible to users. Additionally, designers must address any potential legal risks or issues pertaining to copyright, trademarks or content licensing. By addressing legal considerations, designers can mitigate risks and ensure that the design aligns with regulatory requirements.

Usability and accessibility – to ensure optimal user experience, it is important to conduct usability testing with users, aiming to identify potential usability issues and gather valuable feedback on the interface's ease of use. Simultaneously, it is essential to assess the accessibility of the design by conducting tests with assistive technologies like screen readers and keyboard navigation. This evaluation helps ensure that the interface is inclusive and usable for all individuals, including those with disabilities. By incorporating both usability testing and accessibility evaluation, designers can iteratively refine the design to enhance its usability and accessibility, ultimately providing a more inclusive and user-friendly experience.

Usability heuristics – usability heuristics involves examining factors including the visibility of system status, the alignment between the system and real-world tasks, the provision of user control and freedom, consistency with established design standards, effective error prevention strategies, prioritising recognition over recall, ensuring flexibility and efficiency of use, and embracing minimalist design principles. By systematically evaluating the design against these heuristics, designers can identify areas for improvement and refine the interface to enhance usability, thereby creating a more intuitive and user-friendly experience for users.

Interface metrics to check

When designing a User Interface (UI) for a UX/UI solution, ensuring usability and user satisfaction is important. One way to achieve this is through thorough evaluation and optimisation of the interface using interface metric checks. These checks involve assessing specific aspects of the UI design to ensure it meets established criteria and standards. In this context, three important metrics that are commonly evaluated include the ability to configure the interface, the ability to navigate within the system and the keystroke effort per task.

Ability to configure the interface – the ability to configure the interface is the extent to which users can customise the interface according to their preferences or needs. Designers evaluate the availability and usability of configuration options, such as changing layout settings, adjusting font sizes or modifying colour schemes. A high level of configurability allows users to tailor the interface to suit their individual preferences, leading to increased user satisfaction and engagement. Designers may conduct usability testing to determine the effectiveness of configuration options and adjust accordingly.

Ability to navigate within the system – the ability to navigate within the system is the ease and efficiency with which users can move through different sections or screens. Designers assess the clarity and intuitiveness of navigation elements, such as menus, buttons, links and search functions. They also consider the organisation of content and the consistency of navigation patterns across the interface. A well-designed navigation system enables users to find information quickly and effortlessly, reducing frustration and enhancing the overall user experience. Usability testing can be used to identify navigation issues and optimise the navigation flow.

Keystroke effort per task – the keystroke effort per task measures the number of keystrokes or user interactions required to complete a specific task within the interface. Designers aim to minimise keystroke effort by simplifying workflows, reducing unnecessary steps and optimising user interface elements such as input fields, dropdown menus and buttons. A lower keystroke effort per task indicates a more efficient and user-friendly interface, as users can accomplish their goals with fewer interactions. Designers may use task analysis to identify areas where keystroke effort can be reduced and make the necessary adjustments.

Interface metrics to check

Use of interface metrics on the UX/UI design of an online streaming platform

An online streaming platform is a digital service that allows users to watch and stream audiovisual content over the internet. These platforms provide a wide range of content, including movies, TV shows, documentaries, music videos and original programming, which users can access on-demand from various devices such as smartphones, tablets, computers and smart TVs. Examples of popular online streaming platforms include Netflix, Amazon Prime Video, Hulu, Disney+ and YouTube.

How each of these interface metrics can be used to evaluate the UX/UI design of an online streaming platform:

Ability to configure the interface

- Users should be able to personalise their streaming experience by customising various aspects of the interface, such as the layout, content recommendations and playback settings.
- The platform could offer options for users to create personalised playlists, adjust subtitles and audio preferences and set up parental controls.
- Additionally, users may want to customise their home screen by selecting favourite genres, actors or directors, which will influence the content recommendations displayed to them.

Ability to navigate within the system

- Clear labels, recognisable icons and logical grouping of content will facilitate efficient navigation and exploration.
- Features such as search functionality, filters and sorting options can help users quickly find specific movies/films, TV shows or genres of interest.

- Breadcrumb navigation and back buttons should be available to help users retrace their steps or navigate between different levels of content hierarchy.

Keystroke effort per task

- The platform should offer keyboard shortcuts or voice commands for common actions, such as play/pause, volume control and skipping forward/backward.
- Users should be able to perform tasks with minimal keystrokes or clicks, reducing cognitive load and enhancing the overall user experience.
- Features such as autocomplete suggestions, predictive search and context-aware menus can help users accomplish tasks more quickly and with fewer interactions.

Quick check 10

1 What elements should be included in a checklist when evaluating the UX/UI solution design of an online supermarket shopping website?

2 What UI metric checks should be conducted to ensure that a UX/UI design solution is both usable and accessible?

TA4 Communicate UX/UI solutions

Learning intentions

This topic is about how to communicate UX/UI solutions.

It covers:

4.1 Develop UX/UI solution showcases

4.2 Techniques to deliver UX/UI solution showcases

4.1 Develop UX/UI solution showcases

Showcase formats

A UX/UI solution showcase is a presentation or display of a User Experience (UX) and User Interface (UI) design project. It typically involves detailed descriptions, visuals and sometimes interactive elements that illustrate the process and outcomes of a design solution. These showcases are designed to communicate how specific design challenges were addressed, demonstrating the effectiveness of the design in meeting user needs and business goals.

Developing UX/UI solution showcases involves several steps to ensure that the presentation effectively communicates the design process, decisions and outcomes.

Table 3.22: Showcase formats are appropriate to different audiences and content

Showcase format	Description	Considerations	Example
Live presentation (in-person or remote)	A live presentation involves presenting the UX/UI solution in real-time, either in person or via a virtual platform like Zoom, Microsoft Teams or Google Meet. The presenter can interact with the audience, answer questions and provide additional depth or context as needed based on audience reactions and questions.	• Encourages immediate feedback and interaction, allowing for clarifications and expansions on points as needed. • Highly relevant for interactive sessions, Q&A and discussions where audience participation is essential. • Useful for networking, workshops and training sessions where collaboration and hands-on activities are important. • Ideal for conveying complex information that might require real-time explanations or demonstrations.	A UX designer presents a new mobile app design to a potential client, demonstrating the app's features and user flow, and answering questions on the spot.

(Continued)

Showcase format	Description	Considerations	Example
Slideshow with audio overlay	A slideshow with an audio overlay involves a sequence of slides (often created with software like PowerPoint or Google Slides) accompanied by a pre-recorded narration that explains the content of each slide.	• The content is usually well-structured and scripted, allowing for comprehensive coverage of the topic without interruptions. • Useful for educational content and situations where the audience needs the flexibility to view the presentation at their own pace. • Ideal for training modules, tutorials and marketing presentations. • Useful for providing detailed explanations with visual aids and ensuring consistency in the delivery of information.	A UX team shares a recorded slideshow presentation with a new client, detailing the design process, research findings and design iterations for their review.
Video	A video showcase is a recorded, edited presentation that combines visuals, narration and often animations or screen recordings to demonstrate the UX/UI solution.	• Allows for creative and engaging storytelling, which can help in breaking down complex topics into understandable segments. • Useful for capturing attention and delivering content in an engaging and memorable way. • Effective for reaching broad audiences through platforms such as YouTube, social media or internal corporate communications. • Suitable for a wide range of purposes including educational content, promotional materials, how-to guides and documentaries.	A UX/UI designer creates a video walkthrough of a redesigned e-commerce website, highlighting new features, improved user flows and enhanced visual design, to be shared on the company's website and social media channels.

1 Identify the purpose

Understand the specific goals, such as demonstrating your expertise, highlighting the impact of your design or showcasing your process.

2 Know the audience

Identify who will be viewing the showcase. Tailor the content to their level of knowledge, interests and needs.

3 Select the right format

Choosing the right showcase format for a UX/UI solution is essential to effectively highlight the product's features, cater to the audience's preferences and requirements and ensure the presentation is accessible to all, enhancing overall comprehension and engagement.

- Live presentation is ideal for interactive sessions with immediate feedback.
- Slideshow with audio overlay is suitable for detailed, consistent information that can be reviewed at the audience's convenience.
- Video is best for dynamic, engaging content that can reach a wide audience.

4 Collect all relevant materials

a Research data

Gathering comprehensive research data is essential to understand user needs, market trends and the competitive landscape, providing a solid foundation for the design process.

- User personas provide a detailed representation of the target audience, including their demographics, behaviours, goals and pain points.
- Surveys collect direct feedback from users about their experiences, preferences and pain points related to the design solution.
- **Analytics** provide 'quantitative data' on user behaviour, interactions and engagement with the design solution.
- Competitive analysis, which is a strategic assessment process used by businesses to evaluate their competitors within an industry and any other relevant data that informed the design.

b Design objects

Collecting all design objects, including icons, images and style guides, ensures that the visual elements are consistent and aligned with the overall design vision.

- Wireframes provide a skeletal framework of the product, focusing on layout and structure without the distraction of colours and graphics.
- Prototypes create a realistic, interactive experience that mimics the final product's user interactions and workflows.
- Sketches allow for quick visualisation of ideas, enabling designers to explore multiple concepts without the need for detailed work.
- Final designs provide a complete and polished representation of the product, showcasing the visual design elements such as colours, typography, images and branding.

c Structure the content

Structuring the content involves organising information logically and coherently, making it easier to communicate key ideas and features effectively.

Introduction: provide context about the project, including the problem statement, goals and target audience.

↓

Research: present findings from user research.

↓

Ideas: show initial sketches, wireframes and design concepts, explaining the reason behind each iteration.

↓

Design and development: highlight key design decisions, prototypes, usability testing and final designs.

↓

Results: demonstrate the impact of the design solution, using **metrics**, user feedback and before-and-after comparisons.

↓

Conclusion: summarise the project's success, lessons learned and next steps.

d Develop the presentation

Developing the presentation entails creating a compelling narrative and visual flow that highlights the key aspects of the UX/UI solution, engaging the audience throughout.

- Live presentation: prepare slides or visual aids, rehearse the presentation and plan for audience interaction.
- Slideshow with audio overlay: create a **slide deck** with clear, concise slides. Record high-quality audio narration explaining each slide.
- Video: script the narration, plan the visuals and use video editing tools to create a professional looking final product.

Here are some design tips to follow when developing the presentation. Incorporating design tips involves applying best practices and expert advice to enhance the usability, aesthetics and functionality of the showcase.

- Use a consistent visual style aligned with your brand or project. For example, consistently using a brand's colours, fonts and design elements across all screens and components.
- Ensure readability with clear typography and well-contrasted colours. A showcase presentation should use large, legible fonts and high-contrast colour schemes (such as dark text on a light background) to ensure that all information is easily readable.
- Incorporate visuals such as images, icons and diagrams to enhance understanding. For example, a UX/UI showcase for a travel booking platform could integrate a variety of visuals, including destination images, intuitive icons for navigation and flow diagrams that explain the booking process.
- Keep it engaging with varied content types. This could include a mix of content types, such as explanatory text, tutorial videos, interactive animations demonstrating app features and customer testimonials in both text and video format.

Figure 3.30: Presentation

e Seek feedback

Seeking feedback from peers, stakeholders and potential users is crucial to identify areas for improvement and ensure the solution meets user expectations and requirements.

- Share a draft version with colleagues and gather constructive feedback.
- Make changes based on the feedback to improve clarity, engagement and overall quality.

f Test the showcase

Testing the showcase allows for the identification and resolution of any issues, ensuring that the presentation is smooth, effective and free of errors.

- If it is a live presentation, rehearse it multiple times and test any technical setups.
- For slideshows and videos, ensure all elements work correctly and the content flows logically.

g Present the showcase

Presenting the showcase involves delivering a well-prepared and engaging demonstration of the UX/UI solution to stakeholders, clients or users, emphasising its value and benefits.

- For live presentations, engage with your audience, maintain eye contact and be prepared to answer questions.
- Ensure that your slideshows and videos are easily accessible through appropriate channels like email, websites or social media.

h Follow up

Following up after the presentation is vital to address any questions, gather additional feedback and discuss the next steps, maintaining momentum and engagement.

- After the presentation, provide opportunities for your audience to ask further questions or request more information.
- Collect feedback on the showcase to understand what worked well and what could be improved for future presentations.

Showcase content considerations

When creating a UX/UI solution showcase, it is important to address several key content considerations to ensure the showcase effectively communicates the design process, decisions and outcomes. These considerations help adapt the presentation to suit the intended audience (client/stakeholders, design peers or general public), ensuring that it is engaging, informative and relevant.

Table 3.23: Showcase content considerations

Considerations	Client or stakeholders	Design peers	General public
Type of showcase • Live presentation (in-person or remote) • Slideshow with audio overlay • Video	Present a structured format with a clear agenda. Focus on key business outcomes and include time for Q&A to address specific concerns.	Present detailed case studies and walkthroughs of the design process. Use technical language and interactive elements to engage the audience.	Keep the presentation engaging with visuals and stories. Avoid technical jargon and focus on the user benefits and overall experience.
	Create concise, focused slides that highlight the problem, solution and business impact. Use simple, clear language and professional visuals.	Include detailed slides with insights into the design process, user research data and technical challenges. Provide in-depth explanations in the audio overlay.	Use a narrative style with engaging visuals and straightforward language. Focus on how the design improves the user experience.
	Produce a high-quality, polished video that clearly explains the problem, solution and results. Use metrics and **testimonials** to support your points.	Create a detailed video walkthrough of the design process, including screen recordings, prototypes and interviews with the design team.	Make an engaging, visually appealing video that tells the story of the design. Highlight key features and user benefits, keeping the content accessible and interesting.
Depth of content	Only include detailed analysis if it directly impacts business decisions, such as specific user feedback that led to critical changes or technical details that affected cost and timeline.	Dive deep into the design process, including research methods, ideas, prototyping, testing and iterations. Share insights on design decisions, tools used and lessons learned.	Avoid technical details. Instead, include high-level explanations that are easy to understand and relatable.
Relevance of content	• Highlight how the design meets specific business objectives and user needs. Use relevant metrics, such as increased user engagement, **conversion rates** or customer satisfaction scores. • Include real-life examples and testimonials that illustrate the positive impact of the design.	• Share relevant details about the design process, including user research findings, design iterations and prototyping methods. • Discuss specific challenges faced during the project and how they were overcome.	• Focus on how the design improves the overall user experience. Use relatable examples and stories to illustrate the benefits. • Ensure the content is visually engaging and easy to understand. Use before-and-after comparisons, simple diagrams and clear visuals to convey the message.

Showcase design considerations

When creating a UX/UI solution showcase, it is important to address several key design considerations. These considerations help adapt the presentation to suit the intended audience (client/stakeholders, design peers or general public.

Table 3.24: Factors and elements relating to design and accessibility that need to be planned and implemented when creating an effective and engaging a UX/UI solution showcase

Design consideration	Clients/Stakeholders	Design peers	General public
Colour scheme	• Use a colour scheme that aligns with the client's brand colours or the industry standards to convey professionalism, consistency and trust. • Opt for conservative colours to maintain a formal tone. • Use colours that will highlight key metrics, outcomes and important points without overwhelming the audience.	• Incorporate more vibrant and diverse colours to reflect creativity and innovation. • Use colours that align with design tools and **frameworks** used in the industry. • Use colour coding to differentiate between various stages of the design process, elements or **user flows**.	• Choose an engaging, easy-to-read colour scheme with high contrast between background and foreground colours for better readability and visual appeal. • Ensure colours are accessible to all individuals, including those that have difficulty distinguishing between certain colours or perceiving colours accurately. Use tools like colour contrast checkers. • Opt for a friendly and approachable palette that enhances the overall user experience.
Language and vocabulary	• Use straightforward, business-oriented language. Avoid jargon and technical terms unless they are commonly understood by the audience. • Focus on results, benefits and return on investment. Use language that highlights the business impact and value. • Maintain a formal and professional tone throughout the presentation.	• Use industry-specific terminology and design jargon. Peers will appreciate the depth and detail. • Focus on the design process, methods and technical challenges. Explain design decisions in detail. • Adopt a tone that invites discussion and feedback, reflecting a shared interest in design practices.	• Use plain language and avoid technical jargon. Explain concepts in a way that is easily understandable. • Highlight how the design improves user experience and solves problems. Use relatable examples and stories. • Keep the tone friendly and engaging to maintain interest.

(Continued)

Design consideration	Clients/Stakeholders	Design peers	General public
Layout	• Use a clear, logical structure that flows smoothly from problem statement to solution and results. • Make key points and metrics stand out using larger fonts, bold text and highlighted sections. • Maintain a clean, professional layout with effective use of **white space** to avoid clutter.	• Include detailed sections for each phase of the design process. Use **modular** layouts that can be expanded on. • Incorporate wireframes, prototypes, user flows and design artifacts. Use grids and guides to organise content. • Include interactive elements such as buttons, links, animations that allow peers to explore the design in more depth.	• Use a simple, intuitive layout that guides the viewer through the presentation naturally. • Employ a visual storytelling approach with images, icons and infographics to illustrate points. • Use engaging elements like animations, videos and testimonials to keep the audience interested.
Style	• Adopt a formal style that reflects the professionalism expected in business environments. • Align the style with the client's branding guidelines, including fonts, colours and logos. • Use charts and graphs, to support your points and make the business case.	• Incorporate current design trends and innovative techniques that other designers can relate to. • Provide detailed visuals such as high-fidelity prototypes, design systems and style guides. • Include elements that inspire and provoke thought, such as design inspirations, references and future trends.	• Use an approachable and friendly style that makes the content accessible and enjoyable. • Prioritise visual elements over text. Use large images, videos and icons to convey messages quickly and effectively. • Add a personal touch with user stories, testimonials and real-life examples to connect with the audience.

Good
Bad
Good
Bad
Good
Bad
Good
Bad
Good
Bad
Good
Bad
Good
Bad
Good
Bad
Good
Bad

Figure 3.31: Examples of good and bad colour combinations

Quick check 11

1 What are the different formats for showcasing UX/UI solutions, and how do they differ in terms of presentation style and audience interaction?

2 How should language and vocabulary be adapted when presenting a UX/UI solution to different audiences, such as business stakeholders, design peers and general public?

4.2 Techniques to deliver UX/UI solution showcases

Resources required

Delivering UX/UI solution showcases effectively requires both hardware and software that can deliver high quality presentations to the intended audience.

Computing devices

Computer or laptop
This is the primary device for creating, editing, and presenting the showcase. This will ensure it's capable of running design and presentation software smoothly.

Input devices

Mouse
To hover effects, drag-and-drop functionality, and other interactive components of the UI.

Keyboard
Allows for quick navigation, text entry, and execution of shortcuts to streamline the presentation.

Graphics tablet
Ideal for live sketching, making annotations, and highlighting specific areas of the design in real-time.

Webcam
Use the webcam for virtual meetings and presentations, ensuring clients can see you clearly, which helps build a more personal connection.

Output devices

Display equipment
Use a monitor for design work and a projector/screen for client presentations, ensuring visuals are clear and professional.

Microphone
Ensures that the presenter's voice is heard clearly, allowing for effective narration and explanation of the UX/UI solution.

Speakers/headphones
Enables the audience to hear pre-recorded narrations, sound effects, or any audio components integrated into the UX/UI showcase.

Figure 3.32: Hardware required to deliver UX/UI showcases

Software

- Design and prototyping tools: use these tools to create detailed and interactive prototypes that can be shared with clients for feedback. Ensure you know how to navigate and present designs effectively. For example, Adobe XD is a comprehensive design and prototyping tool with features for wireframing, interaction design and sharing prototypes.
- Presentation software: create a presentation that tells the story of the design process, showcasing key milestones that are significant moments in the project, design decisions and final outcomes. Integrate visuals, metrics and interactive elements to engage the audience. For example, Microsoft PowerPoint is a popular choice because it is a widely used presentation software with extensive features for creating slideshows. In addition to this, it supports multimedia integration and animations.
- Video editing software: use these tools to produce high-quality video walkthroughs of the design, incorporating animations, transitions and voiceovers to explain the design process and decisions clearly. For example, Adobe Premier Pro is professional video editing software with advanced features for editing, effects and audio. In addition to this, it is widely used in the industry for creating high-quality video showcases.
- Collaboration tools: schedule and conduct remote meetings using these tools. Share your screen to present the showcase and use features like chat and Q&A to engage with clients. For example, Slack is a messaging platform that facilitates team communication and collaboration.

How to use resources to deliver UX/UI solution showcases to clients

- Ensure the workspace is organised and free from distractions. Test all hardware (computer, projector, microphone and so on) to ensure they are working correctly.
- Use design tools to create detailed and interactive prototypes. Develop a structured presentation
- Produce a video walkthrough of the design using video editing software, adding voiceovers and annotations as needed.
- Use the projector or large screen to display the presentation clearly.
- Use a high-quality microphone to ensure the voice is clear and professional. Engage with clients by explaining design decisions, showing before-and-after comparisons and highlighting key metrics.
- For remote presentations, use collaboration tools to share the screen and interact with clients. Use chat and Q&A features to address questions in real-time.
- For in-person meetings, encourage clients to ask questions and provide feedback, making the session interactive.
- Share the presentation, video and any other relevant materials with clients after the meeting.
- Ask for feedback on the presentation and the design itself. Use this to refine future showcases and improve the design process.

Techniques for effective communication

Effective communication is key when delivering UX/UI solution showcases to clients. Using techniques such as clarity, coherence, completeness, conciseness, correctness and courteousness ensures that your message is understood and appreciated.

Clarity

Clarity means making your message easy to understand.

- Use simple language: avoid jargon and technical terms unless the client is familiar with them. Instead of saying, 'We implemented a responsive design using a mobile-first approach,' you could say, 'We made sure the design works well on both mobile phones and computers.'
- Visual aids: use clear visuals such as before-and-after screenshots, diagrams and prototypes to illustrate your points.

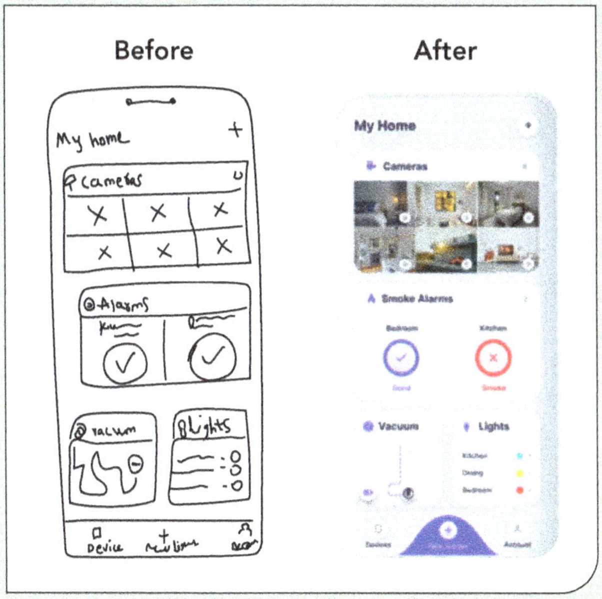

Before
After
My home
Cameras
Alarms
Lights
My Home
Cameras
Smoke Alarms
Vacuum
Lights

Figure 3.33: Before and after shots provide clarity

- Organise content logically: start with a clear agenda, and follow a logical structure (for example, problem, solution, results).

Coherence

Coherence ensures that your presentation flows logically from one point to the next.

- Logical flow: arrange your points in a logical sequence. Start with the problem, then discuss the design process and conclude with the solution and its impact.
- Transitions: use clear transitions between sections. Signal when you're moving from one part of the presentation to another with phrases such as 'Next, we'll look at...'. For example, it is less coherent to jump between topics without transitions such as 'Here's our login screen. Now let me show you the settings page. By the way, our sign-up process is unique'. A better approach would be 'First, let's look at our login screen. Once users log in, they have quick access to their settings, which I'll show next. After settings, we'll dive into the sign-up process and how it streamlines user registration'.

Completeness

Completeness means providing all necessary information. Or, as another example, rather than saying 'Our design is flawless and has no drawbacks', it would be better to say 'While our design addresses many user needs, there may be limitations that we continue to monitor and improve on'.

- Cover all aspects: make sure you address all parts of the project, from initial research to final outcomes. For example, rather than saying 'Our new dashboard looks great. Now, let's talk about the profile page', it would be better to say 'Our new dashboard looks great. It includes features like real-time analytics, customisable widgets and easy navigation. Now, let's talk about the profile page'. Or, as another example, rather than saying 'Our design is flawless and has no drawbacks', it would be better to say, 'While our design addresses many user needs, there may be limitations that we continue to monitor and improve on'.

- Anticipate questions: think about questions clients might have and address them in your presentation.

Conciseness

Conciseness is about being brief and to the point without removing essential information.

- Stick to key points: focus on the most important aspects of the project. Avoid unnecessary details that don't add value to the client.
- Short sentences: use short, direct sentences to convey your message clearly.

Correctness

Correctness ensures that your information is accurate and free of errors.

- Verify information: double-check your data, statistics and facts before the presentation.
- Grammar and spelling: ensure your slides and spoken presentation are free from grammatical and spelling errors.

Courteousness

Courteousness involves being polite and respectful throughout your presentation.

- Positive tone: use a positive and respectful tone, even when discussing challenges or negative feedback.
- Respect client's time: be punctual and stay within the allocated time for the presentation.

Quick check 12

1 How can different formats for delivering a UX/UI solution showcase be effectively structured to meet client needs, including live presentations, slideshows with audio overlays and videos?

2 What hardware and software are necessary for effectively delivering high-quality UX/UI solution showcases and how should they be used to ensure successful presentations to clients?

TA5 Review and improve UX/UI solutions

Learning intentions

This topic is about how to review and improve UX/UI solutions.

It covers:

5.1 Review the fitness for purpose of UX/UI solutions

5.2 Improvements to UX/UI solutions

5.3 Review the processes used to plan, design and communicate UX/UI solutions

5.1 Review the fitness for purpose of UX/UI solutions

Suitability for meeting client, user and solution requirements

Suitability for meeting client, user and solution requirements involves evaluating how well a proposed system or application aligns with the specific needs and expectations of its stakeholders, ensuring that it effectively addresses the defined objectives and delivers the desired outcomes.

How to assess the strengths and weaknesses of UX/UI solutions

Assessing the strengths and weaknesses of UX/UI solutions involves a detailed evaluation of various aspects such as usability, functionality, performance, visual design, accessibility or security, **scalability** and **compliance**. This is crucial because it ensures that the final product is not only functional but also user-friendly and effective.

Table 3.25 provides a framework for assessing the strengths and weaknesses of a UX/UI solution by checking it against key criteria. By evaluating client, user and solution requirements, it is possible to identify areas of success and improvement, ensuring the design meets project expectations and provides an effective user experience.

Table 3.25: How an evaluation of requirements can identify strengths and weaknesses in UX/UI solutions

Requirement type	How it assesses strengths	How it identifies weaknesses
Client requirements	• Ensures the UX/UI design follows the project brief • Checks if the design aligns with the intended theme, purpose and audience • Confirms that all required elements (for example, colours, fonts, branding) are included as specified.	• Highlights any missing elements or changes from the project brief • Identifies inconsistencies in branding, layout or design choices • Reveals whether the final product meets the original objectives set in the task.

(Continued)

Requirement type	How it assesses strengths	How it identifies weaknesses
User requirements	• Assesses usability by testing if the interface is easy to navigate and understand • Ensures accessibility by checking colour contrast, text readability and alternative text for images • Evaluates user engagement by considering visual appeal and ease of interaction.	• Identifies confusing navigation, unclear instructions or poor readability • Highlights accessibility issues, such as small text or poor colour contrast • Shows where improvements are needed to make the design more user-friendly.
Solution requirements	• Checks if all interactive elements (for example, buttons, links, forms) function correctly • Evaluates performance, such as loading times and responsiveness across different devices • Ensures compliance with any specified technical requirements (for example, correct file formats, responsive design).	• Detects broken links, missing functionality or incomplete features • Identifies performance issues like slow loading times or poor mobile compatibility • Highlights any errors related to incorrect file types, poor scalability or failure to meet technical guidelines.

With the data collected from analysing the strengths and weaknesses of an UX/UI solution, a strategic plan should be developed to use the strengths and address the weaknesses to improve the UX/UI solution and enhance the overall user experience.

How to compare UX/UI solutions against requirements

To effectively compare UX/UI solutions against client requirements, user requirements and solution requirements, it is essential to conduct a comprehensive assessment across various factors.

Client requirements

- Revisit the original client brief, user profiles and functional specifications.
- Evaluate how well each UX/UI solution aligns with the client's brand identity, visual style and messaging.
- Assess the extent to which each solution meets the specific features and functionalities requested by the client.
- Analyse how each solution contributes to achieving the client's business goals, such as increasing conversion rates, improving user engagement or enhancing **brand perception**.

User requirements

- Evaluate how well each solution addresses user needs, preferences and pain points, as identified through user research, **personas** and **journey mapping**.
- Consider the outcomes of usability testing sessions, focusing on metrics like task success rates, time on task and user satisfaction scores.
- Incorporate feedback gathered from user surveys, which can provide insights into user preferences, satisfaction levels and areas for improvement.
- Assess how closely each solution aligns with user expectations in terms of usability, functionality and overall user experience.

Solution requirements

- Functional requirements: Evaluate the completeness and correctness of features in each solution, ensuring that all specified functionalities align with client and user needs. This includes assessing features such as user authentication, data input/output, **search functionality** and any custom requirements outlined by the client.
- Interface requirements: Assess the User Interface (UI) and User Experience (UX) design elements of each solution to ensure usability, accessibility and visual appeal. Evaluate the consistency of interface elements, such as navigation menus, buttons, forms and layout across different screens and devices. Incorporate feedback gathered from user testing sessions and usability studies to refine the interface design and improve user satisfaction.
- Non-functional requirements: Check if each solution meets technical requirements, including compatibility with various devices, browsers and operating systems. Ensure that the solution adheres to performance benchmarks for responsiveness, loading times and resource usage. Assess the level of security measures implemented in each solution to protect user data from unauthorised access, data breaches and other security threats. Verify compliance with relevant regulations and standards, such as GDPR (General Data Protection Regulation).

Application of UX/UI design principles

UX/UI design principles are fundamental guidelines that ensure the design of digital products is user-centred, efficient and aesthetically pleasing. Applying these principles effectively can significantly enhance user satisfaction and overall product success.

Usability – usability focuses on making products intuitive and easy to use, ensuring that users can achieve their goals efficiently and effectively. Designers apply usability principles by conducting user research, creating clear navigation structures, organising content logically and providing feedback to users. Usability testing is also crucial for identifying and addressing usability issues throughout the design process, improving overall user satisfaction and productivity.

Accessibility – accessibility involves designing products that are usable by people with disabilities, ensuring equal access to information and functionality for all users. Designers apply accessibility principles by following established guidelines, such as the **Web Content Accessibility Guidelines (WCAG)**, to make interfaces understandable and robust. This includes providing **alternative text** for images, implementing keyboard navigation, ensuring sufficient colour contrast and supporting assistive technologies like screen readers. By prioritising accessibility, designers create more inclusive and usable products that cater to a diverse range of users.

Visual design – visual design focuses on creating visually appealing interfaces that communicate effectively and engage users emotionally. Designers apply visual design principles, such as hierarchy, typography, colour theory and layout, to create aesthetically pleasing and cohesive designs. Visual elements, such as icons, imagery and branding, are used strategically to enhance the user experience and reinforce the product's identity. By balancing aesthetics with functionality, designers create visually engaging interfaces that resonate with users and support their goals.

Performance – performance involves optimising the speed, responsiveness and reliability of products to ensure a seamless user experience. Designers apply performance principles by optimising code, minimising loading times and prioritising content delivery. By prioritising performance, designers create products that load quickly, respond promptly to user interactions and maintain reliability even under heavy usage, enhancing user satisfaction and engagement.

How to assess the application of UX/UI design principles

Assessing the application of UX/UI design principles involves evaluating how effectively these principles have been incorporated into the design and implementation of a product. Here's how you can assess the application of UX/UI design principles:

Usability assessment

- Conduct usability testing with representative users to evaluate the ease of use and effectiveness of the product.
- Use metrics such as task success rate, time on task and error rate to measure usability.
- Gather feedback from users through surveys, interviews or observation sessions to identify usability issues and areas for improvement.

Accessibility evaluation

- Conduct an accessibility audit or review to assess compliance with accessibility standards such as WCAG.
- Use automated accessibility testing tools to identify common accessibility issues and evaluate the accessibility of the product.
- Involve users with disabilities in usability testing to assess the effectiveness of accessibility features and identify any barriers to access.

Visual design review

- Evaluate the visual design of the product against design principles such as hierarchy, typography, colour theory and layout.
- Assess the consistency and coherence of visual elements across the product, including icons, imagery and branding.
- Consider factors such as aesthetics, visual appeal and emotional engagement when assessing the visual design.

Performance testing

- Conduct performance testing to measure the speed, responsiveness and reliability of the product under different conditions.
- Use tools to monitor and analyse factors such as loading times, response times and server performance.
- Identify performance bottlenecks and areas for optimisation to improve the overall performance of the product.

Feedback and iteration

- Collect feedback from users, stakeholders and team members throughout the design and development process.
- Use feedback to iterate on the design, address usability issues, improve accessibility, refine visual design and optimise performance.
- Continuously evaluate and refine the application of UX/UI design principles to ensure that the product meets user needs and achieves its objectives.

Learning in context 14

Assessing the application of UX/UI design principles in an e-commerce platform

An e-commerce platform, 'ShopEase,' is being evaluated to ensure it adheres to UX/UI design principles, providing an optimal user experience for online shoppers. They establish criteria based on UX/UI Principles:

- Usability: ease of navigation, simplicity of checkout process, clarity of product information.
- Accessibility: compliance with Web Content Accessibility Guidelines (WCAG).
- Visual design: aesthetic appeal, brand consistency and visual hierarchy.
- Performance: load times, responsiveness and smoothness of interactions such as button feedback and page transitions.

Usability

They conduct usability tests with real users representing different **demographics** and shopping habits. These are typical behaviours and preferences that consumers demonstrate when making purchases. They observe users as they perform key tasks such as searching for products, adding items to the cart and completing a purchase. They can also check:

- percentage of users who can complete tasks successfully
- average time users take to complete each task
- number of errors users encounter
- gather feedback on their experience and satisfaction levels.

They identify areas where users face difficulties, such as complex navigation or confusing checkout steps. They determine strengths, such as efficient product search and clear product descriptions.

Accessibility

They use automated tools and manual testing to assess accessibility and check for compliance with WCAG standards which can help to identify specific barriers, such as missing alternative text or inadequate colour contrast. This will ensure the platform is accessible to all users, including those with disabilities, by addressing identified issues.

Visual design

They collect user feedback on the platform's design appeal, use of colour, typography and imagery by gathering qualitative data on visual appeal and preferences such as rating aspects such as colour harmony, typography readability and effective use of imagery. This is done to ensure the platform is visually appealing and aligns with brand identity, contributing to a positive user experience.

Performance

They test the platform's performance under various conditions, such as different network speeds and on different devices. This could include measurement of how quickly pages load, evaluating the ease and naturalness with which users can interact with a product or interface. such as scrolling and clicking and to assess how efficiently the platform uses device resources. This will help to identify and address performance bottlenecks, ensuring a fast and smooth user experience.

Quick check 13

1 How does the process of conducting security assessments contribute to evaluating the strengths and weaknesses of a UX/UI solution from a legal perspective?

2 How are design principles used to improve the effectiveness of a UX/UI solution?

5.2 Improvements to UX/UI solutions

Assessing and improving UX/UI solutions demands a comprehensive and structured approach based on user experience, use of UX/UI design principles and psychology and industry and interface standards. By focusing on usability, functionality, performance, visual design, accessibility, security, scalability and compliance, organisations can ensure their products not only meet user needs but also adhere to legal and industry requirements while providing a seamless and engaging experience.

User experience

Improving UX/UI solutions demands a structured approach, incorporating user feedback, usability metrics analysis, expert evaluations and design principles assessments.

Gather user feedback

To enhance a product's effectiveness, designers engage in actively collecting and analysing user feedback, ensuring the solutions connect with user needs and preferences.

- Surveys: deploy online surveys to collect feedback on users' experiences, satisfaction levels and areas for improvement.
- Interviews: conduct one-on-one interviews with users to gain in-depth insights into their pain points, needs and preferences.
- Feedback forms: implement feedback forms within the application or website to capture real-time user opinions.

For example, for an e-commerce platform, user feedback might reveal issues with the checkout process, product search functionality or mobile responsiveness.

Consider design principles

Adhere to established design principles to create intuitive and visually appealing UX/UI solutions, ensuring seamless user experiences and promoting engagement.

- Usability: ensure the solution is easy to learn, efficient to use and error tolerant which means to minimise the negative impact of user errors and help users recover from them easily.
- Visual hierarchy: emphasise important elements such colour and contrast, typography and the use of visual cues like arrows, icons and progress bars to guide users through tasks and indicate the next steps.
- Consistency: maintain consistency in design elements, terminology and interaction patterns throughout the interface.
- Accessibility: ensure the solution is accessible to users with disabilities and complies with accessibility standards.

For example, applying design principles might involve simplifying complex forms, improving contrast for readability or to help users to understand what actions they can perform on interactive elements, such as buttons, links and forms, without needing additional instructions.

Identify potential improvements

Through assessment and analysis, designers can identify areas for enhancement and innovation within their UX/UI solutions, to create user satisfaction and product effectiveness.

- Prioritise issues and pain points identified through user feedback, usability testing, expert evaluations and design principles.
- Consider the impact of potential improvements on user satisfaction, task completion rates and business objectives.
- Generate recommendations for UX/UI enhancements.
- For example, improvements might include redesigning the checkout process for clarity and efficiency, optimising search functionality for better results or enhancing mobile responsiveness for seamless browsing.

Use of UX/UI design principles

As you have already learned, UX/UI design principles are fundamental guidelines that ensure the design of digital products is user-centred, efficient and aesthetically pleasing.

Assessing the use of UX/UI design principles when identifying potential improvements to UX/UI solutions involves evaluating how well the existing design adheres to fundamental principles and identifying areas for enhancement.

Understand UX/UI design principles

Understanding UX/UI design principles is essential for creating intuitive, engaging and effective user experiences that meet the needs of users while achieving the goals of a product or service.

- Usability: evaluate the ease of use, efficiency and learnability of the interface.
- Visual hierarchy: assess the organisation of elements to guide user attention effectively.
- Consistency: check for consistency in design elements, terminology and interaction patterns.
- Accessibility: ensure the interface is accessible to users with disabilities and complies with accessibility standards.
- Surveys: collect feedback from users on their experience with the interface, focusing on aspects related to usability, visual hierarchy, consistency, clarity, intuitiveness and accessibility.
- Interviews: conduct one-on-one interviews with users to understand their pain points, preferences and suggestions for improvement.
- Usability testing: observe users as they interact with the interface to identify areas of confusion or frustration.

Figure 3.34: To continuously improve the user experience of a UX/UI solution, gathering user feedback is crucial to understand user preferences, identify pain points and make informed design decisions

Evaluate visual design elements

Evaluating visual design elements is crucial for assessing their effectiveness in communicating brand identity, enhancing user engagement and creating an aesthetically pleasing and cohesive user experience.

- Typography: assess the readability and appropriateness of typography choices.
- Colour scheme: evaluate the use of colour for aesthetic appeal and effective communication.
- Imagery: check the relevance and quality of images used throughout the interface.
- Layout: assess the organisation and spacing of elements for clarity and visual appeal.

Identify potential improvements

Identifying potential improvements is a key step in enhancing the usability, functionality and overall user satisfaction of a UX/UI solution, ensuring it evolves to meet the changing needs and expectations of its users.

- Prioritise areas where the interface deviates from design principles or fails to meet user needs and expectations.
- Generate actionable insights and recommendations for improving usability, visual design, consistency and accessibility.
- Consider the impact of potential improvements on user experience, engagement and task completion rates.

Use of principles of UX/UI design psychology

UX/UI design psychology involves understanding human thinking and processing patterns, decision-making processes and user needs. It is important to understand these when identifying potential improvements to UX/UI solutions to avoid design mistakes and create solutions that improve user experience and engagement.

Understand UX/UI design psychology principles

Understanding UX/UI design psychology principles is essential for creating interfaces that resonate with users on a subconscious level, influencing their behaviours, emotions and perceptions to ultimately enhance the overall user experience.

- Visual perception: understanding how users interpret and make sense of visual information is crucial for designing intuitive and accessible interfaces such as the use of colours to convey meaning, choosing font and text layouts are that are easy to read and the use of visual icons and other visual indicators to help users understand actions and information quickly.
- Cognitive load: managing the amount of mental effort required to interact with the interface. A simple design to minimise distractions, breaking information down in manageable chunks and revealing information as and when is needed are ways this could be assessed.
- Emotional design: evoking specific emotions and supporting emotional connections with users. This could be assessed through visual design, how well it understands users' needs, preferences and pain points to design experiences and the impact of using feedback mechanisms.
- Behavioural psychology: when understanding UX/UI design principles, assessing behavioural psychology involves examining how users behave and interact with interfaces based on their psychological tendencies and responses. This can be assessed through various methods such as user testing, surveys and interviews.

Gather user feedback on emotional response

- Surveys: collect feedback from users on their emotional responses to the interface, focusing on aspects such as appeal, trustworthiness and enjoyment.
- Interviews: conduct qualitative interviews to explore users' emotional experiences and perceptions of the interface.
- Observation: observe users as they interact with the interface to identify emotional cues and reactions.

Analyse behavioural patterns

- User analytics: Analyse user behaviour data to identify patterns, such as navigation paths, **click-through rates** and **interaction sequences**.
- Heatmaps: use heatmaps to visualise where users focus their attention and interact most frequently on the interface.
- **A/B testing**: conduct A/B tests to compare different design variations and assess their impact on user behaviour and engagement.

Evaluate emotional design elements

- Colour psychology: assess the use of colour to evoke specific emotions and convey meaning.
- Typography: evaluate typography choices for their impact on readability, mood and emotional response.
- Imagery: analyse the relevance, quality and emotional appeal of images used throughout the interface.
- **Micro interactions**: evaluate the use of interactive methods such as triggers and animations for their ability to delight and engage users.

Identify potential improvements

- Prioritise areas where the interface could better use psychological principles to evoke desired emotional responses and behaviours.
- Generate recommendations for enhancing emotional design elements and interactions.
- Consider the impact of potential improvements on user engagement, emotional connection and overall satisfaction.

Use of UX/UI interface standards

UX/UI interface standards are essential guidelines that ensure consistency, usability and accessibility in digital product design. By adhering to these standards, designers can create intuitive and user-friendly interfaces that align with users' expectations and behaviours.

Assessing the use of UX/UI interface standards when identifying potential improvements to UX/UI solutions involves evaluating how well the existing design align with established best practices, guidelines and conventions.

Understand UX/UI interface standards

Understanding UX/UI interface standards is fundamental to creating cohesive, accessible and user-friendly digital products that meet users' expectations and deliver a consistent experience across various platforms and devices.

- Platform guidelines: designers need to familiarise themselves with the specific guidelines for the platforms they are designing for, such as Apple's Human Interface Guidelines for iOS or Google's Material Design Guidelines for Android.
- Web standards: designers and developers should educate themselves on current web standards, such as those established by the World Wide Web Consortium (W3C). For example, use tools and resources such as **accessibility checkers** to ensure that the web design conforms to standards for HTML, CSS, JavaScript and accessibility.
- Industry standards: conduct thorough research to understand industry-specific standards and best practices that are relevant to the project. This may include guidelines for e-commerce, healthcare, finance and so on.

Conduct a compliance review

Conducting a compliance review involves systematically evaluating a UX/UI solution to ensure it adheres to relevant platform guidelines, web standards and industry-specific regulations, thereby guaranteeing a consistent and legally compliant user experience.

- Guideline checklists: use checklists based on platform and industry standards to systematically evaluate the interface for compliance.
- Accessibility audit: assess the interface's accessibility features and compliance with WCAG guidelines.
- Security assessment: evaluate the interface's security measures and compliance with relevant regulations (for example, GDPR).

Figure 3.35: Conduct a compliance review by evaluating the solution

Gather user feedback on usability and accessibility

- Usability testing: conduct usability tests with users to identify usability issues related to **adherence** to interface standards.
- Accessibility testing: include users with disabilities in usability tests to identify accessibility barriers and compliance issues.

Analyse consistency across platforms

- Platform-specific design elements: assess whether the interface follows platform-specific design patterns, conventions and interactions.
- Consistent branding: ensure consistent branding elements and visual identity across platforms and devices.
- Interoperability: evaluate how well the interface integrates with other systems and platforms.

Evaluate compliance with web standards

- **HTML tags**: assess whether the HTML markup follows conventions for accessibility and **Search Engine Optimisation (SEO)**
- Responsive design: assess the interface's responsiveness and adaptability by ensuring the content displays well on a variety of devices and window or screen sizes, from desktops to mobile phones.
- Browser compatibility: in the context of UX/UI interface standards, browser compatibility refers to the ability of a website or web application to function correctly and consistently across different web browsers, ensuring a uniform and seamless User Experience (UX) and User Interface (UI) regardless of the browser being used.

Identify potential improvements

- Prioritise areas where the interface deviates from interface standards or fails to meet user needs and expectations.
- Generate recommendations for improving compliance with standards, usability and accessibility.
- Consider the impact of potential improvements on user experience, accessibility and regulatory compliance.

Learning in context 15

Assess UX/UI solution improvements for a social media platform

A social media platform decided to carry out user testing and feedback on its user interface and design principles. The UX/UI was assessed for:

- user experience
- design principles
- design psychology
- interface standards.

As a result of the feedback, it has decided to implement improvements to the user interface.

Assessment

User experience (navigation issues, responsiveness)

- Weakness: some users still encounter navigation issues, such as difficulty finding specific features or understanding the navigation structure. For example, important sections such as settings or account management might be buried under less intuitive menus, making them hard to locate.
- Improvement: further optimise the solution for navigation by addressing specific issues identified in usability testing. For example, simplify the navigation structure by grouping related features together, using more descriptive labels and providing a clear and accessible site map. Implementing a more prominent and user-friendly search function can also help users quickly find what they need.

Design principles (readability, accessibility, user engagement)

- Weakness: some areas lack visual clarity. For instance, the call-to-action buttons might blend in with other content due to insufficient contrast or unclear positioning.
- Improvement: conduct A/B testing to fine-tune design elements and interactions based on user preferences and behaviour. For example, test different colour schemes and button placements to ensure call-to-action buttons are more prominent and easily identifiable.

Design psychology (behavioural patterns)

- Weakness: not all users respond equally well to the new design elements; some find the animations and dynamic content distracting, which can lead to frustration.
- Improvement: regularly review user feedback and perform iterative testing to refine design elements. For example, offer users the option to reduce or disable animations and ensure that dynamic content does not interfere with the main user tasks.

Interface standards (web standards, industry standards)

- Weakness: there are occasional inconsistencies in cross-browser compatibility, affecting the user experience on less common browsers such as Opera or older versions of Internet Explorer.
- Improvement: regularly review and update the solution to stay aligned with evolving interface standards and user expectations. For example, the use of cross-browser testing, which is the process of testing a web application or website across multiple web browsers to ensure that it functions correctly and appears consistently regardless of which browser is used.

Quick check 14

1 How can principles of UX/UI design psychology enhance the effectiveness of a user interface?

2 What factors should be considered when assessing UX/UI standards to ensure a high-quality and compliant user interface?

5.3 Review the processes used to plan, design and communicate UX/UI solutions

Effectiveness of processes used

Assessing the strengths and weaknesses in the processes used to plan, design and communicate UX/UI solutions involves a comprehensive evaluation of various aspects of the workflow.

Table 3.26: Strengths and weakness in the processes used to plan, design and communicate UX/UI solutions

Process	Strengths	Weaknesses
Evaluate planning	• Clear objectives: determine whether the planning process establishes clear goals and objectives aligned with user needs and business objectives. • Comprehensive research: assess the depth and breadth of user research conducted to inform design decisions. • Stakeholder involvement: determine the level of stakeholder engagement and alignment with project goals. • Flexibility: evaluate the ability of the planning process to adapt to changing requirements and feedback.	• Lack of **user-centricity**: review how user feedback has been collected, analysed and integrated into the design iterations. • Insufficient research: determine whether the research conducted is comprehensive enough to uncover all relevant insights and inform effective design decisions. • Limited stakeholder engagement: assess whether stakeholders are adequately involved throughout the planning process. Limited engagement could lead to potential misunderstandings or conflicts later on. • **Rigidity**: identify any rigidity in the planning process that hinders adaptability to changing project requirements or market dynamics. This could be the insistence on following the original plan without making necessary adjustments.

(Continued)

Process	Strengths	Weaknesses
Review communication	• Determine whether communication channels are established and accessible to all stakeholders. • Transparency: assess whether project progress, decisions and updates are communicated clearly to stakeholders. • Visual communication: evaluate the use of visual aids (for example, wireframes, prototypes, presentations) to effectively communicate design concepts and decisions. • Feedback mechanisms: determine whether feedback loops are in place to gather input from stakeholders and incorporate it into the design process.	• Poor documentation: identify any shortcomings in documenting design decisions, requirements and project progress, leading to misunderstandings. • Ineffective meetings: assess whether meetings are unproductive or lack clear objectives, wasting time and resources. • Misalignment with stakeholder needs: determine whether communication efforts fail to address stakeholder concerns or preferences adequately. • Evaluate whether communication channels are accessible to all stakeholders, including those with diverse needs or working remotely.

How to assess the effectiveness of the processes used to plan, design and communicate UX/UI solutions

Assessing the effectiveness of processes used to plan, design and communicate UX/UI solutions involves evaluating various factors.

- Determine measurable criteria to assess effectiveness, such as user satisfaction, project timeline adherence, stakeholder feedback and meeting project objectives.
- User feedback and testing: conduct usability testing and gather feedback from users to evaluate how well the UX/UI solutions meet their needs and preferences.
- Stakeholder satisfaction: gather input from stakeholders to gauge their satisfaction with the planning, design and communication processes. Assess whether their expectations were met and if they feel adequately informed and involved throughout the project.
- Project outcome analysis: evaluate the final solution against the initially defined project goals and objectives. Measure the extent to which the UX/UI solutions address user needs and enhance user experience.
- Efficiency and timeliness: assess the efficiency of the planning, design and communication processes by reviewing project timelines and resource allocation. Identify any bottlenecks or delays that occurred and evaluate their impact on project success.
- Adaptability and flexibility: evaluate how well the processes adapted to changes in requirements, feedback and external factors. Assess whether the team was able to make necessary adjustments without significant disruption to the project.
- Communication effectiveness: review the clarity and effectiveness of communication channels used throughout the project. Assess whether information was communicated in a timely manner, whether stakeholders were

kept informed and whether feedback was adequately addressed.

- Documentation review: evaluate the quality and completeness of project documentation, including design briefs, meeting minutes and design specifications. Assess whether documentation accurately reflects project decisions and provides useful reference material.
- Assess the level of collaboration and contribution of the individual involved in planning, designing and communicating UX/UI solutions. Evaluate whether the individual effectively used communication and collaboration tools.

Effectiveness of tools and techniques used

Assessing the effectiveness of tools and techniques used to plan, design and communicate UX/UI solutions have been discussed in the previous sections in this unit. Assessing the effectiveness of these involves evaluating various aspects.

Usability and ease of use

- Evaluate how intuitive and user-friendly the tools are for users to operate.
- Assess whether the tools streamline the workflow and make tasks easier to accomplish.
- Gather feedback on the usability and effectiveness of the tools.

Functionality and features

- Review the features and capabilities of the tools to ensure they meet project requirements.
- Assess whether the tools provide necessary functionalities such as wireframing, prototyping, collaboration and version control.
- Evaluate whether the tools integrate well with other software and platforms used in the project.

Collaboration and communication

- Evaluate the effectiveness of communication and collaboration features in the tools.
- Assess the ease of sharing files, providing feedback and communicating in real-time.
- Determine whether the tools facilitate seamless collaboration among stakeholders and clients.

Integration and compatibility

- Assess whether the tools integrate well with existing systems and platforms used in the project.
- Evaluate compatibility with different devices, operating systems and browsers.
- Determine whether the tools support file formats commonly used in UX/UI design and development.

Performance and reliability

- Evaluate the performance of the tools in terms of speed, stability and reliability.
- Assess whether the tools can handle large files and complex projects without lag or crashes.
- Determine whether the tools have a reliable backup and recovery system in case of data loss or system failure.

Cost and value

- Evaluate the cost-effectiveness of the tools in relation to their features and capabilities.
- Determine whether the tools provide good value for money based on their performance and benefits.
- Assess whether the tools offer flexible pricing plans or options for scaling as project needs evolve.

User support and training

- Evaluate the level of customer support provided by the tool provider.
- Assess whether the tools offer adequate documentation, tutorials and training resources for users.
- Determine whether the tools have a responsive support team that can address technical issues and provide assistance when needed.

Security and compliance

- Assess the security measures implemented by the tools to protect sensitive project data.
- Evaluate whether the tools comply with relevant security standards and regulations.
- Determine whether the tools have mechanisms for data encryption, access control and data privacy protection.

Quick check 15

1 How can the strengths and weaknesses of UX/UI solutions be effectively assessed across various factors?

2 What are the key considerations for conducting a comprehensive assessment to effectively compare UX/UI solutions?

Glossary

A/B testing: Also known as split testing. A method used in marketing, web development and product design to compare two versions of a webpage, advertisement, email or app feature to determine which one performs better.

Abstract: A concise and generalised explanation of a concept or an idea.

Abstraction: Focusing on the most important parts of something while ignoring the less important details.

Accessibility: The design and implementation of products, services, environments and facilities that can be used by people with a wide range of abilities and disabilities.

Accessibility checker: A tool or software designed to evaluate digital content, such as websites and applications, to ensure it meets established accessibility standards and guidelines.

Accessibility standards: Guidelines and criteria set to ensure that digital products and environments are usable by people with disabilities.

Active listening: Paying close attention to understand and engage with what someone is saying.

Adherence: The act of following rules, standards, guidelines or requirements.

Algorithm: A list of instructions designed to solve a problem.

Align: To arrange or position things in a straight line or in correct relative positions.

Alternative text: A brief description added to images in digital content, such as websites and documents.

Analysis: The process of breaking down a complex topic or substance into smaller parts to gain a better understanding of it.

Application: One or more programs designed for end-users to be able to complete specific tasks or activities.

Application programming interface (API): A method to allow two or more software applications to communicate with each other, usually via a network.

Architectural design: Plan for how components of a software system will be structured and interact with each other.

Architecture: In Computer Science, architecture means the design of a computer system or part of a computer system. This could refer to hardware and/or software.

Arrow diagram: A visual representation of project tasks and their relationships, showing the flow and sequence of activities using arrows and nodes.

Audit log: A chronological record of the occurrence of an event or action, that has occurred within a system or application. This is often used to record details of attempted logins but can also be used to store details of other events, such as updating information typically used for monitoring and security purposes.

Augmented reality: Technology that overlays digital information or virtual objects onto the real world, typically viewed through a smartphone, tablet or specialised AR glasses.

Authentication: A process that allows the verification of a user's identity, for example, using a username and password.

Biometrics: Defined as 'The automated recognition of individuals based on their biological and behavioural characteristics' by the ISO standards body.

Blueprint: A detailed and technical drawing or plan that outlines the specifications, dimensions and construction details of a building, machine or other complex structure or system.

Botnet: A network of internet connected computers that have been infected with malware. This malware allows the infected computers to be used without the owner's knowledge to perform some form of task.

Bottlenecks: Points of congestion or restriction within a process or system that limit its overall capacity or efficiency.

Brand perception: Refers to how consumers perceive or interpret a brand, including their beliefs, attitudes and opinions about its products, services and reputation.

Breadcrumbs: A navigational aid typically displayed on a website or application interface to show users their current location within the hierarchy of pages or sections.

Budget: The amount of money available to spend on the software project.

Call-to-action: A prompt or directive designed to encourage a specific action or response from the audience.

Click-through rates: CTRs measure the percentage of users who click on a specific link, advertisement or call-to-action within a webpage or email.

Client-defined constraints: Specific rules or preferences that the client has for how the software should be built or what it should be able to do.

Cognitive: Relates to mental processes such as perception, reasoning, memory, attention and problem-solving.

Cognitive impairment: Difficulties or deficits in cognitive functions such as memory, attention, learning, reasoning or problem-solving.

Cognitive load: The amount of mental effort or resources required to process information and perform a task.

Cohesive: Being logically connected and consistent, ensuring all parts of a software application work together smoothly for a unified user experience.

Command Line Interface (CLI): Text-based method of interacting with a computer or software program, where users input commands using a keyboard.

Compliance: The act of adhering to rules, regulations, standards or guidelines, often set by governing bodies, organisations or industry practices.

Consistent: Keeping the same design elements, style and behaviour throughout a product.

Constraints: Limitations, restrictions or factors that impose boundaries or conditions on a project, design or process. These affect how the software project can be done, for example time limits, technology limitations or rules and regulations that need to be followed.

Contrast ratio: Measures the difference in brightness between the foreground (text or graphics) and the background.

Conventions: Established customs, practices, rules or standards that are widely accepted and followed within a particular context, community, industry or society.

Conversion rates: The percentage of website visitors or users who complete a desired action or goal out of the total number of visitors or users.

Corruption: Data corruption refers to errors that occur in data as it is being transmitted or saved.

Crash: When a software application stops functioning correctly. It may not respond at all or it may close.

Critical Path Analysis (CPA): A method used in project management to determine the longest sequence of tasks, known as the critical path, which determines the minimum time needed to complete a project.

Critical Path Method (CPM): A project management technique used to schedule and plan tasks, focusing on identifying critical tasks that directly impact the project's overall duration.

Data flow diagram: A graphical representation of the flow of data within a system.

Data formats: The language or structure that the software uses to understand and store information.

Demographics: Statistical data about a population, typically including characteristics such as age, gender, income, education, occupation, marital status, ethnicity and geographic location.

Denial of Service (DoS): A DoS attack is designed to make a computer system, application or network unusable or inaccessible.

Digital interface: The point of interaction between a user and a digital system, device or software application.

Distributed Denial of Service (DDoS): A Distributed Denial of Service (DDoS) attack is a form of DoS attack where the target system or network is flooded with requests from several computer systems, often using a botnet to send the requests.

Document analysis: The review of existing documentation.

Encryption: The process of scrambling electronic data into a form that is unreadable without knowing the key. Data needs to be decrypted using the key to make it readable again.

End user: A person who will use a software application.

Extended Reality (XR): The umbrella term for Augmented Reality (AR), Virtual Reality (VR) and Mixed Reality (MR).

Extraneous: Something that is not essential or relevant to a particular situation or context.

Extrinsic: The qualities or characteristics that are external or come from outside of something or someone.

Feasibility: An assessment of whether a proposed software project is achievable within the given constraints.

Firewall: A system that monitors incoming and outgoing traffic (in the form of packets of data) from a computer, server or network.

Firmware: A computer program that is embedded into a hardware device to allow it to operate.

Flowchart: A diagram that visually represents a process or workflow, showing the steps involved, decision points and the flow of information or activities using various symbols and connectors.

Focus group: A group of selected people brought together to discuss specific topics related to application development.

Framework: A structured set of guidelines that provides a foundation for developing, building, organising or implementing something.

Function: A self-contained block of computer code that will accomplish a specific task and send some data back (return) to the code that called the function.

Functional requirements: These describe what the software should be able to do, such as features or actions it should perform.

Gantt charts: Visual timelines used in project management to schedule and track tasks over time, showing the start and end dates of activities, dependencies and progress.

Gesture interface: Method of interacting with digital devices or systems using physical movements or gestures.

Graphical mock-up: A visual representation or prototype of a digital interface, such as a website, application or software program.

Graphical User Interface (GUI): Visual method of interacting with digital devices or software applications using graphical elements such as icons, windows and menus.

Hacking: A term used to describe someone gaining unauthorised access to a computer system and the data stored within that system.

Hamburger menu: A Graphical User Interface (GUI) element that typically consists of three horizontal lines stacked on top of each other, resembling a hamburger.

Hardware: Computer hardware is the physical parts of a computer system, such as a keyboard, storage device or a complete computer system.

Hearing impairment: A partial or complete loss of hearing ability.

Heuristics: Problem-solving techniques or mental shortcuts that individuals use to find solutions quickly and efficiently.

House style: The consistent and cohesive design elements, formatting rules and writing conventions adopted by an organisation or brand across various communication materials such as documents, presentations, websites and marketing collateral.

HyperText Markup Language (HTML) tags: The language or code used to create and structure content on the web.

Iconography: The design and use of icons in an application to represent actions, objects or concepts, helping users navigate and understand the interface.

Interaction flows: The step-by-step process a user goes through when using an application.

Interaction sequences: The series of actions or steps that users take when engaging with a digital interface or system.

Interface: A point of interaction between two systems or individuals.

Interface design: Designing the visual and interactive elements of the software.

Intermittent: Occurring at irregular intervals or in a sporadic manner.

Intrinsic: The qualities or characteristics that are inherent to something or someone, rather than being influenced by external factors.

Intuitive: A process that is easy to understand or use without the need for explicit instruction or guidance.

International Organisation for Standardisation (ISO) Body: The International Organisation for Standardisation is an independent, non-governmental organisation that brings experts together to agree on the best way to do something. From this work, a standard is created.

Iterate: The process of repeating a sequence of actions or steps.

Iterative: An approach where the development process is broken down into a series of cycles or iterations.

Iterative models: These models take an incremental approach to project management where the project is divided into small, manageable iterations or cycles, with each iteration building on the previous one.

Journey mapping: A User Experience (UX) design technique that involves creating visual representations of the user's journey or experience across various touchpoints and interactions with a product or service.

Legislation: Laws and regulations that need to be considered and followed during the software development process.

Location hierarchy: The organisation and prioritisation of content based on its importance or relevance.

Malicious spam: Unwanted emails that are sent to a large number of people. Malicious spam is designed to get malware onto a computer system.

Malware: A blended word made from malicious software: a broad term that can be used to describe a wide range of different software that will cause problems for a computer system or network.

Metrics: Used to track, assess and evaluate the performance or progress of a system, process, project or activity.

Micro interaction: A small, specific and often subtle user-interface interaction designed to accomplish a single task.

Milestones: Significant points or achievements along the way towards completing a software project.

Mixed Reality (MR): Technology that combines elements of both Augmented Reality (AR) and Virtual Reality (VR) to blend digital content with the physical environment in real-time, allowing digital and physical objects to interact.

Mock-up: A visual representation or prototype of a design concept, typically used in the early stages of the design process to illustrate the layout, structure and functionality of a product, interface or system.

Modular: A design, system or structure that is composed of separate components or modules.

Modularisation: Breaking something big into smaller pieces or modules that are easier to understand and work with.

Motor difficulties: Challenges or limitations in movement and coordination.

Navigation diagram: A visual representation of the organisation and hierarchy of content within a website or application.

Network operating system: Enables multiple devices and computers on a network to connect and share resources.

Non-functional requirements: These describe qualities or characteristics of the software, such as its speed, security or ease of use.

Non-verbal communication: Sharing messages without using words such as through gestures and facial expression.

Objectives: The goals or aims that a software development project wants to achieve.

Open operating system: An operating system whose source code is freely available for anyone to use, modify or distribute.

Overlay: Adding further information over the top of a picture or video feed.

Packet: A packet is a small block of data that can be sent via a network. Large amounts of data are split into multiple packets before sending.

Packets: A small segment of a larger block of data. Data is split into packets to allow sending on a network.

Pain point: A specific problem, frustration or challenge that users encounter while interacting with a product, service or system.

Parsing of requirements: Examining a list of requirements and organising it into smaller, more manageable parts.

Pattern recognition: Noticing similarities or repeating designs in different elements.

Personas: Fictional representations of target users or customers based on research and data, used to understand their goals, needs, behaviours and preferences in designing products or services.

Personnel: The people who are part of the team working on the software project.

Program Evaluation and Review Technique (PERT) charts: These are charts used in project management to analyse and represent the tasks involved in completing a project, incorporating estimates for task durations and dependencies to identify the critical path.

Phishing: When scam emails are sent that contain links to malicious websites.

Problem reports: Records of issues faced when using applications or software.

Process constraints: The limitations that need to be followed during the development process, such as the timeline or the specific steps that need to be taken.

Program: A set of instructions written to perform a specific task or function on a computer.

Proprietary operating system: An operating system that is developed and owned by a specific company or organisation.

Protocol: A set of rules for transmitting data between different devices, usually via a network.

Prototype: An initial version or model of a product, system or design that is created to test and validate concepts, features and functionality before proceeding with full-scale development.

Prototyping models: These models use the creation of prototypes or early versions of a product or system that are built quickly and refined based on user feedback and testing.

Provider: A system that provides services to another system.

Qualitative data: Non-numerical information or insights gathered from sources such as interviews, observations, surveys or user feedback, providing context, depth and understanding to research findings.

Resources: The tools, materials and people needed to get the software project done.

Responsive design: An approach to web design that ensures a website or application adapts and responds to different screen sizes and devices, providing the best viewing experience for users across desktops, laptops, tablets and smartphones.

RFID: Radio Frequency Identification (RFID) is a technology that can be used to identify a person and allow them to access a building or application using a tag, which responds to specific radio transmissions with an identification number.

Rigidity: Inflexibility or resistance to change within a process, system or organisation, often hindering adaptability and innovation.

Router: A device that passes data between one network and another. For example, a home network is likely to be connected to the internet using a router.

Scalability: The ability of a system, application or solution to handle increased workload, user traffic or data volume without sacrificing performance or functionality.

Scalable: The ability to increase the capacity of a resource according to needs or number of users.

Scope: The breadth and extent of what a project includes.

Screen flow: A visual representation of the sequence of screens or interface states that a user encounters while interacting with a digital product or service.

Search functionality: The ability for users to search and retrieve specific information or content within a website, application or database.

Search Engine Optimisation (SEO): The practice of optimising a website or online content to improve its visibility and ranking in search engine results pages.

Shadowing: Observing users in their natural environment to better understand their experience.

Simulate: To imitate or replicate the characteristics, behaviour or appearance of something, often for the purpose of experimentation, testing or training.

Slide deck: A collection of slides used in a presentation.

Smart speaker: Wireless device equipped with built-in virtual assistant technology that can understand and respond to voice commands.

Smart TV: A television that integrates internet connectivity and interactive features, allowing users to access online content, streaming services and apps directly on the TV screen.

Software development model: A structured approach used to guide the process of creating software.

Stakeholders: Any individual, group or organisation that has an interest or concern in a particular project, initiative or organisation.

Standardisation: The process of establishing guidelines, specifications or protocols to ensure consistency.

Stateless: Does not maintain state': for example, when communicating using a stateless method, a client and server do not need to know about what state each other are in.

Streamline: Simplify, optimise or make more efficient by removing unnecessary steps, processes or complexities.

Success criteria: The specific goals or standards that need to be met for the software project to be considered successful.

Suggestion analysis: Involves examining suggestions for changes or development to an existing product to inform future development.

SWOT analysis: A strategic planning tool used to assess the strengths, weaknesses, opportunities and threats related to a project or organisation, helping to identify key factors for decision-making and planning.

System administrators: People who manage and maintains the servers, networks and security measures to ensure reliable, secure and efficient IT systems.

System deficiencies: Problems or weaknesses in the current system that the new software needs to fix or improve on.

Task flow: A sequence of steps or actions that a user takes to accomplish a particular goal or task within a system, application or process.

Technical blueprints: Detailed plans and diagrams that outline the architecture, components and design specifications of a software application.

Testimonials: Statements from individuals or organisations expressing their satisfaction, approval or support for a product, service or entity.

Tooltips: Small, informative messages that appear when users hover over or interact with an element on a digital interface, such as a button, icon or link.

Transmission: The process of transmitting data from one computer system or application to another.

Two-Factor Authentication (2FA): A security method that requires a user to use two methods (factors) of authentication before access to an application is granted.

Typography: The style, arrangement and appearance of text in design. It includes factors such as font choice, font size, spacing and alignment, which all contribute to the readability and visual appeal of written content.

Uniform Resource Locator (URL): An address of a resource on the internet.

User Experience (UX): The overall interaction and satisfaction users have with a product, system or service.

User flow: The path taken by a user to complete a task within a product or service.

User Interface (UI): The visual and interactive elements of a digital product or system.

User-centricity: An approach to design and development that prioritises the needs, preferences and experiences of end-users at every stage of the process.

Verbal communication: Sharing thoughts or information through speaking.

Verification: The process of confirming or validating whether something meets specified requirements, standards or criteria.

Virtual reality: Technology that immerses users in a simulated environment, typically through a VR headset or goggles.

Virtual world: A computer generated environment, often viewed through a VR headset.

Visual hierarchy: An element of location hierarchy that is the arranging of elements to guide the viewers eye from most to least important.

Visual identity: The collection of visual elements, design principles and branding components that together form the visual representation of a company, brand or organisation, including its logo, colours, fonts and imagery.

Visual impairment: A broad range of vision problems that affect an individual's ability to see clearly.

Visualisation diagram: A diagram to show what the completed application screen will look like.

Waterfall model: A traditional and linear approach to project management where tasks progress in order through predefined stages, like water flowing downstream.

Web Content Accessibility Guidelines (WCAG): International standards developed by the World Wide Web Consortium (W3C) that provide guidance and criteria for making web content more accessible to people with disabilities.

White space: The space between content.

Wireflow: A hybrid design artifact that combines elements of wireframes and flowcharts.

Wireframe diagram: A simplified visual representation of a user interface, focusing on layout, structure and content organisation.

Word-of-mouth: The process of information or opinions being passed from one person to another through oral communication, typically in a casual, informal manner.

Z reading pattern: A term used in design to describe the natural eye movement of users when scanning content in a 'Z' shaped pattern.

Index

Answers

Practice questions and accompanying marks included in this resource are an opportunity to practise examination skills. They do not replicate examination papers and are not endorsed by OCR.

F160: TA1

Quick check 1

1 Discussions might include:
- Both programs and applications are sets of instructions that tell a computer what tasks to perform.
- Both are written in various programming languages and executed by a computer's operating system.
- However, programs are more general and may perform a wide range of tasks, while applications are more specific.

2 For an identified application (such as a mobile app, a web application, a desktop software, or any other type of application), answers should consider the target audience and their needs.

Suitability might include consideration of:
- The main purpose or function of the application
- Its features and how they enhance user experience
- The user interface and experience
- Levels of personalisation and customisation
- Whether the application is accessible to users with disabilities.

Quick check 2

1 Notes should include:
- Compatibility issues
- Support available
- Cost for end user
- Level of technical support required
- Performance
- Customisation options.

2 Responses would discuss a range of operating systems including Windows, macOS, Linux and Chrome OS.

Pros and cons could consider:
- Size of user base
- Developer tools and documentation available
- Compatibility with hardware and software
- Costs
- Security
- User interface.

Quick check 3

1 Summaries of the differences between the software application types should reference:
- Cost and time for development
- Flexibility and customisation option
- Level of support available
- Compatibility with existing software.

2 Answers will reflect on the different factors and suggest reasons why one might be more important than others. They may decide to put this in context to support their answer.

Practice questions 1

1 A program is a set of instructions that tells a computer what tasks to perform **[1]**, however, an application is a specific type of program designed to serve a particular purpose for end users. **[1]**

2 Possible advantages include:

A proprietary operating system has dedicated customer support and documentation so issues can be resolved more quickly. **[1]**

A proprietary operating system usually has a more user-friendly interface so it is more accessible to users. **[1]**

A proprietary operating system is designed for specific hardware configurations so it performs better with specified devices. **[1]**

or other suitable response.

3 **One** from: lifestyle or educational. **[1]**

4 **Two** answers related to answer to question **3a**, e.g. diet and nutrition tracking **[1]** and shopping lists. **[1]**

TA2

Quick check 4

1 Answers might include factors such as:

- Project requirements
- Project size and complexity
- Time constraints
- Budget constraints
- Regulatory requirements.

2 A mind map might include the following points in each section:

Traditional model:

- Sequential approach
- Linear progression through phases
- Emphasises detailed planning and documentation
- Little client involvement until later stages
- High risk of late-stage changes
- Examples: waterfall model.

Prototyping model:

- Focuses on rapid prototyping and feedback
- Iterative process of building, testing and refining prototypes
- Allows for early user involvement and feedback
- Flexible and adaptable to changing requirements
- Examples: rapid prototyping, evolutionary prototyping.

Iterative model:

- incremental development approach
- divides project into small iterations or cycles
- each iteration includes planning, development, testing and review
- allows for frequent releases and updates
- enables flexibility to accommodate changes
- examples: agile, spiral model.

Quick check 5

1 The infographic will give a concise overview of each section and give examples of tasks they might include.

Possible examples include:

- Planning: Requirement gathering and conducting a feasibility study
- Design: System decomposition to identify the modules needed to provide the functionality
- Constructing/creation: Writing code, continually testing code
- Testing: Testing integrated elements, testing whole system
- Implementation: Installation and configuration, training of users
- Documentation creation: Writing end user documentation, creating visual aids
- Maintenance: Bug fixing, improving system performance.

2 Explanations might include the following key points:

- Big bang implementation involves a sudden switch to the new system
- Phased implementation rolls out the new system gradually in stages
- Parallel implementation runs both old and new systems concurrently for a period of time.

Practice questions 2

1 Possible answers include the following:

Advantages of using a waterfall model:

- Simple and easy to understand
- Clear requirements
- Defined deliverables
- Easy to track project progress
- Documentation created to support recordkeeping.

Disadvantages of using a waterfall model:

- Rigid and inflexible
- Late testing
- Limited client involvement
- Difficulties in adapting to change.

Level 3 (high) 7–9

A thorough analysis which includes:

- identification of both advantages and disadvantages
- detailed knowledge and understanding in the context of the question
- clear explanation
- consistent use of subject appropriate terminology.

Level 2 (mid) 4–6

- identification of either advantages or disadvantages
- sound knowledge and understanding in the context of the question
- adequate explanation
- some use of subject appropriate terminology.

Level 1 (low) 1–3

- identification of either one advantage or disadvantage
- limited knowledge and understanding in the context of the question
- basic explanation
- use of subject appropriate terminology is limited.

2 Big bang implementation is where all components of the new system are introduced at the same time.

TA3

Quick check 6

1 Reasons why project planning is important could include:

- Providing a clear vision and objectives for the project
- Clearly setting out the timeline for the project and milestones
- Tracking progress
- Identifying and allocating resources
- Managing budget
- Identifying potential risks and developing strategies to reduce or remove them
- Quality checking
- Supports good communication and collaboration.

2 A mind map might include the following:

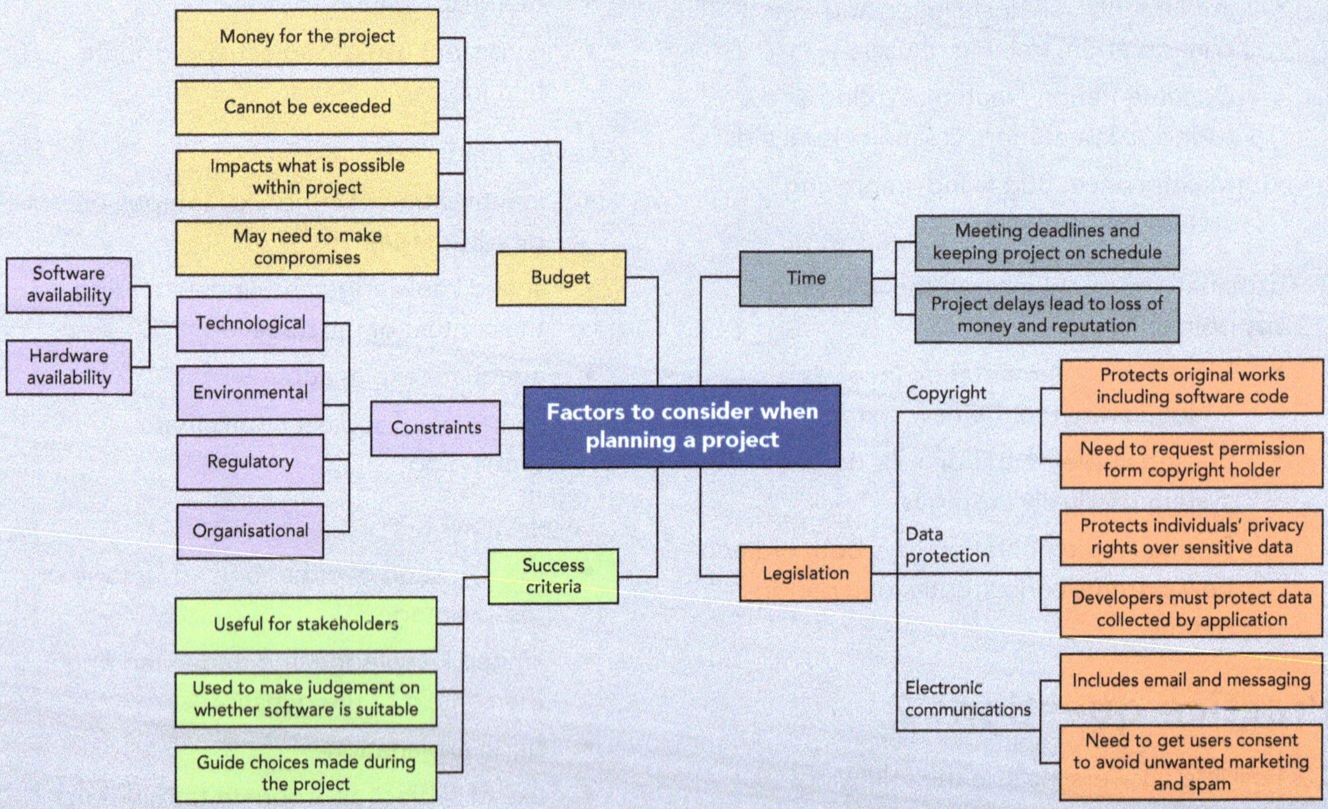
Factors to consider when planning a project
Budget
Money for the project
Cannot be exceeded
Impacts what is possible within project
May need to make compromises
Time
Meeting deadlines and keeping project on schedule
Project delays lead to loss of money and reputation
Constraints
Technological
Environmental
Regulatory
Organisational
Software availability
Hardware availability
Legislation
Copyright
Protects original works including software code
Need to request permission form copyright holder
Data protection
Protects individuals' privacy rights over sensitive data
Developers must protect data collected by application
Electronic communications
Includes email and messaging
Need to get users consent to avoid unwanted marketing and spam
Success criteria
Useful for stakeholders
Used to make judgement on whether software is suitable
Guide choices made during the project

Quick check 7

1 The contents of the SWOT analysis will vary depending on the project selected but might include:

- Strengths such as unique software features or expertise within the team
- Weaknesses such as lack of experience in certain technologies or limited resources

- Opportunities such as market demand for the application or emerging technologies
- Threats such as competition from existing solutions or legal or ethical risks.

2 Notes might include some of the following points:

Gantt chart	Flowchart
• Represents project tasks as bars on a timeline • Shows task dependencies, durations, and progress • Provides a visual representation of project schedule • Can include milestones and deadlines • Allows for resource allocation and tracking • Best used for visualising project timeline and scheduling tasks.	• Represents sequential steps and decisions in a process through symbols • Shows the flow of information or activities from start to finish • Can include loops, branches, and decisions • Helps understanding of logic and decision-making • Best used for mapping workflows and sequences.

Practice questions 3

1 Considering legislation is important when developing an application because it reduces the risk of legal issues or penalties **[1]**, which could result in delays or damage to reputation **[1]**.

2 a Flowcharts provide a clear and visual representation of the project's workflow **[1]**. Flowcharts are a simple way of communicating with stakeholders **[1]**.

b One disadvantage of using a flowchart for project planning is its potential to become complicated **[1]**. As the project grows, the flowchart may become difficult to follow, leading to confusion among team members and stakeholders **[1]**.

TA4

Quick check 8

1 The questionnaire should include both quantitative and qualitative questions that relate to the topic. It may be paper based or digital. Reflections on its usefulness may depend on the quality of the data that is gathered as a result. Disadvantages might include:

- Lack of depth in answers
- Inability to probe with further questions for clarification
- Response rates might be low.

2 Answers might include some or all from:

- Document analysis
- Focus groups
- Interviews
- Meetings
- Observations
- Problem reports
- Questionnaire
- Shadowing
- Suggestion analysis.

Explanations might reflect on time it takes to carry out, cost, availability of information, quality of data gathered or any other justification.

Quick check 9

1 Notes might include:

- Clarify what the client wants
- Agreement of requirements between stakeholders

- Defining the boundaries of the project
- Managing potential risks
- Basis of a roadmap for development
- Communication tool within the client and development team.

2 Client specification document should include:
- Purpose
- Functional requirements
- Non-functional requirements
- Process constraints
- Current system deficiencies
- Data formats
- Client defined constraints
- Version and source control.

Quick check 10

1 The answer will depend on the method chosen but might include:
- Abstraction to focus on specific details and ignore the unnecessary information
- Pattern recognition to identify key themes from different stakeholders
- Modularisation to break the problem down into smaller and more manageable pieces
- Parsing to help organise and prioritise the different requirements.

2 Notes might include:
- Abstraction focuses on simplifying complex requirements
- Pattern recognition identifies common themes or structure
- Modularisation organises requirements into independent modules
- Parsing breaks down requirements into smaller components for analysis and implementation.

Practice questions 4

1 **a** Stakeholder interviews provide first hand information **[1]** directly from someone who is affected by the project **[1]**.

Or any other suitable response

b Stakeholder interviews can be time consuming **[1]** so you may only be able to gather a limited amount of information **[1]**.

Or any other suitable response

2 Choose **one** from:
- Document analysis **[1]**
- Focus groups **[1]**
- Meetings **[1]**
- Observations **[1]**
- Problem reports **[1]**
- Questionnaire **[1]**
- Shadowing **[1]**
- Suggestion analysis **[1]**

3 Possible answers include:
- The application must ensure the protection of customer data **[1]**
- The application should load quickly **[1]**
- The application should be easy to navigate. **[1]**

TA5

Quick check 11

1 Notes and discussions could include advantages such as being intuitive, engaging, accessible, portable and supporting multi-touch gestures like pinch-to-zoom. Disadvantages might include fatigue and strain, limited precision, visibility of fingerprints and lack of feedback.

2 Notes will reflect on one of the following human computer interaction methods: audio, movement/gesture, touch, visual (Command line, GUI). Reasons for suitability might include end user, constraints, device compatibility and accessibility.

Quick check 12

1 The infographic should focus on the main colour groups: red, orange, yellow, green, blue, purple, black and white. For each colour, feelings and emotions associated with that colour should be identified. For example, red is associated with anger, love, passion, danger and joy.

2 The presentation should include a slide for each element of visual design:

- Colours
- Interaction
- Location hierarchy
- Messages (help and error)
- Typography (style and size).

Comments on effectiveness should reflect on the purpose of the application (what it is intended to do) and the audience (who it is aimed at).

Quick check 13

1 Example summaries could include:

- Data flow diagram: shows how data moves within a system
- Flowchart: shows what happens in the process step by step
- Visualisation diagram: shows what each screen will look like in the finished product
- Wireframe diagram: shows a simple view of the interface, focusing on the layout and structure.

2 The visualisation diagram should include a sketch of the images, graphics, text, navigation elements and interactive features. It should include annotations to show the colours, fonts (styles, sizes and colours) and explain any interactivity.

A wireframe differs as it has a simplified appearance, using boxes to show the layout of the content on the screen rather than giving an accurate impression of the overall visual appearance.

Practice questions 5

1

Feature	Letter
Annotation	B
Navigation	A
Logo	C

2 Possible answers include:

Advantages:

- Easy to understand and use **[1]** for end users. **[1]**
- Can interact directly with on screen elements **[1]**, which gives immediate feedback and a sense of control. **[1]**

- A wide range of interactions can be used **[1]** including tapping, swiping and pinching. **[1]**

Disadvantages:

- Touch screens get smudges **[1]**, which can affect use. **[1]**
- Repeated use of touch screens **[1]** can cause pain for the end user. **[1]**
- Touch control can be difficult to control **[1]** for some operations. **[1]**

3 Possible answers include:

- Placing the navigation icons along the bottom of the screen **[1]** to make navigation on a touch screen easier to use. **[1]**
- Using a drop-down box to select type of activity **[1]** to make data entry easier for the end user. **[1]**
- Prioritising space in top left hand corner **[1]** for example, adding search functionality to find key information in the application. **[1]**

TA6

Quick check 14

1 Responsibilities for a mobile application specialist, for example, might include:

- Developing apps for Android and iOS
- Testing apps for Android and iOS
- Collaborating with UX designers.

This will vary depending on the job that is researched.

2 Contributions to the software application development will depend on the responsibilities identified. If mobile application specialist was selected, answer might state:

- Collaborating with UX designers will mean that the mobile application will be designed with the user's journey through the application in mind.

Quick check 15

1 Answers might reference ideas such as:

- Using technical language where required, for example when speaking to developers
- Avoiding technical terms when talking to those without technical expertise so you don't confuse them
- Adjusting level of detail depending on how involved someone is with the project
- Not providing unnecessary details so that communications are not too long.

2 Verbal communication feedback might focus on the language used, the volume, tone and pitch of the voice, the speed of delivery and relevance of the content. Non-verbal communication might focus on the gestures, use of eye contact and body language as well as the use of any visual aids.

Practice questions 6

1 a Possible answers include:

One responsibility of the project manager is to create and manage the project schedule. **[1]**

One responsibility of the project manager is to oversee tasks and activities within the project. **[1]**

b Possible answers include:

By creating the schedule, the project manager make sure tasks are completed on time **[1]** so that deadlines are met. **[1]**

By overseeing tasks, the project manager ensures that everyone knows what they need to do and when **[1]**, which reduces delays and increases efficiency. **[1]**

2 Possible answers include:

The project manager needs to communicate effectively to pass on information to team members **[1]** to make sure project expectations are clear. **[1]**

The project manager might need communication skills to negotiate with the client **[1]** if there is an issue with deadlines or resource availability. **[1]**

F161: TA1

Quick check 1

1 Possible answers include:

- VR can create virtual worlds and is more immersive than AR as it uses a headset that includes screens/sound etc.
- AR is more likely to be run on a mobile phone/tablet and provides an overlay on what the user is seeing.

2 Possible answers include:

- A tablet could provide detail about what the user is seeing, for example it could explain why the Acropolis was build and how it was constructed.
- As the user pointed the device at different parts of the site the information displayed would change to information relevant to what was being looked at.

Quick check 2

1 Possible answers include:

- App could tell user when wash has finished
- App could show how much time is remaining
- App could allow provide advice on what programme to select.

2 Answers might include:

- time spent running
- when a personal best has been reached
- heart rate
- number of miles/kilometres covered
- speed.

Quick check 3

1 Possible answers include:

- File servers can be used to provide access to large numbers of users, whereas a NAS is designed for smaller numbers of users
- File servers require specialist staff to manage whereas a NAS is designed to be easy to setup
- File servers provide more flexibility than a NAS.

2 Possible answers include:

- A SAN consists of an independent network that connects multiple storage devices together to provide storage to a number of servers
- Provide fast access to large amounts of storage.

Practice questions 1

1 Possible answers include:

- Lots of devices can access websites **[1]**

  ...meaning a large number of customers can see details of holidays. **[1]**

- Users don't need to install an application **[1]**

  ...meaning that the company doesn't have to develop for lots of difference devices. **[1]**

- Holiday company website could be found via a search engine **[1]**

  ...meaning that users might search for a holiday using a search engine and view/buy the holiday. **[1]**

2 Possible answers include:

- Virtual reality headset **[1]**
- ...User will be able to walk around the area virtually **[1]**
- ...User will be immersed in the holiday environment **[1]**
- Tablet computer **[1]**
- ...User will be able to click on places to visit and be shown photos/videos. **[1]**

3 Possible answers include:

Advantages:

- Staff could work from home **[1]** as files will be accessible anywhere with access to the internet. **[1]**
- Greater scalability **[1]** so if the holiday company requires more storage this can easily be added. **[1]**
- Collaboration between staff could be improved. **[1]** For example, many people could access a document at one time and edit it.

Disadvantages:

- Cost may increase **[1]** as the cloud storage provider might charge more than using the existing on-site storage **[1]**.
- Concerns over being hacked **[1]**. Data stored in the cloud might be appealing for hackers to try and access **[1]**.
- Should access to the internet not be available **[1]**, then the staff will not be able to access needed files and might be unable to work. **[1]**

TA2

Quick check 4

1 Possible answers include:

- Character: 'c' (any single letter, number or symbol)
- Integer: 5 (any whole number)
- Real: 9.4 (any number with a decimal point and a value after the decimal point)
- String: 'hello' (any number of characters).

2 Possible answers include:

- CSV is human readable
- CSV is a simple format suitable for tabular data
- CSV is not good for complex data
- CSV is ideal for importing data into a spreadsheet
- XML uses tags to structure data
- XML is human readable but not as easy to read as CSV
- XML is highly customisable
- XML is verbose.

Quick check 5

1 Possible answers include:
- Data does not have a context
- Information is data with a context
- Data + context = information.

2 Possible answers include:
- Inputs: number of hours car park space required for, type of vehicle, vehicle registration
- Outputs: price, parking ticket, error messages.

Quick check 6

1
- At rest
- In transit
- In use.

2 Possible answers include:
- At rest: data not in use, stored on a storage device
- In transit: data being sent from one system to another
- In use: data that is being processed.

Practice questions 2

1

	Integer	Real	String
Number plate			✓
Number of hours parking required	✓		
Cost		✓	

[3]

2 Possible answers include:
- Widely used format for exchanging data
- Data can be structured to allow for easy importing of data
- Collection of name/value pairs can allow for structure of data to be organised, for example 'hours parked' : '4'.

Credit any other appropriate response. [4]

TA3

Quick check 7

1 Possible answers include:
- Internal APIs are used within a business. A self-service till in a supermarket might use an internal API to get the product details from a barcode.
- A private API is used to allow communication with internal systems by an application used by external users. For example, a supermarket might use a private API to allow ordering of shopping using a phone application.
- Public APIs allow access by anyone. For example, an app that wants to display the most recent news might use a public API to get the headlines.
- Partner API is used by a business partner. If a business has some data or services it would like to allow access to by some other businesses they would use a partner API. For example, an airline might use a partner API to allow a holiday company to book seats on flights.
- Composite APIs combine multiple other APIs. For example, a large holiday firm might use a composite API when a travel agent books a holiday for a customer. The composite API would reserve flights and hotel rooms from different suppliers.

2 Possible answers include:
- SOAP. SOAP provides authentication and security. The holiday cottage company

would want to ensure that the booking is being made by a customer who is already registered with them and that has paid the deposit.

Quick check 8

1 • A protocol is a set of rules for transmitting data between different devices, usually via a network.

2 Possible answers include:
- Individual layers can be replaced without impacting the other layers. This allows for changes to be made easily.

Practice questions 3

1 API stands for Application Programming Interface.

Answer should include two of the following possible explanations:
- Rules to allow for communication between a client and a server
- A method of requesting data or services from a server
- A method to allow software on a client to communicate with software on a server. **[2]**

Credit any other appropriate response.

2 Answers should include **two** of the following possible explanations:
- REST allows a client (the weather application) to request data from a server
- REST has a GET type of request that is used to retrieve data from a server
- REST is stateless, meaning that the server will not need to know what state the application is in to respond correctly
- REST separates the client and server, so the client does not need to know how the server works. This could be a benefit if the weather provider needs to be changed. **[2]**

Credit any other appropriate response.

TA4

Quick check 9

1 Possible answers include:
- Factor refers to a method of identifying a user
- One factor would be username and password
- A second factor would be a code sent to email/phone or generated using an app.

2 Possible answers include:
- Outdated software, hardware or firmware will have known vulnerabilities. These vulnerabilities will not be patched. Vulnerabilities can be used to access the application/data.
- Lack of updates means that protocols will not have been updated, so could have known vulnerabilities.
- Code libraries will not be updated meaning that known vulnerabilities in the library code might make the application vulnerable.

Practice questions 4

1 Answers should include **two** of the following differences:
- DoS attack has one source.
- DDoS attack uses a botnet to send attacks from multiple sources.
- DDoS is much more difficult to block than a DoS attack.

Credit any other appropriate response. **[2]**

2 • RFID cards can be denied access easily compared to changing a traditional lock
- An RFID card can be given access to just the areas a staff member needs access to
- RFID locks can be set to only be accessed at certain times of the day. **[2]**

Credit any other appropriate response.

- Cameras can act as a deterrent to discourage people from trying to gain unauthorised access
- Cameras can be watched live, and a security response send to the problem location
- Cameras can allow for people trying to get unauthorised access to the location to be identified.

Credit any other appropriate response. **[2]**

TA5

Quick check 10

1 Possible answers include:

The purpose of testing is to ensure that an application works/looks as expected and that errors/bugs are removed.

2 Possible answers include:

Technical testing is done by a developer or quality assurance engineer. Tests should cover areas such as functionality, performance, security.

User testing is done by end users and is more likely to find issues with user interface issues and missing functionality.

Quick check 11

1 Possible answers include:

- Create ghost/image and deployment
  - Disk image created from completely setup computer, image then copied to other computers
- Upgrade
  - involves installing a newer version of the software over an existing installation, retaining user settings and data when possible
- Clean install
  - involves removing the current software and installing it from scratch
- Repair/modify installs
  - allows the repair of an existing software installation that isn't working correctly or modify its features without having to fully reinstall
- Remote install
  - Software is installed on one or many computers from a remote location via a network.
- Unattended installation
  - Installation of software is done automatically without requiring any user interaction.
- Cloud download/install
  - Software is downloaded and installed directly from the cloud, rather than from physical media such as USB flash drives or a local network

- Mobile install
  - installation of software to mobile devices, such as mobile phones or tablet computers, through the app store provided by the device manufacturer
- Network install
  - software applications to be installed over a local network.

2 Possible answers include:

- A clean install involves removing existing software and re-installing it
  - This is likely to remove existing data
- An upgrade involves installing a newer version of an application over an existing application
  - Likely to retain existing data/settings.

Quick check 12

1 Possible answers include:

- what data needs to be backed up
- how frequently the backups should be run
- where the backups should be stored
- how long the backups should be kept for.

2 Possible answers include:

- instructions on how to effectively and efficiently use an application
- overview of the application
- installation procedures
- step-by-step guides on how to use each feature
- troubleshooting tips
- answers to frequently asked questions (FAQs).

Practice questions 5

1 Possible answers include:

Advantages:

- Feedback is from end users, more likely to identify issues with user interface/messages/navigating around the application
- Improved user satisfaction as tested in real life situation
- If wide range of users involved then application will be tested on wide range of hardware/operating systems
- Performance of application tested in a real world situation.

Credit any other appropriate response. **[1]**

Disadvantages:

- Time consuming to get this kind of feedback
- Might only be able to use a limited number of people for testing
- Different users might not agree on user interface or other issues
- Users might not test all aspects of an application.

Credit any other appropriate response. **[1]**

2 Answer should include two of the following possible explanations:

- acceptable and unacceptable use
- potential consequences for breaking the rules
- guidelines for keeping data safe
- what to do if a problem occurs.

Credit any other appropriate response. **[2]**

TA6

Quick check 13

1 Possible answers include:

- Computer Misuse Act: criminalise unauthorised access to computer systems and the data they contain
- Freedom of Information Act: promote transparency and accountability by allowing public access to information held by public authorities
- Data Protection Act: protect personal data by regulating its processing and ensuring privacy rights are upheld
- UK General Data Protection Regulation (GDPR): protect personal data and ensure that organisations process this data in a secure, fair and lawful manner
- Privacy and Electronic Communications Regulations: give people privacy rights when using electronic communication systems.

2 Possible answers include:

- Website must inform the user that cookies are being used and what they are being used for
- The user must accept the use of cookies but there are exceptions for essential cookies.

Practice questions 6

1 a Any **one** from:

- Data Protection Act
- UK General Data Protection Regulation
- Privacy and Electronic Communications Regulations. **[1]**

b Any **one** from:

- Seek permission from existing users to use their data for marketing purposes
- Add an opt-in for marketing when user signs up to use the application or service. **[1]**

2 The Freedom of Information Act does not apply to this business. **[1]** The FOIA applies to public access to information held by public authorities (for example, as government departments or police forces). **[1]**

F162: TA1

Quick check 1

1 User feedback plays a crucial role in refining and enhancing a digital product's user experience. It provides valuable insights into user preferences, pain points and areas of improvement. For instance, if users consistently report difficulty in finding a specific feature in a website, UX designers can redesign the navigation to improve accessibility. Additionally, feedback on the clarity of error messages can prompt UI adjustments to ensure users understand and can resolve issues easily. The iterative nature of UX design relies on continuous user feedback to create a product that aligns with user expectations and needs.

2 UX designers focus on understanding how users consume and discover music to design features such as personalised playlists, recommendations and social sharing. UI designers then implement visual design elements, such as album covers, playback controls and navigation menus, to create an interface that is engaging and immersive.

Quick check 2

1 **Novice/beginner:**

Clear labels/instructions:

- Ensure that all buttons, icons and menus have clear labels that describe their functions in simple language.
- Provide tooltips or brief explanations for unfamiliar terms or features.
- Use intuitive design conventions, such as using recognisable icons and colours, to help novice users understand the interface.

Guided tours/tutorials:

- Offer guided tours or interactive tutorials during the onboarding process to familiarise novice users with key features and functionalities.
- Provide step-by-step instructions with visual cues to help users navigate through different sections of the platform.
- Offer optional tutorials or tips that users can access at any time to learn more about specific features or tasks.

Error messages:

- Ensure that error messages are clear, concise and informative, explaining what went wrong and how users can resolve the issue.
- Provide actionable suggestions or links to relevant help resources to assist users in troubleshooting errors.
- Use friendly and reassuring language to alleviate frustration and encourage users to continue using the platform.

Guidance on how to recover from mistakes:

- Offer prompts or suggestions to help users recover from common mistakes, such as accidental deletion of posts or messages.
- Provide undo options or confirmation dialogues for irreversible actions to give users a chance to reconsider before proceeding.
- Offer links to relevant help articles or support resources that provide guidance on how to address specific mistakes or issues.

Occasional users:

Quick access to key features:

- Ensure that key features such as creating posts, accessing messages and viewing notifications are easily accessible from the main interface.
- Implement shortcuts or prominent buttons to allow users to quickly navigate to commonly used features without searching through menus.

Tooltips:

- Provide tooltips for important features or actions to remind occasional users of their functionality and how to use them effectively.
- Use tooltips to offer helpful tips or suggestions for navigating the platform more efficiently and discovering new features.

Help resources/user guides:

- Offer easily accessible help resources, such as FAQs, user guides and tutorials, to assist occasional users in understanding how to use the platform and troubleshoot common issues.
- Provide links to relevant help articles or support forums within the platform to offer assistance when needed.

Customisation/personalisation options:

- Provide options for occasional users to customise their news feed preferences, such as prioritising content from friends or pages they follow.
- Offer personalisation features that allow users to customise their profile, such as choosing a profile picture, cover photo and bio.
- Allow users to adjust notification settings to control the frequency and type of notifications they receive based on their preferences.

Regular users:

Creating/accessing shortcuts:

- Allow users to create shortcuts to their most frequently accessed features or sections of the platform, such as groups, events or specific profiles.
- Provide options for users to customise their navigation bar or homepage layout to easily access their preferred shortcuts.

Saving preferences:

- Allow users to save their preferences and settings, such as news feed preferences, notification settings and privacy controls.
- Provide options for users to save custom filters or search preferences for easier access to relevant content.

Advanced features:

- Introduce advanced features and functionalities for regular users who are familiar with the platform and want to explore additional capabilities.
- Offer tools for content creators, such as advanced post scheduling, insights and analytics and audience targeting options.
- Provide options for users to integrate third-party applications or services to enhance their experience, such as photo editing tools or productivity plugins.

Collecting feedback from users:

- Implement mechanisms for collecting feedback from regular users to understand their needs, preferences and pain points.
- Offer surveys, polls or feedback forms within the platform to gather input from users on new features, changes to the interface or overall satisfaction with the platform.
- Actively listen to user feedback and incorporate suggestions or address concerns to improve the user experience over time.

Expert users:

Advanced functionality:

- Provide access to advanced features and functionalities that allow expert users to perform tasks more efficiently and effectively.
- Offer tools for content creation, analytics and audience targeting to help expert users optimise their social media presence.
- Introduce advanced privacy controls and security features to give expert users greater control over their account and personal data.

Customisation options:

- Offer extensive customisation options for expert users to tailor their experience to suit their preferences and workflow.

- Allow users to customise their news feed preferences, notification settings and homepage layout to prioritise content and features that are most relevant to them.
- Provide options for users to customise the appearance of their profile, such as choosing themes, layouts and colour schemes.

Keyboard shortcuts:

- Implement a comprehensive set of keyboard shortcuts to allow expert users to navigate the platform quickly and efficiently without relying on mouse clicks.
- Provide shortcuts for common actions such as posting, commenting, liking and messaging, as well as for navigating between different sections of the platform.
- Allow users to customise or remap keyboard shortcuts to match their preferred workflow and habits.

Adjust settings:

- Offer control over account settings, privacy settings and notification preferences to allow expert users to fine-tune their experience.
- Provide options for users to adjust settings related to data usage, security and third-party integrations to optimise performance and security.
- Ensure that settings menus are well-organised and easy to navigate, with clear explanations and tooltips to help users understand their options.

2 On a large desktop monitor, the website may feature multiple columns of content, a navigation bar with numerous options and additional sidebar widgets. However, when accessed on a smaller smartphone screen, the same website needs to prioritise content, simplify navigation and optimise layout to fit the limited screen space effectively.

Screen size directly affects UX/UI design in the following ways:

- On smaller screens, UX/UI designers must prioritise essential content and minimise visual clutter to ensure a seamless user experience.
- UX/UI designers employ responsive layout techniques, such as grid systems, flexible grids and media queries, to adapt the layout of websites and applications to different screen sizes.
- UX/UI designers must ensure that interfaces are touch-friendly and easy to navigate on smaller screens. This may involve increasing the size of interactive elements, such as buttons and links, to accommodate finger taps and gestures, as well as optimising spacing to prevent accidental touches.
- Smaller screens often correspond to mobile devices with varying levels of processing power and internet connectivity.

Quick check 3

1 Strive for consistency: consistency in design elements such as layout, terminology and interaction patterns ensures that users can predict how the interface behaves. For example, in a mobile banking app, maintaining consistent placement and design of primary actions such as 'Transfer Funds' and 'Pay Bills' across different screens helps

users quickly locate and use these features without confusion.

Enable frequent users to use shortcuts: providing shortcuts for experienced users can significantly improve efficiency. For instance, in a graphic design software such as Adobe Photoshop, power users can use keyboard shortcuts for common actions such as selecting tools or applying filters, saving time compared to navigating through menus with the mouse.

Offer informative feedback: informative feedback informs users about the outcome of their actions, helping to confirm successful interactions or alerting them to errors. For example, when submitting a form on a website, displaying a confirmation message or highlighting any fields with missing or incorrect information helps users understand the status of their input and how to proceed.

Design dialogues to yield closure: dialogue boxes and confirmation prompts should provide clear options for users to complete or cancel tasks, ensuring a sense of closure. In an e-commerce checkout process, a well-designed dialogue box confirming the user's purchase and providing a 'Continue Shopping' or 'View Order' option gives users the necessary closure while also offering further actions to take.

2 **Recognition:** in a mobile banking app, the use of recognisable icons and familiar symbols can aid users in navigating the interface effortlessly. For instance, instead of expecting users to recall specific banking terminology or menu options, designers can employ universally recognised symbols such as a magnifying glass for search functionality or a gear icon for settings. By presenting users with visual cues that they can easily recognise and understand, the app minimises cognitive load and enhances usability.

Recall: on the other hand, requiring users to recall information without visual cues can lead to a less intuitive user experience. For instance, if a mobile banking app solely relies on users recalling their account numbers or remembering complex passwords without offering any assistance or hints, it can result in frustration and errors. To avoid this, designers can implement features such as auto-complete suggestions for account numbers or password strength indicators, reducing the cognitive load on users and improving the likelihood of successful interactions.

Quick check 4

1 Intrinsic load: this is the inherent complexity of the task or information being presented. UX/UI designers aim to reduce intrinsic load by simplifying tasks, breaking information into manageable chunks and presenting it in a clear and organised manner.

Extrinsic load: this refers to unnecessary cognitive load imposed by the design itself, such as confusing layouts, cluttered interfaces or irrelevant information. UX/UI designers strive to minimise extraneous load by removing distractions, maintaining visual hierarchy and providing clear and concise instructions.

2 Simplicity and clarity:

- Simplify the main navigation menu by categorising games and content into clear and intuitive sections, such as 'Library', 'Store', 'Community' and 'Profile'.
- Use clear and descriptive labels for menu items and buttons to minimise ambiguity and help users understand their options.
- Streamline the layout of game pages, focusing on essential information such

as game description, screenshots and user reviews, while minimising clutter and distractions.

Reduced cognitive load:

- Limit the number of choices presented to users on each screen, particularly in the main menu and store interface, to avoid overwhelming users with too many options.
- Implement filters and sorting options to help users narrow down their choices when browsing games or content, reducing decision fatigue and cognitive overload.
- Provide clear pathways for users to find specific games or features, such as search functionality and recommended content based on user preferences and behaviour.

Focused user attention:

- Highlight featured or recommended games prominently on the homepage to capture users' attention and guide them towards popular or trending titles.
- Use visual cues such as colour contrast, size and placement to draw attention to important elements, such as sale promotions, new releases or user reviews.
- Minimise distractions and unnecessary elements on game pages and store pages to keep users focused on the task at hand, whether it's browsing for games or making a purchase.

Quick check 5

1 The primary difference between a GUI and a CLI lies in their visual presentation and interaction methods. A GUI provides users with a graphical interface comprising windows, icons, buttons and menus, allowing for intuitive interaction through mouse clicks and gestures. In contrast, a CLI relies on text-based commands entered via a keyboard, with responses displayed as text output. While GUIs are more user-friendly and visually engaging, CLIs offer greater control and efficiency for users proficient in command-based interactions.

2 A Voice User Interface (VUI) and a Touch-based User Interface (TUI) differ primarily in their input methods and interaction models. A VUI enables users to interact with devices using spoken commands or queries, using voice recognition technology to interpret and respond to verbal input. On the other hand, a TUI relies on touch gestures, such as tapping, swiping and pinching, to interact with graphical elements displayed on a touchscreen interface.

Quick check 6

1 Standardisation in UX/UI interface design is crucial because it enhances user familiarity and reduces the learning curve for users. When interface elements such as buttons, menus and navigation follow established conventions, users can quickly understand how to interact with the interface, leading to a more intuitive and efficient user experience. Additionally, standardisation promotes consistency across different parts of the interface and across various applications, which in turn builds trust and reliability among users.

2 Widgets play a significant role in UX/UI design by providing standardised user interface components that enhance usability and facilitate user interactions. These pre-defined elements, such as buttons, checkboxes, dropdown menus and sliders, serve as building blocks for creating intuitive and consistent interfaces across applications and platforms. By incorporating widgets into

design layouts, designers can streamline development, improve learnability and enhance user satisfaction by offering familiar and predictable interaction patterns. Additionally, widgets contribute to the overall aesthetics and functionality of the interface, enabling users to navigate, interact with and manipulate content seamlessly.

TA2

Quick check 7

1 The types of requirement that have a significant impact on the planning and design of UX/UI solutions include client requirements, user requirements, solution requirements, functional requirements, interface requirements and non-functional requirements. Each type of requirement contributes to shaping the design process and ensuring that the resulting UX/UI solution meets the needs and expectations of stakeholders and users

2 UX/UI solution requirements can be sourced and identified through various methods, including client briefs, analysis of current systems, review of existing documents and consideration of user/user profiles. These sources provide valuable insights into stakeholder expectations, user needs and existing system functionalities, helping designers and developers identify the key requirements that must be addressed in the design process.

3 Several tools are commonly used to document UX/UI solution requirements, including requirements specification documents, wireframing and prototyping tools, collaboration platforms and project management software. These tools provide designers and stakeholders with a structured framework for capturing, organising and communicating requirements, facilitating collaboration and ensuring alignment throughout the design and development process.

Quick check 8

1 Designers can use these techniques to document UX/UI ideas and design concepts:

- Wireframing tools enable designers to create skeletal representations of interface layouts, detailing key elements and functionalities.
- Mood boards aid in establishing the visual direction of a project by collecting inspirational images and establishing a cohesive aesthetic.
- Paper prototyping allows for rapid iteration and testing of ideas using physical materials such as paper and sticky notes, facilitating early user feedback.
- Flow diagrams help visualise user pathways and interactions within the interface, ensuring a seamless user experience.
- Sketches and diagrams, whether hand-drawn or digitally created, offer a flexible means of exploring and communicating design concepts, allowing for quick ideation and iteration.

2 Examples of the stages in which an idea evolves into a design concept:

- Initially, designers gather insights through user research, market analysis and stakeholder input to understand user needs and project requirements.
- From these insights, they generate UX/UI ideas, often in the form of sketches, brainstorming sessions or collaborative workshops.

- These initial ideas are then translated into wireframes, which serve as low-fidelity representations of interface layouts and functionalities.
- Mood boards are created to establish the visual direction, gathering inspiration and defining the aesthetic aspects of the design.
- Through iterative prototyping and testing, designers gather feedback from users, stakeholders and usability testing to refine and validate the design concepts.
- Flow diagrams help visualise user pathways and interactions, ensuring a seamless user experience.
- Finally, sketches and diagrams are used to explore alternative design solutions and communicate concepts effectively.

TA3

Quick check 9

1 Diagrams are powerful visual tools that can help designers map out and communicate complex UX/UI design features in a clear and understandable manner. For instance, flowcharts can be used to illustrate the sequence of interactions and decision points within a user flow, allowing designers to identify potential bottlenecks or usability issues. Similarly, navigation diagrams can visualise the structure and hierarchy of a digital interface, helping designers ensure intuitive navigation and information architecture.

2 Graphical mock-ups serve as powerful visual representations of UX/UI designs, allowing designers to communicate design decisions and showcase key features and functionalities. In illustrating navigation style, mock-ups depict navigation elements such as menus, navigation bars, buttons, links and breadcrumbs, demonstrating design choices regarding their placement, appearance and behaviour. Similarly, house style is conveyed through the integration of visual elements such as colours, typography, logos, icons and other branding elements consistent with the organisation's brand guidelines. The layout of the interface is visually represented in mock-ups, showing the arrangement of content, navigation elements and other interface components, along with design decisions related to placement, spacing, alignment and hierarchy. Content is showcased within mock-ups through the inclusion of text, images, videos and other multimedia elements, providing stakeholders with a clear understanding of the content structure and presentation. Additionally, mock-ups simulate system interaction and event handling by incorporating interactive elements such as buttons, form fields, dropdown menus and interactive widgets, along with annotations or interactive prototypes to demonstrate user interactions and interface responses. Finally, mock-ups illustrate error handling and feedback methods, including error messages and success notifications, to show how the interface communicates errors, provides feedback on user actions and guides users through error resolution processes. Overall, graphical mock-ups play a vital role in effectively communicating various aspects of a UX/UI design, facilitating collaboration, feedback and decision-making throughout the design process.

Quick check 10

1 **Navigation:** assess the ease of navigation through the website, including the clarity of menu labels, the presence of search functionality and the accessibility of product categories.

Product presentation: evaluate the layout and organisation of product listings, ensuring clear product images, detailed descriptions and relevant filtering options.

Shopping cart functionality: check the usability of the shopping cart, including the ability to add, remove and update items, as well as view subtotal and proceed to checkout.

Checkout process: review the steps involved in the checkout process, assessing form fields, payment options and shipping methods for simplicity and clarity.

Mobile responsiveness: test the website's responsiveness on various devices, ensuring an optimal viewing and shopping experience across desktops, tablets and smartphones.

Accessibility: ensure compliance with accessibility standards, such as providing alternative text for images, keyboard navigation options and sufficient colour contrast for readability.

Performance: assess the website's loading speed and overall performance to minimise wait times and enhance user experience.

2 **Usability testing:** conduct usability testing to evaluate the ease of use and efficiency of the interface in completing common tasks and achieving user goals. This involves observing users as they interact with the design and collecting feedback on areas of difficulty or confusion.

Accessibility evaluation: assess the design for compliance with accessibility guidelines, such as sufficient colour contrast, keyboard accessibility and support for screen readers. Use tools and techniques such as automated accessibility testing and manual evaluations to identify accessibility barriers and ensure inclusivity for users with disabilities.

Visual design consistency: check for consistency in visual design elements, including typography, colour usage and layout. Consistent design helps create a cohesive user experience and enhances usability by reducing cognitive load and improving familiarity.

Interaction design patterns: evaluate interaction design patterns such as navigation menus, buttons and form fields to ensure they are intuitive and user-friendly. Consider factors such as responsiveness, error handling and feedback mechanisms to enhance usability and provide a smooth user experience.

Content clarity and readability: assess the clarity and readability of content, including text and imagery, to ensure it is concise, informative and easy to understand. Use readability metrics and user feedback to identify areas for improvement and optimise content for usability.

TA4

Quick check 11

1 A live presentation involves presenting the UX/UI solution in real-time, either in person or via a virtual platform. The presenter can interact with the audience, answer questions and provide additional context as needed.

A slideshow with an audio overlay involves a sequence of slides accompanied by a pre-recorded narration that explains the content of each slide.

A video showcase is a recorded, edited presentation that combines visuals, narration and often animations or screen recordings to demonstrate the UX/UI solution.

2 **For business stakeholders:**

- Use straightforward, business-oriented language. Avoid jargon and technical terms unless they are commonly understood by the audience.
- Focus on results, benefits and return on investment. Use language that highlights the business impact and value.
- Maintain a formal and professional tone throughout the presentation.

For design peers:

- Use industry-specific terminology and design jargon. Peers will appreciate the depth and detail.
- Focus on the design process, methods and technical challenges. Explain design decisions in detail.
- Adopt a tone that invites discussion and feedback, reflecting a shared interest in design practices.

For the general public:

- Use plain language and avoid technical jargon. Explain concepts in a way that is easily understandable.
- Highlight how the design improves user experience and solves problems. Use relatable examples and stories.
- Keep the tone friendly and engaging to maintain interest.

Quick check 12

1 Live presentation (in person or remote): use a structured format with a clear agenda. Focus on key business outcomes and include time for Q&A to address specific concerns.

Slideshow with audio overlay: create concise, focused slides that highlight the problem, solution and business impact. Use simple, clear language and professional visuals.

Video: produce a high-quality, polished video that clearly explains the problem, solution and results. Use metrics and testimonials to support your points.

2 **Hardware:**

Computer or laptop: this is the primary device for creating, editing and presenting the showcase. Ensure it's capable of running design and presentation software smoothly.

Monitor/projector/large screen: use the monitor for design work and the projector/screen for client presentations, ensuring visuals are clear and professional.

Mouse and keyboard/graphics tablet: use these tools to enhance precision and efficiency in design tasks, making it easier to create detailed and high-quality designs.

Microphone: use the microphone for recording presentations or voiceovers.

Speakers/headphones: use speakers/headphones to hear audio elements of UX/UI and during remote presentations.

Webcam: use the webcam for virtual meetings and presentations, ensuring clients can see you clearly, which helps build a more personal connection.

Software:

Design and prototyping tools: use these tools to create detailed and interactive prototypes that can be shared with clients for feedback. Ensure you know how to navigate and present designs effectively.

Presentation software: create a presentation that tells the story of the design process, showcasing key milestones, design decisions and final outcomes. Integrate visuals, metrics and interactive elements to engage the audience.

Video editing software: use these tools to produce high-quality video walkthroughs of the design, incorporating animations, transitions and voiceovers to explain the design process and decisions clearly.

Collaboration tools: schedule and conduct remote meetings using these tools. Share your screen to present the showcase and use features such as chat and Q&A to engage with clients.

TA5

Quick check 13

1 The process involves conducting security assessments to find vulnerabilities, ensuring that the solution is robust and resilient against potential threats. The number of vulnerabilities found, and the severity of issues are used to measure the effectiveness of security measures implemented.

This evaluation involves conducting compliance audits and reviews to ensure that the solution meets all relevant standards and regulations governing its use. By employing these methods, organisations can ensure that their UX/UI solutions adhere to industry standards, legal regulations and best practices, thereby mitigating risks and ensuring the solution meets all the relevant standard.

2 **Usability:** usability focuses on making products intuitive and easy to use, ensuring that users can achieve their goals efficiently and effectively. Designers apply usability principles by conducting user research, creating clear navigation structures, organising content logically and providing feedback to users. Usability testing is also crucial for identifying and addressing usability issues throughout the design process, improving overall user satisfaction and productivity.

Accessibility: accessibility involves designing products that are usable by people with disabilities, ensuring equal access to information and functionality for all users. Designers apply accessibility principles by following established guidelines, such as the Web Content Accessibility Guidelines (WCAG), to make interfaces understandable and robust. This includes providing alternative text for images, implementing keyboard navigation, ensuring sufficient colour contrast and supporting assistive technologies such as screen readers. By prioritising accessibility, designers create more inclusive and usable products that cater to a diverse range of users.

Visual design: visual design focuses on creating visually appealing interfaces that communicate effectively and engage users emotionally. Designers apply visual design principles, such as hierarchy, typography, colour theory and layout, to create aesthetically pleasing and cohesive designs. Visual elements, such as icons, imagery and branding, are used strategically to enhance the user experience and reinforce the product's identity. By balancing aesthetics with functionality, designers create visually engaging interfaces that resonate with users and support their goals.

Performance: performance involves optimising the speed, responsiveness and reliability of products to ensure a seamless user experience. Designers apply performance principles by optimising code, minimising loading times and prioritising content delivery. By prioritising performance, designers create products that load quickly, respond promptly to user interactions and maintain reliability even under heavy usage, enhancing user satisfaction and engagement.

Quick check 14

1 **Visual perception:** understanding how users interpret and make sense of visual information is crucial for designing intuitive and accessible interfaces such as the use of colours to convey meaning, choosing font and text layouts are that are easy to read and the use of visual icons and other visual indicators to help users understand actions and information quickly.

Cognitive load: managing the amount of mental effort required to interact with the interface. A simple design to minimise distractions, breaking information down in manageable chunks and revealing information as and when is needed are ways this could be assessed.

Emotional design: evoking specific emotions and supporting emotional connections with users. This could be assessed through visual design, how well it understands users' needs, preferences and pain points to design experiences and the impact of using feedback mechanisms.

Behavioural psychology: when understanding UX/UI design principles, assessing behavioural psychology involves examining how users behave and interact with interfaces based on their psychological tendencies and responses. This can be assessed through various methods such as user testing, surveys and interviews.

2 **Platform guidelines:** designers need to familiarise themselves with the specific guidelines for the platforms they are designing for, such as Apple's Human Interface Guidelines for iOS or Google's Material Design Guidelines for Android.

Web standards: designers and developers should educate themselves on current web standards, such as those established by the World Wide Web Consortium (W3C). For example, use tools and resources such as accessibility checkers to ensure that the web design conforms to standards for HTML, CSS, JavaScript and accessibility.

Industry standards: conduct thorough research to understand industry-specific standards and best practices that are relevant to the project. This may include guidelines for e-commerce, healthcare, finance, etc.

Quick check 15

1 **Usability:** evaluate the ease of use, learnability, efficiency and error management of the solution through usability testing and user feedback.

Functionality: assess the completeness and correctness of features, including the degree of feature completeness and user feedback on feature usability.

Performance: measure load times, response times and resource consumption to ensure optimal performance under different conditions.

Visual design: evaluate the aesthetic appeal, brand alignment and visual consistency against brand guidelines and user preferences, incorporating user feedback on aesthetics and design consistency.

Accessibility: ensure compliance with accessibility standards such as WCAG through accessibility testing and reviews, aiming to identify and remove barriers to access for users with disabilities.

Security: conduct security assessments to identify vulnerabilities and ensure robust protection of user data against potential threats, with metrics including the number and severity of issues found.

Scalability: evaluate the solution's ability to handle increased loads and user growth by assessing maximum concurrent users and performance under stress.

Compliance: conduct compliance audits and reviews to ensure adherence to industry standards, legal regulations and best practices, with methods including encryption protocols, access controls and audit logs for tracking user activities.

2 **Client requirements:** evaluate the alignment of the solution with the client's objectives, business goals and specific feature requests. Consider factors such as increasing conversions, improving user engagement and reinforcing brand identity.

User requirements: assess the usability, functionality and visual design of the solution to ensure it meets the needs and preferences of the target users. Conduct usability testing, gather user feedback and consider factors such as ease of use, efficiency and aesthetic appeal.

Solution requirements: review the technical aspects of the solution, including scalability, performance, security and compliance. Test the solution's scalability under different load conditions, measure performance metrics such as load times and response times, and assess security measures such as encryption protocols and access controls.